Redemptorists of Cuenca

The Redemptorist Martyrs of Cuenca by Belén del Pino

Redemptorists of Cuenca

SIX MARTYRS
OF THE SPANISH CIVIL WAR

Edited by Antonio M. Quesada, CSsR

Translated from Spanish by Gary Lauenstein, CSsR

Liguori

Imprimi Potest:
Stephen T. Rehrauer, CSsR, Provincial
Denver Province, the Redemptorists

Published by Liguori Publications, Liguori, Missouri 63057
To order, visit Liguori.org or call 800-325-9521

Library of Congress Cataloging-in-Publication Data

Names: Quesada, Antonio M., editor. | Lauenstein, Gary, translator.

Title: Redemptorists of Cuenca: six martyrs of the Spanish Civil War / edited by Antonio M. Quesada, CSsR; translated by Gary Lauenstein, CSsR.

Identifiers: LCCN 2019048825 | ISBN 9780764828232 (paperback)

Subjects: LCSH: Redemptorists—Spain—Cuenca—History—20th century.

Christian martyrs—Spain—Cuenca—Biography. | Cuenca (Spain)—Church History—20th century.

Classification: LCC BX4020.M33513 2020 | DDC 272/.9094647—dc23

LC record available at https://lccn.loc.gov/2019048825

ISBN 978-0-7648-2823-2

Liguori Publications, a nonprofit corporation, is an apostolate of the Redemptorists. To learn more about the Redemptorists, visit Redemptorists.com.

Printed in the United States of America

24 23 22 21 20 / 5 4 3 2 1
First Edition

(Originally published in Spanish in 2013 as *Mártires Redentoristas de Cuenca:Misioneros de la abundante Redención (1936-1938),* Antonio M. Quesada, coordinator, copyrighted by Editorial El Perpetuo Socorro, Covarrubias, 19-28010 Madrid, Spain.)

Martyrdom touches upon a mystery about humanity. To understand the human person, one must understand his life, faith, and relationships. We discover that in the littleness of each martyr there is hidden a great treasure.

A martyr is not someone intent upon suicide, no matter how sublime his motivation may be. He is a person who bets on life but puts his faith first. A martyr is not a hero. Among the many martyrs are personalities of great fragility. Also, a martyr is not reckless, not even a brave person, because many martyrs have come up against death without seeking it.

Likewise, martyrdom is not a reward for a dedicated life, although it does follow a trajectory of generosity. Within the martyr is a great love for Jesus Christ that permits him to die with a loving surrender in communion with him who said, "No one takes [my life] from me, but I lay it down on my own. I have power to lay it down" (John 10:18).

The martyr radiates faith and faithfulness to God in a way that is true to oneself. Martyrdom allows a person to step across a threshold away from fear and selfishness. Martyrdom is a sure bet on a culture of pardon and reconciliation. And all of this is pure grace, by which God permits the martyr to confront death with the same attitude as Jesus. This is possible only with the help of the Spirit.

About the cover:

The the cover artwork, beautifully painted by Belén del Pino, shows us the Redemptorist missionary vocation lived in Cuenca (which is presented as a stage) and that is lived in a martyrial way. St. Paul's bridge is presented at the same time as an exit space for the mission of announcing the Gospel and the martyrdom that opens the vocation of the six Redemptorists to identify fully with the Redeemer. The bridge identifies mission and martyrdom; every missionary vocation is called to live in a martyrial dimension.

The six martyrs are moving, roaming; they walk as a community of missionaries. Once again, the artist tells us about the prophetic dimension of the Redemptorist apostolic community, called to join Christ the Redeemer and sign with his life what he announces in his message.

Each of the missionary-martyrs has an element with which to identify the missionary vocation: Br. Victoriano has the Word of God in his hands; Fr. Pozo the missionary cross; Fr. Goñi the icon of Perpetual Help; and Fr. Ciriaco Olarte the rosary—four elements that identify this missionary vocation. Fr. Pedro Romero has his hands in an attitude of recollection and prayer, which recalls the need for prayer to live as missionaries. Finally, the group is preceded by Fr. José Javier Gorosterratzu who carries the palm of martyrdom. The martyrial horizon is the missionary's own horizon, which announces the Gospel of Christ in the midst of any circumstance.

Finally, each of the martyrs carries the element that synthesizes something important in their life. Fr. Gorosterratzu takes the palm for being the head of the group. Br. Victoriano carries the book, for being a missionary who preached from writing, translating the word of God into the spiritual writings that he composed for the lady he directed. Fr. Julián Pozo carries the cross, because his life was a configuration with Christ on the cross of disease. Fr. Miguel Goñi carries the icon of Perpetual Help, which he tries to save as the best jewel of the community, for his Marian devotion. Fr. Ciriaco Olarte is passing the rosary accounts, reminding us that when they were arrested they had just celebrated the Eucharist and prayed the holy rosary. Finally, Fr. Pedro Romero is in an attitude of silence, prayer, and recollection—an attitude in which he lived the last years of his life. Meanwhile his eyes contemplate his companions because he lived two years longer than those, and he had to make sense of his life from what happened to his brothers in the community.

The attitude of the six is to keep walking; there is much to do. The Congregation of the Most Holy Redeemer must continue to announce Christ in word and deed, in the midst of all circumstances. These six Redemptorists invite you to join them, consecrating yourself in the Congregation as a religious or joining the Redemptorist work as a layperson who shares spirituality and mission.

Contents

✂

Dear Reader:

The Redemptorist province of Madrid continues its celebration. It has been 150 years—and counting—since the first Redemptorists arrived in Spain with the mission of bringing to the most remote corner of the continent the abundant redemption of Jesus Christ.

There have been many men who have made this beautiful project possible over the past century and a half, putting into it all their gifts, their dreams and their lives. All of us Redemptorists have in mind great missionaries, formators, confessors, novice masters, or professors who have marked us with their apostolic zeal, their selfless commitment, and their missionary passion.

Some of them have done so by responding in an extraordinary manner, when the circumstances demanded it, with the surrender of their own lives, without moving a step backward, and with giving to their efforts their last drop of blood.

In an especially sad and difficult epoch of the history of Spain, far from the political disputes of the time, twenty-one Spanish Redemptorists died as victims of religious persecution. It was a persecution unleashed in that country in the 1930s. These Redemptorists died simply for being religious, for being missionaries, for remaining firm in their faith and firm in their Christian vocation. A process of beatification is underway to recognize all of them as witnesses for the faith.

For six of them, the Redemptorist martyrs of Cuenca, the process has been completed and, upon their being beatified on October 13, 2013, they have been presented to us as models of what Christian discipleship has come to mean in recent times. They are admirable witnesses of the faith. They have put on the line their very lives. They are Frs. José Javier Gorosterratzu, Ciriaco Olarte, Miguel Goñi, Julian Pozo, and Pedro Romero, and Br. Victoriano Calvo. To read the story of their lives, stories that have been gathered together in this book with fidelity and affection, is an exercise that will bring us to a particularly splendid moment in the history of the Redemptorists of Spain. It will, above all, help us to know men of robust faith, of joyful hope, of impressive missionary zeal, of admirable courage which radiated the Gospel out from the church of San Felipe de Neri in Cuenca.

I sincerely thank all those who have made possible this process, which recognizes the bravery of martyrs in our blesseds. This process has come to a happy conclusion. There have been many confreres who have brought the process to this point, gathering testimonies, writing books and pamphlets, praying that the process comes to a successful conclusion. To all of them, I extend the affection and recognition of the Redemptorist province.

And my most heartfelt thanks to all those who have made it possible that this publication has come to light after many hours of investigation and study. And, thanks to them today, we are able to delve into the hearts and come close to the lives of these brothers of ours, who, with the Church's recognition, now protect and encourage our mission.

May familiarity with the lives of our newly beatified renew our missionary vocation and inspire our availability for what is new and difficult.

Madrid, October 13, 2013
Pedro Lopez Calvo, CSsR
Redemptorist Province, Madrid

Presentation

Today, July 31, we commemorate the martyrdom of Frs. Ciriaco Olarte and Miguel Goñi, currently protomartyrs of the Congregation of the Most Holy Redeemer and first in the procession of persons who died for their faith in Cuenca during the religious persecution of 1936. In these present pages we wish to invite you to get to know the biography and the martyrdom of these six Redemptorists who will be beatified in Tarragona on October 13, 2013.[1]

Those who have prepared this book have entered into the hearts of these Redemptorists, and we have become familiar with their ideas, their feelings, their life and vocation. We remain fascinated with them. Throughout their biographies we are able to glimpse the activity of the Holy Spirit, who has transfigured them, and who has completed his work, giving them the gifts of perseverance and fidelity. We invite you to get close to them while attempting to avoid every ideological label and resistance, allowing yourself to be dazzled by persons called and consecrated to evangelization, people who were faithful to this call in the midst of circumstances wholly unfamiliar to them. Such was the religious persecution unchained in 1936 in the rear guard of the zones controlled by the government of Madrid.[2]

....

1 Translator's note: This presentation was made by the editor of the book, Fr. Antonio Manuel Quesada Montoro, CSsR, on July 31, 2013, before the beatification took place.

2 Translator's note: In 1936, this was the socialist government of the Second Spanish Repubic, which had begun a campaign to limit or destroy the free practice of religion. While the government controlled Cuenca, it had embarked on a "mopping up" operation to eliminate resistance.

From the start we want to make it clear the subjects of this book are not martyrs to some war, since none of these six were enlisted in the military or participated in any act of war. Nor were they prisoners detained in acts of war. They were part of civil society and found themselves trapped by war. They were killed solely for their personal position of being Redemptorist religious, and for this were considered to be enemies of the people. But it was those very people whom they had served through their efforts to evangelize the humblest people of the city.

In this work we have wished to reconstruct the events of the martyrdom of the six Redemptorist blesseds and to walk with them along their personal journeys. Their life stories placed them in Cuenca in July 1936. Their stories ended with them offering their lives for the love of God. All of us who have participated in putting together this work have tried to approach this objective with proper historical rigor. It can be appreciated that there are abundant references in the footnotes, for the purpose of offering the interested reader the possibility of continuing to delve deeper into their histories.

The work is conceived in two parts, which respond to two questions: "What happened?" and "Who are they?" The first question is discussed in the first three chapters of the work. Beginning with a presentation of the scene where the events took place, Cuenca of 1936, we position the Redemptorists in such a way as to present the tragedy of the events and the martyrdom that these missionaries endured, just as the six blesseds suffered it, and just as the people in Cuenca did with whom they shared these same tragic moments. To the question "Who are they?" we will respond by offering the biographies of the six martyred Redemptorists, full biographies, in which is revealed the identity of each one, his life's journey, and his apostolic and missionary ministry.

At the time of writing this microhistory of the Redemptorists martyred in Cuenca, we were concerned to establish ties with world history. For this reason, many references to other people are found where we describe the religious persecution and martyrdom of the Redemptorists. For the same reason, mission chronicles are cited when we refer to the missionary activity of these Redemptorists, so that we can tie in the relationship each had with all the places where each of them had worked.

To the Redemptorist missionaries who read these pages we would like to say that the six blesseds constitute six different profiles of the same ecclesial vocation, that of the Redemptorist missionary, molded in each one of them in a distinct manner. Among the six we have a Redemptorist coadjutor brother, an intellectual, various missionaries, two chronically infirm confreres, and an old man. Each one develops, at different stages of life, a personal form of living our unique vocation. Each one offers us a way to be a Redemptorist missionary; and together, in community, they call our attention to developing our life as missionaries in a communitarian way. Today, the Church and our society need communities that live their testimony and holiness in a communitarian setting. Approaching the martyrdom of these confreres we discover the power of communal martyrdom.

Regarding the authorship of the present work, we have to relate that it has been composed in three stages. Fr. Manuel Gómez Ríos (1942-2004) began the investigation and redaction before the year 2000, when it was thought that the beatification would be imminent. Cancer and his premature death left the present work barely started. Subsequently, Fr. Roberto Bolaños, using the material of Fr. Gómez Ríos, finished the work. He handed over to the Redemptorist province a manuscript of the finished work titled *They Gave Their Lives for Abundant Redemption*. The date of its publication was delayed, and when that date was decided upon, it was seen as appropriate to include in the manuscript the latest investigations that had been done in preparation for the beatification, besides including other recently published investigatory works. In order to do so, a commission was formed consisting of Fr. Laureano Del Otero and myself. We revised the previous texts, corrected those dates that were incorrect, and incorporated things we were asked to include. So, to be completely fair, we believe that this has been a collaborative effort among the four of us who have put a hand to it: Manuel Gómez Ríos, Roberto Bolaños, Laureano Del Otero, and Manuel Antonio Quesada.

The sources used for editing this book, besides the works already cited, have been the *Actas* of the process of martyrdom of the blesseds, in which are gathered the testimonies of witnesses for the process. Also, we have found useful the data that the investigators of the 1940s and 1950s had discovered, and which are found registered in the archives of the Redemptorist province of Madrid. To complete all of this and to reconstruct the biographies, we have made use of the local chronicles of those communities where these Redemptorists lived or of the chronicle of the Redemptorist province of Madrid. In that way, we have managed to fill in missing data, which the religious persecution caused by the destruction of the files, and chronicles of some of our communities. We have also looked for all those personal documents that mark out the biography of each of these six Redemptorists, in order to thus make precise by cross-referencing the dates we offer. At the end of the book we offer a list of works consulted and of documents on which we have depended for this publication.

Before concluding, I wish to express my gratitude for the effort put forth by everyone who has helped in the investigation and in verifying the facts researched by Fr. Manuel Gómez Ríos. I would like to single out Frs. Emilio Lage and Tirso Cepedal for their quick responses in the various consultations made to the Redemptorist General Archives in Rome, as well as to the Redemptorist provincial archives in Madrid. I also thank the chroniclers and archivists of the communities of Perpetuo Socorro in Madrid, Granada, Astorga, El Espino, Pamplona, and La Coruña for their cooperation in researching the local archives to find facts about the apostolic ministry of the six Redemptorists. Also, the general and provincial secretariats of the Oblates of the Most Holy Redeemer and of the Marianists have helped verify facts and offer details. Likewise, I am grateful for the cooperation of the archivists of the diocesan archives of Pamplona and Vitoria, the contribution of the Delegation for the Cause of Saints of the Diocese of Cuenca, as well as for the generous cooperation of the pastors in the hometowns of each of the blesseds and of other places where the blesseds had lived. All of these contributors are also in part authors of these lines which we are inviting you to read, leaving you to be impressed by the personal mystery of these six Redemptorist missionaries whom we present to you.

Antonio Manuel Quesada Montoro, CSsR (editor)
July 13, 2013, Seville
Commemoration of the martyrdom of Ciriaco Olarte and Miguel Goñi

Frequently Used Abbreviations

A. B. RODRÍGUEZ, I	A. B. RODRÍGUEZ, *La Guerra Civil en Cuenca (1936-1939). Vol.I. Del 18 de Julio a la Columna del Rosal* (Madrid, 2006).
A. B. RODRÍGUEZ, II	A. B. RODRÍGUEZ, *La Guerra Civil en Cuenca (1936-1939). Vol.II. La pugna ideológica y la revolución* (Madrid, 2006).
AGA	Archivo General de la Administración (General Archives of the Administration)
AHDV	Archivo Histórico Diocesano de Vitoria (Historical Archives of the Vitoria Diocese)
AHGR	Archivo Histórico General Redentorista de Roma (Historical Archives of the Redemptorist general government in Rome)
AHMC	Archivo Histórico Municipal de Cuenca (Historical Municipal Archives of Cuenca)
AHN	Archivo Histórico Nacional (National Historical Archives)
Anales	Anales de la Provincia Española (Annals of the Spanish province)
APRM	Archivo de la Provincia Redentorista de Madrid (Archives of the Redemptorist province of Madrid)

A. B.RODRÍGUEZ Y R.DE LA ROSA	A. B.Rodríguez y R.De la Rosa, *Represión y Guerra Civil en Cuenca. Nuevos testimonios y fotografías* (Cuenca, 2009).
BPE	Boletín de la Provincia Española (Bulletin of the Spanish province)
C.Beatificationis - Declaraciones	*Causa Beatificationis et Canonizationis seu Declarationis Martyrii Servorum Dei Declaraciones* Josephi Xaverii Gorosterrazu Jaunarena et Sociorum eius. Acta Processus Ordinarii Informativi super "Fama Martyrii." Conchae 1962–1965; 3 vols.
C.Beatificationis - Escritos	*Causa Beatificationis et Canonizationis seu Declarationis Martyrii Servorum Dei Escritos* Josephi Xaverii Gorosterrazu Jaunarena et Sociorum eius. Acta Processus Ordinarii Diligentiarum seu super "De perquisitione scriptorum." Conchae 1962–1965.
Causa	Archivo Histórico Nacional, Fondos Contemporáneos, Causa General. (National Historical Archives, Contemporary Collection, General Cause)
Crónica de Cuenca	APRM. *Crónica doméstica de la comunidad Redentorista de Cuenca.* (House chronicle of the Redemptorist community of Cuenca, 1939–1940)
Crónica Madrid PS.	A. MADRID-PS, *Crónica doméstica de la Comunidad Redentorista del Perpetuo Socorro de Madrid.* (House chronicle of the Redemptorist Community of Perpetual Help of Madrid)
Curriculum	*Curriculum vitae*
D. DE FELIPE	D. DE FELIPE, *Nuevos Redentores* (Madrid, 1962).
d.c.	Documento citado (Cited document)
EGET	Archivo General del Ejército de Tierra (General Archives of the Army)
Exp.	Expediente (File)
F.	Folio (Folio, page)

Leg.	Legajo (File or bundle of papers)
Reg.	Registro (Record or Register)
S. CIRAC ESTOPAÑÁN	*Martirologio de Cuenca. Crónica diocesana de la época roja.* (Barcelona, 1947).
Sec.	Sección (Section)
Sum.	Sumarísimo no. (Summary Number)
T.	Tomo. (Volume)

List of Photos and Illustrations

PART ONE

What Happened?

The Events Surrounding the Martyrdom

CHAPTER ONE

The Revolution and Religious Persecution of 1936 in Cuenca

On December 26, 2007, the Spanish Parliament approved the *Law of Historical Memory*, which condemned the reprisals made behind the lines on both sides of the Spanish Civil War against the civilian population "for political, ideological reasons or for reasons of religious belief," (art. 2) and during the dictatorship, as well as "declaring the illegitimacy of the tribunals, juries, and whatever other penal and administrative organs which, during the Civil War, were constituted to impose for political or ideological motives or because of religious belief, condemnations or sanctions of a personal character, as well as their resolutions" (art. 2). Although not the only cause of violence and reprisal, violence originating from beliefs about the Catholic Church in the zone loyal to the government of the Second Republic is well-established. The government minister of Largo Caballero, Manuel de Irujo[3] himself, read a memorandum before the Council of Ministers on January 9, 1937, about this religious persecution, which said:

The actual situation of the Church, beginning this past July, in all the loyal territory, except the Basque territory, is the following:

a) *All the altars, religious images, and objects of worship, save for a very few exceptions, have been destroyed, mostly with vilification.*

b) *All the churches have been closed against worship, which has been totally and absolutely suspended.*

c) *A great many of the churches in Cataluña, of the normal type, have been burned.*

d) *Parks and official organisms have received the bells, chalices, monstrances, candelabras, and other objects of worship; their materials have been melted down and even have been made use of for the war or for industrial purposes.*

e) *In the churches, all sorts of things have been warehoused by the official institutions which have taken over occupancy of them: markets, garages, paintings, living quarters, shelters, or they have been used in other diverse ways, resulting in the construction of facilities of a permanent character.*

f) *All the monasteries and convents[4] have been emptied out and religious life in them has been suspended. Their buildings, objects of worship, and goods of all types have been burned, looted, occupied, and destroyed.*

....

3 Manuel de Irujo Ollo (1891-1981), Director of the Basque Nationalist Party, minister without portfolio (September 1936-May 1937) in the two administrations of Largo Caballero, Minister of Justice in the cabinet of Negrín (May 18-December, 1937) and again minister without portfolio until August of 1938. [Translator's note: Juan Negrín y López was a leader of the Spanish Socialist Workers' Party and president of the Second Spanish Republic from 1937 to 1939.] In a government meeting, which took place in Valencia on January 9, 1937, he presented the memorandum cited in the above text about the religious persecution. His was the only vote of support.

4 Translator's note: The word *convento* in Spanish is used for religious houses of men as well as religious houses of women. In colloquial English, a convent is the residence of religious women, while a monastery is the residence of religious men. That is the meaning to those words, which we will employ in this translation.

g) *Priests and religious have been detained, submitted to prison, and shot without due process in the thousands; these actions, even though well diminished, still continue, not only in rural areas, where people have been hunted and killed savagely but in the cities. Madrid and Barcelona and the other great cities add hundreds of prisoners to their jails without any other known cause than that they are priests or religious.*

h) *It has come down to an absolute prohibition of keeping in private any images and objects of worship. The police in charge of home searches go through the interiors of homes, including the areas of personal and family intimacy, and destroy with ridicule and violence the images, holy cards, religious books, and anything related to worship or which can remind someone of worship.*

In this chapter we do not pretend to do an exhaustive study, but present a summary of the facts to help us understand the microhistories of people within the context of other greater historical processes. Given that a great deal has been written about the Spanish Civil War and its religious persecution, the product of repression in the Republican rear guard, we refer our readers to those studies.[5] In this work we will concentrate on the city of Cuenca. To do this, we will make use of the study done by the historian Ana Belén Rodríguez Patiño,[6] one of the few works that deals with development of the Civil War in the provincial capital of Cuenca.

It would be impossible to gather all the viewpoints and to point out the multiple aspects that come to the fore in such a complex process. Given that the object of this work is to present the lives of the six Redemptorists, we examine that part of the Civil War and of the revolutionary process which permits us to understand how events came about. The reality is much fuller than we can present in these brief pages.

....

5 The most complete work is A. MONTERO, *Historia de la persecución religiosa en España 1936-1939.* (Madrid, 1961)

6 A. B. RODRÍGUEZ, *La Guerra Civil en Cuenca (1936-1939). Vol. I. Del 18 de Julio a la Columna del Rosal* (Madrid, 2006); A. B. RODRÍGUEZ, *La Guerra Civil en Cuenca (1936-1939). Vol. II. La pugna ideológica y la revolución* (Madrid, 2006). Later, the author published materials that did not appear in the first works: A. B. RODRÍGUEZ PATIÑO Y R.DE LA ROSA, *Represión y Guerra Civil en Cuenca. Nuevos Testimonios y Fotografías* (Cuenca, 2009).

In final consideration, this history is told from the viewpoint of six innocent victims. It is important that the reader understand from the first that the events are related as seen and felt by the victims—that is, these six Redemptorists. In this way we can understand what they went through in the first person: "The war is experienced at the front, yes, but no less at the rear. And the silent and atrocious war that the unarmed and undefended civilian population endures is the most disgraceful of all wars."[7] To scrutinize the hearts of the victims is to place ourselves before each individual. In these pages we go beyond the causes and statistics of the Civil War and instead portray as human beings those who died in rear-guard actions due to repression. We give a face and a history to the protagonists.

The City of Cuenca at the Beginning of 1936

Cuenca was a small capital of a poor province[8] situated between provinces of greater social, economic, and political significance, such as Madrid, Valencia, and Toledo. It was the seat of a bishopric, for which reason all the diocesan institutions were centralized there. The province was predominantly rural, for which reason the capital was tied to traditional agriculture, and fundamentally depended upon the other populated areas of the province.[9]

The city enjoyed a good social climate. With hardly any industry, the social ills stemming from conflicts between business and labor were rare. Social relationships in Cuenca were rooted in networks of friendship, family, and function. From the beginning of the 1930s, Cuenca experienced growth brought on by emigration from the farm to the city. The city absorbed this demographic increase without modernization of its urban, social, and economic structures.[10]

In 1936 the city could count 20,086 inhabitants.[11] Socially, it was

....

7 A. B. RODRÍGUEZ Y R. DE LA ROSA, 175.

8 Translator's note: In 1833, Spain was divided into fifty provinces. In 1978, with the democratization of Spain, provinces were grouped into seventeen autonomous regions. These regions did not exist as a political entity at the time of the Spanish Civil War, but their distinct cultural differences were well established.

9 Cf., A. B. RODRÍGUEZ, II, 17.

10 *Ibid*, 17-20, 142.

11 A. B. RODRÍGUEZ Y R. DE LA ROSA, 180.

divided into two large groups of people:[12] the elite and the popular masses. The elite consisted of the bourgeoisie, the political class, and the clergy, which exercised great influence throughout the province. The popular masses were made up of some very heterogeneous groups, such as the artisans, employees, small merchants, dependents, servants, gardeners, agricultural day workers, other temporary workers, and salaried workers in small factories and workshops. The political leanings of these groups were largely conservative.

The economy of the city was based on crafts, produced in families: "It consisted of sixty-nine businesses with 516 workers…The only two bases for production were food—olive oil and wheat—and a small industry of wood products, situated mostly on the roadsides leading to Madrid and Valencia. Too scanty a business base for a capital city of 20,000 inhabitants."[13] The labor unions in all of this were small and weak, their demands more social than political. This was for two reasons: on one hand, the size of the proletariat was not very big; on the other hand, each factory or workshop offered employment to a small number of workers who maintained tight relationships with the management. Nevertheless, beginning in 1931, an anarchistic influence was brewing among them.[14] With an increasing population and an industrial base which could not at the same time absorb that population, Cuenca soon saw itself overrun with a collection of vagabonds and beggars.[15] This difficulty disrupted a fragile social system. Since the nineteenth century, the city authorities could not find any solution for two problems that deepened the misery and marginalization of people in the poor barrios. Both problems had to do with hygiene: deficiencies in the sewage system and in the water supply.

The geographical distribution of the city was peculiar, and composed of three zones:[16] the upper, or old zone; the lower, or new expansion; and

----

12 A. B. RODRÍGUEZ, II, 25-26.

13 *Ibid*, 27.

14 Cf., *Ibid*, 28ff. As a curious fact, in Cuenca was the only case in all of Spain where the anarchists controlled the Union Hall, which became the headquarters of the CNT (Translator's note: *Confederación Nacional de Trabajo*, association of anarchist labor unions affiliated with the International Workers' Association).

15 A. B. RODRÍGUEZ, II, 19-20.

16 Cf., *Ibid*, 22-25.

the barrios on the periphery. The *upper zone* occupied in former times by comfortable families, suffered an economic and social decline in later years. And in the decade of the 1930s this upper zone was inhabited principally by priests, religious,[17] and by those who sought to install themselves in cheap apartments in the less convenient part of the city. The *lower zone,* inhabited by the bourgeoisie class, owners of smaller industries, businesses, and liberal professionals, had become in the 1930s the social and economic center of the provincial capital. Finally, there were the impoverished *barrios* on the periphery, established with the arrival of migrants from the countryside to the city, and made up of masses of day laborers, servants, and liberal professionals of low social condition.

As we have pointed out, politically it was a city that voted conservatively.[18] Until then, extremist political organizations were insignificant, on the right and left, in the province or in the city. This was due to a lack of class consciousness in the small group of the proletariat about the fact that the conservative vote belonged to CEDA,[19] and also about the fact that most conservative young people belonged to the Association of Catholic Students.[20] But the social and structural crisis that was lived out in this small capital of a rural province and seat of a bishopric "contributed to the discomfort of the bourgeoisie, in disagreement with the measures of the republic, and to the increasing discontent of the popular groups, which saw themselves as ever more impoverished. As a result, and while the first did not organize protest movements, the second began to gestate a broth of culture which transformed itself into a militancy nearer to that of their

....

17 According to Redemptorist Dionisio de Felipe, who lived around 1930 in San Felipe de Cuenca, the clergy lived in the upper part of the city in order to have easier access to the bishopric and the cathedral. (D.De Felipe, *Nuevos Redentores* [Madrid, 1962] 139-140).

18 Cf., S. CIRAC ESOPAÑÁN, *Martirologio de Cuenca. Crónica diocesana de la época roja.* (Barcelona, 1947) 687.

19 Cf., A. B. RODRÍGUEZ, II, 39, 44 ff. [Translator's note: CEDA stands for *Confederaciones Españolas de Derechos Autónomas* (Spanish Confederations for Autonomous Rights), a coalition of groups under the leadership of José María Gil Robles, a law professor from Salamanca who had headed *Acción Popular* (Popular Action), an influential Catholic political youth group.]

20 The Association of Catholic Students was an organization that, after 1931, included the Republican youth more active politically in the country, among whom were an abundance of those in well-positioned families. In other cities many of them in 1933 formed part of the Spanish University Union, tied to Falange.

related parties and a notable affiliation with the two unions."[21] This contributed to the fact that the neighborhoods on the urban periphery became a focus for the unions who, with the revolution of 1936, saw the moment as an opportunity to prosper.[22]

As we have pointed out, the anarchist option was growing among the labor unions, formed into the CNT-FAI[23] and Libertarian Youth, which, while small in number, were well organized. Little by little, they would form a notable presence in Cuenca society. The Socialist Youth were a growing force in the province, but not in the city, and the members of the PCE[24] in Cuenca city were few and disorganized. While *Falange Española*[25] already existed and enjoyed great strength in other parts of the province, its emergence in the city of Cuenca was late.[26] At the beginning of 1936 its membership consisted of a dozen young men and a similar number of women; a number which, in spite of their growth in the months to come, never succeeded in having a greater political influence due to the inexperience and youth of its members. One place that served its diffusion was the Institute of Secondary Education in the city, where young Catholics studied. This is where the *Falange Española* germinated in Cuenca, bringing together "youth of a hard-working mentality, based in the Catholic religion, and of middle-class background, although not always comfortably so, by which they longed for political change which would give them a more solid base, spiritually and socially."[27]

....

21 Cf., A. B. Rodríguez, II, 31.

22 D. de Felipe writes from his knowledge of Cuenca that "*in Cuenca, capital and, because of the strong character of the region and of the conditions of social life, Marxism were able to find ground well-prepared to receive its seed of resentments and to make it germinate with freshness, vigorous in its system more than in the desire for social betterment.*" (D. De Felipe, 142)

23 Translator's note: CNT = *Confederación Nacionalista del Trabajo*, which is translated "National Confederation of Labor"; FAI = *Federación Anarquista Ibérica*, which is translated "Iberian Anarchist Association." The two groups joined in an affiliation of anarchist and labor union movements.

24 Translator's note: PCE = *Partido Comunista de España*, which is translated the "Communist Party of Spain."

25 Translator's note: *Falange Española*, translated "Spanish Phalanx," was a nationalist political movement founded in Spain in 1933 by José Antonio Primo de Rivera, son of the dictator Miguel Primo de Rivera.

26 Cf., A. B. RODRIGUEZ, II, 39.

27 *Ib.*, 40.

The Transformation of Society in Cuenca
from February to July 1936

When elections were called for February 16, 1936, most voters supported conservative figures who represented Cuenca's electoral traditions, such as General Joaquin Fanjul Goñi (candidate for Cuenca from 1919 to 1936).[28] Until 1935 the majority of the electorate on the right in the province belonged to CEDA while a small group of Acción Popular gravitated to Calvo Sotelo. Sotelo swung his voters to Falange in 1936, which began growing that year.[29] "The Falange was trying to fill with more tradition and less revolution a niche which Catholic parties on the right already occupied. And in Cuenca, the majority of the conservative electorate, party to the Republic or not, voted for CEDA in February and May."[30]

These elections of February 1936, gave power to the Popular Front in the rest of the Spanish state.[31] However, candidates on the right triumphed in Cuenca. But the Commission of Acts of the Courts annulled the electoral results of the provinces of Granada and Cuenca, publishing in the *Gazette of Madrid* on April 8 a Decree of Governance which declared null the elections for deputies to the courts in both provinces and called for new elections for May 3 in both districts.[32] This will produce a change in the political horizon of the city, since "after the month of February 1936, it began to be perceived clearly that the national ideological context was catching on in Cuenca, slowly but progressively. The increase of public activity of the right and of the left contributed to a greater examination of conscience also in the province."[33]

Before the development of these events, the vote on the right in Cuenca

....

28 Translator's note: Joaquin Fanjul Goñi held a licentiate in law, was a leader of the Morrocan War on behalf of Spain and became a general. He was first elected to the Spanish parliament in 1919, and again from 1931-36 as a member of the conservative *Partido Agrario* ("Agrarian Party"). In 1936 he resigned from Parliament and partnered with Franco among those who rebelled against the Second Spanish Republic.

29 Cf., *Ib.*, 47.

30 *Ib.*, 45.

31 Translator's note: the Popular Front was a coalition of left-wing political parties in the Spanish Second Republic.

32 Cf., *Ib.*, 50, 51.

33 *Ib*, 55.

swung to a more combative party against the regime, for which reason Falange was popular with conservative voters. Also, statistics showed most members of Catholic groups, such as the Association of Catholic Students, the Youth for Catholic Action, and the Franciscan Youth, were favoring that party.[34] The Falange was growing gradually so that in the spring of 1936 there were already some twenty affiliates and forty sympathizers.[35]

The little capital in the spring of 1936 saw itself at the center of political interest for all parties. On April 30, Miguel Primo de Rivera, seeing the importance of the elections for Falange, went to Cuenca to establish a party organization there.[36] On the next day, May 1, the party was convoked by a political decree that called for all the followers of his brother, José Antonio, to light the match for his sympathizers, beckoning them to the polls.

On the same day, May 1, the International Day of the Worker, the city found itself involved in a protest organized by the unions and workers' parties, which ended with a public disturbance.[37] Sadly, the monastery of San Pablo was attacked:

> On May 1, two anarchist friends went with a hunting rifle out to the nearby mountains, separating themselves a bit from the rest of the noisy crowd that was celebrating the day. One of them let loose a shot, or they were firing shots while doing a little hunting. The sound caught the attention of the other workers, who believed it was an attack on the part of the religious at the monastery, toward whom they maintained a great distrust. In a few moments, the feelings of indignation exploded, fanned on by the poor atmosphere that already existed between both communities. The perpetrators of the mistake either did not want to or did not know how to defuse the situation. At the last moment, the whole

....

34 Cf., *Ib.*, 39-42. 47-48.

35 Falange tried to introduce the candidacy of José Antonio Primo de Rivera in Cuenca to secure his liberation. Fanjul conceded the post to him and withdrew from the elections. In view of the circumstances, Falange believed it presented an opportunity to take a step forward in the political panorama. Ignoring the dictate of the government, which understood the vote as a runoff election, Falange put José Antonio at the head of the list in Cuenca. For his part, Franco, who had been included in the first balloting, withdrew from continuing on the list (Cf., *Ib.*, 50-54).

36 Cf., *Ib.*, 56. 62-63.

37 Cf., *Ib.*, 56 and 63.

group gathered there decided to take justice into their own hands and to attack the monastery.[38]

Due to the inaction of the authorities, the religious had to abandon the place. On the night of May 1, the monastery was attacked and the groups of strikers, out of control, seized the possessions inside. The religious were surprised, humiliated, and attacked. The right-wing parties, in view of the reaction of the masses of workers, accused the strikers of wanting to intimidate conservative voters. Every newspaper told the story from its own ideological viewpoint, contributing to an increase of violence among each ideological bloc. The Popular Front press promoted the false rumor and the conservative press condemned the events. Thus, on the eve of the elections, the streets of Cuenca were the scenes of fights, confrontations, and of groups of agitators disrupting the peace.[39]

The poll results in May were diametrically opposed to the results in February, giving the victory to the Popular Front. This time José Antonio was the leader on the right who received the most votes.[40] The official number of voters in the capital of Cuenca was 8,655, and those who exercised the vote were 4,754; the right-wing parties protested the climate of coercion that caused only 54 percent of the electorate to vote:

> *The revolutionary events of that time coerced the electorate, and fear made them believe it was better to not go out to vote in those circumstances. Also, they denounced the passive attitude of the governor, Antonio Sánchez Garrido, and the small amount of liberty with which they had been able to hold their meetings in the province. In view of this, López Villaverde argued back that the low participation was due to the saturation of the electorate of Cuenca, called to the polls three times in the first six months of the year. Without a doubt, this exhaustion also favored Falange.*[41]

---

38 *Ib.*, 82 According to D. De Felipe, the assault on the monastery of San Pablo "*was remembered in the Union Hall. Before the elections the unions had to expel the Vincentians, who with their students had a great number of votes...*" [for candidates on the right.] (D. DE FELIPE, 143).

39 Cf., A. B. Rodríguez, II, 63. 80-82.

40 Cf., *Ib.*, 70-71.

41 *Ib.*, 68.

The elections of 1936, with their two convocations, contributed to inflaming the social climate and to creating a spiral of violence. Since 1934 extremist youths of both sides had already begun to arm themselves. This spiral of violence was encouraged by the political debate maintained by the newspapers. Some of the headlines in the press were open proclamations of violent reaction against their enemies, as were the attacks on religion by the newspaper *La Lucha*.[42] There was also a lack of governance by the civil governor, who did nothing to stop the increasing spiral of violence, which created the hostile climate leading up to July 18, 1936.[43]

The Development of Events in Cuenca from July 18-30, 1936

Although it had grown recently, the Falange in Cuenca scarcely had the organization necessary to stage a revolt on July 18.[44] When Calvo Sotelo[45] was assassinated on July 13, there was a group of young and combative Falangists in the city. They were few in number, disorganized and not coordinated enough to act, since their leaders were imprisoned.[46] Events obliged them to remain in waiting, convinced that it was the military that must take the initiative.

The military governor of Cuenca, an enthusiast for the conspiracy, was unable to declare a state of war in the province, since he had very few troops to carry such a thing out; besides, the army in the neighboring provinces was loyal to the government in Madrid.[47] The uprising remained the responsibility of the Civil Guard,[48] the biggest military detachment in the province.

....

42 Translator's note: *La Lucha* ("The Struggle") was the name of a Communist newspaper, which began publication in Teruel, Spain, in 1936.

43 *Ib.*, 79-81.

44 Translator's note: The Spanish Civil War was initiated on July 17-18, 1936, when General Francisco Franco and several other Spanish generals, who had been fighting a war for Spain in Morroco, turned their troops against the Socialist government in Madrid.

45 Translator's note: José Calvo Sotelo was finance minister during the dictatorship of Miguel Primo de Rivera and was a leading right-wing extremist. He was assassinated in revenge for the assassination of a leftist political figure.

46 Cf., *Ib.*, 42; A. B. Rodríguez and R. De la Rosa, 138.

47 Translator's note: The government in Madrid was leftist.

48 Translator's note: The Civil Guard is the oldest law enforcement agency in Spain, semi-military, under the command of the Ministry of the Interior and the Ministry of Defense. It enjoyed then and today still enjoys a reputation of honesty and is nicknamed the *benemerita* ("the honorable ones"). At the time, it attempted to remain neutral and to defend the innocent.

But the chief in command, Gárcia de Ángela, begged for prudence in view of the circumstances.

Under the umbrella of the parties of the Popular Front, the anarchists (CNT-FAI and the Libertarian Youth) were the most organized. When news of a military revolt was broadcast on the radio, the Committee of the CNT of Cuenca received orders from the National Committee. By radio they learned that the working masses had taken to the streets in other capitals and they urged those of Cuenca to do the same. Such was the situation when…

> …*on the night of the 17ᵗʰ of July, a small group of anarchists of CNT, FAI, and JJLL[49] met in 'El Colmado Conquense'[50]—a place frequented by union members and governed by César Martínez. They decided to take the initiative when they heard the news of the revolt….Among them were Pablo Requena, Agustín Álvarez, Adolfo Álvaro, Antonio Méndez, Gerardo Alcañiz, and Elías Cruz Moya. This last was the president of the local federation. It was they who approached the Civil Governor about putting into effect the first measures dictated by the Popular Front, although the Governor had no intention of joining them.*[51]

The civil governor, Antonio Sánchez Garrido, refused to give them arms, while at the same time calling for calm and confidence in his powers of public order.

The next morning, July 18, all militants gathered in the union hall to act quickly to suffocate any flames of revolt. The Socialists and Republicans did the same. Anarchist groups began patrolling with pistols and hand tools, taking control of public streets. Searches, arrests and confiscations began. "At midday on July 18, the first of these happened: three members of the right-wing, bathing together in the river, far away from everything going on, were arrested on the outskirts of the city."[52] On July 19 there was a second

----

49 Translator's note: JJLL stands for *Juventudes Libertarias* ("Libertarian Youth") or *Federación Ibérica de Juventudes Libertarias* ("Iberian Federation of Libertarian Youth").

50 Translator's note: literally, "Cuenca Grocery Store."

51 A. B. Rodríguez, I, 79.

52 *Ib.*, 80.

request to the civil governor for arms. With a second refusal, the militiamen who had already been organized, made an assault on the armories. With weapons in hand, the power of the CNT, FAI, and JJLL was reinforced. That same day, the governor, who had received reports of the advancing troops in revolt, called up all the forces of the Popular Front and on the next day, July 20, the Committee of the Antifascist Alliance was set up. It was also referred to as the Committee of the United Popular Front.[53] The union movements acted quickly, occupying buildings and strategic bridges.

In the barracks of the Civil Guard, situated in the upper part of the city, were the guards charged with advancing the rebellion; Lieutenant Benítez González and Captain Carmelo Martínez, who were trying to convince the chief of command, Francisco García de Ángela, and on the other hand, the military governor.

Isolated shots were heard in various places in the upper part of the city, where retired military men confronted the militiamen who were trying to attack the monastery of San Felipe:

> [But] the true fight was not on the streets...and was kept fundamentally small in the enclosure of the siege of the Civil Guard. If in the first days in the Court of Flags of the Headquarters of the Commandant an uprising was on the point of being staged in earnest,...these processes were resolved in a unique manner. In the first case, in the meeting which involved those chiefly in command, a rapid inventory was made of the Guard's forces and of those of the militias and an uprising was ruled out. The militias then cordoned off the barracks and the area surrounding the Civil Government building. They lifted the hose from a gasoline pump and threatened to burn down the whole building if the Guard were to resist. Those who were under siege asked for safe passage for the women and children out from the enclosure, before beginning talks. After this, the negotiations produced the Guards' definitive surrender.[54]

....

53 Translator's note: in Spanish this last was *Comité de Enlace del Frente Popular*.

54 *Ib.*, 102-103.

The rapid action of the leaders of the different parties of the Popular Front tipped the balance in the small conservative city of Cuenca. A few days after the beginning of the war, the military governor, Lieutenant Colonel Manuel Romero was arrested.[55] In a report prepared by the Committee of Cuenca, Elías Cruz Moya, Pablo Requena, and Gerardo Alcañiz maintained that: "it seemed that the Civil Guard could not agree among themselves or that they felt intimidated because we workers had surprised them in their attempt to take to the streets, with the result that their betrayal did not bear fruit in the capital.[56] After this, the governor and the Popular Front decreed, in agreement with the government, the transfer of all the forces of the Civil Guard to dispersed sites."[57]

The activity of the United Committee of the Popular Front focused its efforts on controlling the institutions holding real power in the city: the political institution, centralized in the control of the civil government building, which was cordoned off by the union leaders; the forces for public order, through the control of the command headquarters of the Civil Guard, watched night and day; the religious institution, by the control of all religious buildings and persons: "On the 19th of July, the archbishop's palace was cordoned off and any movement of the bishop or his curia was prohibited. Also, the cathedral was vacated as well as all monasteries and convents in the city: that of the Discalced Carmelite Sisters, that of 'las Blancas,'[58] that of the Order of the Immaculate Conception....The monastery of the Vincentian Fathers was already vacated due to the events of May. San Felipe Neri...attacked after a small bomb exploded at the front entrance."[59]

....

55 "What makes Cuenca so unique is that just a few months prior nobody would have foreseen such activity. And only the enthusiasm and effervescence created by the situation of war made it possible that the three institutions holding actual power in the city were put under pressure." (*Ib.*, 87)

56 Translator's note: This report from the group of socialists, anarchists, and communists who took over Cuenca indicates that the Civil Guard thought the people in Cuenca would support the rebellious military leaders.

57 *Informe del Comité local de la Federación CNT de Cuenca*: Causa, Leg.1538, Exp.3, p. 44.

58 Translator's note: *Las Blancas* were an order of nuns called the Slaves of the Most Blessed Sacrament and of the Immaculate Mary.

59 A. B. Rodríguez, I, 87-88. The device at the church of San Felipe exploded on July 20.

Apse of the church and monastery, San Felipe

Everyone went into action, but at the same time everyone carefully followed orders. For some there was spontaneity, for others indecision. In general, there was little organization. Only the anarchists did not await orders; on July 20 they exploded a bomb at the bishop's palace and another at the entrance of the Monastery of San Felipe.[60] It generated a climate of disorder and fear in the civil population. Businesses closed and, after July 20, only the militiamen circulated through the streets, stopping everyone they met.[61]

On July 21, amid suspicions of a revolt by the Civil Guard in their barracks, a group of CNT men, among them Elías Cruz Moya,[62] went off to Madrid to ask for reinforcements, which did not arrive until July 26. On that date, the elite of the Spanish anarchists amassed in Cuenca. Among them was their leader, Cipriano Mera.[63] Mera returned to Cuenca on July 28 with various trucks in which were transported some 150 armed militiamen. There they managed to dominate the situation, with the greater part of the anarchists joining the Rosal Column.[64] They also managed to concentrate the provincial Civil Guard in the city of Cuenca, preparing to depart for the front at a later date. With the Benemérita,[65] away from the city, public order was increasingly in the hands of the Rosal Column and the militiamen.[66]

In view of the uncertainty, the city's Civil Guard remained concentrated from July 22 in one part of the seminary building in order to better

....

60 Cf., *Ib.*, II, 90.

61 "No one dared to go outside because people were afraid. There were only military men outside and, if they saw you on the street, they stopped you right away and demanded to know who you were," (Interview cit., *Ib.*, I, 86).

62 Translator's note: Elías Cruz Moya was part of a group of sixteen from the various socialist, anarchist, and communist organizations that were then governing the city.

63 Cipriano Mera, member of the National Defense Committee, was the one who chose Lieutenant Colonel Francisco de Rosal to be at the head of a column of militiamen who came through Cuenca.

64 Translator's note: Various groups of militiamen were formed among the socialists, anarchists, and communists of Spain. One group was the "Rosal Column," which was guilty of many of the atrocities against religious in Cuenca.

65 Translator's note: The colloquial name of the Spanish Civil Guard was *la Benemérita*, "the Meritorious."

66 "Our demand was finally met, since around eight o'clock that night the Civil Guard left for Madrid, thus ceasing to be a threat to Cuenca. The city was won for the cause" (C. Mera, Guerra, exilio y cárcel de un anarcosindicalista. Memorias [France, 1976], 25: A. B Rodríguez, I, 105).

control it. From July 26, Civil Guard officers from all of the provincial posts began arriving to join the concentration of troops there, and they remained until they were sent to the front in Madrid on August 2, 1936. From that date on,[67] in the other part of the building, the bishop together with some religious and priests were under the care of the Civil Guard.[68] When the Civil Guard went off to the front and the militia patrols took responsibility for public order, they also assumed responsibility for the care of the seminary building, keeping (at their own expense) all the ecclesiastics taking refuge there.[69]

From July 18-30, a veritable revolution took place in Cuenca. It broke out with a great deal of violence in response to the military uprising in Africa. The Republican government was deeply affected by this uprising, and the extremist groups on the left, whom they wanted to eliminate,[70] took advantage of the situation. The results of all this was an explosive revolution with an authoritarian tinge, mixed in with a violence that increased daily and which surprised the civilian population. Fear fomented by violence and the constant threat of personal denunciations served to control the rear guard in little time.[71]

July 31, Beginning of the Spiral of Violent Reprisal

The revolutionary response to the uprising in Cuenca, inasmuch as it was a small city with little political or social conflict, cannot be compared to that

....

67 Translator's note: from July 26, 1936.

68 A. B. Rodriguez, I, 105.

69 Translator's note: To make it clear what the author is saying: The Civil Guard, also called the *Benemérita*, was expected to favor the call of the military generals, such as Francisco Franco, who had rebelled against the Spanish Second Republic; as a result, on July 21 Elías Cruz Moya, representing the socialists, communists, and anarchists, went to Madrid to ask the Socialist government there to move the Civil Guard out of Cuenca to fight on the front in Madrid against the generals. On July 22 the members of the Civil Guard in the city of Cuenca came to the seminary to defend the bishops and priests. On July 26, all the Civil Guard from everywhere in the province of Cuenca came to the seminary to concentrate their forces there. On July 28 Rosal's Column of militiamen came into Cuenca. On August 2, 1936, the Civil Guard followed orders from the Socialist government to leave Cuenca for Madrid. The Civil Guard was no longer able to protect the bishop, priests, and religious. The militiamen took over the responsibility to care for the needs of the religious, priests, and bishop, whom the same militia regarded as their enemies.

70 Translator's note: The Socialist government in Madrid was suspicious of some of the more extreme elements of the left, especially the anarchists.

71 A. B. Rodríguez and R. De la Rosa, 170. 180-181.

in surrounding cities and provinces.[72] Personal relationships after July 18 became a problem, because everyone knew each other. Personal and family grudges became aggravated in this climate. There was progressively more violence and repression, which brought with it the loss of personal liberty and social trust. Groups of armed militias in cars rushed through the streets and began the searches, confiscations, detentions, and later, the assassinations.[73] The disorder generated by the abuse from these groups and the way the authorities supposedly in control caved in to them resulted in the population remaining holed up in their houses. "Cuenca became peopled by armed individuals, who changed the normal greetings, salutations and atmosphere of the streets....Fear followed when the 'phantom cars' passed by, when the sound of blows with rifle butts against doors at dawn and shouts were heard, and when detentions were made."[74]

As we have already pointed out, when the Rosal Column arrived, violence increased exponentially. The arrival of anarchist militiamen, outsiders coming in, produced a contagion that spread to places like Madrid.[75] With the anarchist militia came lootings, church burnings, kidnappings, and killings from July 31 on. A horror like none before broke out in the city, encouraged by rumors and the advance of terror. "The first two assassinations of religious occurred on July 31, without there being other criminal acts of great importance in the meantime."[76]

Until July 31 there had not been deaths in Cuenca.[77] On that last day of July, in full daylight, after having traversed the whole city without hiding anything but in the sight of everyone, the first assassination of religious— two Redemptorists—initiated a spiral of violence which did not end until the beginning of 1937. Beginning August 4 or 5, crimes became more generalized. Throughout the whole month of August 1936, autonomous groups from the Rosal Column and local anarchist militiamen rode in dark-col-

....

72 A. B. Rodríguez, II, 111. S. Cirác wrote in *The Martyrology*: "We can affirm that the Cuenca diocese was one that had less victims of persecution, less deaths in the war, and also less war criminals." (S. Cirác Estopañán, 18)

73 Cf., A. B. Rodríguez, II, 85. 143.

74 A. B. Rodríguez and R. De la Rosa, 183.

75 Cf., A. B. Rodríguez, II, 91-93.

76 AHMC. City Police, General Affairs, Leg. 2389-2, esp. 105: Cit. A. B. Rodríguez, II, 117.

77 Cf., A. B. Rodríguez, II, 91-92. 115-116; A. B. Rodríguez and R. De la Rosa, 138.

ored cars called the Phantoms. To these were joined some people from UGT[78] and Socialist Youth. They formed vigilante patrols, which, began to make *los paseos*.[79] These followed the same pattern: particular individuals would be taken from their homes during the night and would be driven by car to the place of their assassination.[80] Even though the executions took place at night, everyone was talking about the deaths the next day.[81] With these deaths, they intended to cleanse the rear guard of disaffected individuals, justifying the deaths from motives of security in the rear guard. Those killed were deprived of any type of defense or judicial guarantees, presenting this action as "the people's justice."[82]

The two bloodiest months were August and September, which in the capital produced fifty deaths in August and 31 in September. Beginning in October the number of victims decreased until January 1937. The groups of dead never were large, the biggest being made up of seven people.[83] The place most used for assassinations was the garden walls of the cemetery.

According to a statistical study by A. Belén Rodríguez Patiño from multiple sources,[84] 144 persons died through reprisals in the city of Cuenca, of whom only forty-seven were of households in the capital. Of the thirty-six ecclesiastics who were murdered, only twenty lived in the city of Cuenca. The chosen victims were outstanding members of right-wing parties, people with ties to the Catholic Church, and others known for their political sympathies. The most significant group of reprisal victims, because of their faith, were religious priests or laypersons. The second group was that of outstanding militants in right-wing parties, and the third group was composed of activists[85] from each locality. As we have seen, there was a

....

78 Translator's note: *Union General de Trabajadores (UGT)*, translated as "General Union of Workers," was a major Spanish trade union.

79 Translator's note: Literally, "excursions." This became the nickname for the practice during the Spanish Civil War, of militias abducting people, driving them out of town and then shooting them, usually leaving the bodies on the road as a warning to others.

80 Cf., A. B. Rodríguez, II, 118-119. 122; A. B. Rodríguez and R. De la Rosa, 189-190.

81 Cf., *Ib.*, 144.

82 Cf. *Ib*, 85-88.

83 Cf., *Ib.*, 116-119.

84 Cf. *Ib.*, 114-119; A. B. Rodríguez and R. De la Rosa, 201.

85 Translator's note: activists against the socialist government in Madrid.

selective search for those who were to suffer repression, and in their selection of targets the persecutors especially aimed their violence at the Catholic Church—its priests, religious, churches, monasteries, and convents:[86]

> *They shot many religious and those affiliated to political parties on the right not because of any concrete actions on the part of the victims, but for the simple fact of their belonging to an ideological group. They killed out of fear of a rear guard that would be openly republican; out of anger and because that was what was being done in other towns nearby. That's why many individuals who had behaved normally until then became executioners or signed orders for searches and killings. Nobody asked why these things were happening. It was war and that was good enough.*[87] [88]

This violence continued until December 1936, in which the nighttime sequestrations gave way to the arrests by the SIM.[89] The provincial jail,[90] housed in an old castle, was full of prisoners crowded into the cells. The control of the jail was given to the labor unions. When the number of arrests made by the militiamen and the Committee of Public Health increased, the provincial prison ended up being inadequate and other places had to be

....

86 A. B. Rodríguez & R. De la Rosa, 205.

87 A. B. Rodríguez, II, 128.

88 Translator's note: It is surprising to read that members of the Second Republic would kill those who were openly in favor of the Republic. The reason for their anger and fear, it seems, is that the radical union members and students, who were all sympathetic to Communism, especially as it was lived in Russia at the time, did not want conservatives to participate in the democratic process. The number of radicals was comparatively small, while the number of conservatives, especially in rural areas, was large. In an open and fair election, the conservatives could have regained control of the Republic.

89 Cf., *Ib.*, 146. The SIM was the *Servicio de Investigación Militar* ("Service for Military Investigation") of the republican government, which had a notable role in the repression of the rear guard in the cities loyal to the government in Madrid (Cf., A. B. Rodríguez and R. De la Rosa, 149.)

90 The provincial jail depended on the General Administration of Prisons. It required a file on each prisoner, who should be assigned one man per cell (Cf., A. B. Rodríguez, II, 101-104.) These guarantees were changed as of July 18, 1936. The registration ledger of the provincial prison in Cuenca with its admissions and releases was copied in the section on jails listed in the *Causa General* to give us an idea of the number of prisoners. [Translator's note: *la Causa General* was an extensive investigation done after the Civil War by the Franco government to see what crimes against justice were committed by the Republican government] (*Pieza 3, Cárceles y sacas: Causa*, Leg. 675. Exp.2, pp.7-38).

pressed into service, such as the conciliar seminary and the monastery of the Carmelites.

Religious Persecution in the City of Cuenca

In 1936, the city of Cuenca had many religious institutions. Besides the cathedral and the diocesan conciliar seminary,[91] there were three parishes (Santiago, El Salvador, and San Esteban); the churches of San Pedro, San Miguel, San Andrés, San Antón, and La Virgen de la Luz; the seminary of the Vincentians in San Pablo; and the monastery of the Redemptorists in San Felipe. To these can be added the convents of the Discalced Carmelites; the Sisters of the Sacred Heart of Jesus and of the Holy Angels; the Justinian nuns; the Benedictines and the Order of the Immaculate Conception (the Conceptionists); the religious women's communities of the Servants of Jesus; the Servants of St. Joseph; the Mercedarians; the Daughters of Charity in the Hospital of Santiago and in the offices of the municipal charity; and the Little Sisters of the Poor in the nursing home. According to the census done the year before, living in the city were eighteen canons and curial priests, twenty-seven pastors and chaplains, eleven religious men, and 111 religious women. Also, one should add the seminarians of the conciliar seminary and those of San Pablo, together with their professors.[92]

Religion was one of the more controversial topics during the Second Republic,[93] giving rise in the working classes to a class hatred against the Church, named enemy of the people. This hatred in Cuenca, given the religious idiosyncrasy of the city, took flesh little by little, giving rise to various protests until July 1936, when it was transformed into assaults on churches—and later, in the murder of priests and religious.

At the end of March, in a session of the city council, Republicans and socialists demanded the closure of the churches and the expulsion of all the religious from the city as enemies of the people.[94] This act will not be relevant until the May elections, when the first attack on the Church occurred: on May 1 and 2 the Monastery of San Pablo is assaulted, and the

....

91 S. Cirac Estopañán, 162.

92 Cf., A. B. Rodríguez, II, 124.

93 Cf., *Ib.*, 125; A. B. Rodríguez and R. De la Rosa, 185.

94 Cf., A. B. Rodríguez, II, 82.

Vincentians there were falsely accused of having shot at some demonstrators as they passed by the monastery. All of this was a false rumor, because the shots were fired by a person near those demonstrators.[95] This incident provoked a distancing between the city's Republican government and the local church.

The latent hatred toward the Church once again came to the fore with the beginning of the Civil War. Priests did not have problems during the first weeks, although many of them sought places to hide.[96] And although there was not a single death until July 31, acts of violence were perpetrated against religious buildings from July 18 through 31: on July 20, two devices were exploded, one in the episcopal palace and the other at the door of the church of San Felipe, which then was assaulted. The Sisters Servants of St. Joseph were expelled on July 22, and their high school confiscated.[97] On July 28, the bishop's palace was searched.[98] On July 29 and 30, the bishop's palace and the cathedral were sacked.[99] Various acts of violence commenced against religious buildings in the city, but with the arrival of the militiamen from Madrid the pillaging of buildings was forgotten and the persecution of Church people began.

From July 27 on, priests gathered at the diocesan seminary in the belief that it would be a safer place for them. The bishop also went there after the militiamen made a meticulous search of the episcopal palace. The Mercedarian religious women, who lived in another wing of the building, saw to

....

95 "On May 1, two anarchist friends went with a hunting rifle out to the nearby mountains, separating themselves a bit from the rest of the noisy crowd that was celebrating the day. One of them let loose a shot, or they were firing shots while doing a little hunting. The sound caught the attention of the other workers, who believed it was an attack on the part of the religious at the monastery, toward whom they maintained a great distrust. In a few moments, the feelings of indignation exploded, fanned on by the poor atmosphere that already existed between both communities. The perpetrators of the mistake either did not want to or did not know how to defuse the situation. At the last moment, the whole group gathered there decided to take justice into their own hands and to attack the monastery" (*Ib.*, 82; cf. *Ib.*, 82-83; A. B. RODRÍGUEZ Y R. DE LA ROSA, 185). According to D. De Felipe, the assault on the monastery of San Pablo "was remembered in the Union Hall. Before the elections the unions had to expel the Vincentians, who with their students had a great number of votes..." [for candidates on the right]. (D. DE FELIPE, 143).

96 Cf. A. B. RODRÍGUEZ, II, 124.

97 Cf. A. B. RODRÍGUEZ Y R. DE LA ROSA, 129.

98 Cf. A. B. RODRÍGUEZ, II, 125.

99 In *Martirologio* (S. CIRAC ESTOPAÑÁN, 163-170) all the looting that the churches suffered is described.

the needs of the priests. Each had a room assigned to him. They could say Mass each day, pray the rosary and Divine Office in common, and have the Blessed Sacrament reserved there.[100] The Civil Guard, concentrated there, protected the building. Once they were sent to the front, a group of militiamen took their place, making the seminary a veritable jail.[101] The militiamen that came from outside[102] tried to copy what was done in the surrounding provinces. The spark of the head-on persecution of the Church was lit.[103] After the attack on the monastery of San Pablo, two facts must be pointed out, for they relate to the way events developed.

The first of these events, as we have already pointed out, was the assassination of the first victims in the city of Cuenca, two Redemptorists. "Their macabre selection was random, with the only reference being to choose members of the Church."[104] Taken from the home of an old priest near the cathedral, they were assassinated in the Cantera del Batán.[105] It was commonly known that the killings involved two religious from San Felipe. From then on, the practice of "anything goes" raged.[106]

The second event was the assassination of the bishop, D. Cruz Laplana y Laguna.[107] Confining him in the episcopal palace since July 19, the militiamen did a search, after which he was obliged to leave the palace and go to the seminary, together with his sister, Ascensión; his cousin, Manuel Laplana Torres; and his administrator, D. Fernando Español Berthier.[108] In the seminary there was already a group of fifteen priests. The Rosal Column began to pressure authorities to have the bishop given over to them, thus taking him away from the priests.[109] When the Civil Guard was sent to the front, the mayor, fearing for his own life, offered the bishop the option of

....

100 Cf. S. CIRAC, *Vida de D. Cruz Laplana, Obispo de Cuenca* (Barcelona, 1943), 123-124.

101 Cf. A. B. RODRÍGUEZ, II, 125.

102 Cf. *Ib.*, 95.

103 Cf. A. B. RODRÍGUEZ Y R. DE LA ROSA, 199.

104 Cf. A. B. RODRÍGUEZ, II, 117.

105 Translator's note: literally, the Millstone Quarry.

106 A. B. RODRÍGUEZ Y R. DE LA ROSA, 193.

107 Cf. M. E. GONZÁLEZ, *Los doce obispos mártires del siglo XX en España* (Madrid, 2012) 71-74; S. CIRAC, *Vida de D. Cruz Laplana...*, 122-127.

108 Cf. S. CIRAC, *Vida de D. Cruz Laplana...*, 71.

109 Cf. A. B. RODRÍGUEZ, II, 125-126.

leaving the city along with the *Benemérita,* who were committed to defend him. But the bishop refused to abandon his diocese. During the morning between August 7 and 8, the local committee of the Popular Front decided to do away with him. Taken away from the seminary along with the priest D. Fernando Español, they drove them in a car five kilometers up the highway toward Villar de Olalla and killed them.[110] The martyrdom of the bishop took on a symbolic dimension in the religious persecution: the general population realized that no one was safe.

Although the Church did not participate in the military uprising, this was the accusation made by the Popular Front. The Church members could have an affinity with those who had housed them in the headquarters of the Civil Guard, but they did not maintain contact with any of them.[111] But the mere suspicion of their siding with subversives was sufficient pretext on the part of the militiamen to place the Church at the center of the bull's-eye. The undercurrent was a strongly anticlerical sentiment, which was encouraged by the press. For example, on August 3, 1936, an article published in *El Heraldo de Cuenca* was a call to revolution: "May not a single church stand; may all the clergy in Spain disappear; we do not want the teachings of people hostile to God and to men who are promoting and commiting crimes."[112]

The militiamen of Puente de Vallecas, led by Cipriano Mera, awoke the instinct for doing away with the "enemy," which consisted of poor, defenseless religious.[113] "The population lived in a veritable state of shock and incomprehension, of fear and powerlessness, since the executioners of those who were killed along the walls of the municipal cemetery and in the ditches had been their neighbors in Cuenca. They knew them perfectly well and the families to which they belonged."[114] The group of those who carried out the religious persecution in Cuenca amounted to forty persons. Their nicknames remain in the collective memory: *el Sustos* (Frights), *el Picias* (Pranks), *el Viruta* (Shaving), *el Cestero* (Basket Weaver), *el Guerra*

---

110 M. E. GONZÁLEZ, *o. c.,* 72-73. D. Cruz Laplana and Fernando Español were beatified in Rome October 28, 2007.

111 Cf. A. B. RODRÍGUEZ, II, 123.

112 B. MARTÍNEZ PÉREZ, *Sin compasión, ¡¡A la picota!!* in *Heraldo de Cuenca,* 83 (3-8-1936) 1.

113 Cf. A. B. RODRÍGUEZ Y R. DE LA ROSA, 199.

114 *Ib.,* 138.

(War), *los Pambaratos* (Cheap Bread), *el Cangrejero* (Crab), *el Polaco* (Pole), *el Vinagrero* (Vinegar Seller), *el Pesca* (Fishing), *el Barbero* (Barber), *Roque el Danzas* (Rook Dances), *el Finito* (Finished), *Peñaranda* (Punishing), *Garrote* (Club), *Sariñana* (translation not found, but *Sariña* means "Navy"), *Pulgarcito* (Little Thumb), *los Cacharreros* (Homebuilders).[115]

The religious persecution had another consequence: the destruction of the religious patrimony of the city.[116] One of the first acts of violence was the destruction of the religious buildings in the upper part of the city: the churches of San Pedro, Santa Cruz, el Salvador, San Esteban, and the hermitages of San Jerónimo and San Antonio. Also, the monasteries and convents were assaulted, robbed, and bricked up. The Benedictine nuns were driven out from their convent, which was converted into a barracks, and the nuns were taken to the Little Sisters. The Discalced Carmelites, the Sisters of the Sacred Heart of Jesus and of the Holy Angels (known also as the *Petras*)[117] and the Conceptionists (*Concepcionistas misioneras de la Enseñanza*) were evicted and the convents were converted into jails. There was destruction of sacred images, looting of places of worship, and the theft of religious works in gold and silver. To this must be added the destruction of libraries, as happened to the 10,000 volumes in the cathedral school. Finally, the destruction of parish records should be mentioned, the loss of documentation which the government tried to gloss over by issuing a decree for their conservation dated February 28, 1937; a measure which came too late. This attack against the patrimony was symbolic of the violence against the Church. As a columnist in the *Heraldo de Cuenca* put it when, a few days later, with the bishop and many priests already killed, the argument was made for church destruction due to the enemies of the Republic taking safe harbor in them:

....

115 *Ib.*, 199ss. Their names appear among the militiamen of Cuenca (*Pieza especial de milicianos*: CAUSA, Leg. 675, Exp. 11), responsible for the repression in the city (*Pieza 4. Checas*-CAUSA, Leg. 675. Exp. 3). Many of them died at the front. Those who did not, after the war, were judged by military tribunals. These military judgments are kept in AGET in Madrid (see the references to the summary judgments at the end, in the documentation in the archives).

116 Cf. A. B. RODRÍGUEZ, II, 132-142.

117 Translator's note: the author appears to think that the *Angelicas* and the *Petras* were the same religious order. It seems, though, that besides the order associated with the Holy Angels, there was a distinct order, called "the Justinian Order of St. Peter" which was known as *las Petras*. Both were located in Cuenca.

Cuenca's Convent of the Discalced Carmelites, later converted to a jail

Fascism shall die, undoubtedly, for the glory of the Proletariat, and, with its death, we shall be able to signal also the definitive abolishment of that former empire of friars, priests, and nuns, of the Catholic Apostolic Roman Church, so poorly administered by all the Spanish clerics, and especially by their highnesses....The art should be esteemed by all people of culture; but life and liberty should be more esteemed. They become stronger in the most famous Christian churches, and, from them, they still attempt to sow terror and to snatch away from us our rights as free human beings. It doesn't matter. With sorrow, with true sorrow, Spain will be seen to need to tear down those artistic jewels in order to dislodge from its precincts the traitorous and factious criminals. Before seeing the Nation and the Republic drowned in blood and enslaved to a power that bears the spirit of Torquemada, let all the cathedrals come down, all the schools, all the magnificent architecture. Do they care? Hardly.[118]

Here is a summary of the religious persecution in Cuenca:

Jailing of all priests, the tortures they were made to suffer, the assassinations of which they were the victims constitute further evidence of the official religious persecution out of hatred for Jesus Christ and his Church. The priests of the Diocese of Cuenca, almost absolutely all, were poor, simple, humble, profoundly pious, with the millennium-long kind of piety from the traditional Spanish family and with a well-proven priestly vocation. They were dedicated exclusively to the care of the Church and to care for the souls of the faithful. They were charitable to the needy and to all, as best as they could be. The fines and the imprisonments and the threats previous to all that, at the outbreak of the revolution, turned into the slogan, which also was a command: "Kill all the priests!"....And thus began the tragedy of the priests of the Diocese. Some hid and lived for days and days behind walls, in basements or in caves; others fled through the fields and mountains, without knowing where to go, as if hunted by wild animals. Others were taken prisoner

------

118 B. MARTÍNEZ PÉREZ, *El sacrilegio de la clerecía española* en *Heraldo de Cuenca*, 85 (10-8-1936) 1.

by armed gangs: these men blasphemed satanically to terrorize the priests, they insulted them and hit them, threatened and pushed them, they tortured them, beat them cruelly, mutilated and mocked them, they martyred them and killed them, stomped on them, cut them into pieces, they sprinkled them with gasoline and set them on fire, they left their bodies on the highways and in the mountains....The persecution of priests extended to anyone and anything connected to them: their homes, their books, their belongings, family members, parents, siblings and in-laws, their nephews and nieces, their friends—all because they were related to the priest. They did all this to the priests, solely when they were good priests and worthy ministers of Jesus Christ....The official religious persecution in the Diocese of Cuenca reached the lay faithful themselves as well, as is proven by hundreds of bloodied testimonies.[119]

Members of the Redemptorist community of San Felipe Neri in Cuenca were victims of this persecution, as we shall show in the following pages.

....

119 S. CIRAC ESTOPAÑÁN, 693-694.

CHAPTER TWO

The Community of Martyrs of San Felipe of Cuenca

The civil province and diocese of Cuenca have a special place in the memory of Redemptorists. In 1864 Fr. Victor Loyódice established in Huete (Cuenca) the first foundation in Spain. The same priest founded the second Redemptorist presence in Alhama (Granada), but both were closed by the liberal Revolution in 1868.[120]

The residence in Huete scarcely lasted four years, but it was the first witness of the community life and the missionary charism of the congregation founded by St. Alphonsus. That is where they initiated the popular mission campaigns. Also in Huete the first authentic copy of the icon of Our Mother of Perpetual Help, Mother of the Redemptorist popular missions, arrived. In that same town there occurred the first miracle in our country wrought by that venerable icon. But Cuenca was also significant at the level of vocations in that the first to join the Redemptorist Congregation in Spain, the priest Pedro López, was born in Torrejoncillo del Rey (Cuenca) and was pastor in Jabalera (Cuenca) when he came to know the missionaries. Finally, the first Spanish Redemptorists who had to abandon

---

120 Cf. MISIONEROS REDENTORISTAS, *Los Redentoristas en España. Primera fundación (1863-1879)* (Madrid, 2013); D. DE FELIPE, *Fundación de los Redentoristas en España* (Madrid, 1965) 331-335.

their homeland because of revolution, were called from this community to go into exile in other countries. Therefore, it is not surprising that, since the first foundation was frustrated for political reasons, the Redemptorists in Spain thought of Cuenca when they had the opportunity to rebuild a second foundation.

The restoration of the Congregation was begun with the arrival in Madrid of Fr. Meinral Jost on December 15, 1878. Two years later he opened the community of Nava del Rey (Valladolid), Granada. El Espino (Burgos)[121] followed that, then Villarejo de Salvanés (Madrid), Astorga (León),[122] and the communities of Madrid—first Santa Barbara, then San Miguel and el Perpetuo Socorro (Perpetual Help), Cuenca, and Pamplona (Navarra). It was in these residences that all the witnesses to the faith from Cuenca spent the greater part of their lives.[123]

The Community of San Felipe de Neri of Cuenca

On February 1, 1895, the Redemptorists opened the first foundation in the city of Cuenca. The community consisted of four priests and two brothers. Fr. Pedro López, a native of Cuenca, was the founding superior. He was a Redemptorist from the beginning of the Redemptorist presence in Spain, and was outstanding in his preaching and missionary work.

The bishop, D. Pelayo González Conde, the former dean of the chapter

....

121 The monastery of Nuestra Señora de El Espino is an old Benedictine cloister closed by the property alienation of Mendizábal. [Translator's note: Juan Álvarez Mendizábal was a Spanish economist and politician. In 1835 he became Minister of the Treasury. To restore the Spanish treasury to solvency, he issued a series of decrees, which closed and sold off church property, with the proceeds going to the treasury.] The monastery is situated near the River Ebro, almost at the dividing line between Álava and Burgos, in the township of Santa Gadea del Cid. It was acquired by the Redemptorists in 1879, and once it was rehabilitated, it was inaugurated in 1882 as the minor seminary of the Spanish Redemptorists. The majority of Spanish Redemptorists, including the protagonists of this book, passed through this minor seminary, what is called a *juvenatus* (juvenate) in France.

122 The monastery of Astorga was inhabited by Franciscans since 1272. The French occupation [Translator's note: by Napoleon's troops in 1808] damaged it severely. It was again inhabited in 1818 until the exclaustration of 1836 [Translator's note: when church property was confiscated by the Spanish civil government.] In 1883 it was given to the Redemptorists by Bishop Brezmes and in October, 1884, it became their theological center. In these first years, Fr. Edward Bürhel created the formation structure to prepare Spanish Redemptorists for the priesthood. We emphasize the importance of this place as the major seminary in which the greater part of the Redemptorist priests mentioned in this book were formed.

123 Cf. D. DE FELIPE, *Fundación...*, 399-421.

in Astorga,[124] was a great friend of the Redemptorists and especially of Fr. López. He gave the Redemptorists the Oratorian monastery and the church of San Felipe de Neri, a baroque work from the eighteenth century, abandoned since the time of the confiscation of Church property under Mendizábal in 1835. It is located in the upper zone of the city, the so-called "Vatican of Cuenca" because of the presence of the cathedral, episcopal palace, seminary, and other convents and churches. It is an area favored with a wonderful view of the rift created by the rivers Huécar and Júcar, so much admired by poets and painters. But at the same time, it suffered from an absence of residents because of its geographical location, an abundance of churches in the area, and the displacement of the population to the lower part of the city, caused by a new urbanization.

The house that the community inhabited was a big, uncomfortable place, vacant for many years. Since the time that the Oratorian Fathers left it, it had been used as a barracks for the Civil Guard, a school, living quarters for poor families, and as a recreation area.[125] The church, nevertheless, was a lovely jewel.[126] It was a single edifice in the form of a Latin cross with side chapels on both sides. It was decorated in a florid and baroque style, with paintings in the vaults by the brothers González Velázquez.[127] Below the church, an ample crypt opened up. A beautiful retable rose behind the main altar gilded with paintings on wood. A statue of the patron saint of the church was in the center. The Redemptorists placed in the center an icon of Our Lady of Perpetual Help made of bronze at the workshop of Marco Pérez in Cuenca. The face and hands were made of marble. An image of Our Lady of Sorrows, attributed to Salzillo,[128] was also venerated in the church and another of St. Francis attributed to Zurbarán,[129] which was in the Iberoamerican Exposition of Seville in 1928.

....

124 Translator's note: The dean is the official who presides over the chapter, or clergy, of a cathedral.

125 Cf. R. TELLERÍA, *Un instituto misionero* (Madrid, 1932) 390-392.

126 Cf. D. DE FELIPE, *o. c.*, 141.

127 Translator's note: In the eighteenth century, three brothers, Luís, Alejandro, and Antonio—all sons of the sculptor Pablo González Velázquez—collaborated with one another on a variety of paintings.

128 Translator's note: The Spanish sculptor Francisco Salzillo worked in the neoclassical style during the eighteenth century.

129 Translator's note: Francisco de Zurbarán painted in Spain in the seventeenth century.

Twenty-six years after leaving Huete, Fr. López was enthusiastically welcomed at the station in Cuenca as the superior of the new community, but—it also has to be said—with heavy criticism from the old liberals who kept intact their old anticlerical attitudes. They were a minority, but they made themselves heard in the city's press.

As with every foundation,[130] things were not easy in the beginning. The crypt had been used for keeping horses. The first task of the new tenants was to get rid of the troughs that lined the right wall and to get it ready to receive the missionary icon of Perpetual Help. In addition, it was the only house for religious in the city, which soon made it one of the most beloved and frequented places of worship by the citizens of Cuenca in the upper zone. Two other factors contributed to the splendor of the church of San Felipe: one was the special cultivation of the sacrament of reconciliation, which brought about a closeness to the faithful, and the encouragement of frequent Communion. When the Redemptorists first arrived in the city, frequent Communion was rare. The second factor had to do with the religious communities, especially of women. They came to the Redemptorists of San Felipe to ask for preachers for their annual and monthly retreats, or other preaching events in the boarding schools. Their requests were always generously attended to.

One segment of the clergy did not receive the arrival of the Redemptorists with the same enthusiasm, as frequently happens in small clerical cities where there is fear of "competition." However, they soon realized that the newly arrived religious at the community of San Felipe were, by their charism, missionaries. And the Redemptorists soon dedicated themselves to evangelization in the city as well as throughout the large rural areas of the diocese and in the neighboring region of La Mancha. A report sent to Rome in 1897 said:

> *Until now, because of a lack of personnel, we have given few missions, though we could give relatively many. In this diocese of Cuenca we will always find difficulties, either on the part of the clergy or on the part of the people. The faith here has received many blows. The bishop here has*

....

130 R. TELLERÍA, *o. c.*, 390-392; T. CEPEDAL, *Las Comunidades de la Provincia. Cuenca-San Felipe*: BPE XXVII, 151 (2000) 73.

given the Fathers what is necessary to meet the costs of giving missions. He has set aside 3,000 pesetas for this purpose.[131] For missions of ten days, they have 100 pesetas, for others that are longer, 200 pesetas. If the local priests don't want to have anything of this, all this stays with us for the benefit of our house.

However, the report concludes: "The community, in general, is esteemed in the city and in the diocese."[132]

The popular missions were the principal apostolic work of the community. In 1896 they preached eleven; six missions and three renewals[133] the following year; the number rose to twenty-two missions and twelve renewals in 1898. To this has to be added novenas[134] and brief sermons in rural areas. In the year 1897, with few missions for lack of personnel, "they preached more than one-hundred sermons on special occasions."[135] In Cuenca it was the custom that the missionaries precede and accompany the bishop to prepare the people spiritually for his pastoral visits in rural towns. Moreover, throughout the forty years of the Redemptorists' presence, they preached the gospel—not only throughout this province, but even in other neighboring provinces, such as Teruel, Guadalajara, Valencia, Toledo, Madrid, and reaching as far as Málaga.[136]

The community of San Felipe always had an average of eight to twelve members. Twelve was the number of which the community was formed

....

131 Translator's note: a Spanish gold peseta in 1897 weighed about .29 grams; in 2016 values, each would be worth $11.68 U.S. dollars, for a total of 3,000 pesetas calculated at around $35,000.

132 AHGR 30150002, 0006h. We must clarify that normally two Fathers would go on a mission. This would mean that the contribution given by the bishop was five pesetas a day, including costs. The mission was offered free to the people. This clarification is necessary because of the ongoing accusations stemming from the anticlericalism of the age about the wealth of the clergy.

133 Translator's note: A *renewal* was a follow-up series of talks given after a mission had been preached and for a much shorter period of time than the mission itself would have required. It was an innovation of St. Alphonsus himself with the purpose of cementing in the good results achieved by the mission.

134 Translator's note: A *novena* comes from the Latin word for "nine" and refers to a preaching event of nine days duration. It is modeled after the nine days that the Apostles and Mary spent praying for the coming of the Holy Spirit after Jesus ascended into heaven (Acts 1:14).

135 D. DE FELIPE, *o. c.,* 382.

136 R. TELLERÍA, *o. c.,* 395-397. Translator's note: The distance from Cuenca to Málaga is 564 kilometers, more than 350 miles.

when the Civil War broke out. Sometimes, there were those who were sick with tuberculosis within the community—a frequent illness at that time. They were sent there to recuperate in the dry air of La Mancha. But its high number corresponded to an intense evangelization activity throughout the whole city.[137] Along with the missionary campaigns throughout the diocese and the neighboring dioceses, we need to remember the ordinary apostolate of the church itself: well-planned liturgies, careful attention to confessions, labor-intensive conferences, spiritual exercises for laypeople, devotions, pious associations, for example. Because of the decree about frequent Communion by St. Pius X, San Felipe became one of the churches most attended for the celebration of the Eucharist, where the necessity of frequent Communion was drummed into the laypeople. During the forty years of Redemptorist presence, San Felipe was an evangelization center known throughout the city of Cuenca, "bringing about a flourishing of the Christian life."[138]

---

137 Cf. *Ib.,* 393-394.
138 *Ib.,* 393.

Community of San Felipe of Cuenca, 1929

This was the scenario and apostolic field where some of the witnesses to the faith that we are going to present worked for years. Others were in the community less time. The witnesses for the process of beatification remember all of them as apostolic men, men of prayer and study, popular missionaries in the vineyard of the Lord. The Church was always open to welcome those who came to her and was totally removed from any political themes.

The presence in Cuenca of the sons of St. Alphonsus was so significant that in the year 1915 the Redemptorists began a second foundation in the city, although only for a short time—the monastery of San Pablo,[139] which they converted into a minor seminary (1915-1920). The idea came up in 1913. Father provincial Marceliano Gil thought that the minor seminary in El Espino (Burgos) was inadequate for receiving the vocations from Spanish regions far from the north. The new minor seminary was established in the old monastery of the Dominicans, situated outside the walls of Cuenca in a charming landscape, the gorge of the River Huécar across from *Las Casas Colgadas*.[140] On April 7, 1915, the two upper classes made up of thirty-four teens arrived from El Espino. Among them were Julián Pozo and Miguel Goñi, who finished their courses there during the two years prior to novitiate. Classes began on April 14, and on April 25 the solemn inauguration was celebrated and included the participation of practically all the Fathers of San Felipe. A group of missionaries also lived in the minor seminary. They were relocated to the south of the country. Just the same, this seminary of San Pablo did not survive. It was closed in August 1920, and professors and students returned to El Espino. The Vincentians occupied San Pablo in 1922, doubling the number of religious orders of men in the city.[141]

According to Sebastián Cirac Estopañán, when the time of difficulty for the Church arrived, the church of San Felipe was outstanding in the 1930s for "the splendor of the liturgy, both in the morning and in the evening; the great number of the faithful who came there, the solid piety

---

139 *Ib.*, 400-404; T. CEPEDAL, *a. c.*, 75.

140 Translator's note: The "hanging houses" of Cuenca are several buildings that seem to rest on very little base but which rise three or more stories above the gorge at the edge of the cliff.

141 S. CIRAC, *Vida de D. Cruz Laplana, Obispo de Cuenca* (Barcelona, 1943) 99-102.

that was cultivated there, the prudent and efficacious spiritual direction that was given there; the spirit of sacrifice and the zeal of the religious, who traveled about the whole diocese at the slightest wish of the Prelate."[142] The relevance which the Redemptorists had in Cuenca made it likely that they would become the focal point of anti-clerical currents, and even more so when they had become the only male religious order present after the expulsion of the Vincentians.

The Winds of Persecution

The Second Republic was declared on April 14, 1931, and with it came difficult times for the Catholic Church in Spain. The old anticlericalism of the nineteenth century survived in certain political sectors that put the religious question at the center of political debate. The successive governments of the Republic had openly anticlerical and antireligious manifestations, since they saw the Spanish Catholic Church as a powerful force opposed to many of their republican projects. The Church had declared some projects contrary to the faith, if not to the religious liberty proclaimed by the Republic itself.

The fall of the monarchy and the arrival of the new republican regime unleashed a series of acts of vandalism against churches and Church personnel. Priests, religious men and women, and laypeople suffered martyrdom, handing over their lives as a consequence of the out-of-control hatred against the faith. Cuenca, although peaceful, was no stranger to this kind of reaction. The Redemptorist community of San Felipe also suffered this antireligious violence. Fr. Raimundo Tellería ends his presentation on the community of San Felipe of Cuenca in his work *Un Instituto misionero*[143] by making reference to the problems beginning in April 1931:

....

142 15 S. CIRAC ESTOPAÑÁN, *Martirologio de Cuenca. Crónica diocesana de la época roja* (Barcelona, 1947) 170.

143 Translator's note: A missionary institute.

The incendiary torches which in 1931 blackened with the smoke of Averno[144] the clear skies of Spain and which profaned with its tongues of flame the sanctity of the altars, were at the point of reducing to ashes the venerable church of San Felipe and the rest of the city, not excluding the seminary and the episcopal palace. Fortunately, the names of the instigators and of their accomplices in the attempted coup were discovered and the criminal plot was aborted. Later there were not lacking some unjust taunts against the community; but with God's help and that of Our Mother of Perpetual Help they managed to shake them off and happier days dawned and shed their light on their evangelizing efforts for the good of souls.[145]

After the storm came the calm, but the life of the community remained altered by the new winds which, in the Spanish phrase, "ran through the skin of the bull." There is not much data regarding the life of the community during this period, but it can be clearly seen that social tension affected them and made problems for them.[146] They had to suspend apostolic activity in provincial towns like La Roda or Madrigueras.[147] Little by little, the community was limiting itself only to liturgical ministry and to sporadic preaching events in the city:

Time of the Republic when the masses are unleashed. Impossible to think about missionary campaigns. Nor can the bishop go out for pastoral visits. Consequently, a ministry special to this house is disappearing: The Tridua[148] preparatory to episcopal visits. There is not much work beyond the walls of the house. The work within the house continues more or less the same, to judge by the number of Communions. Cuenca is a

----

144 Translator's note: Averno is the name of a volcanic crater in Campania, Italy, which the Romans and the Greeks thought was the entrance to the underworld.

145 R. TELLERÍA, *o. c.*, 395.

146 The community chronicles were destroyed during the Civil War.

147 "They had already announced a Loyalty Campaign for the weeks of Lent, but with the political effervescence leading up to the Republic, especially in those centers, La Roda, Madrigueras, ...it had to be suspended." Comunidad de Cuenca 1931, Anales X, 77-78.

148 Translator's note: a *Triduum*, Latin for "three days," was a three-day preaching event, in the case referred to here to prepare a parish for the visit of the bishop; the Latin plural for a Triduum is *Tridua*.

city where the right wing triumphs, but the people have been thoroughly worked over by socialism. And because of the current atmosphere they are pressed into compliance on the streets.[149]

The apostolic thrust during these years was a continuous apostolic retreat. Father provincial José Machiñena did the canonical visitation[150] to Cuenca on June 10, 1935, accompanied by Fr. Vicente Renuncio. In the report, which they put together and sent to Rome, we find an echo of the situation in which those missionaries were living: "Regular observance is kept well. Liturgy in the church normal, outside activity, little."[151] After the visit, with the hope of reenergizing the missions, Fr. Ciriaco Olarte was sent to the community.

In the first days of 1936 the Redemptorist community consisted of seven priests and four brothers, among whom five will be martyred:[152] Frs. Inocencio Tirapu Leoz (superior), Javier Gorosterratzu, Pedro Romero, Isidro Fernandez Posado, Ciriaco Olarte, Julián Pozo; and Brs. Clemente López, Marcos Álvarez, Victoriano Calvo, and Benjamín López de Murga. In that same month of January, Fr. Miguel Goñi came to the community and in March they welcomed a very young priest who had just finished the second novitiate, Fr. Eloy Gómez Jorge.

The date for the elections was set for February 16. From January on,

....

149 Comunidad de Cuenca 1932: *Ib.,* 133. In the statistical data reflected in the provincial chronicle throughout the years, the splendor of the liturgy can be clearly seen as well as the real decline in outside work. Taking as reference the years 1932 and 1933 we can arrive at some idea of this. In 1932 (*cf. Ib,* 133) the pastoral ministry which took place in the church of San Felipe consisted of the following: 35,340 Communions in the church, 211 sermons, 206 instructions, forty-eight conferences to associations with 450 members, and two series of spiritual exercises to laypeople; apostolic work done outside of San Felipe was: one mission, six condensed missions, four Tridua, seven novenas, six retreats for religious women, two series of spiritual exercises for major seminarians, two series of spiritual exercises for girls, and twelve sermons on special occasions. In 1933 (*cf. Ib,* 188) the pastoral ministry was: 28,500 Communions, twenty-three sermons, seventy-two instructions, fifty-nine conferences to associations which counted 550 members and two series of spiritual exercises; the pastoral work outside of San Felipe was: two missions of ten days each, one condensed mission, one mission renewal, six Tridua, two novenas, twelve retreats for religious women, one series of spiritual exercises for major seminarians, twenty-three sermons on a variety of topics. This is the tone of what continued in the following years until 1936.

150 Translator's note: A canonical visitation was a visit prescribed by the Rule to a house or province; it was done by the superior general, the provincial superior, or their delegate.

151 AHGR 30150002, 0034.

152 Cf. Comunidad de Cuenca 1936: *Anales* XI, 36.

the electoral campaign was upsetting the peace throughout society. In the midst of this unsettled situation, the community celebrated a festival on February 2. On that day the whole city turned its attention to San Felipe, where they celebrated the golden anniversary of Br. Clemente Lopez's religious profession. His presence in Cuenca was somewhat forgotten because of his long time there. At least one person said that they had seen him there already at the beginning of the twentieth century. The bishop of Cuenca, Msgr. Cruz LaPlana, came to honor him together with various priests of the city who came to attend the renewal-of-vows ceremony. Also, Father provincial, Marceliano Gil came from Madrid and, representing the brothers of the province, was Br. Aniceto Lizasoain.

After the elections, the battle was joined. On the long-awaited day, February 16, the elections were held. In Cuenca, CEDA won but the results were annulled due to pressures from the Popular Front. Elections were rescheduled for the following May 3. The political confrontation between the two blocs became sharper, and before the date for new elections tensions were so high that acts of vandalism, disrespect, and humiliations were common. For two and a half months there was an increasing spiral of violence and intolerance.

On Labor Day, May 1, 1936, in response to the burning of the monastery of San Pablo and the circulation of constant rumors about the Vincentians, the superior of the Redemptorists, Fr. Leoz, sent Br. Benjamin with a letter to the superior of the Vincentians, offering them hospitality and refuge in San Felipe. The brother was able to deliver it without problems. But the situation was tense and menacing false rumors were increasing throughout the city. For that reason, the superior tried contacting various friendly families to spend the night in their homes, for fear that uncontrollable groups of workers might assault San Felipe. With the exceptions of Brs. Victoriano and Benjamin, the rest of the community spent the night elsewhere. A few of the Civil Guard, advised of the fear of the religious, spent the whole night watching the grounds.

The next morning, May 2, the community gathered in their residence, with the exception of Fr. Romero and Br. Clemente, who had spent the night in the nursing home of the Little Sisters and remained there. They remembered to again offer the Vincentians who still remained in Cuenca the opportunity to move over to San Felipe. In order to give the message,

Fr. Leoz sent Fr. Miguel Goñi and Br. Benjamin, dressed in lay garb. Upon their return, they found themselves in danger of death.[153] Br. Benjamin tells us about their arrival in the neighborhood of the monastery:

> *Fr. Goñi and your servant were sent, dressed as men from the country-side, he with a jacket, myself in overalls. On the way up to the bridge of San Pablo, which you have to cross first, we didn't see anyone; at the end of the bridge were some young ladies, who seemed to be ladies of the night. They said whatever came into their minds. Near the bridge and on the other side, there was a pair of Civil Guard. When we wished to go by on our way to "the superintendent's office," they came to tell us we could not go by. We said we were tourists and that we wanted to cross over in order to see the Gorge of Huenca, and so they let us. We went on our way, but not to the superintendent's office. There were several trucks at the door, carrying things away. We pretended that we were admiring the marvelous view that you can get there, but since, until this point we had not seen anything special, we opted to go down into the city instead of going back by the same way, to be able to pick up some further detail.[154]*

Because it was impossible to get to the house of the Vincentians, the Redemptorists decided to go back to the community by another route, going along the lower part of the city, where there was a fair amount of public agitation. Taking them to be Vincentians, the demonstrators chased them, throwing rocks and, when they caught up to them, beat them. The missionaries had to escape to a business establishment, where they were saved. Outside, the demonstrators did not cease yelling slogans against the Church and in favor of the Popular Front. They ended up in the Civil Government building.

....

153 Both protagonists, each on his own part, have left us several accounts of the events; texts which are in agreement in all their details. Fr. Goñi did so in a typewritten letter written to his family and dated June 30, 1936 (M. GOÑI, *Carta a su familia* en: *C. Beatificationis—Escritos*). Br. Benjamin has left us two descriptions of the events: one written as memories, dated July 25, 1940 (APRM. Mártires 0400105.4) and the other as the first of three writings sent to the vice-postulator, Fr. Lucas Pérez, in June 1944, and entitled *Dos años en zona roja (Two Years in the Red Zone)* (APRM. Mártires 0400105.1).

154 APRM. Mártires 0400105.1, 4-5.

As we were walking and at a few meters' distance from the Puerta de Valencia[155] we began to see groups of young men who were looking for or waiting for the Fathers. As we continued to approach the groups, they were getting larger and making us feel uneasy, but now it was too late to turn back. They began to suspect that we were Vincentians, something which they asked us as they came up to us. Our answer was negative, but their suspicions did not go away. One dared to say that he had seen me with a gun and shooting out from the monastery of San Pablo. With that, a car full of assault guards appeared on their way up to the residence of the Vincentians. They stopped the car and told the guards that they should frisk us because we were carrying firearms. The search was negative in all regards. But from that moment and with the guards now absent, they began to really give us a hard time. Naturally...once we passed the bridge of the Puerta de Valencia we headed home, but Fr. Goñi took the road toward the parish of El Salvador....I followed behind him....Since things were getting worse by the moment, we decided to speak with them. For our part the first condition was that they not touch us and that they convince themselves that we were not Vincentians. We could go to the barracks or to the Civil Government building, though the two places were a bit at a distance. They agreed that...they would take us to the Civil Government. But we had not gone but a few meters, we had not finished walking the flight of stairs which end at the Calle del Agua,[156] when they began to go back on their word. They began their insults and began hitting us. They broke Fr. Goñi's glasses and they must have struck him a blow with their fists, because blood was coming from his nose and his mouth....In the Civil Government building, and after the rigorous questioning from the chief of the Commissar, we made our statements and insisted that we had been mistreated....[157]

They had left the house at nine in the morning and it was nearly nine in the evening when they returned. They only escaped from that trap, which

---

155 Translator's note: "the Gate of Valencia," one of several ancient gates into the city.

156 Translator's note: the word *calle* means "street."

157 APRM. Mártires 0400105.4, 2-4.

could have been fatal, by being escorted by the police, who accompanied them to the door of the monastery of San Felipe. Apart from a few blows and bruises, they were able to return unharmed. The next day the election took place in Cuenca, with the victory going to the Popular Front in that provincial district.

In the midst of this climate, on June 10 the appointments for the triennium of 1936 to 1939[158] arrived at the monastery, and with them changes in the Redemptorist community of Cuenca.[159] The superior, Fr. Inocencio Terapu Leoz, left Cuenca to go to Astorga (León); to take his place was Fr. Agustín Pedrosa Misol, who arrived around July 8, coming from the community of San Miguel in Madrid.[160] In July 1936, therefore, the Redemptorist community in Cuenca consisted of twelve religious, eight priests, and four brothers:

1. Br. Clemente López Aguilló, seventy-eight years old. He had been in Cuenca since 1894 and, now as an old man, helped however he could.

2. Br. Marcos Álvarez García, seventy-three years old. He had been in Cuenca since 1920 as a cook.

3. Fr. Pedro Romero Espejo, consultor,[161] sixty-five years old. He had been in Cuenca since 1921, fundamentally dedicated to the services in church.

4. Fr. Augustín Pedrosa Misol, superior, sixty-five years old. Recently arrived in Cuenca.

5. Fr. José Javier Gorosterratzu Jaunarena, admonitor and minister, fifty-nine years old. He had lived in Cuenca since 1933 where, besides writing his books, he took care of the services in church.

....

158 Translator's note: in the 1930s Redemptorist assignments were for periods of a *triennium*, three years. In 2011, the terms of office of provincial and local superiors and assignments in general were lengthened to four years. *Triennium* means "three years." *Quadrennium* means "four years."

159 Cf. Comunidad de Cuenca 1936: *Anales* XI, 37-38.

160 According to a note we found, he was in Cuenca ten days when the Civil War broke out (cf. APRM. Mártires 0400118, f. 3).

161 Translator's note: The position of consultor in a Redemptorist community is as an advisor to the superior.

6. Fr. Isidro Fernández Posado, consultor, forty-five years old. Present in the Cuenca community since 1932, dedicating himself fundamentally to the missions.

7. Fr. Ciriaco Olarte Pérez de Mendiguren, forty-three years old. In Cuenca for one year and a half, dedicated to the missions.

8. Br. Victoriano Calvo Lozano, forty years old. Lived in Cuenca since 1924 as sacristan.[162]

9. Fr. Miguel Goñi Áriz, thirty-four years old. Arrived in Cuenca in January 1936 to recover from an illness and to attend to church services.

10. Fr. Julián Pozo Ruiz de Samaniego, thirty-three years old. Came to Cuenca in 1927 for the purpose of recovering from an illness. He helped in the confessional.

11. Br. Benjamín López de Murga Equíluz, twenty-five years old. Arrived in Cuenca in August 1935 as receptionist and tailor.

12. Fr. Eloy Gómez Jorge, twenty-six years old. Arrived a few months before to reinforce the work of the missions.

Missing from this list is Fr. Rafael Ferrero, who was in Nava del Rey (Valladolid) and who did not end up coming into the community. He was in this city of Valladolid province waiting for another priest to take his place in order join the community at his new assignment. The other priest was sick. That situation saved his life. Of the twelve Redemptorists in Cuenca, six received the grace of a martyr's death.

The Dispersion of the Community

The electoral triumph of the Popular Front made the situations of the priests and religious of Cuenca critical. This situation became complicated in a special way beginning July 18. In response to the uprising of the troops in Africa against the government of the Republic, groups of anarchist workers and members of the parties of the Popular Front took the city of Cuenca and initiated a wave of revolution:

....

162 Translator's note: The sacristan is typically appointed to prepare the church for Mass and other liturgical celebrations.

Suddenly in July 1936, everything stopped. The week that followed July 18, 1936 was a week of terror in Cuenca. During it commerce was shut down; night and day bombs frequently exploded and shots were heard, by which the Marxists tried simply to create terror in the population and to keep the patriots locked in their homes and to intimidate the Civil Guard. The streets and plazas, the gates of the city, and the bridges were seen to be full of riflemen, militia dressed in a mechanic's overalls and armed with rifles and pistols. They detained everyone who was going by, between blasphemies and threats, demanding documentation, while aiming their rifles at them or they pointed the gun at their chest or in their back. And the Revolutionary Committee and gangs of militiamen dominated and began to take charge in the city, leaving the Civil Guard, which was concentrated in the seminary building, powerless.[163]

The community of San Felipe was not indifferent to the situation they were living through. Fr. Dionisio de Felipe describes it this way:

From July 18 they could not continue on in the monastery without exposing themselves recklessly to mass extermination. Friendly persons did not fail to pass warnings along about the dangers which threatened San Felipe; but the most pressing advice was that of a long-time friend, D. Nicolás Belinchón, by means of a letter carried to the monastery by a boy, since Belinchón could not leave the house. He was under threat as much as the religious. In the letter, he communicated—according to Brother Benjamín—that in the Union Hall it was agreed in a session to throw them in jail or to beat them or to kill them, as the more radical wished to do.[164]

July 18 and 19[165] passed with a certain amount of tranquility, but uncertainty and fear were perceptible everywhere. Alarmed by the news that various people were bringing them, on both days the outside door was

....

163 S. CIRAC ESTOPAÑÁN, 162.

164 D. DE FELIPE, *o. c.*, 144.

165 From this moment, the only primary source of information is Br. Benjamín (cf. APRM. Mártires 0400105.1, 12-17; 0400105.4, 7-11), referring to the rest of his narration.

locked. Eucharist was celebrated also with the church locked, and none of the members of the community, who were dressed in secular clothing, went onto the street. In the afternoon of the July 19 they began to see armed men and to hear gunshots. Some groups of militiamen prowled about outside the monastery. During the early morning hours, an uproar alarmed everyone. On the following morning they found out that a firecracker had been placed at the door of the church of "las Petras."

On the morning of July 20, the Civil Guard of the city received orders to remain quartered in the seminary and the streets were at the mercy of groups of armed militia:

> *During dinner that day an altar server arrived with a letter from Nicolás Belinchón. He wanted to come to our residence, but they were following him, so he could not. He tried several times, without being able to do so. He went in search of the altar boy who lived next door to his house. In the letter he told me that before nightfall we should abandon our house. They had talked about us in the Union Hall. He knew about it from a neighbor whom he had had in his house who had attended the meeting, and who still cared for him. He was there doing some work, and as soon as he got out of the Union Hall, he went to tell D. Belinchón about it, so that he could tell us. He remembered that, concerning the inhabitants of San Felipe, they were of several opinions. Most wanted to kill us, and others to give us a beating.*[166]

Because the situation for San Felipe was untenable, the superior Fr. Pedrosa, who that day was on retreat, convoked a meeting to decide what had to be done. At the meeting, by common accord, they decided to look for refuge in private homes of friends of the community. Each one received some money from the superior for expenses and an order not to compromise the families that welcomed them. Each one went to the house designated for him and by eight o'clock that evening no one was left in the monastery. Everyone passed that night outside of San Felipe. Fr. Pedroso took up lodging in the house of Amparo Hortelano, president of the Archconfraternity of Perpetual Help. Fr. Gorosterratzu went to the house of

---

166 APRM. Mártires 0400105.1, 12-13.

María García. Frs. Posado, Olarte, Goñi and Jorge went to the house of D. Acisclo and his sister. In the home of the Muñoz family were Fr. Pozo and Br. Victoriano. The Little Sisters of the Poor took in Br. Marcos. Fr. Romero and Br. Clemente went to the house of the Camareras de la Virgen;[167] and Br. Benjamín, to the house of the Román Magro family.[168]

That night the militiamen knocked down the wall that protected the doors of the church of San Felipe, they placed some artifacts at the doors and, three explosions knocked the doors down. On the morning of July 21 members of the community returned to celebrate the Eucharist. As they arrived they discovered the condition of the church now after the explosives had been used. Br. Benjamin tells of his impressions: "Fr. Romero was celebrating Mass as Fr. Pozo and Br. Victoriano arrived. Others had celebrated Mass already in the convents of the religious and some in the cathedral. The smell of explosive powder hung over the church. We tried to close up the church as best we could so that no one could gain entrance from outside. From now on, it would not be open to the public."[169]

....

167 Translator's note: a lay association.

168 Cf. B. LÓPEZ DE MURGA, *Cuenca en el Recuerdo* (Pamplona, 1996) 27-28; APRM. Mártires 0400115, 3.

169 APRM. Mártires 0400105.4, 9.

Retablo Mayor before 1936, San Felipe

Burned interior of San Felipe

They all spent that afternoon in the community setting and at nightfall each returned to his hiding place. Early in the morning, Br. Benjamin, who was staying across the street from San Felipe, returned to the monastery with an altar server. Along the way, they hid their faces from the president of the Union Hall, who was prowling about the house of the Redemptorists. It was all very frightening. Little by little, a few religious returned to the house on July 22: Pedrosa, Romero, Pozo, Posado, and Victoriano. This last was the one who prepared dinner for whoever was there. According to Isidro Posado, while they were eating "we received a letter from a committee which said that a directive had been issued telling us that they were not taking responsibility for our lives and if at six in the evening we saw a train from Madrid decorated with flags and we heard shots, then we should run for our lives, because they were not taking responsibility for our lives."[170] In view of this message, at six o'clock that evening each of them left for his house of refuge. This was the last day the majority of the community would see each other.

....

170 I. POSADO, *C. Beatificationis—Declaraciones* I, 147.

Br. Benjamin at the door of the house where he was hidden

Posado continues, during the night "since we were no longer there in the house...they went into the house, tore down the sacred images, desecrated the church and stole everything."[171] On the July 23 only Fr. Romero and Br. Benjamin went there. They boarded up the house and the church as best they could and went back to their hiding places. From that moment, each one lived out his own odyssey.

The Redemptorists who had concealed themselves in the houses of those connected to the community, tried in every way to follow a normal rhythm of life: celebrating Mass, praying, dedicating hours to study, bringing Communion to the sick, and doing all those things that are part of priestly ministry—even going out, at danger to their own lives, to help the dying. They would communicate with one another through people in whom they had confidence, to find out about one another's welfare and to exchange news regarding the unfolding events. In this case, children were the least likely to raise suspicions in the persecutors.

The situation became increasingly tense, violent, and chaotic. Insecurity grew for the religious in hiding, and they endangered the charitable families who were taking care of them. Fr. Pedrosa communicated to the members of the community that it would be better for some to find a more sure refuge. Two places seemed adequate for this task: the nursing home of the Little Sisters of the Poor and the diocesan seminary. In spite of this, others preferred private homes.

....

171 *Ib.*, 147.

Little Sisters of the Poor (left) and San Julián Seminary (right)

On July 24, there was a search of the house where Fr. Gorosterratzu was hiding, so he decided to leave that place. On July 25,[172] those who were lodged in the house of D. Acisclo, who had gone to the lower part of the city, felt harassed and decided to seek other hiding places. Frs. Romero, Posado, Jorge, and Br. Benjamin went to stay with the Little Sisters. Frs. Olarte and Goñi opted to go to the house of the priest D. Enrique María Gómez Jiménez, just next door to the cathedral. Fr. José Javier Gorosterratzu asked permission to go to the seminary, where other priests had taken refuge and where the Civil Guard was garrisoned. Fr. Pozo and Br. Victoriano, who lived in the apartment below that of Fr. José Javier, accompanied him that morning to his new refuge.

In the following days, the militiamen entered the monastery several times with the excuse of looking for weapons hidden by the priests and brothers. They forced the door open and made a minute search without finding the weapons they were looking for, though they requisitioned everything they wanted.[173]

On the afternoon of July 26, Br. Benjamin received two missives: one from the superior asking him to fetch an envelope of money (an envelope already taken by those who did the search) and another message from Fr. Olarte asking him for a chalice with which he could celebrate the Eucharist in the house of D. Enrique without having to go to the cathedral. Together with the request, through the altar server, he told him: "We are lost, now that everyone knows where our hiding place is; be careful that they don't catch you."[174]

A few days later, vandals entered into the monastery of San Felipe and created such destruction that it rendered it practically unusable. The work of destruction would be completed some months later with the arrival of the ringleader of the Rosal Column. Br. Benjamin looked on with tears in his eyes at how they had made barricades of the confessionals and dressed the statue of St. Alphonsus in a miltiaman's uniform.

----

172 Cf. APRM. Mártires 0400105.1, 16-17; 0400105.4, 10; 0403003, 5.

173 Cf. APRM. Mártires 0400105.1, 16-17; 0400105.4, 12-13.

174 APRM. Mártires 0400105.4, 13.

The Plight of the Redemptorist Community of San Felipe

Before narrating in detail the martyrdom of some of the Redemptorist community of Cuenca, which took place in the first two weeks of August 1936, we shall record the situation of the religious not martyred as well as the residence and the community church during the entire Civil War. Fr. Pedro Romero joined the five martyred Redemptorists, although he did not suffer a violent death. He died in jail as a consequence of the punishments he endured because of his priestly status.

Fr. Augustin Pedrosa,[175] superior of the community, after a time in the house of Esperanza Molero, holed up with the Little Sisters of the Poor so as not to compromise the Molero family. On September 27, 1936, the CNT placed a political delegation of control within the nursing home.[176] According to what he himself testified, "there I suffered the indescribable. I was belittled, made fun of, threatened with blows that made my teeth rattle. They turned their backs on me with marked indifference."[177] So as not to continue to suffer this bad treatment on the part of the militiamen, he left there and took asylum in the house of María Zanón. In 1938, Fr. José María Ibarrola traveled from Madrid to bring him back with him.[178]

Br. Clemente López Aguilló[179] was the oldest in the community. He spent almost all of his life in Cuenca. When the community dispersed on July 20, since he was somewhat infirm he hid in the house of the Little Sisters of the Poor as one more old person. There he dedicated himself to prayer. While in exile, he got sick with acute bronchitis and he received painstaking care. Nevertheless, he died there on December 19, 1937, because of gangrened varicose veins.

....

175 Cf. *Ib.,* 21; Comunidad de Cuenca 1936: *Anales* XI, 38. Agustín Pedrosa Misol (cf. Apéndice 2).

176 Cf. E. JORGE, *Declaración ante el Tribunal militar; Cuenca 13-5-1939:* AGET. Leg. 5927 / Sum. 33.

177 Comunidad de Cuenca 1936: *Anales* XI, 38.

178 Fr. J. M. Ibarrola tells us: *"I took a train to Cuenca, where I picked up the superior, an old man, now dead, who laughably called me 'grandson.'"* (J. M. IBARROLA, *Un redentorista en el Madrid rojo* [Madrid, 1965] 212).

179 Clemente López Aguilló (Cf. Apéndice 2).

Br. Marcos Álvarez,[180] although also old, was a little younger than Br. Clemente. When he left San Felipe on July 18 he went to live with the Little Sisters of the Poor. He had to leave there in July 1937. He went to the house of Doña Paca Echebarría, where he arrived fairly sick from a heart ailment. He received visits there from Fr. Pedrosa, who brought him Communion occasionally. On November 23, 1937, he died suddenly of asystole,[181] provoked by the deprivations and sufferings of that time.

Fr. Isidro Fernández Posado[182] ended his asylum at the Little Sisters of the Poor. As we said, in September 1937, the militiamen of the UGT and of the CNT assumed the direction of the asylum at the time that Fr. Isidro left, fooling the militiamen at the entrance by being disguised as a beggar. These militiamen, "on seeing him in the street, thought he was a beggar and took him to their barracks. He slipped out of the barracks and by a tortuous route along the streets, he arrived at the house of the Zanón family."[183] He was hidden in the house of María Zanón for some months. Fr. Isidro did not feel safe in the city and for that reason decided to move out to the small towns of the province. In Cuenca again in September 1938, he decided to cross to the zone controlled by Franco but was discovered, arrested, and later taken to the jail on Calle Sorni. After a month, he was transferred to the jail of San Juan de los Reyes and from there again to Cuenca, to the jail installed in the Carmelite monastery, until the end of the war.[184]

....

180 Marcos Álvarez García (Cf. Apéndice 2).

181 Translator's note: "flat-lining," no cardiac electrical activity.

182 Isidro Fernández Posado (Cf. Apéndice 2).

183 Cf. Comunidad de Cuenca 1936. Vicisitudes Fr. Posado: *Anales* XI, 40.

184 After the war, Fr. Isidro F. Posado was the chronicler of the community at Cuenca. On some separate sheets, he was putting together the chronicle of the community. In it he leaves us the story of his own odyssey during the religious persecution: "*He was caught by the red police and taken to a jail in Valencia and stayed there. He was the object of poor treatment for thirty-six days. From the jail, he was transferred to the Cárcel Modelo in the same city.* [Translator's note: the name of the jail was *Cárcel Modelo* because in the nineteenth century it was one of several which embodied the latest thinking in rehabilitation of prisoners]... *Sufferings...Why detail them all? In the prison, he exercised the ministry of Apostle, hearing confessions, distributing Communion, and celebrating the Holy Sacrifice of the Mass and being the consolation of the afflicted. Five months later, he was taken to the jail in Cuenca, where he remained twenty-five days. From there he was released to celebrate the triumph of the troops of Generalissimo Franco*" (*Crónica de Cuenca*, año 1939, 2).

Br. Benjamín López de Murga Eguíluz[185] had been two years in the community as tailor and receptionist. When the time to abandon the religious house arrived, he was housed nearby with the Rodrigo Grueso family, the family of the altar boy of San Felipe. They lived in what was popularly called "the house of the priests," a huge house on Calle Andrés Cabrera, where the *Centro Sacerdotal de San Julián*[186] was set up. Besides being able to see the church and the monastery, Br. Benjamín felt safer because the head of the family was also a municipal guard. Escaping from a meticulous search by the militiamen on August 13, 1936, he continued hidden there until June 1937, trying not to so much as look out a window. From there he went to the house of Eugenia Muñoz, where he remained until May 1938. In January he presented himself to the Republican authorities as someone who had escaped from the Nationalist zone and enlisted in the army as a militiaman. On May 23, 1938, he set out on foot toward the front but, once outside of Cuenca, instead of heading in that direction, he crossed a mountain range and went to the contrary battle front. On May 25, the army of Franco arrested him. Inducted into the army again in Saragossa, he was discharged at the end of the war.

Fr. Eloy Gómez Jorge[187] was the youngest of the community, barely twenty-six years old, and of a very unstable character. Once he saw that he might be discovered, he became an easy target for the SIM, which arrested him as a collaborator. We will let him describe the situation he lived through during three years of religious persecution:

He[188] found himself in this capital at the beginning of the Glorious Uprising,[189] and stayed there from the month of February 1936, without having been the subject of correction by any of my superiors.

....

185 Br. Benjamín himself has left us narratives of his adventures in various writings (APRM. Mártires 0400105.4; APRM. Mártires 0400105.3). To know more about Br. Benjamín see Appendix 2.

186 Translator's note: St. Julian's Center for Priests.

187 About Eloy Gómez Jorge Appendix 2.

188 Translator's note: Fr. Eloy begins by using the third person to refer to himself in this narrative, then switches to the first person.

189 Translator's note: This was the name that the Franco government gave to its rebellion against the Republican Government, starting on July 17, 1936.

On July 23, 1936, all the Fathers had to leave the monastery because they had gotten news that there was going to be an assault on the monastery, as then happened. And he passed the afternoon when he left the monastery and the whole night in the house of a Canon[190] named D. Acisclo, who lived on Calle Cabrera, number nine. The next day he went out to get a place at the Little Sisters of the Poor, where the superior of the monastery, Agustín Pedrosa had taken refuge, along with Frs. Isidro Fernández, Pozado, Romero, who died of natural causes and two brothers who also died a natural death. He was in the monastery until the 27th of September, 1937. In all this time, he stayed hidden so that no one knew that's where they were. They didn't receive visits from anyone, nor did they speak with anyone as if he weren't in hiding with the others and the Little Sisters. Only on the 14th of August of 1937, I mean '36, he attempted with Fr. Posado to go to Teruel. For which reason this narrator went out first in order to see if that would go well. But on leaving Cuenca, militiamen detained him and asked for his safe-conduct paper. Since the narrator told them that he was going to go for a bath and he didn't think it was necessary and the militiamen insisted upon seeing it, he said that he was going to look for it. He tried to do the same by another way out, but the results were the same. He went back to the monastery and did not leave there.

On September 27 of 1937, because the CNT placed a Delegate in the asylum for the Little Sisters of the Poor as administrator, saying that that Delegate was somebody by the name of Elias, and he lived in the Convent, those of us who were hiding there had to look for another place in order to survive. The narrator went to the house of Doña Raimunda Escudero, who lived on Calle San Pedro, number 24. There the narrator remained once again hidden and maintained the same way of life, not seeing anyone outside the house. He only went down to the apartment below to get a haircut. On that same floor there were other Fathers in hiding. On that occasion he received from Doña Raimunda one hundred pesetas so that the one who is writing this might say Masses in suffrage

---

190 Translator's note: originally, a *canon* was a priest who lived with other priests attached to a cathedral and who had the right to vote on the Vicar Capitular, or diocesan administrator, when there was no bishop in a diocese; later, it became an honorary title given to senior priests who had contributed significantly to the life of the diocese.

for her priest-brother. He also received one hundred or one hundred and fifty pesetas from Doña Ana Coello, whom the narrator did not know, in order to say Mass for her intention. That money came through the mediation of a religious Sister. He stayed in that house until January 19, 1938; in the afternoon, a Captain of the Brigade Líster and some soldiers came to demand beds. In doing so, they discovered where the narrator was. They arrested him and brought him to the Battalion, then to the Commissary, where they took his statement. They searched him and found medals and a rosary. He could not deny he was a priest. He told in the statement where he had been, without giving details, simply that he had been in the Asylum of the Little Sisters of the Poor and in the house of Doña Raimunda Escudero. He asked if as a consequence of this Doña Escudero was arrested, and they said no. They said she was detained, but much later. They didn't bother the Little Sisters. Then he was handed over to SIM, where they again took a statement. He gave the same answers, and they brought him to the jail of the seminary. On the day that the narrator was arrested, they posted a guard in the house and after it was searched they found Fr. José Galende Sentín, on whom they found a list of people belonging to "Socorro Blanco" who had helped him.[191] Once Fr. Galende made his statement, they summoned the narrator and showed the narrator the statement that Fr. Galende had made. They pointed out to him the contradiction, since the narrator had not said there was anyone else in the house, to which the narrator replied that indeed that was so, since that Father was in the apartment below.

The narrator was held six days incommunicado in the seminary, until they brought him to the seminary offices and told him, without any further explanation, that he was to stay there, taking care of the office so that no one took anything. The narrator can only guess that this was so because the Chief of the Prison, Félix Arrellano, was from the same area that the narrator was from. In a few days, Félix himself gave him the charge that he write up a list of those held in the semi-

---

191 Translator's note: the *Socorro Blanco* ("White Help") was a group of Nationalists who helped families of those put in prison and which acted as a fifth column behind the enemy lines. They were named *Socorro Blanco* in contradistinction to the *Socorro Rojo* ("Red Help") of the Communists.

nary and the narrator did so, putting his own name down first. Now he was charged every day to do this report which he created from books of searches done high and low. Later, they let him go out into the street once, for which he had to ask permission from the Chief. And later, he went down to Cuenca on a daily basis to hand in the list at the offices of SIM without doing anything else there, that is, without giving any statement nor rendering any service. After a great deal of time had passed, sometimes he was the prisoner-in-charge in the aforementioned prison. He welcomed prisoners who came in under guard and accompanied by an official. On such occasions, he assigned the cell where the prisoner would be incarcerated. This was true whether it was to be their normal cell or punishment cell. When he was asked what kind of treatment he gave the prisoners, he answered that he never dealt with anyone directly as long as he had this mandate. Nor did he insult anyone. Only it is possible that on some occasion he spoke words in a tone a little louder than usual. Concretely, the narrator has been accused of treating a prisoner poorly whom he found at a window. The narrator does not know how this happened, because he was not present. But what really happened was this. There was a prisoner there by the name of Fermín Garrido Moya, a lawyer whom the narrator knew since he was a prisoner there for a long time. On this occasion, the prisoner went to the window, which was relatively high up, to see his wife. She had brought him clothes and food. This lawyer was seen by the guard. And then the acting Chief of the prison, named Millán, ordered that he be transferred to a punishment cell.

When asked what persons he had denounced, he clearly declares that outside of the persons that he had already cited in his statement, he did not denounce anyone—and this in spite of the fact that they asked him to do so on a number of occasions. Once when they asked him where the superior of the community was, he declared that his name was Gorrosterrazu. In reality, that was not his name, since that Father had been assassinated in the first days of the Movement. By saying that was his name, they would not look for him anymore. Moreover, he knew where many priests were hiding, where their precious stones were hidden and the other sacred things, where there were radios for communication and which would pick up the station from Salamanca, where right-wing people were hiding. Nevertheless, he said nothing. He had connections with little groups of Falangists, such as Victoriano Martínez, a chauffeur, neighbor from San Lorenzo de Parrilla, who would stand at bars and sometimes shout, Viva Franco! Moreover, a brother of Victoriano in an attempt to escape to the Nationalist zone was discovered before he could do so. They arrested him and took him away. When the narrator found out about it, he told Victoriano. He warned him that, since they were Falangists, the two brothers were taking a risk. He advised him that he should hide a 9mm long-slide pistol which he had and that he should go to the Nationalist zone, which he then did. All the details the narrator could get about his situation, he communicated to Victoriano, keeping him apprised of many details. Thus it was that the militiamen began to distrust the narrator, principally Alfonso Juárez Juárez, secretary general of the service. He prohibited the narrator from using the telephone. And this being the case, at times he was followed on the street. Amparo Pardo Cárcel can testify to this detail. She lives at Fifteenth of July, No. 43. The narrator has gone so far as to call upon this young lady to confirm what things she had spoken about with the narrator, because of suspicions that they were things having to do with his service in the jail. The narrator was in this situation until his trial along with thirteen others, among whom was Doña Raimunda Escudera. All were pardoned.

On various occasions he wanted to leave the prison to go to the Department of Health, but the SIM answered that he was a prisoner at their disposition and he could not leave. On being asked where he wanted to go, he said to Health, now that there had been a provision that permitted him to serve in that Corps, but always this request was denied. Concretely, when he was absolved he went to the CRIMP where he was classified as of the auxiliary services and with that classification he went another time to SIM to say that he wanted to leave. This happened March 12. The Secretary General, Alfonso Juárez, ordered him to continue in the same place, that is, the seminary prison to do the list of the detained and to do intake on those who were brought in, showing them to their cells. I remained in the same situation until the liberation.... [192]

192 E. GÓMEZ JORGE, *Declaración indagatoria* en: AGET. Leg. 5927 / Sum. 333, 3-4.

Only Fr. Eloy Gómez Jorge remained in the city during the whole civil contention. He was arrested by the Franquista troops[193] for his collaboration with the SIM, when these troops entered Cuenca, and was subjected to a military trial.[194]

After the war, the superior, Fr. Agustín Pedrosa, returned from Madrid in April 1939 to see the condition of the church and the house of the community.[195] There he found Fr. Eloy Gómez, incarcerated, and Fr. Isidro Posado, recently released from jail. Br. Benjamín joined them. They verified with their own eyes the lamentable state of the house and church after suffering sacking and then conversion into a barracks where first columns of anarchistic militiamen were housed and later the "nationalist" troops. This explains why San Felipe was in a state of total ruin. Sebastian Círac Estopañán describes for us what happened in the church of San Felipe:

> *It isn't possible to get an idea of the artistic, religious, and material losses caused in the monastery of San Felipe, of the Redemptorist religious, in its crypt and in the main church, which were the scene for sacking, fire, and destruction. There is no comparison as to how the holy enclosure and the religious community brought forth the sacrilegious, iconoclastic, and criminal fury of the enemies of Christ....The cause of such a Satanic persecution was evident: the splendor of the liturgy, both in the morning and in the evening; the great number of the faithful who came there, the solid piety that was cultivated there, the prudent and efficacious spiritual direction that was given there; the spiritual sacrifice and the zeal of the religious, who traveled about the whole diocese at the slightest wish of the Prelate. Among the most striking losses in the church of San Felipe we should mention the following: the monumental baroque retable and other good retables, good paintings by Francisco Preciado and Antonio G. Velásquez: the devout sculpted image of Christ of a Good Death and the impressive group of Our Lady of Sorrows, attributed to Salzillo.[196]*

....

193 Translator's note: those of Generalissimo Franco.

194 When Eloy Gómez Jorge was sentenced to six years or more, the Church (the diocese of Cuenca and the Congregation of the Most Holy Redeemer) asked for a review of the judgment. The sentence was reduced to less than six years. Once he completed his sentence, he was freed, living his life out as a diocesan priest in his native area. (Cf. *Ib.*)

195 Cf. *Crónica de Cuenca,* año 1939, 2ss.

196 S. CIRAC ESTOPAÑÁN, 170.

Because of the persecution suffered by all the members of the community, the martyrdom of six of its members, the destruction and profanation of the temple and of the monastery, we can call the Cuenca Redemptorist community a community of martyrs, because the whole community suffered from religious persecution.

CHAPTER THREE

Martyrdom:
When Love Is Greater than Death

We have all heard that the twentieth century was the century of martyrs, an expression of St. John Paul II, which is true due to the clash of the Church of the twentieth century with totalitarian and exclusionary worldviews. Indeed, there were more martyrs in the twentieth century than in any other during the 2,000 years of Christianity. Martyrdom is not just the stuff of legends. It's a current reality that accompanies the Church contemporaneously.

How do we understand martyrdom in a society of tolerance?
Martyrdom is the supreme testimony of faith. But behind this testimony is an unjust death, suffered by one or several persons because of a persecution unleashed for motives contrary to the Christian virtues of faith, hope, charity, or for other reasons derived from them. It is born out of the continuing conflict of the "already of the kingdom" and the "not yet" spoken of by the Second Vatican Council. People who want to live in faithfulness to the kingdom have to live it in a present, which although already on the way to fulfillment, is a situation in which grace and sin grow together. The gospel itself puts on the lips of Jesus the prospect of the martyrdom of his followers, to live in communion with the one who was the first Martyr:

Blessed are you when they insult you and persecute you and utter every kind of evil against you [falsely] because of me. Rejoice and be glad, for your reward will be great in heaven. Thus they persecuted the prophets who were before you (Matthew 5:11-12).

If the world hates you, realize that it hated me first. If you belonged to the world, the world would love its own; but because you do not belong to the world, and I have chosen you out of the world, the world hates you. Remember the word I spoke to you, "No slave is greater than his master." If they persecuted me, they will also persecute you. If they kept my word, they will also keep yours. And they will do all these things to you on account of my name, because they do not know the one who sent me (John15:18-21).

In one way or another, throughout all the periods of Church history, there have been martyrs, since persecution is connatural to the pilgrim Church. If this were not so, one would have to ask the question whether it was faithful to the gospel of Jesus or if the Church had not succumbed to two temptations: accommodation to the present, with the subsequent loss of the prophetic dimension, or collusion with power, leaving aside charity. The Second Vatican Council itself reminds us:

Since Jesus, the Son of God, manifested His charity by laying down His life for us, so too no one has greater love than he who lays down his life for Christ and His brothers. (see 1 John 3:16; John 15:13) From the earliest times, then, some Christians have been called upon—and some will always be called upon—to give the supreme testimony of this love to all men, but especially to persecutors. The Church, then, considers martyrdom as an exceptional gift and as the fullest proof of love. By martyrdom a disciple is transformed into an image of his Master by freely accepting death for the salvation of the world—as well as his conformity to Christ in the shedding of his blood. Though few are presented such an opportunity, nevertheless all must be prepared to confess Christ before men. They must be prepared to make this profession of faith even in the midst of persecutions, which will never be lacking to the Church, in following the way of the cross.[197]

In order to know the causes of martyrdom, one has to look at it from two sides: on the part of the persecutor and on the part of the Church. When we look at the history and the geography of the martyrdom event, the causes that have unleashed persecution have been numerous. In the case with which we are concerned in this book, the reasons have been, for one part, a class resentment, understanding the Church as a factual power and oppressor which must be destroyed; for another part, an ideological motivation sustained by a narrow world vision as happened with Communism, Nazism, and Fascism in the period between wars. On the part of the Church, the Vatican Council itself recognized that the very life of the Church could on occasion awaken hatred and resentment toward her. When it speaks of the roots of atheism, it tells us:

Believers themselves frequently bear some responsibility for this situation. For, taken as a whole, atheism is not a spontaneous development but stems from a variety of causes, including a critical reaction against religious beliefs, and in some places against the Christian religion in particular. Hence believers can have more than a little to do with the birth of atheism. To the extent that they neglect their own training in the faith, or teach erroneous doctrine, or are deficient in their religious, moral or social life, they must be said to conceal rather than reveal the authentic face of God and religion.[198]

While it is not speaking directly about religious persecution, the references which the Council makes are able to serve us in discovering the causes which awakened the *odium fidei*[199] in a people who are Christian by tradition and culture, such as are the Spaniards.

Confronting the persecutor is the martyr. Through this word *martyrdom*

....

197 (LG 42, 2; http://www.vatican.va/archive/hist_councils/ii_vatican_council/documents/vat-ii_const_19641121_lumen-gentium_en.html)

198 (GS 19, 3; http://www.vatican.va/archive/hist_councils/ii_vatican_council/documents/vat-ii_const_19651207_gaudium-et-spes_en.html)

199 Translator's note: "hatred toward the faith."

we touch upon a mystery about humanity in that it affects our understanding of the person, life, faith, and relationships. Certainly, in the littleness of the person there is hidden a great treasure. Because it is a mystery, we run the risk of misinterpreting it. A martyr is not someone intent upon suicide, no matter how sublime his motivation may be. A martyr is a person who bets on life, who loves life, and who does not flee from his life, but who puts his faith first. A martyr is not a hero, ethical or otherwise. Among the many martyrs there are personalities of great fragility, both personal and moral. Nor is the martyr a reckless person—not even a brave person—because many martyrs have come up against death without seeking it. Likewise, martyrdom is not the reward for a dedicated life, although it does follow a trajectory of generosity. Within the martyr is a great love for Jesus Christ, which permits him to die with a loving surrender to him who said, "No one takes [my life] from me, but I lay it down on my own. I have power to lay it down" (John 10:18).

The martyr speaks to us of faith, of a faith lived which becomes faithfulness to God in a way that is true to one's self. This faithfulness allows a person to step across a threshold away from fear and selfishness in order to put his confidence in God. Martyrdom is a sure bet on a culture of forgiveness and reconciliation, since the martyr dies pardoning and becomes a call for pardon. But all of this falls short if we do not talk about grace. To speak about martyrdom is to speak about the grace of God, which permits a person to confront death from the same perspective that we have been talking about. When we speak about the grace of martyrdom, we are not speaking about death as a gift, but rather about the gift of experiencing that death with the same attitudes as Jesus, and this is only possible through the Holy Spirit.

Today martyrdom continues to have a great social force as a testimony of faith in the midst of unbelief, as a proof of charity, and as an affirmation of the right of liberty of conscience.[200] A new rereading of martyrdom[201] offers us an authentic Christian anthropology, from which came a "new martyr paradigm," very much developed in European theology as in that of Latin America. With these words we offer some clues that may help the reader to understand this chapter in which we deal with the martyrdom of the six Redemptorists who gave their lives in Cuenca.

Two important themes fill out what has just been said: the conscience of the martyr and the testimony of martyrdom. Stopping to consider the first, it has not been easy to gain access to the conscience of these six martyrs in order to see to what measure they assumed their tragic destiny as self-surrender and communion with Christ. In them a process unfolds which includes fear of death, nervousness about their helplessness, and uncertainty about the more immediate future until they are able to accept all of it. In all of this they had the support of their companions, the mutual words of exhortation to faithfulness, prayer, and the Eucharist. They all made the novitiate of martyrdom, perceiving the tragic destiny that awaited them, and they put into play at that time the fourth Redemptorist vow—the vow and oath of perseverance—through which they placed their confidence in the fidelity of God who called them. They persevered in this fidelity until the definitive moment of their lives, beyond the circumstances in which it was their lot to live. Their existence became a testimony and word about the Redemption of Christ. Not keeping anything for themselves, not even what was their right to keep by way of inheritance, in giving themselves they were all the more missionary.

Finally, martyrdom needs to be told in story form. The Cistercian Bernardo Olivera writes, referring to the martyred monks in Algeria in 1996:

....

200 "The affirmation of a right to freedom of conscience in the face of unlawful intrusions of human power. This was the orientation that martyrdom had in the worthy and radical proposition of the author of Apocalypse. To affirm the value of one's own conscience supposes, at the same time, to place Power in the position which corresponds to it and to impede that it go beyond its limits in its functions. The Christian martyr has created an atmosphere favorable to the appearance and development of this right, perhaps the most basic and the generator of all the others, which is freedom of conscience and of religion in the face of every form of totalitarian self-importance of whatever type of power, especially political power" (M. VIDAL, Concilio Vaticano II y Teología Pública, [Madrid, 2012] 211).

201 In the year 2003 the international magazine of theology CONCILIUM published an edition entitled Repensar el Martirio [Rethinking Martyrdom] (Concilium 299). The authors think through the theme from different points of view and locales.

The death of a small group of men does not have great significance in the bellicose world of today. But not every death is a mere disappearance. On the contrary, there are those who commence living when they die. Such is the case of the seven Trappist monks assassinated in Algeria in May of 1996. But they are not alone; they represent very many others who, as their way of confronting the ultimate, were born in their dying....These letters and conferences refer to the seven monks and, just as much, to so many other consecrated persons in religious life. By way of baptism, their religious profession, and martyrdom, the Lord God consecrates his own....One tries to touch life in its crudity and glory in order to find traces of God passing through our history....One day, Friday, more infamous than holy, Jesus of Nazareth died on a cross, just like so many others, disfigured and outraged. In front of this ignominy, someone, a pagan centurion, could describe the dignity of that man and exclaimed: "Truly he was the Son of God!" These pages were written with that purpose. To show that the dignity and transcendence of the human being is capable of conquering death and of revealing the tender love of Him who created us. If religious life, through the evangelical counsels, does not reveal this reality, it has to be said that it veils the light and life of the One whom we profess to follow.[202]

The witnesses to the self-surrender of the six Redemptorists had the same role. Among them was Br. Benjamín, who became a reminder of his six confreres who were faithful to their religious profession in the midst of difficulties. And together with Br. Benjamín, the Congregation of the Most Holy Redeemer has gone on elaborating about the memory of its martyrs in Cuenca until they have become the heritage of the Church through their beatification.

The Memory of the Martyrdom

Saint Alphonsus wrote a book titled *The Victory of the Martyrs*, in which he offers us not only a description of the torments suffered by the martyrs, but also describes how fragile men and women lived through those sufferings and gave a yes to God in their weakness. In that work he exhorts Redemp-

---

202 B. OLIVERA, *Martirio y consagración. Los mártires de Argelia* (Madrid, 20112) 78-80.

torists of each generation to confront the difficulties that they encountered in the development of their missionary vocation. We remember how these difficulties began in the foundational period under Neapolitan regalism and later under Austrian Josephinism.[203] These difficulties were found in France and Italy; also in Spain with the repression of religious communities in 1868 and in neighboring Portugal in 1910. But these situations of difficulty did not constitute a systematic persecution for the Congregation of the Most Holy Redeemer[204] until the coming to power in Mexico of Plutarco Calles in 1926, who "begins to apply with every rigor the antireligious laws of the Constitution of Querétaro."[205] As a matter of fact, one of those who found himself overtaken by this wave of anticlericalism was Fr. Ciriaco Olarte, who returned from Monterrey[206] to his homeland fleeing the anticlerical Mexican hurricane. Although in that persecution the Church was suppressed, and at least forty priests were martyred, plus some laity and religious, there were no victims among the Redemptorists.[207]

....

203 Translator's note: *Regalism* was the notion that the king had complete authority over the Church. *Josephinism* was the attempt by Emperor Joseph II of Austria to reform Austrian law to reflect the values of the Englightenment.

204 D. RUIZ, *Hacia los altares. Nuestros mártires*: BPL XXVII, 151 (2000) 149-152. The magazine *El Perpetuo Socorro* XXXV, 425 (November 1933) published a collection of articles under the title "The Redemptorists and Persecution." Through these, the persecution suffered by the Congregation of the Most Holy Redeemer in the two centuries of its existence was exhibited, with the intention of demonstrating "with testimony from various countries to the fact that the Congregation of the Most Holy Redeemer has not been far from the cross of Christ" (*Ib.*, 520). Thus it moves from the persecution suffered in Spain (*El Perpetuo Socorro* XXXV, 425), Italy (Fr. RICCARDO, *La Provincia Romana en las revueltas políticas de Italia (1798-1873)*: *Ib.*, 473-479), Switzerland (M. JAKOBS, *Suiza, regazo de la Congregación*: *Ib.*, 481-491), Austria (J. RUDISCH, *Austria en la brecha*: *Ib.*, 493-496), France (J. BILLET, *La Tercera República y los Redentoristas franceses*: *Ib.*, 499-504), Germany (G. BRANDHUBER, *Las botas del príncipe de Bismarck*: *Ib.*, 513-517) and Poland (ANÓNIMO, *¡Polonia!*: *Ib.*, 518-520).

205 L. MIGUÉLEZ, *Viceprovincia de México*: BPL XXVII, 151 (2000) 352. Translator's note: Plutarco Elias Calles was president of Mexico from 1924 until 1928. The constitution of Queretaro was approved in 1917, but six of the articles of the constitution were anticlerical. These Calles sought to enforce strictly.

206 Translator's note: Monterrey, Nuevo León, México.

207 Some of the Redemptorists in Mexico returned to Spain, others went to Venezuela, Central America, or Cuba, where they established the Congregation. Others lived difficult lives in hiding and others ended up in jail for a time. But with time there came calm. To sum things up, Fr. R. Bayón says about these Redemptorists: "During the many years of the persecution unleashed on them, and sometimes in the peak of the most difficult periods, they had time not only to preach missions, but even to multiply foundations....I believe our Mexican Fathers did work which was more fruitful and long-lasting in the years of persecution than in the years of peace." (*Ib.*, 471)

Situated in a context of hostility between Church and state during the Second Republic and motivated by the second centenary of the birth of the Redemptorist Congregation, Fr. Bayón did an analysis in which he reflected on how the sons of St. Alphonsus had developed in the middle of persecution, with the aim of giving encouragement to their companions, and faced with the discouragement in which they were living in Spain. In finishing his explanation of the difficulties lived by the Spaniards, he concludes: "We do not know what days are ahead of us, or what men may scheme, or what God may decide. When God leaves us, it is to make us miss him so that we will seek him, as the eagle leaves its eaglets to provoke them to fly. We are thus the artificers of our own destiny; our souls are never at the mercy of our persecutors, but in our own hands. *Anima mea in manibus meis semper.* ['My soul is always in my own hands']" (Psalm 118:34).[208]

The hostile environment in which the Spanish Redemptorists were living in the decade of the thirties in the twentieth century is clear. The chronicles tell us that when the community in Cuenca got together to prepare for their dispersion, in the minds of all was the possibility of dying a violent death. On July 24, in the face of the complications that were cropping up around the situation and after the search of the lower floor of the house where Fr. Julián Pozo was hiding with Br. Victoriano, Fr. Pozo commented: "The Redemptorists do not yet have martyrs. We'll see if we become the first ones!"[209]

Before introducing the martyrs, it is necessary to note that they are being given in pairs or in groups. This method helps us describe the ecclesial character of religious persecution, since they were not martyred for being certain individuals, but insofar as they were members of a group. On the other hand, grouping them this way helps and gives strength to them in enduring the experience of their martyrdom with a gospel attitude. Lastly, it speaks to us of a community dimension which martyrdom acquires, a peculiarity of marked importance to the Redemptorist missionaries, a Congregation formed of communities of missionaries. Fr. Dionisio Ruíz offers us his own interpretation: "None of the six (who died in Cuenca)

....

208 *Ib.*, 471.

209 APRM. Mártires 0405001; 0400115, 8; D. DE FELIPE, *Fundación de los Redentoristas en España* (Madrid, 1965) 186.

faced the harshness of death alone. All went to their deaths two by two. It could be said that Christ repeated his evangelical scenario: 'He sent them two by two.' Frs. Olarti and Goñi, Fr. del Pozo and the diocesan priest Juan C. Escribano, Fr. Gorosterratsu, and Br. Victoriano. And for Fr. Romero... since he had no companion, God gave him an angel."[210]

Now that we have presented the framework of the story, we present the martyrs of the Redemptorists of Cuenca. Grouped in two blocks, we shall present the end of life of the three groups of martyrs, beginning with the places where they were staying, and we shall conclude with the special case of Fr. Romero.

The Group in the House of Don Enrique María Gómez: Ciriaco Olarte and Miguel Goñi

Frs. Ciriaco Olarte, Miguel Goñi, and Eloy Gómez Jorge were welcomed into the house of the priest D. Acisclo,[211] cathedral canon, on Calle Andrés Cabrera, No. 9, until July 25.[212] The priest had gone to live in the lower zone of the city in view of the critical situation in the upper zone, and had left them free use of the house. His nephew, Nicolás Ortega, and his niece, Emiliana López, lived with him. They helped the Redemptorists in their daily needs. On July 25 there were explosions on that same street and everyone was frightened. The daughter of the niece of the canon let it slip that her parents were hiding some priests in their uncle's house. The nephew of the priest, D. Nicolás Ortega, warned the Redemptorists about what happened and they left their refuge. Frs. Ciriaco and Miguel were received in the home of another priest, D. Enrique María Gómez,[213] friend of the community. He lived next to the cathedral, on Calle Pilares, No.17, on the second floor. This priest was served in household tasks by a housekeeper, Segunda Mateo Cañada.

....

210 D. RUIZ, *De camino* 1, 2-3 (APRM. Mártires 0400124). We have to point out that, according to studies done since then, in the group consisting of Fr. Pozo and D. Juan Escribano and that which is formed of Fr. Gorosterratzu and Br. Victoriano there were more persons, as we shall show at the appropriate time.

211 Translator's note: We are leaving the abbreviation "D." in place throughout the book; it stands for *Don*, an honorific title for a man, including priests or bishops. *Doña* is the female equivalent.

212 Cf. APRM. Mártires 0403003, ficha 5; 0403001; 0404003, 9-20.

213 D. Enrique María Gómez Jiménez (cf. Apéndice 3).

Home of Don Enrique

Given how close the cathedral was, the next day they went out early to celebrate the Eucharist there. But when they recognized the danger that this involved, they decided to make the house of D. Enrique a monastery. Br. Benjamin received a note from Fr. Ciriaco Olarte—delivered by the altar server from San Felipe—in which he indicated that by way of the child "he was sending a chalice with which to say Mass in the house, while everything else they already had there."[214] Also in the note that the altar server brought him, he counseled his confrere to hide well since, according to them, everybody in the zone knew where they were. And Ciriaco concluded: "We are lost, now that everyone knows where our hiding place is. Be careful that they don't catch you."[215] With what was necessary to celebrate Mass, and realizing the social context that surrounded them, the three priests began to consciously prepare for martyrdom. Each morning they celebrated Mass and prayed the Office in common. They lived feeling as if they were on a continual retreat, the three preparing themselves for an uncertain future, since they could see that every day things were getting worse.[216] Doña Segunda later gave a faithful reflection of what they lived through. She had heard Fr. Ciriaco say on July 30 or 31: "We will spend the feast day of our father St. Alphonsus very happily; we will be spending it in heaven."[217]

It seems it was a baker who informed the Committee of the Union Hall about them.[218] They got up, as any other morning, on July 31. About eight o'clock in the morning the three priests celebrated the Eucharist. They then

....

214 APRM. Mártires 0400105.2, 10.

215 APRM. Mártires 0400105.4, 12.

216 The only witness to what happened in that apartment to have survived the Civil War was Señora Segunda Mateo Cañada, assistant to D. Enrique. She was considerably old then, more than seventy years of age. She later told two persons what happened. They are the ones who have passed the tale along in their turn. The first to whom she told it was Br. Benjamin, who insists in his writings that he heard it from her. "What I am about to tell is the story from the woman who was with D. Enrique, from her own tongue" (cf. APRM. Mártires 0400105.2, 13). "She was an assistant to D. Enrique. I don't know her name, but I know where she lives, and I would recognize her, but I don't know the address of the house. What follows I heard her say in her own voice" (APRM. Mártires 0400105.2, 10). The other source, who credits Doña Segunda, is Lucas Pérez (APRM. Mártires 0403001, 1), who in his manuscript notes, in the year 1944, writes the name and the age of the old lady, seventy-nine years, in the margin of the page, and puts phrases between quotation marks taken from the interview with her. Both versions are in agreement, although they add complementary details.

217 APRM. Mártires 0403001, 1; 0400105.2, 11.

218 Cf. APRM. Mártires 0400105.2, 10.

went into the office to pray the Divine Office in common. It would have been about nine o'clock when two militiamen from the Libertarian Youth, *El Chepudo* and *El Borrachines*,[219] called at the door and broke into the apartment to search for arms.[220] However, what they really wanted was to verify the presence of the two Redemptorist religious. "D. Enrique attends to them and they examine the whole house minutely. They open the office and find there the two Fathers. 'They are two priests,' D. Enrique explains. The militiamen close the door and leave. In a whisper, the Fathers exchange words about this first brush with danger in the house search. These militiamen have not behaved too poorly."[221] They had not yet recovered from that scare when the militiamen come back, but in greater numbers: "They asked for those gentlemen, to see who they were. D. Enrique tells them that they are two friends. They tell them that they should quit the pretense and come along with them, that they must sign a little statement,"[222] and they arrest them and take them away. D. Enrique and his assistant try to stop them from taking them, but a militiaman pushes them away and shouts at them, "You, get away if you know what's good for you!"[223] The two Redemptorists, guessing their fate, say goodbye to D. Enrique, telling him: "Until heaven!"[224] Upon going out and closing the door, the militiamen took the habits off the priests, then frisked and searched them. Doña Segunda watched "through a peephole what they were doing to them and saw that they took all the papers from their pockets and viciously tore them to pieces.

....

219 APRM. Mártires 0403001, 1. Translator's note: these were nicknames, the first meaning "Humpback," the second "Boozers."

220 Cf. APRM. Mártires 0400105.2, 10.

221 APRM. Mártires 0400115, 6.

222 Cf. APRM. Mártires 0400105.2, 11.

223 APRM. Mártires 0403001, 1.

224 Cf. APRM. Mártires 0400105.2, 11. The boldness of D. Enrique (to be a priest and to take in so generously the two religious of San Felipe) is going to cost him his life. On August 12, 1936, around 10:00 PM, four militiamen came to the house on Calle Pilares and asked him to accompany them to clear up a few things with the police. As they go out, they attempted to take him to the Bridge of San Pablo, thus to do away with the body in the river and to be able to say that it was a suicide. But he resisted them, sitting down on the steps of the Plaza Mayor. So they put him into a car right then and there and headed in the direction of the Puerta de San Juan and then toward the Plaza de Toros (cf. S. CIRAC ESTOPAÑÁN, *Martirologio de Cuenca. Crónica diocesana de la época roja* [Barcelona, 1947] 192-193). His body was recovered the next day with a bullet in the head at kilometer 15 on the highway to Alcázar (*Pieza principal de Cuenca ciudad*: CAUSA, Leg. 1062. Exp. 10, 136).

Then they half-pushed the priests down the stairs while cursing terribly at them"[225] When they searched Fr. Miguel they found a photograph, which they then tore up.

Because of where the house of D. Enrique was and the hour in which these things happened, a lot of people saw what was going on: the clock on the Tower of Mangana struck ten in the morning when they saw a dozen militiamen shouting blasphemies and hurrahs for Russia, insults and a profusion of threats against the Church and the priests. The militiamen took the two religious away, hitting and pushing them, in rhythm to "The International," through the streets of Cuenca. One priest was wearing glasses, the other a beret.[226] The group was made up, among others, of *El Picias, El Vinagrero, El Frutos, El Guerra, El Borrachines, El Chepudo, El Garrote, el Hijo del Gaire,* and at the front of all of them, *El Sustos.*[227] Armed with pistols in hand, they took them away in a rough manner.[228] Together with them was an unidentified person with a rifle. They crossed through the center of the city,[229] along Calle Pilares, Calle Severo Catalina, down the descent to Las Angustias, side gate of the Discalced Carmelites, by the hermitage of the Virgin, and the Descalzos Bridge. Upon arriving at the bridge, they took a path that went inside, to the bank of the Júcar River, in the direction of the power station of Batán.

....

225 APRM. Mártires 0400105.2, 11.

226 Cf. FLORENCIO DÍAZ, *Declaración ante el Tribunal Militar*: AGET. Leg. 4131 / Sum. 1064, 56 r.

227 Cf. *Ib.*; APRM. Mártires 0404004.

228 Cf. APRM. Mártires 0404003, 17.

229 Fr. Dionisio de Felipe, who knew Cuenca very well, since he had lived at San Felipe various years, describes thus the *via dolorosa* of the two Redemptorists: They went along Calle del Severo Catalina, which borders the left side of the plaza in front of the cathedral, the main plaza, and went down Las Angustias [Translator's note: *angustias* means "sorrows"], called such because it leads to the hermitage of Our Lady of Sorrows, very much venerated in Cuenca...." D. DE FELIPE, *Nuevos Redentores* [Madrid, 1962] 171-172); cf. APRM. Mártires 0400107, 4.

Descent to the Hermitage of Our Lady of Sorrows

As they passed, there were many witnesses to this improvised Way of the Cross. Simona Hidalgo saw how the priests were pulled out of the house of D. Enrique. She went to confession and spiritual direction with Fr. Ciriaco Olarte, and when they saw each other they greeted one another. Encarnación Muñoz, who was coming back from Las Angustias, also saw them come out.[230] Halfway, Felisa Mata, who went out to do some shopping, ran into the little group of ten men, equipped with small arms. She stopped and let them pass. Later, she learned it was the religious who were with these men.[231] Genoveva Ayllón, who was going from the Plaza to Las Angustias where she lived "saw a group of armed men who were dragging along two men whom she did not know...saw the son of 'Frutos' and saw 'Guerra,' who were just kids."[232] When they passed the hermitage of Las Angustias, the caretaker of the shrine, María Yuste, seeing the commotion, asked what was happening. She was told it was two of the Fathers from San Felipe. She and others with her shut down the hermitage. Later, they heard the shots.[233] Further on, Anastasio García saw them when they arrived at a fountain in front of a quarry. Among those he knew was a man, whom he did not know, armed with a rifle. He continued onward and when he arrived at the Descalzos Bridge, he heard the shots.[234] Only D. Florencio Díaz challenged the militiamen:

"What are you people going to do? Don't you see this is a barbarity? You don't win the war this way!"

To this *El Sustos* responded:

"You have to kill these pests of the rear guard to assure the victory."

Not only was there some doubt about the place, but for a time even about killing them. But *El Sustos* said:

"If we're not going to kill them, why did we bring them here?"

El Sustos went ahead to find a place. In a clearing of a quarry they made them go up a terrace. Fr. Olarte said:

....

230 Cf. *Ib.*, 13.

231 Cf. *Ib.*, 12.

232 *Ib.*, 15.

233 Cf. *Ib.*, 10.

234 Cf. *Ib.*, 16.

"If you are going to kill us, do it now. Why walk further, treating us this way?"[235]

The militiamen, from above and below, fired their shots in an irregular way at the two martyrs.[236] Ángeles García heard one of the two say, "Don't do anything to us. We are just some poor friars."[237] Various persons were witnesses to the macabre execution. One of them describes it thus:

At the end of July 1936, she happened to be returning from selling some items, produce from an orchard that her parents cultivated. She arrived at a spot near Descalzos Bridge. She was able to see that a group of some eight or ten individuals had taken the same road as she. The group was composed of "El Sustos" and other militiamen armed with pistols and shotguns and two other individuals. She deduced from the expression on the faces of these two individuals that they were under arrest. She stayed behind them until they arrived at a clearing that is on the path that leads to the orchards, above the spring of Caquito. The group stopped there and the narrator also stopped there. One of them told them to let her pass by. So the one who is making this declaration went further on and she was going up in the direction of the path toward Las Angustias, along a slope that leads to it. She heard El Sustos telling them to wait. After a bit of time the witness turned her head to hear El Sustos from a clearing that there is below the path to Las Angustias. El Sustos told the group to go up, which they did. She was able to tell also that the men who were under arrest, instead of bringing them up along the path, forced them to go across the rocks and rugged terrain. When the witness arrived at the house of Batán and stopped to talk... she heard shots which, without any doubt, were those that occasioned the death of the poor prisoners.[238]

....

235 Cf. APRM. Mártires 0400105.2, 11; 0400107, 5.

236 Cf. APRM. Mártires 0400107, 5.

237 Cf. APRM. Mártires 0404003, 11.

238 ÁNGELES GARCÍA FRÍAS, *Declaración ante el Tribunal Militar* en: AGET. Leg. 4131 / Sum. 1064, 56.

Doña Juana Soria heard the shots from the water ditch where she was washing.[239] Another witness, when the Redemptorists were shot, heard them say: "Viva Christ the King! Viva St. Alphonsus!"[240]

When they were shot, they fell to the embankment and stayed stretched out there at its foot. The militiamen drank from a fount that was there on the side and left, leaving two guards to make sure no one got near.[241]

....

239 Cf. APRM. Mártires 0404003, 9.

240 Cf. APRM. Mártires 0400107, 5; 0400105.4, 13.

241 APRM. Mártires 0400105.2, 12; 0404003, 11.

Hoz del Jucar, the place where C. Olarte and M. Goñi died

Upon hearing the shots, some people came close to find out what was happening.[242] The witnesses saw them both still alive, lying there at the foot of the slope,[243] the one going over to the other to console him. One of them, we cannot know which, died within minutes;[244] his companion went through a long and painful agony, slowly bleeding and crying out for help.[245] Many heard him over a period of hours. Even though we cannot determine with exactitude who lived longer, it was probably Fr. Goñi. Although Fr. Ciriaco received shots in the chest and bled out little by little,[246] when he was exhumed, a shot to the neck was discovered, which was without a doubt the *coup de grace*. Fr. Miguel Goñi, on the contrary, was shot in the head, which caused a cranial hemorrhage and the destruction of the cerebrum,[247] although his death had to be slow. Anastasio García, a neighbor in that place, says he went over to the pair around six in the afternoon, and by then both were dead.[248]

The bodies were not taken away until eight o'clock in the evening. At that time, officials of the court came to take them away. They obliged some curious bystanders to carry them from the quarry area up to the road, leaving behind them a trail of blood:[249]

....

242 Cf. APRM. Mártires 0404003, 15.

243 Cf. *Ib.*, 11.

244 Fr. Isidro Posado echoes this confusion about the data: "They were still alive for some time; one of them for three hours; some say it was Goñi, others that it was Olarte; I don't know." (I. POSADO, *C. Beatificationis - Declaraciones* I, 156). According to Br. Benjamin, it was Fr. Goñi who had a prolonged agony (Cf. APRM. Mártires 0400105.4,14). According to Fr. Retana, it was Fr. Olarte who lived some hours more (Cf. APRM. Mártires 0400117, 5); this is the version that another witness to that day transmits, Maximino Muñoz (APRM. Mártires 0404003, 20); Anastasio García is also of this opinion, who says the fatter one is the one who remained alive longer, transmitting what was said to him by a witness who was present on that very July 31 and who was a shepherd (cf. ANASTASIO GARCÍA, *C. Beatificationis - Declaraciones* I, 186). We are inclined toward Fr. Goñi, the balance tilting in the direction of the more life-threatening wound.

245 Cf. APRM. Mártires: 0400107, 5-6; 0404004; 0404003, 11.

246 Cf. *Acta de defunción de Ciriaco Olarte Pérez de Mendiguren*: REG. CIVIL DE CUENCA, Sec. 3.ª, T. 42, F. 304, N.º 603; it was written on August 3, 1936.

247 Cf. *Acta de defunción de Miguel Goñi Áriz*: REG. CIVIL DE CUENCA, Sec. 3.ª, T. 42, F. 305, N.º 604; written on August 3, 1936.

248 Cf. APRM. Mártires 0404003, 16.

249 Cf. *Ib.*, 16; ANASTASIO GARCÍA, *C. Beatificationis - Declaraciones* I, 186-187.

He arrived at the courthouse at twenty hours. The guards had arrived at nineteen hours. He observed how they had dragged them over the slope, with the dirt disturbed by the action. The two bodies were about a meter and a half apart. Fr. Olarte was face up without shots to the head, but shot in the chest, a pool of blood near the cadaver. Fr. Goñi was propped up on the ground with five shots to the head (the right temple from top to bottom), the brain destroyed.... He still had his glasses on. They took them down the road and there they put them in boxes painted black. They carried them on their shoulders to the bridge. A lot of blood was pouring out. Then from the bridge a van took them to the cemetery.... They arrived at the cemetery about ten o'clock at night. [250]

The news soon got around all of Cuenca. It was on everyone's lips that the ones who had been carried off like lambs in broad daylight, executed while crossing the city, and killed near the hermitage of Las Angustias, had been some Redemptorists from San Felipe.

On April 10 and 13, 1940, the exhumation of the bodies of the six martyrs took place from the common grave at the cemetery, and they were transferred and reburied in the Redemptorist mausoleum. The whole community was present at the moment and witnessed the horrifying facts that the bodies of the missionaries offered regarding their passion and death. The chronicler has transmitted it to us in all its detail. Fr. Miguel Goñi had "his sternum destroyed; the right arm broken in an improbable posture. The left shoulder was lowered. Without a doubt, it was after shooting and killing him that he suffered these breaks. The effects of the prolonged and very painful agony were evident in his face."[251] In the 2008 medical report done during the identification of his remains,[252] it has to be noted that "in the posterior part of the right parietal lobe appears an orifice that could correspond to a wound from a firearm, without there appearing very clearly an exit wound,"[253] in spite of the fact that in the rear part there

....

250 MAXIMINO MUÑOZ GABALDÓN, *Declaración* en: APRM. Mártires 0404003, 16.

251 *Crónica de Cuenca, 1940, month of April.*.

252 Cf. *Informe médico pericial de los restos. Madrid 2008* en: *Actas de la recognición y traslado de restos,* 48-51. [Translator's note: the Spanish means *"Medical expert's report on the remains. Madrid 2008* in *Records of the identification and transfer of remains 48-51"*

253 *Ib.,* 48.

is a loss of the temporal bone, as much on the left as on the right, which well could be the exit wound of the projectile, with an orientation from the top to the bottom. The cranial cavity showed in the frontal bone the lack of a closure for the medial suture, the two portions of the frontal parietal separated on two sides. The sutures of the upper part of the brain were torn and the two occipitals separated. The ribs appeared broken in fragments of approximately ten centimeters and some large broken bones of the upper and lower extremities.

Regarding the cadaver of Fr. Ciriaco, the chronicler of 1940[254] points out that it had the head intact, although on opening the mouth they could see the exit wound of the bullet, since they had shot him in the nape of the neck. They could also see on his face the expression of sharp pain. The doctor who did the medical examination of the remains in 2008[255] also made note that he had the cranium intact, although the jaw was partially destroyed. Some ribs were broken and, among the bones of the extremities, the right humerus bone and the right fibula appeared broken.

The Seminary Group:
José Javier Gorosterratzu, Julián Pozo, and Victoriano Calvo

On July 24 there was a search conducted of the home of D. Elpidio Miranzo, situated on the second floor of No. 22, Calle Andrés Cabrera. In that same building, on the first floor, the home of Eugenia Muñoz and her sister Isabel, Fr. Julián Pozo and Br. Victoriano were hiding.[256] Eugenia warned the religious of the danger that the search of the floor above suggested and asked them what they would say in case a group of militiamen appeared in the house. She wanted to make sure that all the inhabitants of the apartment would offer the same version. Fr. Julián commented: "We will represent ourselves as that which we are, Redemptorist religious. We do not have martyrs. Let's see if we'll be the first."[257] Conscious of the danger, during the succeeding days the three hidden Redemptorists prepared to live their

---

254 *Crónica de Cuenca, 1940, month of April.*

255 Cf. *Informe médico pericial de los restos...*, 51-53.

256 *Ib.,* 48.

257 APRM. Mártires 0405001, 1. Br. Benjamín recorded similar words (APRM. Mártires 0400105.2, 13) as did Fr. Retana (APRM. Mártires 0400107, 13).

presentiment, nurturing their spiritual life with daily prayer and the celebration of the Eucharist.

Fr. Pedroso was alarmed by the increase in the number of house searches. He sent a note to all the religious of the community that they leave the families where they were and hide at the diocesan seminary or at the Little Sisters of the Poor. Since the forces of the Civil Guard of the province were concentrated at the seminary, those staying there felt safer from the extremist groups that were patrolling the city. At the Little Sisters of the Poor, under the control of the provincial deputation, and converted for the most part into an asylum for the religious sisters of the city, they could remain unnoticed among the elderly and the employees. Fr. Julián Pozo and Br. Victoriano Calvo heeded the warning of the superior and went off to the seminary with Fr. J. Javier Gorosterratzu. On the morning of July 25, grateful for her help, they took their leave of Doña Eugenia. They were convinced they would be gone only a few days, and they went off to their new home.[258]

Since the Civil Guard was concentrated at the seminary, many priests sought help and safety in this great building. It ended up housing a dozen priests and, from July 28 on, the bishop of the diocese himself and his family members. Each had his own room and all were assisted by the Mercedarian Sisters, who previously had served the seminarians. They prayed the Office in common, celebrated the Eucharist each morning, had access to the chapel for prayer before the Blessed Sacrament, celebrated the sacrament of reconciliation with other priests, and in these ways helped one another to live through those moments. Without a doubt, their adversities helped them to experience more strongly the reality of the local Church, in union with their diocesan pastor, D. Cruz Laplana.[259] The news of the execution of the two Redemptorists also came to them rather quickly: "The news of the deaths of Frs. Olarte and Goñi became quickly known throughout the whole city. Where it had its greatest impact, without doubt, was in the seminary, where a dozen priests were concentrated."[260]

The priests remained at peace, hiding in the seminary until August 2,

---

258 Cf. APRM. Mártires 0405001, 1.

259 Cf. S. CIRAC, *Vida de D. Cruz Laplana, Obispo de Cuenca* (Barcelona, 1943) 123-124.

260 APRM. Mártires 0400115, 8.

when the captain of the headquarters of the Civil Guard of Cuenca, García Ángela, was transferred to Madrid and all the forces of the unit were sent to the front. This decision left the seminary at the disposal of the anarchist militiamen,[261] without the protection the Civil Guard had given the priests. "If at first that place had been a defense and a shelter, now with the departure of the Civil Guard it became a veritable prison. In effect, the priests enclosed there came under scrutiny and confinement in their respective quarters. They were not permitted to leave their rooms, while on the lower floors of the building dungeons and the headquarters of the secret police were authorized for construction. Later, these would be supervised by the SIM."[262] One of the priests who was in the seminary at the time offers us a description of the surroundings in which they were living:

We all tried to prepare ourselves spiritually, since we thought that the time was imminent in which they could kill us. I can especially refer to Fr. Gorosterratzu. In one of the meetings in which we were talking about the probability of our death, he showed himself to be pious and innocent. He told us that he had talked to Jesus in the chapel and told him that he was ready to die as a martyr, but that it would be better if it were later on; he said he would be grateful to be able to finish the history he was writing.[263]

Gradually the consciousness was growing among the priests that, more than likely, theirs would be the destiny of martyrs. This fact appeared as much in their usual conversations as in the spiritual exhortations they gave one another, encouraging each other to give testimony of their faith. Every night before retiring to their respective rooms, they made confession to each other.[264] The three Redemptorists lived out those days in this spiritual envi-

....

261 Cf. A. B. RODRÍGUEZ, *La Guerra Civil en Cuenca (1936-1939). Vol. I. Del 18 de Julio a la Columna del Rosal* (Madrid, 20063) 72-73.

262 APRM. Mártires 0400115, 8.

263 CAMILO FERNÁNDEZ DE LELIS, *C. Beatificationis—Declaraciones* I, 284-285. This was the priest who at the time was superior of the seminary and chaplain for the Mercedarian Sisters. He was in the seminary at the same time as the three Redemptorists until August 6, 1936, when he left there.

264 REMEDIOS ACEDO MAEZTU, *Ib.,* II, 667.

ronment, without contact with the outside world. Fr. Julián and Br. Victoriano spent the greater part of each day in prayer in chapel before the Blessed Sacrament and with the rosary in hand. Fr. J. Javier,[265] besides his personal absorption in prayer, heard the confessions of the Mercedarian Sisters who were taking care of them and gave them spiritual talks to comfort them in those moments.[266] While he was doing this, he also continued writing his work about Cardinal Carranza, which he left unfinished.[267]

On August 8, a rumor put the prisoners in the seminary on alert. At midnight, the militiamen had taken away Bishop Cruz Laplana, along with his family member D. Fernando Español. The news alarmed everyone and they knew what had been the destiny of those two.[268] Fr. J. Javier was nervous by nature. When he heard of the events, he fell apart and suffered an anxiety crisis, seeing clearly the future that was awaiting them.[269] Trapped into a situation of martyrdom, grounded in his vow of perseverance as a Redemptorist, and strengthened in his interior life, gradually he accepted the tragic fate that was presenting itself. That is what the few witnesses tell us who survived from that time.[270]

....

265 "I know the kind of life that they led in the seminary—through Francisco Martínez, now deceased—that every night Fr. Gorosterratzu heard their confessions and encouraged them to become martyrs. He had a presentiment that they would be led to their deaths because the very fact that he was urging others to accept a martyr's death was a clear sign of it, the sign of the danger that all detected." (M.ª NATIVIDAD CUENCA PÉREZ, Ib., 408-409)

266 Cf. Ib., 654. 659. 667-669.

267 "He was writing a history and they sent the original proofs from the printer in those days so that he could correct them; the 'militiamen' intercepted one of the proofs and in their ignorance decided they could see in those papers some evidence of espionage. For this reason, they demanded that he appear before them. In these circumstances, in order to defend himself, he said quite innocently that he was an historian and a man of science. The militiamen, with malicious irony, responded that he was flattering himself with a lot of hot air. He received the rebuke with humility and, as always, with his own peculiar nervousness." (CAMILO FERNÁNDEZ DE LELIS, Ib., I, 281)

268 D. Cruz Laplana was called out at midnight by the porter of the seminary, who told him that the militiamen were requiring this. He was dressed in his cassock and pectoral cross accompanied by his faithful family member D. Fernando Español. They were put into a car and assassinated at kilometer 5 of the highway to Villar de Olalla (Cuenca). Their bodies were carried away and buried that same day in the common grave at the cemetery of Cuenca (cf. S. CIRAC, o. c., 124-128).

269 "According to testimony...Fr. Gorosterratzu was very nervous when they took away the Bishop...since he was by temperament a nervous person." (M.ª NATIVIDAD CUENCA PÉREZ, C. Beatificationis - Declaraciones II, 409).

270 Cf. CAMILO FERNÁNDEZ DE LELIS, Ib., I, 285; REMEDIOS ACEDOMAEZTU, Ib., II, 660.

At dawn on August 9, Fr. Julián Pozo was taken out of the seminary for his execution. In the Union Hall, a list was drawn up of ten people whom the gangs of militiamen would assassinate that morning. Among those who carried out the executions were *El Sustos*, in charge, and together with him, *Pambarato* and *El Finito*.[271] Fr. Julián did not face the final moment of his life alone. With him they took D. Juan Crisóstomo Escribano,[272] who also was in the seminary. Another two people[273] were brought into the group, probably the priest Alfonso López-Guerrero Portocarrero and Francisco Torrijos Ruiz. A line of militiamen waited at the door of the diocesan seminary as guards. They later transferred the prisoners to the adjacent plaza, where they were put into a car.[274] Some of those who led them out were impressed with the composure that D. Juan Cristósomo demonstrated. He asked them to allow him to go vested in his soutane, and was exhorting the militiamen, forgiving them, before they would kill the prisoners.[275] Fr. Julián Pozo maintained an attitude of recollection and resignation.[276]

....

271 Cf. FÉLIX LORCA URANGO, *Declaración* en: CAUSA, Leg. 1062, Exp. 7, 139.

272 Juan Crisóstomo Escribano García (Cf. Appendix 3).

273 There are discrepancies in the sources about who the two people were who accompanied Julián Pozo and Juan Crisóstomo Escribano to martyrdom. Sebastian Cirac (cf. S. CIRAC ESTO-PAÑÁN, 173-177), who uses as his principal source the registry of the cemetery for which he takes as reference the day of burial, tells us that they died with "two gentlemen of Cardenete" (*Ib.*, 229); looking at the general list (cf. *Ib.*, 174), on August 10, 1936, the cadavers of two men of Cardenete were buried, belonging to Francisco Ruiz Escribano and Francisco Torrijos Ruiz; from the details which the general list gives about their martyrdom it tells us that they died together and embracing each other (cf. *Ib.*, 105-106 y 108). The other source is the lists in the *Pieza Principal* (Translator's note: this refers to the capital, Cuenca) in the *Causa General* of the city of Cuenca (Translator's note: this is the investigation done under Franco regarding the conduct of the "People's Tribunals" during the Second Republic) (CAUSA, Leg. 1062. Exp. 10, 136 y 140). These were taken from the Civil Register of Cuenca; it asserts that on August 9, 1936, three people died from the neighborhoods of Cuenca (*Ib.*, 136) and seven persons from outside the city (*Ib.*, 140), a total, then, of ten men; four of the cadavers were found at kilometer 8 or 9 of the highway to Tragacete; four in El Pinar de Jalaga, one on the highway to Alcázar and another on the road in the cemetery. Because of the access that we have had to this last source, which gathers the data from the Civil Register, and knowing that the death certificates were higher on the days on which the assassinations occurred, without closing the issue, we are inclined to think that the group formed by the four persons whose cadavers were collected between kilometers 8 and 9 on the highway from Tragacete consisted of: Julián Pozo, Juan Crisóstomo Escribano, Alfonso López-Guerrero, and Francisco Torrijos (C.f., Appendix 3).

274 Cf. APRM. Mártires 0400115, 8; 0405001, 1.

275 Cf. APRM. Mártires 0405001, 2; 0405004, 19.

276 Cf. APRM. Mártires 0400120.

Taken to kilometer 8 on the highway from Tragacete, D. Juan[277] took a cross in one hand and a rosary in the other. At the moment of gunfire, with his arms in the form of a cross, he had the strength to shout, "Viva Cristo Rey!" The executioners, full of rage, said to him, "You still dare to shout?" And immediately they hit him again with a new discharge of gunfire.[278]

Fr. Julián Pozo[279] faced the definitive moment of his life with the gentle and humble attitude that always characterized him. He knelt, gripped his rosary, and began to finger the beads while saying the Hail Mary. One of the militiamen fired his gun at Fr. Julián's head. At that very moment, he fell dead with his characteristic smile on his lips. We have no data about the other people who shared that martyrdom. The death certificate points out that Fr. Julián Pozo "died in the early hours of the morning on the ninth day of the present month, at the second hectometer of kilometer eight on the highway from Cuenca to Tragacete, close to the capital. He died as a result of a wound to the head."[280] The body was recovered the same day, August 9, and was buried in the common grave in the cemetery in Cuenca.

When the body was exhumed in 1940,[281] they could only see that it was totally decomposed. In the examination of 2008 they were able to tell from the remains that the cranium presented "on the right front section…a rectangular hole of 1.5 x 2 cms., which is not typical for the entrance wound of a bullet, although it could correspond to it. The rest of the cranium had a missing fragment on the left temporal lobe of 1.5 x 6 cms.,"[282] which could have been the exit wound.

Scarcely had they learned the news of what happened to Fr. Pozo, when it became the turn of Fr. José Javier Gorosterratzu and Br. Victoriano Calvo. At eleven o'clock at night on that same August 9, the militiamen interro-

---

277 Cf. S. Cirac Estopañán, 189-190; APRM. Mártires: 0405001, 2; 0405004, 19.

278 When they went to recover the body of D. Juan Cristósomo, he had the scapular around his neck and the rosary in one hand and the cross in the other. No one was able to take them from him. (cf. *Ib.*)

279 Cf. D. DE FELIPE, 188; APRM. Mártires: 0405004, 5 y 11; 0400107, 9; 0400114, 5.

280 *Acta de defunción de Julián Pozo Ruiz de Samaniego:* REG. CIVIL DE CUENCA, Sec.3.ª, T. 42, F. 324, N.º 642.

281 *Crónica de Cuenca, 1940, month of April.*

282 *Informe médico pericial de los restos…,* 46.

gated the sisters about the rooms of the priests.[283] In the first hours of the dawn of August 10, they came to the seminary to finish their work. That night they carried off in the so-called "death car," five to seven of the seminary prisoners.[284] Moreover, with total certainty we know that, besides the two Redemptorists, D. Manuel Laplana,[285] got into that car, as did D. Victoriano Pérez[286] and Fernando Pérez del Cerro,[287] and probably the priests who were brothers, D. Lucio[288] and D. Juan Félix Bellón Parrilla.[289] When they called them, D. Manuel asked the militiamen: "May we know where you are taking us?" And another of the priests answered him: "We are going to our death; we are going to martyrdom for God and for Spain!"[290]

Some religious sisters, among them the niece of Fr. Javier Gorosterratzu, Sr. Escolástica Nuin Gorosterratzu, a Benedictine nun[291] of Cuenca, saw him from the windows of their rooms in those dramatic moments: "I saw him exactly when they brought him out, because that night we were awake and a Little Sister of the Poor told us, warned us, that they brought

....

283 Cf. REMEDIOS ACEDO MAEZTU, *d. c.*, 659.

284 On that day, August 10, 1936, the bodies of eight people were recovered (CAUSA, Leg. 1062. Exp. 10, pp. 136 y 140; S. CIRAC ESTOPAÑÁN, 174, with the exception of this last reference, which puts as the date the 11th of August, the date in the cemetery registry). Of them, one was a layman from Caracenilla (Cuenca) who died in Pinar de Jalaga; the rest were six priests and a lay religious. According to the data in the *Causa General*, five of them died on the right side road of the cemetery: J.Gorosterratzu, Victoriano Calvo, Manuel Laplana, Victoriano Pérez and Fernando Pérez; the bodies of the other two priests were found on the highway from Cuenca to Arcos de la Cantera, near the shortcut which goes to the cemetery. According to S. Cirac Estopañán (*Martirologio*, 61 y 209; *Vida de D. Cruz Laplana...*, 125-126) the three who died on the cemetery road were brought out from the seminary; S. Cirac (*Martirologio*, 181-182) does not say where the Bellón Parrilla brothers were detained, though he does say that they died with D. Victoriano Pérez, D.Manuel Laplana and other priests. Although the data can be coincidental, we do not have access to information to close the question, but rather are leaving open the list and the number of those who suffered martyrdom in that early morning of August 10, 1936, on the cemetery road.

285 Manuel Laplana Torres (cf. Appendix 3).

286 Victoriano Pérez Muñoz (cf. Appendix 3).

287 Fernando Pérez del Cerro (cf. Appendix 3).

288 Lucio Bellón Parrilla (cf. Appendix 3).

289 Juan Félix Bellón Parrilla (cf. Appendix 3).

290 Cf. S. CIRAC, *Vida de D. Cruz Laplana...*, 126.

291 The Benedictine nuns were taken from their monastery and brought to the nursing home of the Little Sisters of the Poor, adjacent to the diocesan seminary of San Julián.

him out and then I myself saw my uncle for a short space of time, and I, along with Sr. Nieves, saw that he had his hands tied because you could see that at least he had them behind his back."[292]

One of the Little Sisters of the nursing home, Sr. Luisa de la Asunción, saw them leave the seminary about two in the morning. The militiamen escorted them and continually pushed them around. Among the militiamen was Elías Cruz Moya, one of the directors of the CNT of Cuenca, who had participated in the death of the bishop of the diocese. The religious men were serene and tranquil as they went along. When he saw how many they were, the driver of the van complained that they were a lot and that not all would fit in. So they took them to a nearby spot.[293]

Fr. José Javier Gorosterratzu and Br. Victoriano Calvo were martyred in the early morning of August 10, on the right side of the road of the cemetery of Cuenca, near a fountain. The cause of death of both was a cerebral wound provoked by shots received to the head.[294] When the bodies were recovered, they were buried in the common grave of the cemetery of Cuenca.

When they exhumed the body of Fr. Gorosterratzu in 1940,[295] they perceived an expression of horrible agony on his face. In the investigation of 2008, the cranium and the jaw of Fr. José Javier[296] appear conserved in fragmentary form. The bones of the upper extremities have their ulnas broken and the right radius deteriorated.

In 1940, when the casket of Br. Victoriano was opened, his body appeared "with the thorax destroyed by blows."[297] In the investigation of 2008[298] there was discovered in his cranium "in the right parietal bone... behind the face there appears a cylindrical orifice which could be from a bullet wound. In the left tempo-occipital there appear various fracture lines in a detached fragment which could correspond to the exit orifice of

....

292 ESCOLÁSTICA NUIN GOROSTERRATZU, *C. Beatificationis—Declaraciones* II, 422.

293 APRM. Mártires 0401002.

294 *Acta de defunción de Victoriano Calvo Lozano*: REG. CIVIL DE CUENCA, Sec. 3.ª, T. 42, F. 326, N.º 647; *Acta de defunción de Javier Gorosterratzu Jaunarena*: REG. CIVIL DE CUENCA, Sec. 3.ª, T. 42, F. 327, N.º 648.

295 *Crónica de Cuenca, 1940, month of April.*.

296 *Informe médico pericial de los restos...*, 42. 45.

297 *Crónica de Cuenca, 1940, month of April.*

298 Cf. *Informe médico pericial de los restos...*, 40-42.

a projectile."[299] Also, the ribs on the left side appear broken and the upper extremity on the left side has the ulna and radius broken.

---

299 *Ib.,* 40.

Place where J. J. Gorosterratzu and V. Calvo died

The Case of Fr. Pedro Romero

Fr. Pedro Romero, age 67, experienced a bloodless martyrdom. Although his sufferings extended through a longer time than the martyrdom of his companions and did not end up in his shedding blood, his health was weakening and he finally died in a jail cell, exhausted on account of the religious persecution. In July 1938, a terrible dysentery took him to his death in a few days' time. According to the death certificate "he died in the provincial prison on the fourth day of the present month (July), at eight hours and thirty minutes, as a consequence of tuberculous enteritis according to results from the medical certificate and the examination which was done."[300] Although he was not assassinated, the loss of his life was recognized by the ecclesiastical tribunal as truly that of a martyr, and the decretal of martyrdom has confirmed it.

He hid with other confreres in the nursing home of the Little Sisters of the Poor on July 25, where he went unnoticed as one more old person. There he did pastoral work with the residents of the home and with the Little Sisters.[301] The day he took to the road for the nursing home, they saw him head there with a crocheted blanket and a trunk on his shoulder.[302] He stayed there until September 20, 1937,[303] the day on which the CNT assumed control of the nursing home. Then, like the other Redemptorists, he had to look for another place. He concealed himself in the house of Doña Bienvenida Herráez, on Calle San Miguel. She offered him a dark room in which he could not only live, but also hear confessions of those who came to him. He stayed in this house until the mother-in-law of Doña Herráez denounced him. The mother-in-law had a mental problem. Fr. Romero had to go to the civil government building to give a statement. There they ordered that he be included on welfare assistence. He registered for a room at the charity hospital but he could not endure the blasphemies and ridicule. He left there and lived as a beggar on the streets of the city.

....

300 Cf. *Acta de defunción de Pedro Romero Espejo*: REG. CIVIL DE CUENCA, Sec. 3.ª, T. 44 F. 300. N.º 599.

301 Cf. ISIDRO FERNÁNDEZ POSADO, *C. Beatificationis—Declaraciones* I, 170.

302 Cf. APRM. Mártires 0406005, 1.

303 Cf. APRM. Mártires 0406007, 11.

People saw him every day wandering about the streets of Cuenca,[304] with a book in one hand, wearing a worn-out habit, carrying a rosary, and with a crocheted quilt around his shoulders.[305] He ate by the charity of others. He slept under the bridge, as would any beggar. He mumbled prayers under the trees of the park.[306] For a while he went to sleep at the so-called Posada de Ruperto[307] in the Puerta de Valencia, where he slept in the stable. A few pious families of Cuenca offered him something warm, which was the only thing he would accept. There were offers to take him in, first from friendly families and then from his Redemptorist confreres, but he refused them. He didn't want to compromise or complicate anyone's life. Besides, in this way he was freer to exercise the apostolate as he wished. He also rejected an offer to leave Cuenca so that he would not leave abandoned and without a priest that city where he had spent a considerable part of his life. But with this kind of life he felt more tired every day and his health was breaking. He even came to think of jail as a kind of public lodging.

On June 5 he was arrested for saying the rosary and reading books of prayers in the street. He was taken to the civil government building,[308] where he was in jail for twenty-four hours. From there, on June 6, 1938, he was registered in the jail installed in the monastery of the Discalced Carmelite Nuns.[309] He was accused of disliking the regime.[310] When he saw the meal they gave him, which consisted mostly of lentil soup, he would joke: "A few pork chops would do me just fine!"[311] There he found a veritable guardian angel in the person of the young man Gabriel Lozano, sacristan of Rubielos Bajos (Cuenca). Gabriel has left us his testimony in a letter,

....

304 Cf. APRM. Mártires 0400105.2, 2-6; 0400107, 10; 0400114, 1-2; 0406001; 0406002; 0406005.

305 Cf. APRM. Mártires 0406002, 1.

306 Cf. APRM. Mártires 0400105.2, 5; 0406007, 15.

307 Translator's note: "Rupert's Inn" may have been a shelter for the homeless in the days of the Second Republic.

308 APRM. Mártires 0406001, 1.

309 Cf. *Libro de registro de la Prisión Provincial de Cuenca; copia:* CAUSA, Leg. 675, Exp. 2, F. 26, N.º 1316.

310 Cf. APRM. Mártires 0406002, 1.

311 TRIFÓN BELTRÁN, C. *Beatificationis - Declaraciones* I, 178; APRM, Mártires 0406002, 1.

in which he gives us a firsthand account of the life of Fr. Pedro during the month that he was in that place:

In 1938…Fr. Romero arrived at the prison of the Discalced Carmelite Nuns with a dark shirt, umbrella, a bag of clothes, a blanket, his books, two or three crucifixes, a big rosary and a small one, and with eyes bathed in tears that ran to the floor. Right away I got up to greet him and to console him in his deep bitterness, and he answered right away with an agreeable smile, which calmed him a great deal. I invited him to my apartment with the purpose of helping him in whatever way I could, but since there were forty of us who spent the night there, he said he preferred an isolated spot. And in fact I took him to a room that no one occupied. I prepared for him a bed on the soft soil, a bag with straw, two blankets and his own, with the bag of clothes as a pillow, so that he could rest and I offered him some food. He said it would be better for him to eat later. But I went off to look for a glass of milk and I gave it to him and I spent the afternoon with him to keep us entertained and to give him encouragement. At this time and on other occasions we talked…. Since the food they gave him in jail made him feel bad, I had to beg alms from some very wealthy gentlemen, like D. Julián Izquierdo, Chief Engineer of Montes; D. Rafaél Ripollés, Architect of the Casa Real; D. Trifón Beltrán, Capitular Vicar; D. Ramón Melgarejo, Marqués de Melgarejo; D. José Echevarría; D. Felipe Quintero, medical dentist; and others. People brought them food from outside. But since they had been stripped of everything, they were living by charity. But because of the small amount that Fr. Romero ate, he did not lack anything. He spent all day in fervent prayer, sometimes with the rosary, sometimes reading Thomas à Kempis, which he lent me, sometimes with the prayer of the breviary, and in a great deal of meditation. Also he heard some confessions and gave very good and useful advice. From time to time I would fluff up his bed, wash things for him, clean, etc. He was overcome by dysentery. He suffered a lot in those days and nights, but without ceasing his profound prayer. Finally, he was so weak despite the helps that I gave him…When I returned one day, it was a sad and pitiable sight. A plague of flies covered him in that infected atmosphere. He had a most alarming and almost agonizing appearance. I could tell he was saying some short prayers.

I asked him: "How are you, Father?"

"You can see for yourself," he replied.

I tried to get him up. With effort he got to his feet. He was wrapped in a blanket and was leaning on me. I took him to a private room where I washed him from head to foot. I changed his clothes and dressed him. And since I was getting a good reputation in the prison, I asked for a few useful materials for the Father: I got a decent room for him, a bed, pillow, mattress, sheets. After he got in bed, he opened his arms and indicated that he wanted me to approach him. He gave me a long and strong hug and said over and over, "God reward you! God reward you!"

I went out into the prison to ask for food. They gave me milk, eggs, sugar, coffee, and everything. He asked for a crucifix and rosary. He took some food and, while praying the rosary, fell asleep. Afterwards, I had to take off his sheets and put others on and the same for part of his underwear. He got better and got to the point where he could get up to do his devotions. The news of his liberation arrived in those days and he became happy, saying he would be leaving. But they annulled the decision, causing him deep pain. But he complained about nothing. Finally, the enterocolitis[312] became evident....I was washing his things day and night. He did not let go of the crucifix or rosary. Now he could not take food. He only said over and over: "Fresh water! Fresh water! Jesus, Mary, and Joseph!" Since now he could not be left alone and I was worn out, an Augustinian Father from Zamora, called Fr. José, kept him company at night. He was from the same town, Rubielos, as D. Trifón and I.[313]

Seeing him so seriously ill, I said to him: "Father, are you mindful of God, the Virgin, the next life, the account we have to give to God of our life?"

He answered me with his eyes fixed on the crucifix which he held in his hands: "Of course, since I have preached about it to others all of my life!"

....

312 Translator's note: inflammation of the colon and intestines.

313 Translator's note: Rubielos de Mora is a small town in the province of Teruel in Spain.

*He went into his agony. I called D. Trifón, who read to him the
commendation of the dying. They gave him two injections of camphorated
oil.*[314] *...He raised his arms. I knew he wanted me to approach him. He
embraced me strongly and in a few moments died in that way. This was
at night. The Augustinian Father, Luciano Checa, and I laid him out
and watched over him. The next day the gentlemen I've just mentioned
told me to take care of getting a coffin at their expense....When they
came for the deceased, they gave me permission to accompany him as
far as the public road.*[315]

From the very beginning, everyone regarded him as a martyr.[316] There
have even been those who have said, *He is more of a martyr than anyone.*

The Testimony of the Martyrs

A *passio* was what the first Christians called a narrative about martyrdom.
The churches published such narratives about the believers who had given
the supreme testimony to their faith. We now limit ourselves to some testimonies of the Redemptorists who lived out in their own flesh the disasters
of the war or were present to the events in Cuenca. We have chosen letters
from the first moments, when news was fairly confusing. These letters do
not appear in the later diocesan process. We include them here because we
think that these letters demonstrate the dimension of martyrdom, which
the Spanish Redemptorist province and the Congregation of the Most Holy
Redeemer experienced in the events narrated.

The initial news about the violent death of the Redemptorists of
Cuenca was confused, hard to come by, and slow due to the circle of fire
that surrounded the city because of its geographical position in the division
of Spain. On the other hand, the beginning of the war came as a surprise
to the provincial superior of the Spanish Redemptorists, Fr. Carlos Otero.
He was visiting the communities in Portugal and was not able to go back to
Madrid, in spite of trying to do so on repeated occasions.

....

314 Translator's note: Camphor oil was injected for pain and inflammation, but is no longer
recommended because it can have fatal side effects.

315 Cit. D. DE FELIPE, 227-229.

316 Cf. APRM. Mártires 0400115, 13; TRIFÓN BELTRÁN, C. *Beatificationis—Declaraciones* 179-180; GABRIEL LOZANO, *Ib.*, II, 615.

On the March 6, 1937—almost eight months after the martyrdom—the provincial superior sent to Rome reports about the rumors, which now were taking on the form of news. For prudence's sake he did not give the names of the cities but only the name of the local superior of the communities. He wrote about Cuenca: "Community of Fr. Pedrosa: News has arrived of some being shot, others seem to have been saved, among whom is the superior."[317] They are still faces without names, but just the same, tragic faces.

A few days later, on March 12, Father provincial writes from Astorga (León) to congratulate Fr. Patrick Murray, the superior general of the Congregation of the Most Holy Redeemer, on his name's day. On this occasion he offers the prayers, sufferings, and sacrifices of a part of the province and the blood of a number of martyrs.[318] He does not give names, as in the preceding letter, but he expresses the martyrs' testimony with evidence of those who have surrendered their lives to jail and to death. On April 25 he sends a new letter to Rome with news about the brothers and the communities in the "red zone." He gives the names of several who have been shot, though he continues to have no news from Cuenca. In the middle of the sorrow of it all, there clearly appears this appeal: "May the Most Holy Redeemer make fruitful the blood of these generous Martyrs of the province and the sufferings of all the rest."[319]

On December 10, the superior general, Fr. Patrick Murray, repeats the names of the victims of Cuenca, among many others from the various communities:[320] Frs. Gorosta, Olarte, and Pozo with Br. Victoriano. Fr. Goñi is not mentioned. And on December 12, Fr. Otero confirms the facts: "We finally have news from Cuenca. The Rector there, Fr. Pedrosa, has written to Fr. Ibarrola, who in turn has communicated this to me: Frs. Gorosterratzu, Olarte, and Poza and Br. Victoriano are dead. (We suppose they were shot.) The others are OK."[321]

On July 8, 1938, Father provincial confirms the rumors that have

317 AHGR 30150001, 1918.

318 112 AHGR 30150001, 1919.

319 AHGR 30150001, 1921.

320 APRM. VIII, 6/1937.

321 AHGR 30150001, 1939.

been circulating with the news brought from Cuenca by Br. Benjamin. In his letters, he describes as martyrs the confreres who persevered in their missionary vocation. For this reason, they are "honored with the palms of the martyrs":

> By way of Br. Benjamin, who has managed to get out of the red zone, we have verified the martyrdom of five of our members: Reverend Frs. Gorosterratzu, Olarte, Goñi, Pozo, and Br. Victoriano. Those five endured scorn and taunts during the first month of the movement, faithful to their faith and their vocation, honored with the palms of the martyrs of Christ....It is sad, but at the same time very much an honor for the province. For this reason, in the midst of the pain one feels a certain...consoling satisfaction to see how those who had been honored to wear our holy habit offered willingly to God the greatest thing they could offer: their lives.[322]

On August 10, 1938, with the war in its second year, the provincial wrote to Rome a very pessimistic letter about the Spanish situation. No one could have imagined that the war would have lasted so long and would have been so devastating. In the middle of such pain and crushing treatment the bright glory of "our dear martyrs" is illuminating the intense night of "these so tragic hours" with their witness and their intercession, with a taste of Easter morning, with the firm hope of a new day:

> God is making Spain pass through this terrible test of war. I am afraid that our province will come out of it fairly broken, partly due to the extensive diminishment suffered by our houses in the red zone, partly due to the defections because of military service, in part for other reasons. It is the hour of testing and I don't know if we are up to the test. It seems to me we have learned little from such a tremendous situation....May our dear martyrs intercede for us and that they attain for us the generosity which the Most Holy Redeemer asks of the province in these so tragic hours.[323]

....

322 C. OTERO, *Carta circular; El Espino 8/7/1938*: A. Espino.

323 AHGR 30150001, 1956.

It is a precious affirmation in the life of all the brothers, beyond hatred, division, and the barbarity of the war that was in its most agonizing moment. "These are the ones who have survived the time of great distress; they have washed their robes and made them white in the blood of the Lamb. For this reason they stand before God's throne and worship him day and night in his temple....and God will wipe away every tear from their eyes" (Revelation 7:14-17).

After the persecution and the Civil War, on February 28, 1941, Fr. Patrick Murray sent a letter of reply to Fr. José María Nuin Gorosterratzu, who was finding himself in a delicate situation. For unknown reasons, Fr. José had communicated to Rome his desire to abandon the Congregation but to continue as a priest. Father general asks him to indicate which bishop it is who will receive him into his diocese. The superior general asks him to convey this information to him via Father provincial. Fr. Murray says he will then communicate with the Holy Father, asking that Fr. José receive a three-year leave of absence, according to law. And he adds: "I hope that you will be able to continue in the Congregation which your uncle, Fr. Gorosterratzu, has honored with his virtue, apostolate, and holy martyrdom and in which you yourself have worked, until the present, fruitfully and to the satisfaction of everyone."[324]

As in good stories, this one has a happy ending: Fr. José María persevered in his Redemptorist missionary life. But it is worth pointing out in the document the explicit recognition of the holy martyrdom of Fr. Gorosterratzu on the part of the superior general. The martyrdom had occurred only five years previous. The whole Congregation gave the same recognition of martyrdom as the superior General.

On November 6, 1941, Fr. Agostín Pedrosa wrote to Rome. He was still the juridic superior of the nonexisting community of Cuenca. He explained his reasons for continuing on in the city where he had spent two years hidden in the home of friends. Once the war had ended, the superiors thought to abandon the foundation, since the house and the church lay in total ruins. It was impossible to rebuild them without some kind of help, including that of the bishop. Fr. Pedrosa admits that all this is true, but he could choose some other area of the city and begin all over, from poverty as a starting point,

....

324 118 AHGR 30150009, 445.

because the faithful would lend a hand. Moreover, the field of apostolic work they have before themselves seems in every way the kind beloved to St. Alphonsus. And six brothers who are martyrs are in the cemetery. They should be cared for: "My opinion is that we should continue in Cuenca; we should not abandon it. It is fully in the spirit of the foundations of our Holy Father Alphonsus. Cuenca is a diocese which is very uninstructed and very abandoned. Missionary religious are necessary. And since there are no others than ourselves here, we should not abandon the city. We have six martyrs in the cemetery and we need to take care of their ashes. The faithful promise to help us. Our daily bread will not be lacking to us."[325]

In our opinion, this is the most important testimony as to the martyrdom of the Redemptorists of Cuenca. The one who speaks in its favor is the superior of the whole group—a seventy-year-old from Zamora who shared in the life of the same community, knew their human and religious limitations, as well as their great personal values and their dedication to the Redeemer in their apostolic life. Well, Fr. Pedrosa, a truly good man loved by everyone, does not have the slightest doubt that the members of his community—his "subjects," in juridical language—were witnesses to the faith. They loved Christ to the extreme of giving their very own lives. He venerates them as martyrs, cares for their remains with tenderness and the intensity of the first Christians. He states it spontaneously in a letter to the superior general, who had not asked him for it.

It is surprising to discover that, before this letter of Fr. Pedrosa, the death of the six Redemptorists, victims of reprisals in Cuenca because of the religious persecution, was communicated as martyrdom in various official communications which the Congregation sent out, as much in the Spanish province as in the general government. The war ended in May 1939. The official publication of the general government narrated what had happened in each of the houses of the Spanish province. Then it presented a narrative about those who fell victim to the persecution in Spain.[326] A little later, in February 1940, the bulletin of the Redemptorist province of Madrid[327]

....

325 AHGR 30150010, 011-1.

326 *Elenchus eorum qui Hispania saeviente persecutione perierunt*: Analecta Congregationis SS. Redemptoris XVIII-3 (May 1939) 150-153.

327 *Necrológica. Las Comunidades bajo el poder rojo*: BPE 8 (2 de febrero de 1940) 3-7.

begins its new venture with the list of the Redemptorists who were killed out of hatred toward the faith. The edition is introduced in these words: "Let the distinguished names of our martyrs serve as a glorious portico into this brief review. Their blood will not only be the fertile seed germinating new sons of St. Alphonsus. It was also, without a doubt, an effective preservative against the irreparable harm to other members and to our property." Afterward, in talking about the events that happened in our communities, it introduces those who gave their lives as martyrs.

The Fame of Martyrdom over the Years

Once the news became known, the Spanish Redemptorist province had a clear consciousness that the six religious of Cuenca were true martyrs. They had been killed because of their faith. This consciousness was both spontaneous and real. It became apparent from the first moments, grew with the passing of the years, and remains in force until the present day, as much within the geography of Spain as beyond its frontiers.

With real veneration, once the war was over, the chronicler tells us "rigorous procedures were taken to get permission to transfer the remains of our martyrs and deceased from the common grave used during the red period. On the tenth at 9:30 in the morning the whole community was present at the municipal cemetery of the city and the bodies were exhumed....They were reburied on the tenth in our gravesite. May they rest in peace until the final resurrection and we ask that they intercede for us."[328]

The war had no more than ended when the Spanish province produced a holy card with the names of the twenty-one Spanish martyrs, to perpetuate their memories.[329] It had the following caption: *Et laverunt stolas suas in sanguine Agni* (Revelation 7:14).[330] Fr. José María Ibarrola was to then publish a biographical sketch and facts about the deaths of the six Redemptorists under the title "Our Martyrs" in the magazine *El Perpetuo Socorro*.[331] This was fruit of the fame of martyrdom that they had among Redemptor-

....

328 *Crónica de Cuenca, 1940, month of April*, 312-313.

329 *Estampa:* APRM. Mártires 0000001; cf. BPE 8 (2 de febrero de 1940) 15.

330 Translator's note: "And they washed their robes in the blood of the Lamb."

331 J. M.ª IBARROLA LATASA, C.Ss.R. *Nuestros Mártires*: El Perpetuo Socorro XLI (1940) 101-104. 132-137. 185-190. 309-310.

ists. Fr. Luis Fernández de Retana[332] also had the same intention, although the final result was frustrated.

332 APRM. Mártires 0400107.

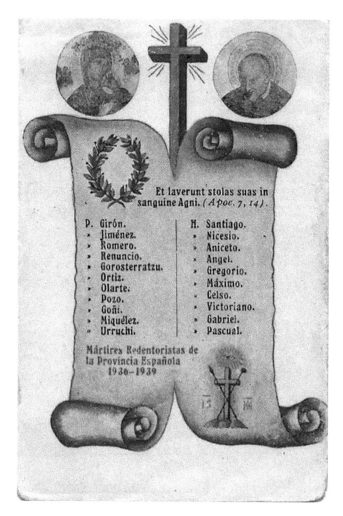

Holy card with the names of the 21 martyrs

The provincial government quickly initiated arrangements to find witnesses who had been present and to collect all the data, with the idea of initiating a process of the recognition of their martyrdom. Reverend Fr. Lucas Pérez began this task of compilation. He put forth a great effort in an investigation, aided by Br. Benjamin López de Murga. Both gathered every testimony possible and as much documentation as was within their reach. Fr. Ricardo Colmenares continued this enormous task beginning in 1952, together with Frs. Javier Iturgáiz and Dionisio de Felipe. These three made every effort to keep the memory of the martyrs alive, repeatedly presenting their brothers as new martyrs for the twentieth century. In 1952, Fr. Ricardo Colmenares produced a series of laminated and framed prints[333] with the photographs and names of the twenty-one martyrs of the province.[334] Fr. Javier Iturgáiz attempted to write a book about them. Fr. Dionisio de Felipe published his book *Nuevos Redentores*,[335] in which he gathered together all the preceding investigations. Finally, Fr. Dionisio Ruiz Goñi spread the fame of the martyrdom of the six Redemptorists, beginning in 1996, with the publication of a bulletin called *De Camino*, or "On the Way."[336]

The opening of the process of canonization was requested through Fr. Dionisio de Felipe. The session of initiation was celebrated on April 11, 1962, in the cathedral of Cuenca and the diocesan phase of the process was closed on May 28, 1965, with the superior general present. After a period of inactivity for the cause,[337] a decree of legal validity was obtained on May 27, 2000. The *Positio*[338] was presented on April 26, 2001. This was studied and approved by the experts first of all, and dated June 11, 2011; then later by

....

333 Translator's note: large size paper, 297 mm x 420 mm, or 11.7" x 16.5," a paper size which is typically used for drawings and diagrams.

334 Orla de los Mártires Redentoristas de la Provincia de España; 1952: APRM. Mártires 0000002.

335 Translator's note: *New Redeemers.*

336 APRM. Mártires 0400124.

337 Prudence dictated that during the pontificate of Paul VI, the proceedings and talk about them, were silenced due to the political process that was going on in Spain. However, memory of the martyrs continued on.

338 Translator's note: A *positio* in a canonization process is a position paper advocating the decree of holiness based on the biography of the proposed saint and a collection of all the evidence of holiness and witness testimonies already gathered.

the cardinals and bishops on November 6, 2012; and His Holiness Benedict XVI signed the decree of martyrdom on the following December 21.

Parallel to the canonical process, the remains of the martyrs were exhumed in May 1977 by the Ecclesiastical Tribunal of Cuenca and were transferred to Madrid, where they were placed in the crypt of the parish of the Most Holy Redeemer. In December of 2008, after the identification, study, and treatment of the bones, they were placed in the chapel of the Coronation in the Shrine of Perpetual Help in Madrid, where they remain to this day.

Even though the process was not always constantly active, since on many occasions it had been put on pause, the renown of the martyrdom was always maintained among the Spanish Redemptorists. Its memory had been present in the important moments of the life of the province. So in 1943, as the celebration of the golden anniversary of the Shrine of Perpetual Help was getting under way, two marble slabs were discovered:[339] the first with the names of the martyrs from the provincial residence, and the second with the names of the martyrs from the whole Spanish province, among which are also the six Redemptorist martyrs of Cuenca. Later, in the year 2000, the centenary of the foundation of the Redemptorist province of Madrid was celebrated. On that occasion a special bulletin was published in which appears an article by Fr. Dionisio Ruiz.[340]

....

339 Cf. *Por nuestros Mártires* en *Crónica Madrid-PS.* V (May 17, 1943) 246-248. These stones were taken out of the church around 1970, during the Pontificate of Paul VI, although they are preserved in the attic of the house.

340 D. RUIZ, *Hacia los altares. Nuestros mártires*: BPE XXVII, 151 (2000) 149-155.

PART TWO

Biographies
Who Are the Martyrs?

José Javier Gorosterratzu Jaunarena

CHAPTER FOUR

José Javier Gorosterratzu Jaunarena[341]

His Infancy in the Valley of San Sebastián

José Javier was born in a small town of northeast Navarre[342] at that time called Urroz de Santesteban (today Urrotz) on August 7, 1877.[343] He was the second of eight children from the marriage of José María Gorosterratzu and María Tomasa Jaunarena. Theirs was a Basque-speaking family of farmers who, despite their properties, had to work to earn their daily bread.[344] The child received the waters of baptism the day after his birth and was given the name José Javier.[345]

341 We take the transcription of the first names and last names from the baptismal and religious profession records. In the official documents, sometimes he appears as José. However, in his personal writings he prefers Javier or simply X. Regarding his first surname, in the official documents it appears indistinctly as Gorosterrazu, Gorosterratzu, and the more familiar Gorosta.

342 Translator's note: Navarre is a Basque autonomous province in Spain.

343 Cf. JUZGADO DE PAZ DE URROTZ (NAVARRA), Sección 1.ª, T. I, f. 6.

344 José Javier tells us that his family "was middle class with regards to temporal goods. Although they had property they had to work in order to live and to sustain their family." (J. J. GOROSTERRATZU, *Curriculum Vitae; Nava del Rey 1896*, 1: *C. Beatificationis - Escritos*). The brief biography of his brother Martín Gorosterratzu, also a Redemptorist, sets the background saying "his most Christian parents" José and Tomasa were "comfortable farmers, benefactors of the parish and of the pastors": *C. H. Martín Gorosterratzu (1885-1955)*.

345 PARISH OF SAN MIGUEL DE URROTZ (NAVARRA), *Libro de Bautismos* n.º 2.º, f. 96 vto. n.º 3. The first name that appears is José Gabriel. Over that is written José Javier. And in the margin there is a note, which affirms the change.

He lived out his infancy in the environs of the Valley of San Sebastián. It is one of many such valleys, up against the Pyrenees of Navarre. A traveler is surprised to come upon these places behind the mountains, sleepy places in the clouds. The hollow, which is no more than 600 meters[346] above sea level, gives the place a temperate microclimate such as is found in mountain villages along the Atlantic. It is a place of rivers, streams, and springs where, at the same time, forests of beeches and oaks, flocks of sheep, and simple ferns can be seen. Among them are the dolmens[347] thousands of years old. They stand there, as if dreaming of the ancestral culture which set them up. Except for his paternal grandfather, who was from Urrotz, the rest of his grandparents came from the neighboring town of Labayen (Navarre).

Urroz de San Sebastián is a small Navarrese municipality[348] of ranches and farms where they produced cheese, *kaikus*,[349] and *zuecos*,[350] made good use of the firewood, charcoal, and lumber, and had a flour mill near the brook Ameztia. "The hamlet of Urroz stands out as very well cared for, especially the assemblage of houses in the main square and its church dedicated to St. Michael." A charming and popular image of the Virgin and Child is venerated there and in the nearby hermitage dedicated to St. Christopher.[351]

Javier attended the school in Urrotz[352] for only three years. For this reason, when he entered the postulancy, the only language he knew was Basque, his mother tongue. The family grew and it became necessary that

....

346 Translator's note: 1,968 feet.

347 Translator's note: A *dolmen* is a Druid monument that consists of a large horizontal rock resting on two upright ones.

348 Translator's note: The municipality is the basic level of local Spanish government. Municipalities make up provinces, which then make up autonomous regions. In the regions of Asturias and Galicia, civil parishes are a more basic unit, making up a municipality.

349 Translator's note: The *kaiku* is a wooden bowl for boiling milk and making yogurt in the Basque area. It is also the name of a woolen jacket worn by people in that area.

350 Translator's note: wooden shoes.

351 A. FLORISTÁN, *Recorridos por Navarra. Valle de Santesteban-Basaburúa menor* (Estella, 1992), 323-332.

352 Translator's note: alternative spelling for *Urroz*.

the older brothers work in order to help the family.[353] At the end of the nineteenth century the thinking about childhood was much different than it is today. Javier himself describes[354] the situation: "When he was twelve years old, they sent him to the house where his mother had grown up to help his grandparents, who were lifelong farmers; the grandfather was out pasturing a part of his flock of sheep. He could not bring them all together because he had so many, hundreds. Javier worked with his grandfather for two years. At the end of the two years, his grandfather died."[355] In fact, he spent two years as a shepherd in the hidden little town of Labayen, smelling of the field, the sheep, and the clean air of the mountain with the sonorous silence of Ave Maria's in the warmth of his grandfather's presence.

When Juan Antonio Jaunarena died on March 1, 1892, at age 64, Javier returned to his parents, in his account "because he was of no further use there, and in his own home he could go to school in the winter; and so it was, when winter came he began to go to school and, after attending there for three months, dropped out and never went back again."[356] The passage describes his sparse formation, his lack of interest in farming and being a shepherd, and the influence of the grandfather Juan Antonio on his life.

If his academic initiation was not very well begun, the same did not happen with his initiation as a Christian. At scarcely four years of age he received the sacrament of confirmation from the hands of the bishop of Pamplona, José Oliver y Hurtado, in the parish of the village of Santesteban (Navarre) on August 30, 1881.[357] The rest of his initiation as a Christian he will receive in the context of his family. When he was a novice he remembered how "his grandfather was very devoted to the Virgin and recited

....

353 Javier was the second of the brothers (cf. PARISH OF SAN MIGUEL DE URROTZ (NAVARRA), *Libro de Bautismos* n.º 2, *Libro de velaciones y casados, Libro de defunciones* n.º 1). Older than Javier was José Antonio (1876), who married Francisca Michelena; the six remaining siblings were younger: José Miguel (1879), who married in Argentina; Isidoro (1881), married María Josefa Urroz; Balbina (1883), married Juan José Nuin; Martín José (1885), who made vows as a Redemptorist; Joaquina (1889), who married Florencio Machiñena; and Juana Josefa (1892), who married Antonio Agesta.

354 Translator's note: in the third person.

355 J. J. GOROSTERRATZU, *Curriculum...*, 1.

356 J. J. GOROSTERRATZU, *Curriculum...*, 2.

357 PARISH OF SAN MIGUEL DE URROTZ (NAVARRA), *Libro de confirmados* n.º 1, ff. 30-31 (30-8-1881).

rosaries to the Virgin, called his son to say the rosary with him, but his son grew tired of it and for that reason asked the grandfather why he prayed so much. The grandfather told him that, after death we do not know whether we will be condemned and so that we might not be condemned, we had better ask for that favor from the Virgin while still in this world."[358] His fellow villager, Fr. José Machiñena, six years his junior, recalled that José Javier's parents "were very good and very religious; the father, although he was not the sacristan, fulfilled the function of one many times singing at Mass and doing it with a great deal of gusto and grace....Since the family was very Christian (as they tend to be in the town) he was raised with much piety, well raised. In school, he learned his first letters."[359]

His Vocation: Called from the Sheepfold

Restiveness regarding his vocation had to have awakened in José Javier very early in his life, since his niece, a religious herself, declared during the process for beatification: "I heard it said by my mother that he cried when he was small and he was going out for his sheep-tending duties, because they would not let him go to become a religious."[360] In April 1888, when he was eleven years old, the Capuchin Franciscans opened a center for vocations in Lecároz (Navarre) and went around promoting vocations in the surrounding villages. There awoke in José Javier the desire to become a Capuchin in the recently opened preparatory school,[361] together with other friends, among whom was another student from Urrotz "nineteen years of age, advanced in his studies."[362] He was José Javier's friend and naturally influenced him in his decision to accompany him "in order to save his own soul and to preach to others." José Javier spoke to his parents. José María did not pay much attention, considering it all to be "the pretensions of a child." However, his wife, María Tomasa, took the part of her son when Javier "begged her to take him to the school and that he would persevere." Father and son showed up at the minor seminary of Lecároz. No luck: when the Capuchins

---

358 J.J. GOROSTERRATZU, *Curriculum...*, 2.

359 11 J. M.ª MACHIÑENA, *C. Beatificationis—Declaraciones* I, 91.

360 SISTER ESCOLÁSTICA NUIN, *C. Beatificationis—Declaraciones* II, 418.

361 Translator's note: *Colegio* in Spanish refers to a prep school, beginning in junior high.

362 13 J.J. GOROSTERRATZU, *Currículum...*, 3.

asked the age and his educational background of Javier, they concluded that "he was too old, didn't have enough schooling, and they could not take him in."[363]

After the interview, José Javier and his father went to the church, since it was Sunday and they had not been to Mass yet, and they also wanted to see the solemn Mass that the Capuchins chanted. The sincere but ungainly notes written by novice José Javier have allowed us previously to see into the openness of Javier to the sense of mystery he had before nature; now he does the same before the beauty of the liturgy:

> *When the time of Consecration came, all the friars prostrated on the floor. When he saw this,[364] it added all the more to his desire to be a Franciscan (sic) but, since they had not accepted him, he began to cry a little; it was due to the commotion of it all. So he promised the Virgin that he would say six Ave Maria's each day for her to show him some religious order that he could enter. Then they went home; he paid no more attention to it all, said his Ave Maria's to the Virgin and that was it.[365]*

And the Virgin did not let loose the hand of Javier. Where the human reach ends, the reach of the Almighty begins. God, who was the one to awaken the desire for religious life in Javier, offered him an answer, but first two years had to pass by. In 1894, when Javier was only sixteen years old, two Redemptorist missionaries from the community of San Ignacio in Pamplona, Fr. Bueno (Antonio Capocci Buoni[366]) and one of Javier's countrymen, Fr. Prudencio Eviti Gorosterratzu,[367] gave a parish mission in Santesteban. It began on March 5[368] and lasted ten days. Among those attending was D. Dionisio Erviti, the father of one of the missionaries. The missionaries asked him if he knew of a boy who might want to become a

....

363 *Ib.,* 3.

364 Translator's note: José Javier is speaking about himself in the third person.

365 *Ib.,* 4.

366 Antonio Capocci Buoni (*Bueno*): cf. Apéndice 2.

367 Prudencio Erviti Gorosterratzu: cf. Apéndice 2.

368 Cf. *Crónica de Pamplona* I, 41.

Redemptorist. Javier himself said that it was D. Dionisio who gave his name to them. When the mission was over, the boy spoke to his father about it, and his father once again set out, this time to Pamplona, to speak with the superior of the community, the Frenchman Fr. Lorthioit.[369] Although the last names were difficult on both sides, they immediately clicked. However, given Javier's age and lack of studies, the Redemptorist offered to receive Javier as a Brother with the job of carpenter. José Javier wrote: "He told him, yes; and within five days, the two of them (father and son) were off so that Javier could be on his way from there to Nava."[370] They presented themselves punctually for their appointment. Seeing the boy, Fr. Lorthioit said "he was small for his age."[371] In spite of the fact that he once more showed desires to study, the three came to an agreement that José Javier would enter the novitiate in Nava del Rey (Valladolid) as a brother and with the appointment of being carpenter. José Javier concludes his notes with a picturesque detail: "All the while Fr. Lorthioit never stopped laughing, seeing how small José Javier was and how he had left no door untried."[372] This fact reflects three constants in his character: power of observation, tenacity, and nervousness.

José Javier left Pamplona at the beginning of April 1894, accompanying a French Redemptorist, Fr. Praly, who had been passing through that community. The French priest fell sick and remained in El Espino (Burgos) to recuperate. So the teen continued his journey by train to Medina del Campo (Valladolid) where Fr. Antonio Mariscal went out to meet him on April 10[373] and brought him to the Redemptorist community in Nava del Rey (Valladolid). The chronicler gives us the first impression that he has of our protagonist: "In May a postulant for the lay brotherhood arrived, named Javier Gorosterratzu, about seventeen years of age. He did not know even a single word in Spanish."[374] After José Javier had spent a month as a postulant and in view of his level of cultural understanding and difficulty in expressing himself, they decided to send him to the juvenate to learn

....

369 Pablo Lorthioit: cf. Apéndice 2.

370 J. J. GOROSTERRATZU, *Curriculum...*, 5.

371 *Ib.,* 6.

372 *Ib.,* 6.

373 Cf. *Crónica de Nava* I, 213.

374 Cf. *Anales* II, 480.

Spanish. The chronicler of Nava del Rey recorded that on June 1 "Brother Pío and a young postulant from Navarre, José Javier Gorosterratzu, left for El Espino. They wanted to have him pursue studies, but he has no inclination for books."[375] He stayed scarcely a month in El Espino, because on July 2 he went as a postulant to the community in Astorga (León).[376] The philosophy and theology students prepared for priesthood there. He was a postulant in Astorga for a whole year. The chronicle of Nava del Rey notes that on July 16, 1895, "Two lay brother postulants arrived from Astorga, Fortunato Méndez, who was given the name 'Camilo,' and José Javier Gorosterratzu, who kept the name 'Javier.' Later they will go to the novitiate."[377] The choice of names points out the admiration he had for the great men of his homeland, Navarre.[378]

His Formation Years

He spent the month of August 1895 with the other postulants preparing themselves for the beginning of the novitiate. After the retreat days, which are prescribed by the Rule, he was invested in the Redemptorist habit on September 8, 1895, at the hands of Fr. Francisco Colloud, the novice master, and began the novitiate.[379] From the green, echoing valleys of his native Navarre he had gone to the dry Spanish mesa, with a whole new light and that internal murmur that is discovered only by listening, in silence, to the infinite barrenness of the land—ideal for this period of novitiate.

....

375 *Crónica de Nava* I, 216.

376 Cf. *Anales* II, 487.

377 *Crónica de Nava* I, 239. In the Chronicle for Astorga (*Crónica de Astorga* I, 181) it notes that on July 23, 1894, Brs. Fortunato and José went to the novitiate.

378 In the Congregation of the Most Holy Redeemer, it was not the custom to change the name of the person entering the Congregation, although it frequently happens to lay Brothers in the case in which the name of a new arrival is the same as an already professed brother. José Javier, in coming into the novitiate as a coadjutor [Translators' note: *Coadjutor* is a term used for lay Brothers, that is, members of the Congregation who are not clerics], adopted the name *Javier*. When he became a chorist, he professed his vows with the name *José Javier*. [Translator's note: *Chorist* is the term for clerical students who would recite the Divine Office in community with two sides, or "choirs," alternating.] Just the same, he used indistinctly the names José Javier, Javier, or Xabier. We shall use José Javier or Javier.

379 His inscription appears in the book for the taking of the habit for Brothers (cf. APRM. *Liber Primus Inscriptionis Vestium mutationis Laicorum—1866-1967*, n.º XXXVIII).

In Nava del Rey, the formators noticed very quickly that the novice carpenter Javier was especially capable when it came to studies. For this reason, in March 1896 they put him forward for studies so that he would profess his vows as a clerical religious.[380] Father Master wrote up the petition for religious profession to the provincial of France, Fr. Gavillet, in which he comments that cultural "backwardness" was at fault for the novice's lack of education. But there was a well-founded hope that he would progress rapidly in his studies:

His way of being is good and docile and on occasions "cunctabenda."[381] In his way of relating to others he is open and seems younger than his years. He has conducted himself well during novitiate. There is nothing that is particularly noticeable, save his docility and obedience in everything to superiors. He has a love for the Congregation, a spirit of prayer and gets along well with everyone, all of which in the future will get even better. Br. Gorosterratzu will progress in his studies and will be a very useful worker in the vineyard of the Lord, though not outstanding, because of his knowledge of the Spanish and Basque languages.[382]

....

380 His investiture in the habit was noted also in the records for the clerical novices: "*Josephus Xaverius Gorosterrazu et Jaunarena. Dominica, 8 Septembris 1895, Nativitate B. V. Maria sacra, in hac domo Seraphicae Teresiae de Jesu, in civitate Nava Regis, a Franc. Colloud, Nov. Magistro, in Novitiatum admissus est adolescens Josephus Xaverius Gorosterrazu, laicus, e pago Urroz, prov. Navarrensi et dioc. Pampelunensi, natus 7 Augusti 1877, nempe annos 18, mensis 1, dies 1*". [Translator's note: In English this reads: "*Joseph Xavier Gorosterratzu y Jaunarena. On Sunday, 8 September 1895, on the holy Nativity of the B. V. Mary, Joseph Xavier Gorosterratzu, an adolescent, born on 7 August 1877, 18 years of age, one month and one day, from the village of Urroz, the province of Navarre and the diocese of Pamplona, is admitted into novitiate in this house of the Seraphic Teresa of Jesus by Francis Colloud, Master of Novices.*"] [*And in another handwriting*] "*Ad professionem admisus choristas, 8 Septembris 1896*" [Translator's note: "*Admitted into profession as a clerical novice, 8 September 1896.*" [*And another handwriting*] "*Mortus in domo Conquensis 1936*" [Translator's note: Died in the house in Cuenca 1936] (APRM. *Liber Primus Inscriptionis Vestium mutationis Choristarum—1866-1934*, n.º C). Mention is also made of his change from lay brother to clerical novice in the chronicle of the community: "*1896, September 8. Br. José Javier Gorosterratzu makes his profession. The same was invested in the habit a year ago as a lay brother; but he was assigned to studies in March, and seeing that he advanced somewhat, he leaves for Astorga. God give him perseverance!*" (*Chronicle of Nava, I, 266*)

381 Translator's note: the word *cunctabenda* is not in any dictionaries, but the context indicates a degree of goodness and docility beyond average.

382 AHGR 30150009, 0290.

All that led him to ask the superiors in the Congregation to admit him to the religious profession, which he did on September 8, 1896, before the master of novices, Fr. Francisco Colloud. Frs. Jorge Collin and Francisco Masson were the witnesses.[383]

Once novitiate was finished, he was assigned to Astorga to begin his studies in preparation for the priesthood. Life in the Redemptorist seminary in Astorga was hard because of the direction that Fr. Bührel imposed on it and because of the great scarcities of the times: food was spare and poorly prepared, clothes were old and unpresentable, the library was very poor, because it was just beginning to get organized and they did not have adequate resources. Their health suffered a lot in that place and that climate, to the point where they had to bury many students in the blossoming of their youth, afflicted with tuberculosis. Nor could the accommodations be improved until years later. Fr. Ramón Sarabia writes about it: "For recreation, we students had nothing more than a patio some forty meters long and twenty wide.[384] To protect ourselves from the rain in winter and the heat in summer, we only had a shed up against the city walls. It was seven meters long and four wide.[385] It was a certainty that religious life in this shed was going to be very hard, for the present, and detrimental to the health of the students as well, unless the Lord gave us his grace and protection."[386]

To bring his level of studies up to par, he received special classes for a time from Fr. Pardo. The main body of his class professed vows on October 15. Five of them who were a little older[387] were sent to the novitiate before finishing their courses at the juvenate. It was hoped that thus they could avoid being called up to enlist in the army to go to the war in Cuba.[388] After their profession, Br. José Javier Gorosterratzu joined them for studies in the next two academic years (1896-1897 and 1897-1898). They studied human-

....

383 APRM. *Liber secundus inscriptionis Professionis Religiosae Perpetuae in Congregatione SS. Redemptoris,* Año 1896, n.º 86.

384 Translator's note: about forty-four yards long by twenty-two yards wide.

385 Translator's note: about twenty-three feet long and thirteen feet wide.

386 APRM. R. SARABIA, *Mis memorias* I, 190-191.

387 José Faúndez, Gregorio Sanromán, Domingo Ruiz, Aniceto Lizasoain and Gregorio Lobo.

388 Cf. *Anales* II, 516-520. Translator's note: The Cuban war of independence from Spain took place from 1895 to 1898.

ities and rhetoric and so all were able to make up for the various missing elements in their scanty initial formation.[389]

In 1899, Br. Javier Gorosterratzu began his philosophical studies in Astorga, which extended to six academic years in length. He took two years of philosophy (1898-1900), two years of theology (1900-1902), and two years of moral theology (1902-1904). The grades that he received during these six years of the major seminary[390] have been preserved and we are able to see the good results he was able to attain. Moving ahead, at the end of his studies he was appointed to be a professor. It's clear proof that the young Navarrese, who came to the novitiate in the role of carpenter, took intense advantage of his stage of formation.

We have little information about those years. They were difficult materially speaking and spartan in religious discipline. We consider of interest a fact that a chronicler gently recorded, though it does not appear to fit in with the rigidity of the period:

> *[On May 7, 1900, they had] a very agreeable event. A representative of Casa Edison came to the city with his cinematography. We managed to have it in our own monastery and to see it function from the fifth through the seventh. On the fourth he turned on the electric machine for us, which he installed in the lower cloister. The town council and the priests of the city were invited. And since it was evident that there was enough room for the residents of the seminary, they were invited as well. Nobody missed, and everyone arrived delighted and highly satisfied with the monastery for having offered them this favor. Everyone was eager to see this new marvel, while at the same time they did not dare to go to a theater so as not to scandalize the people. And they knew how to respond to this courtesy, not paying anything.*[391]

In the Redemptorist historical general archives in Rome is preserved a congratulatory album which the Redemptorist students of Astorga sent

....

389 *Anales* III, 55-62; *Anales Prov. Hispanicae CSSR*. Vol. 3, Madrid 1928, 49 and 86.

390 AHGR 30150007, 0004/8; APRM. Mártires 0401001, 2.

391 *Crónica de Astorga* II, 89. The chronicler was Anselm Jung, French, who lived in Spain for 29 years. The postscript, written in a distinct handwriting is a clarification made by Fr. Bürhel.

to Father General Matthias Raus for his fiftieth anniversary of religious profession on November 1, 1903.[392] The whole thing is a song of filial affection and of love for the Congregation, which was still young in Spain. Br. Gorosterratzu offered him this token gift of prayers: "I promise to make Holy Communion five times for the intention of Your Paternity.[393] I will recite the rosary once a week for a year and to recite each day this month a Te Deum[394] to help give thanks to God."[395]

Secondly, the album recalls an excursion in the environs of Astorga on "a bright afternoon in May, at that hour in which the light of the sun is its purest, when the songs of the birds are the most inspired, when the aroma of the flowers is the most perfumed and intoxicating." With Fray Luís de León[396] as background, the story unfolds among four students, from different areas of Spain, all about ready to move on from the scholasticate:[397] a Catalan, a Galician, a Basque, and a Castilian.[398] They meditate about the future of the Spanish province. Throughout the text, they express their love for their country and their Congregation; to realize the dream of founding the Redemptorist Congregation in Galicia, the Basque Country,

....

392 *Los estudiantes de Astorga al Rmo. Matías Raus en los 50 años de su profesión* en "*Obolo de los Estudiantes al Reverendísimo Padre*": AGHR 30150010, A/4. Each of the class members wrote of his own offer of prayers.

393 Translator's note: *Your Paternity* was an honorific given to superiors general of religious orders of men at the time, but no longer in use.

394 Translator's note: The *Te Deum* is a Latin prayer typically said in thanksgiving to God.

395 *Ib.*

396 Translator's note: Luís de Leon was a Spanish Augustinian who lived in the sixteenth century and was a poet, theologian, and teacher.

397 Translator's note: The college level of seminary studies.

398 [Translator's note: The four students were each from different Spanish provinces, respectively, Catalonia, Galicia, the Basque Province, and Castile. The author of the poem in Galician had to have been Julio Domínguez Yánez, native of Puebla de Trives. Puebla de Trives, officially "A Pobra de Trives" in Galician, is a city in the province of Ourense in the Galician region of northwest Spain.] He wrote a Pregárea a Virxe d'as Ermidas. [Translator's note: Galician for "Prayer to the Virgin of As Ermidas." As Ermidas is a Marian shrine in the region of Bolo-Valdeorras in the province of Galicia, overlooking the Bibei River, and is considered one of the best examples of Galician Baroque architecture.] The Catalonian poet would be Domingo Saa González, native of Asnurri (Lerida, Catalonia) who dedicates it to the "Moreneta de Montserrat." [Translator's note: "the black Virgin of Montserrat" is one of the two principal patrons of Catalonia. The statue is located at the Monastery of Montserrat.] The Castilian student who was involved in the conversation did not give a poem and we do not know who it could have been because there were several Castilians in the class, with the others we have mentioned; all were ordained on December 28, 1903.

and Catalonia, they compose a prayer-poem asking Mary for it. None of the poems is signed, but it is undoubtable that the Basque must be Br. Gorosterratzu, the only Basque in the class, the only one who knew the language and could write it. He presents the narrative in this way: "a native of Vasconia,[399] he had a great deal of the romanticism of his country in him and not a little of zeal for the splendor and culture of its inhabitants."[400]

In the dialogue that precedes the poem, Javier reveals the key to understanding it. He is happy because there is a Redemptorist community in Pamplona...

> ...*at the very doors of Vasconia; but "he desired to soon see two or three Redemptorist communities in the heart of Escualerria (sic)[401] because... the faith of those mountain people raised in their patriarchal customs ran the risk of being eviscerated by the odor of evil doctrines, if that faith did not have near it focuses of life and warmth in which to feed itself and renew itself; from which fact he concluded that our communities of El Espino and La Nava[402] would be better placed among their countrymen, catechizing them and preaching to them the eternal truths...in the environs of Aralar, or in the Valley of Baztán."*[403]

The dialogue ends this way: "And what do you ask of the Virgin of Aránzazu?" asked the Catalonian. "I ask her," answered the Basque, "that she bring us soon to her land, that she bless our Most Reverend Father, and

....

399 Translator's note: *Vasconia* is an ancient name for the northern regions of Navarre, which is in Basque Country, and Aragon, which is not part of Basque Country. Despite the similar sound of the words "Vasconia" and "Basque," there is no definitive evidence that the two are identical. Nevertheless, since the Middle Ages, Vasconia has come to be identified with Basque Country.

400 *Ib.*

401 Translator's note: *Escualerria* is the Spanification of the Basque words for Basque Country: *Euskal Herria*. The word *sic* indicates that the author must have felt it was simply a misspelling, but is in fact found in several older references to Basque Country.

402 Translator's note: two formation communities, El Espino where the juvenate was housed and La Nava del Rey where the novitiate was.

403 Translator's note: Aralar is a region of mountainous terrain with one peak in particular considered the "Matterhorn" of Basque Country; the Valley of Baztán is the area surrounding a city in Navarre where Basque is the principal language spoken.

that we see him soon in Spain."[404] With this backdrop we offer the complete poem-prayer in the original Basque:[405]

Mariari Aitarenzat Otoitza	Prayer to Mary for Father General
Nere Ama Birgiña	My Mother, Virgin
Aranzazukoa,	of Aránzazu,
belorizen gera	we come enthused,
gutzit biotzekua,	from the bottom of our hearts
zuri eskazeko,	to request of you
nola gu goitua	that from on high
eman dezakezun	you give us
agiz on gogua.	a great grace.
Gure nausiari	For our good superior,
ongi bizizeko,	a happy life
nola lur onetan	now on the earth,
alaitsen betiko	just as later,
baitere berzian.	eternal happiness.
Zuk, Ama, onelako	Mother,
otoitza arzadazu	receive this prayer;
ezez utzizeko.	do not disregard it.
Zuk dakizu bada,	You well know,
nere, Ama Maria,	My Mother, Mary,
ain pollit, ederra,	so pretty, so beautiful,
ta aimbeste garbia,	and so pure,
nola gure Aitak	that our Father,
aurtengo urtengo	now and in the past,
duen poziz eta	is so happy
onetaz betia.	and full of goodness.

....

404 *Ib.*

405 Translation into Spanish by the Redemptorist Dionisio Ruiz Goñi. [Translator's note: The English translation is from the Spanish.]

Zer onak diraden	How good he has been
oyek badakizu	you well know
zuk, nere Ama, ongi,	my Mother.
aurten betezendu	This year he completes
berrogey eta	fifty years since he entered
urte, zela, sartu	the Congregation
Congregaziuan,	and since he was received into it.
ta zen emen artu.	

Orreren gatikan	For that reason,
eska eldu gera	we came to ask
euskaldun guziak	all the Basques,
zure aiztiñera.	in your presence,
eman dezayazun	that you give him
orain eta beti,	now and always
biziza agiz ona	a very happy life.
gure on Aitari.	

This poetic, juvenile literary attempt expresses the religious sentiments of José Javier a few days before his ordination and, at the same time,
the affection he had for his small land, with the nuances that he himself
introduces about the limits and the differences between Vasconia and
non-Basque Navarre. He considers himself a native-born Vasconian.

On December 28, 1903, José Javier Gorosterratzu and ten classmates
received priestly ordination in Astorga. We have not preserved personal
notes that would permit us to know his attitude in receiving the sacrament
of the oils for service to the Church as a member of the Congregation. The
chronicles record some interesting facts about similar celebrations which
allow us to take a guess about the surroundings of spiritual rigor which was
lived in the Redemptorist major seminary.[406] The bishop of Astorga was

....

406 A few years earlier, in 1900, there were ordinations on March 31 and first Masses on
April 1. The chronical underlines this day: "There were few people. Since no family members of
the recently ordained came for the day, an in-house celebration could be held. Most Reverend Fr.
Rector had the goodness to give an extraordinary recreation day in common. The recently ordained
sat at the Fathers' table. There were formalities in prose and in poetry, and music was not lacking."
(Chronicle of Astorga 11, 7-8)

not able to confer the sacred orders. So, on December 26, the feast of St. Stephen "the Most Reverend and Most Illustrious Lord Tomás Mazarraso... apostolic administrator of Ciudad Rodrigo[407] came very early to the house. Over the next three days he conferred sacred orders on the moral theology students": on the twenty-sixth they were ordained subdeacons, on the twenty-seventh, deacons, and on the twenty-eighth, priests. The chronicler adds: "On the twenty-ninth all the priests offered the most august sacrifice of the Mass, without any solemnity; there was class on that day and the next days, so that all the joy was purely spiritual. Who doesn't know that blessed Clement[408] served at table on the day of his priestly ordination?"[409] At the time the provincial superior was Fr. Teodor Runner (French), superior of the house Fr. Otmaro Allet (Swiss), and prefect of students[410] Fr. Eduardo Bührel (French).

His priestly ministry unfolded in two phases differentiated by the apostolate in which he was engaged: first as a professor and later as a missionary.

First Period of His Priestly Life: Professor (1904-1913)

When he had finished his theology courses in Astorga, young Fr. J. Javier Gorosterratzu received his new appointment: professor of the first-year class of Latin in the minor seminary (juvenate) in El Espino (Burgos).[411] It was September 11, 1904, when he arrived with two other companions at the station in Pancorbo (Burgos) to begin his time as professor. It was midnight, nobody was waiting for them, and the old monastery stood at quite a distance from the train station. So, leaving their cargo at the train station,

....

407 Translator's note: Ciudad Rodrigo is a small cathedral town in the province of Salamanca.

408 Translator's note: The "blessed Clement" referred to is St. Clement Mary Hofbauer, a Redemptorist priest. He was canonized in 1909.

409 *Die 29 omnes presbyteri primum augustissimum missae sacrificium obtulerunt, nulla pompa; schola fuit ac diebus caeteris, tota denique laetitia fuit spiritualis. Quis nesciat B. Clementem diae ordinationis suae presbyteralis ad mensam ministrasse?* (Chronicle of Astorga II, 117). [Translator's note: this is the original Latin text taken from the chronicle which the author had translated above into Spanish, in italics.]

410 Translator's note: The prefect of students was in charge of the students on the philosophy/theology levels.

411 We do not know for what reason the chronicler in Astorga writes that he was transferred on September 10 to S. Miguel (the second community in Madrid) with other companions: *"hospitio nostro S. Michaelis destinatus"* (Ib., 132).

they set out on foot. He spent two years introducing the students of the first academic course to the Latin language.

On September 7, 1906, for unforeseen reasons which are not mentioned, the provincial Otmaro Allet asked Fr. general Matthias Raus to name Fr. J. Javier Gorosterratzu professor of the first year of philosophy.[412] In the appointments made that month, Fr. José Javier appears as professor of philosophy and sciences, but in El Espino. The two first courses in philosophy were transferred to El Espino since space in the house in Astorga was very much reduced because of all the students. In the meantime, room was made for them in the community of the studendate.[413] Ramón Sarabia relates that in 1893, when he arrived in Astorga, "there were not a few students who were two to a cell"[414] because of lack of space. In its apparent simplicity the new assignment signified a decisive change in the life of J. Javier Gorosterratzu. From now on, a new period of intense intellectual activity begins which is prolonged, with distinct variations, until the moment of his death.

El Espino did not offer conditions for higher learning. Faced with this lack, on March 7, 1907, Fr. Javier was sent to Miranda de Ebro[415] to collect physics instruments. On March 23, for the first time his students presented a philosophy thesis which ended up being fairly good.[416] On August 13, when the course had concluded, the chronicler notes that the exams of the students of philosophy were good.[417] Fr. J. Javier stayed three years in El Espino: two as professor in the minor seminary and one as professor of first-year philosophy for students who had already professed religious vows. Before leaving for the Astorga community, we offer a synthesis of the pastoral work that took place at this time. Opportunities for pastoral work

....

412 AHGR 30150001, 1282.

413 *Crónica del Espino* IV, 3. 52. Translator's note: *Studendate* was the name of the last six years of seminary training and consisted of two years of philosophy studies and four years of theology studies; it was also called the major seminary, as opposed to the juvenate or minor seminary.

414 R. SARABIA, *d. c.* I, 190. Translator's note: The word *cell* is used for the small bedroom or study of a religious in a community.

415 Translator's note: Miranda de Ebro is a city in Burgos, which is a hub for the chemical industry.

416 Translator's note: Physics was still considered in seminaries part of Aristotelian philosophy.

417 *Crónica del Espino* IV, 28. 29. 50.

were very few and the reason for it has a very simple explanation. For the first five years after ordination, the young Fathers could not hear confessions without passing an examination of their capabilities. For that reason they seldom went out to preach, since both ministries—preaching and hearing confessions—are very much related. This norm remained in force in the Redemptorist Congregation until the second half of the twentieth century.

Fr. J. Gorosterratzu

In spite of this, Fr. Javier went out to preach on December 8, 1904, in honor of the Immaculate Conception of Mary. It was his debut and he did it in the tiny village of Guinicio, near El Espino. It was another ten months before he went out again to the nearby town of Santa Gadea del Cid, on September 25, 1905, to give thanks to God for the new harvest. A year later he preached again in the same town on October 3, 1906.[418] At the end of March 1907, he traveled to Salinas (Álava) to preach during Holy Week. In 1906, he preached on the feast of Our Mother of Perpetual Help at the monastery: "This year it was celebrated with total solemnity. What contributed to it was the outstanding weather today. Since very early in the morning there could be seen in the church a great number of people wanting to go to confession and to feed themselves with the Bread of Angels. The Mass of General Communion[419] was celebrated at 7:30 AM, as was the custom. At 10:30 AM, the Solemn Mass took place, sung by Fr. Rector. During it Fr. Gorosta preached."[420] In the last sermon in his time in El Espino, he preached in Santa Gadea, on June 26, 1907, the feast of St. Peter.

During his time in El Espino, Fr. J. Javier lived in an environment of recollection, characterized by study, prayer, and devotion to the Eucharist and to Mary. The chronicle points out forcefully the date of April 5 of that same year:[421] "This will be a day that will always be memorable in the annals of the Spanish province. It is the day chosen on which to consecrate the whole province to the Eucharistic heart of Jesus."[422] And the chronicle gives a full page to record all the events that the community and the seminarians participated in that day.

On September 7, 1907, the chronicler of El Espino wrote: "Fr. Gorosta, a professor who has been here for three years, two in the juvenate and one

....

418 *Ib.,* 14.

419 Translator's note: in 1910, St. Pius X issued a decree called *Quam Singulari* allowing children to receive Communion as soon as they had reached the age of reason. In the decree he called upon pastors to have a celebration once a year of a General Communion, in which all the children and any others who had already received Communion, would take part. Some days of instruction were to proceed the event. This service was offered by the Redemptorists as well as by others.

420 *Ib.,* 2.

421 *Ib.,* 30-31.

422 Translator's note: In the late 1800s and early 1900s, an effort was made by the Redemptorists to create a new devotion to Christ under the title of "the Eucharistic Heart of Jesus," somewhat parallel to the Jesuits' devotion to the Sacred Heart of Jesus.

with the students of philosophy, is changing residence and going off to Astorga, passing through Nava del Rey."[423] This stay in Nava is the week of vacation, which the professors in the major seminary enjoyed at the end of the academic year. On September 12, Fr. Gorosta arrived from Nava. Six days later, the students gathered again in Astorga. These were the students who, for lack of space, had been displaced to El Espino.[424]

At the head of Fr. Javier's new community was Fr. Teodoro Runner, and Fr. Marceliano Gil was prefect of students. From its foundation, Astorga gave a great deal of importance to popular missions. At this time there were eight Fathers dedicated to that ministry.[425] It was, with its great internal variety, the most diverse community and the most numerous of the Madrid province.

The following academic year, Father provincial proposed to Rome various changes of professors in Astorga with a view to gaining more missionaries. Fr. Javier Gorosterratzu would take charge of teaching philosophy in both courses in Astorga. In this way, Fr. Ortíz became available for preaching missions. The same things happened with Fr. Turiso, who would become an excellent missionary.[426] But because Fr. Gorosterratzu at the period "is preparing a manual of philosophy and wishes to have a little more time available to write his work," the provincial proposed, in an August 15, 1910, letter to the consultor general, Fr. Van Rossum—future cardinal and prefect of the Congregation *Propaganda Fidei*[427] that Fr. Gorosterratzu could continue with his two philosophy courses, provided that it were convenient that he be the only professor in the second year and that Fr. Toribio Alonso Santamaría teach the first course. This priest "is a young Father with very good dispositions for philosophy."[428] The change was accepted and had a double advantage: "Fr. Gorosterratzu would have more time free to work on

----

423 *Ib.,* 51.

424 *Crónica de Astorga* II, 255.

425 *Ib.,* 218.

426 O. ALLET, *Letter to the Superior General; 31 of August, 1908:* AHGR 30150001, 1345.

427 Translator's note: The translation of the Latin *Propaganda Fidei* is "Congregation for the Propagation of the Faith," the Roman Curia's department in charge of the Church's evangelization programs.

428 AHGR 30150001, 1377.

his manual and, at the same time, Fr. Alonso Santamaría could train more easily at the side of Fr. Gorosta in the teaching of philosophy."[429]

An interesting fact about the unease of Fr. Gorosterratzu as a professor was his decision to write a manual of philosophy for the reason that none existed that his students could follow.[430] He never managed to get it published. Dionisio de Felipe, who came as a student to the Redemptorist seminary in Astorga the year that Fr. Javier left off teaching, gives this description of the professor, interesting because it gives us a knowledge of aspects of his personality: "When he had finished his studies, he was sent as a professor of philosophy and science. That says a lot about his talent and how brilliant he was in his studies. He would be a good philosopher, he had the temperament for it, he was profound in his thought and sufficiently nebulous to associate with the philosophers of the highest category."[431]

The year 1910 came and went with normalcy for Fr. Javier. He kept the same offices and services to the community until the beginning of the new academic year 1910-11. On September 2 the number of professors was changed and the two courses of philosophy were divided up. Fr. José Javier was given the second-year philosophy course, the sciences, and elocution, and Fr. Alonso had the first-year course.

During his stay in Astorga, besides teaching, Fr. Gorosta had the confidence of his superiors and between 1908 and 1912 he fulfilled the delicate office of zelator.[432] Although during this period of being a professor Fr. Javier did not distinguish himself with pastoral activity because he was busy with his teaching duties and in editing his philosophy manual, he had a few sporadic preaching dates. In January 1908, he preached in the

....

429 *Ib.*

430 "As a backup to that book we had other reference works, but few and none of them had the seriousness of contemporary philosophical science....We had the books by Cardinal González and a few others; but they were very few, and in addition they had the rudiments of a very antiquated science." (R. SARABIA, d. c. I, 214).

431 D. DE FELIPE, *Nuevos Redentores* (Madrid, 1962) 153.

432 Translator's note: The zelator's task in the community was to see to the exact adherence to the Rule by community members, including reporting infractions at community Chapters of Faults. A Chapter of Faults was the meeting of the community at which the zelator would make public accusation against members who had failed to observe the Rule.

Redemptorist church for all the Saturday evening services.[433] In April he went to Bembibre[434] for Holy Week. And in the month of May, a month dedicated to Mary, he was in charge of preaching during the first week, developing the theme "Mysteries in the Life of the Most Holy Mary." On July 25 he preached on the feast day of the patron saint of Spain, St. James the Apostle, and on December 20 he did the same in honor of Our Lady of Perpetual Help.[435]

In 1909 he preached a little more.[436] Again in May, Fr. Javier was busy from May 5 to May 9, giving a commentary on the Salve Regina. And from May 20 to May 31, he preached on the Magnificat. 1910 and 1911 were similar to the previous years, pastorally, with one exception that deserves to be mentioned: from March 27 to April 7 of the second year, Fr. Javier preached a mission with Fr. Vadillo in Moreiras (Orense), for the first time that we know of.[437]

During the 1912 academic year, Fr. Javier was released from teaching to prepare his manual. For this reason he was not able to be readily available for preaching. But at the end of March, a group of missionaries gathered for the mission in Rosal, a large parish in the diocese of Tuy (Pontevedra).[438] The chronicler takes time to describe the confrontation between the scandalous assistant and the pastor of the parish, which had the people divided.

....

433 The theme was especially dear to all Redemptorists, in that it fit in nicely with the promise of St. Alphonsus to preach every Saturday in honor of Mary.

434 Translator's note: another town in the province of Leon, about 45 kilometers (28 miles) northwest of Astorga.

435 *Crónica de Astorga* II, 254. 255. 277.

436 In January he preached on the Epiphany in-house. In March he preached on the feast day of St. Joseph and on the third Sunday of March, which was dedicated to Perpetual Help. In Holy Week he went to the city of Puebla de Trives (in the province of Orense). On September 5 he preached on the Sunday dedicated to the Sacred Heart. On December 19 he preached the sermon on the day of St. Lucy in the small town of Bierzo of San Miguel de las Dueñas in the province of León. (cf. *Ib.,* 324. 330. 360).

437 160 people from the neighboring area. The Chronicler writes: "This mission was regular; they are simple people; good customs prevail in the town. With 600 people coming to Communion, others in the annex of the church were left without Communion. Almost all of them came to Communion two or three times during the mission. The conferences given were the usual: to single women, to married women, to married men and to young men. With faculties from the bishop, they solemnly blessed a beautiful statue of Our Lady of Perpetual Help, which they carried in procession" (*Ib.,* III, 14).

438 Translator's note: Tuy, also spelled Tui, is a town in the province of Pontevedra in the Galicia region on the left bank of the river Miña. South and east of it is Portugal.

This made the missionary work difficult. Nevertheless, "the mission had very good results. There were confessions of people away from the Church for fifteen, twenty, or thirty years. Many of the scandals were stopped, but not all. Number of Communions 2,400."[439] A little later, on March 5, 1913, he preached the first novena of which we have record in Valdespino.[440]

1913 was the last year in which the name of Fr. José Javier appears as prefect of the Church and Mass prefect[441] as a member of the community in Astorga. He was relieved from teaching duties and entrusted with that of being prefect of the academy of moral theology while he continued working on the manual of philosophy. We do not know for what reasons he was still working on this manual. Either he had not finished it or he had not handed it in to be printed. Perhaps for that reason—and because he had been a year and a half away from teaching—the superiors decided to transfer him to Pamplona. The chronicle in Astorga limits itself to relating the news without any comment: "on July 4, Fr. Gorosta has been transferred to the house in Pamplona."[442] On July 6, 1913, he left for the community in

....

439 Frs. Nicolás Lorenzo Grandal, Javier and Domingo Saa González, his companion from their student days in Astorga (cf. *Ib.*, 38) preached from March 27 to April 7. In that same year he preached in the chapel connected to his community during the second day of the Triduum of Carnival. [Translator's note: A Triduum is a three-day event which includes prayer and preaching; Carnival usually occurs before the beginning of Lent in most Catholic countries and includes parades, wearing of masks and costumes, excessive consumption of alcohol and a carnal atmosphere in general. In 1912 Ash Wednesday was on February 21] His *audience was rather large*. On May 11, the May Devotions took place. [Translator's note: this pious practice consisted of saying certain prayers to the Virgin Mary during each day of May and decorating an altar to Mary with flowers.] July 7 was a community day of retreat and he was named *interim confessor* for it. On September 8 he preached at the profession and reception of the habit of two Poor Clare nuns. On the 14th he went to Brimeda *to help Fr. Lorenzo with confessions*. On October 20th he preached at *the Perpetual Help meeting* [Translator's note: probably the confraternity of Our Mother of Perpetual Help.] A month later, November 19, he gave the panegyric of St. Elizabeth in the monastery of the Holy Spirit in Astorga. [Translator's note: The panegyric of St. Elizabeth was a sermon given on the feast day of St. Elizabeth of Hungary which honored her many virtues] On December 7 he returned to Brimeda *for the purpose of hearing confessions for the people and preaching the sermon on the Immaculate Conception of Mary* (*Ib.*, 28. 31. 34. 42-43. 45).

440 *Ib.*, 49. He preached two sermons in Villoria on the day of St. Thyrsus, the 24th of January; the second day of the Triduum during Carnival in the church connected to the community, February 3; a sermon in Bustillo del Páramo on the 30th of May and one on St. Peter in the parish of Rectovía in Astorga, June 29 (*Ib.*, 48. 50. 53).

441 Translator's note: The prefect of the Church was a responsibility assigned to one community member who saw to it that the church was supplied with what it needed; the Mass prefect was assigned to keep track of requests for Mass intentions and donations given for them.

442 *Ib.*, 53.

Pamplona. At age 36 he concludes his phase as formator to which he had dedicated for eleven years.

The Longest and Most Fruitful Stage of His Life: Missionary in Pamplona, Madrid, and Cuenca (1913-1936)

On August 29, 1913, the provincial superior, Fr. Marceliano Gil, wrote the general consultor in Rome about several matters. Among them, he suggested "for consultor in Pamplona,[443] R. Fr. José Gorosterratzu, who is there and is a serious person and who conducts himself well."[444] The house chronicle gives the information that he arrived on July 6, 1913, to form part of this community and to replace Fr. Prudencio Erviti in the missions in the Basque language. As his community assignment he is made the chronicler. On August 31 he notes: "He[445] remains in charge of the Archconfraternity of Perpetual Help."[446] He stayed uninterruptedly in Pamplona until March

....

443 Ever since their restoration in Spain, the Redemptorists had a desire to make a foundation in Navarre. An offer from Bishop Luís Cabral came to them, which asked them to be missionaries in his diocese. He offered them "the pompously named Royal Basilica of San Ignacio; it was in fact a small chapel." They accepted it in 1891. The residence also was very small. It was found to be "almost solitary at an extreme end of the city. Nor could it be envisioned that there would develop around there the present magnificent new suburb of the city." (R. TELLERÍA, *Un instituto misionero* [Madrid, 1932] 379). The place retained the living memory of the fall of Íñigo López de Oñaz, who fought with the Castilian troops in the siege imposed on Pamplona by the French. In the year 1607 the Viceroy Juan de Cardona built a commemorative arch to the fall of the city. Later they built the little Basilica of San Ignacio, inaugurated on October 10, 1694. In 1704, another Viceroy permitted the building of a little house, with garden attached, for the chaplains of the isolated basilica. With the suppression of the Society of Jesus in 1767, the basilica was handed over to the diocese, which attached it to the nearby parish of San Nicolás. On December 12, 1891, Fr. Pablo Lorthiot arrived in Pamplona, accompanied by Br. Luís. They took possession of the little house and the royal basilica of San Ignacio, so generously offered by Bishop Ruiz Cabral. *It wasn't the first offer made to us.* At the end of 1901, Fr. Pedro López initiated "the construction of a more fitting residence, which could substitute for the damp refuge which the community had lived until then." This was begun on the feast of St. Alphonsus, 1903. [Translator's note: The feast of St. Alphonsus was celebrated on August 2 in those days.] Gorosterratzu lived there for thirteen years in his first stay in Pamplona. He carried out his pastoral ministry in the small, Baroque, royal basilica. He only was able to enjoy the modern new basilica, for which he fought so hard, in the second, short stage of his stay there, which we shall see at its proper time.

444 The provincial adds: "I ask Your Reverence [Translator's note: "Your Reverence" is the honorific title given to the Consultors General and other superiors in a religious order] to grant me this, because they are constantly asking me about it and urging me to find out for the sake of the missions in Cuenca and Pamplona" (AHGR 30150001, 1436).

445 Translator's note: Fr. Javier is speaking in the third person about himself.

446 *Chronicle of Pamplona* II, 20. 21.

15, 1927, when he was sent to the Redemptorist community of San Miguel in Madrid.[447]

When Javier arrived in Pamplona,[448] he met up with Fr. José Machiñena,[449] from his same town, assigned there since 1911 to preach missions in Basque with his other countryman, Fr. Prudencio Erviti, who would die in March 1913. Fr. José Javier will be sharing his life and his missionary task in the Castilian and Basque languages[450] with Fr. José Machiñena until 1924, at which time Fr. Machiñena will be sent to Granada. During the long period in which Fr. José Javier resides in the community of San Ignacio, he will be living with a large number of confreres, both priests and brothers. Among these will be Fr. Donato Jiménez, who will be the superior of the community during various periods.

....

447 *Ib.*, 20.

448 Cf. *Anales* VI, 111. 206. 274. 353. 413; *Anales* VII, 61. 205. 462. 522; *Anales* VIII, 33. 127. 198; *Anales* IX, 55. 112. 173.

449 José María Machiñena Aríztegui (1883-1962); c.f., appendix 2.

450 Translator's note: Castilian is the language we would identify as "Spanish" today; it was spoken in Castile and eventually became widespread throughout Spain and the world. It is a romance language derived from Latin. Basque is the language, which was proper to the Basque Country and is unrelated to any other known language. It predates the Indo-European languages of Europe.

Community of Pamplona, 1915:

J. Gorosterratzu, front row, far right

During this assignment Fr. José Javier was at various times consultor to the local superior and admonitor.[451] The assignments for August 29 confirmed Fr. Donato Jiménez as superior for the 1918-1921 triennium. Fr. Jiménez was given as consultors to Frs. Enrique Esprit Chaubel and Javier Gorosterratzu. These appointments did not please everyone.[452]

One event that is going to require some attention in this period and in which Fr. Javier is going to intervene directly will be the matter of the "peaceful possession" of the Royal Basilica of San Ignacio. The business started to become complicated when the city council approved the project of an urban extension in 1917. It included, among other things, the partial demolition of the Royal Basilica to fit it in with the new alignment for the Avenue of San Ignacio. The bishop protested, and things apparently quieted down for a while. Despite this, on April 18, 1920, Fr. Rector visited with the new mayor, Mr. Sardá, to talk with him "about our aspirations for the lands around our house and church, that they might remain free, so that we may acquire them when the new suburb is expanded." The mayor answered that the rector should be at peace because the Redemptorists had preference. On May 26, a royal order permitted the expropriation of the property for the expansion. Two months later, the chronicle mentions that they now asked for "650 square meters[453] on which to build in the new suburb, at the price of twenty pesetas per meter. The new church will be thirty-one meters

---

451 Translator's note: In Redemptorist governance, the consultor in a local community is a member of the house council who gives advice to the local superior at the superior's request. The admonitor had as his duty to admonish the superior with regards to the superior's duties and personal conduct. Today the position of consultor is still in use, while that of admonitor is no longer appointed.

452 Fr. Enrique Chaubel wrote the following commentary to Fr. Sordet, consultor general: "What's sure is that Fr. Donato Jiménez is very immature, not very serious or formal about things, not able to keep a secret and changes his ideas from one moment to another. Your Reverence will see whether he can be a superior. Fr. Gorosterratzu (judging from exterior appearances) is very prideful, not very charitable, no one can talk with him or tell him anything. You have to stifle yourself, even though he is voicing errors, in order to avoid a quarrel. I understand this Father is missing something in his head; it's the excuse I will give him. That's my opinion. Fr. Gil found out a lot of things and shut up. I don't want things to go on simply out of ignorance" (E. CHAUBEL, *Letter to Fr. Sordet; Pamplona 4-October-1920*: AHGR 30150009, 170-21). The general consultor did not pay much attention to this accusation, fruit of envy, to judge by something else that is said in the same letter (cf. *Visita canonica della Provincia Spagnuola. 1934*: AHGR. 30150002, 0033).

453 Translator's note: 650 square meters equal 6,996 square feet.

in length and twelve in width,[454] with galleries for the men." On December 22, the land was officially conceded to them.[455]

That same year, the Jesuits began to apply pressure in different ways to regain the Royal Basilica, appealing to the Crown, the Royal Academies,[456] the press, and by paying intimidating visits to the Redemptorists. The local press questioned whether the Bishop had a right to the Royal Basilica or whether it was property of the royal patrimony. The bishop declared the Redemptorists "the owners in perpetuo of the Basilica, in spite of all royal donations."[457]

In the middle of all of this, the king communicated to the mayor his desire to conserve intact the Royal Basilica. The Redemptorist community answered in the Navarrese press the accusation that attributed to them "the proposal to build a church on the same site with a different name."[458] This made their intentions quite clear. First, in the records regarding the expansion the protest against the plan to mutilate the chapel is verified. Secondly, "the Redemptorists, faithful to their constant objective, have the intention

....

454 Translator's note: 101 feet in length by 39 feet in width.

455 *Chronicle of Pamplona* II, 365. 367; *Chronicle of Pamplona* III, 6.

456 Translator's note: In Spain, as in France and other countries, there are a number of Royal Academies serving to foster various branches of science or literature, such as the Royal Academy of the Spanish Language, the Royal Academy of Economic and Financial Sciences, the Royal Academy of Engineering, for example.

457 At the end of December 1918, two gentlemen came to the house of the Redemptorists with the proposal that they abandon the Basilica in exchange for receiving the Church of Jesús María with an adjoining section very adequate for serving as a house. It had formerly belonged to the Jesuits and now belonged to the city government (*Anales* VII, 209). On September 12, 1920, Fr. Francisco Escalada, S.J., a resident of Javier, [Translator's note: Javier is a town in Navarre], published the first article in *El Pensamiento Navarro* [Translator's note: a daily newspaper in Navarre that was published between 1897 and 1981, which served as a voice for the Royalists], making it clear that the Royal Basilica and the new lands ought to be subject to the disposition of the Royal Patrimony (*Crónica de Pamplona* II, 376-384). The Redemptorists were in ongoing contact with the bishopric, but hardly ever made use of the media because it was the duty of the bishop to defend their rights. The bishop did so, affirming those rights and rejecting the pretended rights of the Royal Patrimony. Thus, the legitimacy of handing over the Basilica and adjoining house to its actual possessors, the Redemptorists, remained clear.

458 The Redemptorists at no time intended to tear down the old basilica in order to construct the new church which they hoped for, which would be larger and more spacious; in fact, the name would be preserved in that new church: San Ignacio. Besides, the decision to shorten the basilica by a few meters was approved by the majority of the City Council of Pamplona, not to benefit the Redemptorists, but to widen the Calle de San Ignacio according to the plan of the Commission of Expansion (D. DE FELIPE, *De hojalatero a Obispo* [Madrid, 1945] *104*).

of not touching a single wall of the referred-to Basilica," as it was announced at the time. The Commission for Historical and Artistic Monuments of Navarre has responded that there is no evidence that the Redemptorists had the desire to tear down the old Basilica. The Redemptorists, in their article, wondered "about the people who had been able to bring to the attention of his Majesty the King such inexact news, which could disturb the King, when it is certain that loyal subjects ought to tell the King the truth." The rector signed the article, in order to give it an institutional character. We know that Fr. Gorosterratzu edited it. "It created an excellent impression, above all upon people who were loyal to the Redemptorists, as is natural."[459]

The problem was resolved in favor of the diocese, and thus in favor of the Redemptorists. And so we come to October 12, 1924, the date when the diocesan bishop, D. Mateo Múgica, blessed the cornerstone of the new church. Fr. Gorosterratzu acted as subdeacon.[460] On March 25, 1927, we read in the chronicles: "Memorable date for this community...This is the day, finally, on which the solemn blessing of the new church took place."[461] On May 15, Fr. Gorosterratzu left for his new residence at San Miguel in Madrid, where he was to be admonitor to the superior.

As in his previous period in Astorga, his principal activity was academic. In this stage of his life in Pamplona, his principal activity, though not exclusively, was preaching parish missions in Castilian and Basque. To follow him on his missionary itinerary, we will make use of the chronicles of the community in Pamplona, which contain an unexpected and unexplored source of socioreligious data about the rural populations to which he went and the response to the mission in each place.

Scarcely had he arrived in Pamplona on July 6, 1913, when Fr. J. Javier

....

459 The authorship of the article is clear from the house chronicle: "...written by Fr. Goros-terratzu" (*Ib.*, 24).

460 Translator's note: In solemn Masses, such as the one for the blessing of a church, there would have been three liturgical ministers: the bishop, a "deacon" (who was actually a priest), and a "subdeacon" (who also was a priest). It would not have been a concelebration, but a Mass at which the bishop alone presided with the assistance of two priests.

461 *Crónica de Pamplona* III, 238. 395. The bishops who took part in the first solemn Mass which followed the blessing were the following: "*His Excellency, the Papal Nuncio, Tedeschini. Those who accompanied him were His Excellency Irurita, bishop of Lerida and friend from childhood of Fr. Mutiloa; His Excellency Melo, Archbishop of Valencia, and His Excellency Múgica, Bishop of Pamplona.*" And the Navarrese author adds, "*The Spanish flag waved on the spire of the slender tower, singing of the victory to the new city and to the old city, after many years of fights and fatigues (Ib., 107).*"

Gorosterratzu initiated the most intense stage of his apostolate. With regards to popular missions and renewals alone, he preached more than eighty-five, almost all in Navarre. Fr. Dionisio de Felipe writes: "Pamplona was his residence for seventeen years. He dedicated himself to preaching missions, sometimes in Basque, other times in Castilian, for the towns of Navarre. His voice was somewhat harsh and unpleasant, his ideas cloudy, partly because he had difficulty in expressing himself and partly because that was his way of thinking. These notable characteristics were not the best suited for making a preacher of Fr. Gorosterratzu, but that is secondary. What is important is that they did not prevent him from being a great apostle, and even a great missionary."[462]

Fr. Javier preached some of these missions in his native tongue. Fr. José Machiñena or Fr. Leoncio López de Armentia frequently accompanied him. The chronicles note that Fr. Javier reencountered his own people, his native surroundings, its landscape and culture in these towns in the north of Navarre. It is true that things were changing notably in those places, due to the influx of Castilians. Fr. José was a competent witness to these changes and knew how to adapt himself to the pastoral needs of his countrymen, firm in his determination to bring the gospel to all and faithful to his love for his beautiful language.

The summer of 1913 had scarcely ended when in September he preached a mission in Igúzquiza. The chronicles leave us with the following notations:

> *This town of Igúzquiza in which, according to the liberals, the horrible crimes were committed by the Carlistas.*[463] *The Republican soldiers who fell into their hands were thrown into the frightful abyss which lay about ten minutes from the town. It is a half-league*[464] *from Irache and one league from Estella. The parish priest, D. Aurelio Álvarez, had requested the mission, and it was preached by Frs. Gorosterratzu and Páramo. It was a complete success and was met with great enthu-*

....

462 D. DE FELIPE, 153.

463 Translator's note: The Royalists, who supported King Carlos, opposed to the Republicans, who were socialists.

464 Translator's note: a "league" is three miles; while the measurement was common in Europe and Latin America at one time, it is no longer used.

siasm by the people. Everyone in the village went to confession, as did those from the adjoining village of Labeaga. All went to Communion several times. The village only has forty households, but the number of Communions surpassed 800. Also, everyone in the neighboring village of Azqueta went to confession, and many people from some other eight villages as well. In the Procession of the Cross[465] *there were three times the number of people who lived in the parish, with people coming from great distances. It lasted from the 14th to the 21st.*[466]

The next four missions were the only ones Fr. Javier preached outside his native Navarre. They were "in the celebrated region of Cinco Villas de Aragón,[467]in the province of Saragossa and the diocese of Jaca: Faradués, the first town to have the mission, had more than a thousand souls. Nine men went to confession, there were twenty-four confessions and 260 Communions." Malpica, Biel, and Luesia each had ten days of missions, with various results.[468]

In 1914 he preached missions in Arizala, Guetádar, Gordalain,[469] Vidángoz,[470] Olleta, in the parish of San Agustín in Pamplona, Salinas de

....

465 Translator's note: The procession of the cross occurred in the Redemptorist mission at the end of the mission. A cross of twelve or more feet in height was put up as a reminder of the mission.

466 *Crónica de Pamplona* II, 25.

467 Translator's note: Las Cinco Villas de Aragon is named for five historical towns.

468 *Ib.,* 32-33.

469 "The arrival of the two Redemptorist missionaries Gorosterratzu and Páramo was a major event for the two little parishes of Guetádar and Gordalain...and very crowded, as it might be expected from these simple Christian people, even though more than once they had to pay with costly and extraordinary sacrifices" (*Ib.,* 65).

470 In Vidángaz, Valle de Roncal, the parish had seventy to eighty households [Translator's note: The Spanish uses the word *vecino*, which today means "neighbor." However, in older documents it meant a taxpayer—either people who owned property in the town or residents who had to pay taxes. It was made up of family members, relatives living with them, servants, and so on. The term excluded the nobility, clergy, and the indigent, since they did not pay taxes. In more modern times there was an interest in counting everyone in a census, so that the word *habitante* in Spanish means "inhabitant." For our purposes, we will translate the word *vecino* as "household" and the word *habitante* as "inhabitant."] Against the will of Fr. Javier, they had to shorten the mission by three days because of typhoid. Very good participation, with better participation from the men than from the women (*Ib.,* 386-387).

Monreal,[471] and in the parish of Santa María de Tafalla. In 1915 he preached in Iracheta,[472] in Basque in Larrainzar,[473] Milagro, and Peralta.[474] In 1916 in Acedo, Aizpún, Baños de Fitero, Garralde, Imarcoain, and Maquirriain. In 1917 in Abaigar, Cía, Elvetea, Lazagurría, Mendavia, Orbaiceta, Torres, Zabalegui. In 1918, in Auza, Senosiain, and in Zufía (in Basque). In 1919 in Arrarás (in Basque), Burguete, Garzarón (in Basque), Lacunza (in Basque), Murieta and Oroquieta (in Basque). In 1920 in Arróniz, Legasa (in Basque),[475] Murillo del Conde,[476] and Vidángoz. In 1921 in Almandoz, Ciga, Espinal and Leoz. In 1922 in Cizur Mayor, Elgorriaga, Ortiz, Santesteban[477] and Yanci. In 1923 in Áriz, Auza, Echarri, and Vidaurre. In 1924 in

471 From May 18-23, 1915: "Perfect attendance by the people, in spite of having to move very quickly through their work in the fields. For this reason, it was necessary to cut short the duration of the activities.... Fruits of the mission that were conserved: frequent reception of the Sacraments, faithfulness to Reparatory Adoration [Translator's note: Reparatory Adoration was the practice of prayer before the Blessed Sacrament which was offered as reparation for the sins of the world.] "Great enthusiasm for the Obra de la Defensa de la Fe, in which every family enrolled itself." [Translator's note: This may have been an association for the defense of the faith at a time when it was coming under attack from secularizing forces in Spain.]

472 Frs. Cámara and Gorosterratzu preached the mission to this town in Valdorba; they received a simple, but affectionate, welcome; people from nearby villages participated in the mission (*Ib.,* 77).

473 February 1915: This mission was preached by Fr. José Javier and Fr. J. María Machiñena. In it was manifested the elegance of the missionary spirit welcoming and including people who did not know the language. The population consisted of thirty-one households, scarcely more than a single household. "... a serious obstacle came up against the general and universal success of the mission in that the greater part of the people knew only Basque and several families could only understand Castilian. And so, these, who were of a smaller number, asked the missionaries that they would at least direct a few talks to them so that the mission could benefit them as well. These people lived farther away and the missionaries usually preached a sermon for them in the afternoons. Not only did those who spoke the Spanish language come to those sermons, but the Basques who understood Castilian....In the morning and in the evening, the missionaries preached in Basque" (*Ib.,* 77-78).

474 Peralta was a big Navarrese town with a problem: the inhabitants were divided over the issue of communal lands. The mission began on May 12 and had a great turnout of people. The best fruit from the mission was that "there were reconciliations made among families who sought out one another to ask each other for mutual pardon" (*Ib.,* 82-83).

475 Frs. Gorosterratzu and Machiñena preached: "It was an event not only for the town of Legasa, but for the area. Many came to the mission from Santesteban, Navarrete, Gaztelu, Donamaría, Urroz de Santesteban, and other places. Everyone was happy with the mission....It was all preached in Basque" (*Ib.,* 349).

476 From February 21 to March 1, 1920. The missionaries were Frs. Gorosterratzu and Padilla (*Ib.,* 234).

477 In this mission "there were three events each day, two in Castilian and one in the morning in Basque" (Report by Fr. Gorosterratzu. *Crónica de Pamplona* III, 121).

Arráiz; in 1926 in Echalen, Torrano and his own town, Urroz de Santest-eban. His last mission in Navarre was in 1927 in Zabalegui.

In all these missions, a favorite theme of the missionaries was reconcili-ation and social peace, signs of the arrival of the Savior and affirmation that the kingdom had come. Fr. Javier was especially conscious of this peace, for which reason the chronicler notes in the renewal of Guetádar: "Since the mission, the frequency of the people in going to the sacraments has doubled; two persons, who had become enemies because of self-interests, reconciled with each other. One of them renounced his own rights for love of peace."

Besides worship in the basilica of San Ignacio and in preached missions, he gave assorted sermons, Tridua, and novenas in various towns throughout Navarre: Triduum of San Alphonsus in the basilica of San Ignacio (August 1-3, 1913), Larumbe (September 1913), Triduum of the Immaculate Conception in Ororbia (December 6-8, 1913), Triduum in Igúzquiza (June 17-19, 1914); Triduum of Carnival in the church of the Oblates in Pamplona (February 14-17, 1915); May Devotions in the basilica of San Ignacio (May 1-7, 1915), Triduum in Villaveta (June 3-5, 1915); sermon on fulfilling the Paschal duty of receiving Communion[478] in Cirarda (April 1916), Triduum in Cía (May 1916), Tridua to the Sacred Heart in Cía (June 23-25, 1916), Burlada and Oyo, patronal feastdays of Garinoain (November 11-13, 1916) and Triduum to the Sacred Heart in Murillo de Yerri (June 6-9, 1918), as well as preaching in various churches in Pamplona.[479]

Fr. José Javier reached his intellectual, priestly and Redemptorist matu-rity in Pamplona. He lived these three dimensions within the life-giving

....

478 Translator's note: Since 1526 in Spain the obligation to receive Communion at least once during the year was able to be fulfilled any time between Ash Wednesday and Trinity Sunday, which occurred the first Sunday after Pentecost. In other countries it had to be fulfilled between Easter and Pentecost.

479 In the cathedral, he preached ten days in March, 1918, substituting for Fr. Mariscal, and also the week of October 14-20 the same year. In S. Cernin, one of the parishes most beloved to the people of Pamplona because of its historic and artistic significance, he preached five alternate days in the Lent of 1921 (cf. *Ib.*, 71). In S. Agustín he preached a mission from March 17-25, 1914, Ash Wednesday, the Sundays of Lent, Good Friday, and Easter Sunday (cf. *Crónica de Pamplona* II, 37. 38). However, the parish he most often went to was S. Nicolás, near the basilica of San Ignacio and used by the community for great celebrations that could not fit into the tiny basilica.

soil of Basque-Navarrese culture,[480] which helps us understand better those dimensions just mentioned. Thus, the chronicle of 1918 recalls a curious fact, of nationalist suspicions. On May 20, the Second Sunday of Pentecost, Fr. Javier preached in the Royal Basilica a sermon about the fall of St. Ignatius,[481] a glorious fall for God, for Navarre, and for the saint himself. The chronicler, Fr. Antonio Mariscal González, from Granada,[482] who is frequently mentioned for his excessive imagination, comments:

> *Those who heard him say that he was very erudite in historical matters, with many curious and unknown facts. The brave and generous Navarrese came out on high ground sparing the life of St. Ignatius. Those who came out something underhanded were the "Castilian cowards" who let themselves be conquered, since they were so few against so many. So, finally, since St. Ignatius fell and the few who accompanied him capitulated, it was stipulated that everyone's life would be saved. The Navarrese conducted themselves as generous people keeping the treaty, while their enemies, the French, wanted to do away with the prisoners without respect to their surrendering. The sermon was, at least, original: it was listened to attentively and with interest by those who were from afar and those who were from nearby. Thankfully, there weren't very many Castilians.[483]*

Let us recall that Fr. Mariscal González himself was not present and he relates what those who heard Fr. Javier say, certainly people who were not part of the community. The fact and the way of telling it came to be heard by Fr. Javier, who got upset and communicated it to the provincial, Fr. Mutiloa, on a canonical visit to Pamplona. That allows us to understand the note which the provincial signed in the margin of the chronicle: "The

---

480 It is well to remember that Javier Gorosterratzu arrived at the Redemptorist novitiate speaking his mother tongue, Basque, with a total lack of knowledge of Castilian. Also, when he began his novitiate, he chose to call himself Javier, his second name, which identified him with one of the great men of Navarre, the Jesuit saint Francisco Javier.

481 Translator's note: The Basque saint, Ignatius of Loyola, who was wounded in battle as a soldier and experienced conversion as a Christian during his recuperation.

482 Translator's note: Granada is a southern province in the autonomous community of Andalusia, and so Fr. Mariscal González would not have had much sympathy for Navarrese pride.

483 *Crónica de Pamplona* II, 224-225.

person involved does not admit nor do those who heard him recall that he had said those words in his sermon or anything 'offensive' about any race or nation, in the form in which it is reported."[484]

Three elements go into configuring this nationalist identity of the subject of our biography:

1. The shrine of San Miguel *in excelsis*, where he went on pilgrimage several times. Perfect expert that he was on Basque-Navarrese history, the devotion to St. Michael awakened in him the collective memory of his people. The chronicle of July 2, 1920, points out that the whole community made its way there on their day of rest: "From the twentieth to the twenty-second, Frs. Villoslada, Chaubel, and Gorosterratzu stayed at San Miguel."[485] In the entry for April 7, 1921, we read: "The community traveled to the shrine of the angel, as in other years."[486]

2. Roncesvalles,[487] which for Fr. Gorosterratzu was the most celebrated shrine in Navarre. He visited the college church several times. Once it was to receive the relic of St. Francis Xavier on the third centenary of his death, and the celebration of the Congress of the Missionary Union of the Spanish Clergy, which took place from September 20-25, 1922.[488] The remaining visits are not described in the chronicle, but there are traces of them in his book *D. Rodrigo Jiménez de Rada*.[489] In his book we find the following: "Because Roncesvalles, with its heroisms of charity, with prodigies of hospitality, with the splendor of its Christian virtue and religiosity is, in the middle ages in partic-

....

484 *Ib.*

485 *Ib.,* 370.

486 *Crónica de Pamplona* III, 86.

487 Translator's note: Roncesvalles is a village in the Pyrenees, northeast of Pamplona and near the French border.

488 "Those who went from the house to the Francis Xavier event also went to receive the relic at Roncesvalles." Among them, Fr. Gorosterratzu (*Ib.*, 138).

489 Translator's note: Fr. Javier published two books in his lifetime, one the biography of a Navarrese nobleman; the other a translation from the Latin of a classical piece of historical literature.

ular, one of the timbers of the most pure glory of the Pyrenean kingdom and even of all Spain and of all Christendom."[490]

3. St. Francis Xavier, prototype and ideal of the Navarrese; he felt admiration for him and had a special devotion to him. On April 11, 1920, he went on pilgrimage to his shrine with Fr. Padilla. At the time, he was the chronicler for the community and notes: "From Sangüesa they came and went by foot. The Jesuits very much urged them to stay and eat, but they would not."[491] Moreover, not only was he present at the Congress of the Missionaries' Union, in honor of the glorious apostle of the Indies, St. Francis Xavier, which began on September 20, but he was official representative of the provincial at it. The chronicler offers us this report about the inauguration:[492] "From our house, the Most Reverend Fr. Rector and Frs. Gorosterratzu, Machiñena, González, and Felipe participated in the event [at the cathedral]. According to reliable sources, they came back from the event satisfied." On September 23, there was a procession to the shrine of St. Francis Xavier: "The Fathers left for the shrine of St. Francis Xavier who also went to receive the relic at Roncesvalles: the Rector, Machiñena, Gorosterratzu and Munárriz. As they told it, everything went very well. They paid them the twenty-five pesetas, which was the cost for each person for the journey there and back by car, plus the food, which certainly was of good quality and abundant, distributed to each person in paper bags. Each bag contained bread, wine, liquor, chicken, etc. Fr. Gorosterratzu went from our house as representative of Most Reverend Father provincial and to take part in the election of the national president of the Union and of the Cathedral Council. His Eminence Cardinal Benlloch, Archbishop of Burgos, was elected."[493]

....

490 J. J. GOROSTERRATZU, *D. Rodrigo Jiménez de Rada, gran estadista, escritor y prelado* [Translation: *D. Rodrigo Jiménez, great statesman, writer, and prelate*] (Pamplona, 1925) 40.

491 *Crónica de Pamplona* II, 335.

492 *Ib.*, III, 137. 138. 142.

493 *Ib.*, 142.

He remained uninterruptedly in Pamplona until March 15, 1927, on which date he was assigned to the Redemptorist house of San Miguel in Madrid[494] where he resided for three years. But we have a lack of data from this period in the capital because the chronicle disappeared during the war.[495] When the triennium had ended, on May 5, 1930, he was again assigned to Pamplona. This time he remained only a short while, until 1933. In these three years he barely preached eight missions, two in 1931[496] and six in 1932.[497] Of these, two were in Basque.

On January 6, 1933, he again left the community of San Ignacio in the Navarrese capital because he was going temporarily to Cuenca on personal business, as he said.[498] However, what was provisional became permanent, since he was to be found in the city of the Júcar River on August 10, 1936, when he gave the supreme testimony of his faith offering his life for his friend. Ángel Rodrigo, the altar server from the church of San Felipe, remembers him in those years in Cuenca: "This Father dedicated himself to preaching, sometimes going out for missions in villages; he had a considerable gift for preaching. We enjoyed his preaching. It was especially his Basque accent that charmed us...He became nervous especially when he had trouble saying something, because of pronunciation, etc."[499]

....

494 *Ib.,* II, 20.

495 According to the provincial chronicle, the Fathers of the community of San Miguel in Madrid in the year 1927 (cf. *Anales* IX, 166), preached nine missions, four renewals, two novenas and eight Tridua; in 1928 (*Ib.,* 229), they preached seventeen missions, one renewal, eight novenas, and nine Tridua; in 1929 (*Ib.,* 289) the same number as the year before was recorded. Although it is not clear because of the lack of data, Javier Gorosterratzu would have participated in some of these events.

496 Mission in Noáin from January 17 through 25, 1931, with Fr. Ramos; and the mission with Fr. Navarro in Echarri-Larrauri (in Basque) from March 9 through 19, 1931 (cf. *Crónica de Pamplona* III, 91. 93).

497 The mission in Tabar with Fr. Ramos from January 9 through the 20; the mission in Torrano (in Basque) with Fr. Navarro from February 13 to 22; the mission in Elgorriaga with Fr. Navarro from January 25 to February 2; the mission in Zugarramurdi from March 5-14 with Fr. Navarro; the mission in Urzainqui with Fr. Ramos from November 3-13; and the mission in Cilveti with Fr. Goy from December 2 to 12.

498 *Crónica de Pamplona* IV, 46.

499 ÁNGEL RODRIGO, *C. Beatificationis - Declaraciones* II, 512.

Confessor, Spiritual Companion, and Director

The apostolic activity of Fr. Javier in the communities in Pamplona, Madrid (San Miguel), and Cuenca was not limited to popular missions nor to preaching. He spent many hours in the confessional and in spiritual direction besides preaching spiritual exercises to communities of religious—more than fifty groups—especially the Oblates of the Most Holy Redeemer, the Redemptoristine contemplative nuns in the nearby monastery of Burlada, and to the Piarist Sisters.[500] It was the apostolic work which was for him the most undelineated and which demanded the most travel. As distinct from the missions, in which almost always he preached in the dioceses where he lived, he was called to preach the spiritual exercises to communities that were different from one another and distant from where he lived.[501]

A companion and biographer of his, Fr. Dionisio de Felipe, does not manage to explain the power of attraction of his manner, the very many friendships that he had, and the continual series of requests for him to preach the spiritual exercises "in spite of his fumbling way of speaking in conversation and his almost painful effect on his listener, because of his blunders. He could liven up a conversation with his grammatical errors and turns of phrase which caused laughter."[502] Antonia León Viñals, a native of Pamplona, knew Fr. Javier around 1919, before her profession of vows in the monastery of Burlada. She would go to confession to him at San Ignacio. She declared: "When he preached or conducted the spiritual exercises in the church of San Ignacio in Pamplona, although he said sublime things, nevertheless, the public almost left him there by himself...because of the

....

500 Dionisio de Felipe gives as a unique case that "he had preached fourteen years in a row the spiritual exercises to the Piarist Sisters in the same high school" (D. DE FELIPE, 154). Also among those to whom he preached is the frequent mention of the Salesians, Ursulines, and the Little Sisters of the Poor. Less frequently mentioned are the Sisters of Perpetual Adoration, the Discalced Carmelites, the Josephine Sisters, the Servants of Mary, the Conceptionists, and the Teresian Sisters.

501 Thanks to the Redemptoristine nuns of Burlada, who had the sensitivity to transcribe the spiritual exercises and keep them in a notebook, we still have the transcript of the preaching of Fr. Javier to them. In November 1932, the retreat he preached to them had the title "The Five Duties of the Redemptoristine Spouse to her Redeemer Husband"; in September 1934, the theme was "The Life of Faith," and in November 1935, it was "the Beatitudes." (J. GOROSTERRATZU, *Ejercicios Espirituales*: APRM. Manuscripts n.° 119).

502 D. DE FELIPE, 154.

difficulty he had in expressing himself in the Castilian language."[503] But it is evident that, beyond those deficiencies in language, Fr. Javier had that certain something, and something special, which reached the deep interior of his hearer. His word went in conformity with his testimony of life. And for that reason they called him repeatedly to preach retreats. Antonia herself says that very thing:

> *I know that he had nothing of egoism or a spirit of seeking comfort for himself; in his talks and in my dealings with him, I always got the impression that he had great confidence in God. His love for God was manifest in his life of prayer and self-renunciation; in everything else, he gave to others, forgetting himself....In my opinion, he was outstanding in his love of God.*[504] *Other Burlada nuns said that "he had great faith in God and, as an indication of that, I can cite that he demonstrated a very great zeal for the spiritual perfection of the community. He did not act on human motivations, but for supernatural reasons and motives. It didn't matter to him what people said."*[505] *"He had an intense faith and he demonstrated it in exhorting us in the epoch of the Republic to be faithful unto martyrdom....Admirable in his charity. In his conduct and his teaching, he insistently inculcated charity."*[506]

But the greatest prestige gained by Fr. Gorosterratzu in his priestly ministry was in the confessional. He was a great confessor and a great spiritual director, gifted with an extraordinary gift of counseling and deep insight. He seemed to possess the gift of prophecy and left those he interacted with wondering. His success as a confessor and a director of consciences had to be attributed to his competence in moral theology, to his natural talent, to his gift of counsel, to his piety, and to his gentleness in dealing with others. He had a lot of honey in his onrush of words, and a lot of care in his enlightened perceptions. His was an unconditional dedication in service to the sheep. Some very eloquent people thought they could

....

503 ANTONIA LEÓN VIÑALS, *C. Beatificationis - Declaraciones* III, 741.

504 *Ib.*, 742-743. 744.

505 TEODORA BELZUNEGUI, *Ib.*, 749.

506 DOMINICA ZOZOYA, *Ib.*, 761.

easily displace him on some occasions, but they came to be convinced that there was no one who could replace him. Persons who were outstanding for their knowledge, their position or prominence in society came to Fr. Gorosterratzu as to a sure and irreplaceable counselor.[507]

Fr. Javier had the charism to be able to make young women enthusiastic about religious consecration. Sr. Javiera says it this way: "Although in appearances he seemed a little dry, I don't know what he had, but it's certain that he attracted people like no one else."[508] Teodora Belzunegui (Sr. María Josefa) responds in the diocesan process that she came to know Fr. Javier when he came to preach a Triduum of the Sacred Heart in Unciti[509] and he was given lodging in her house in 1917: "He told me then that I had a religious vocation; I had something to do with him later, but not much." The following year, she joined the monastery of Redemptoristine nuns in Burlada. And she adds, he had "a reputation of prudence in the administration of the sacrament of penance and spiritual direction of souls. I heard about him from penitents before coming into the monastery and after my entry."[510]

In 1935, he accompanied his niece, Josefa Nuin Gorosterratzu, to the Benedictines in Cuenca. He preached the Triduum in preparation for taking the habit, and he gave her the name of Scholastica. In the same diocesan process, she testified that her uncle told her: "If you persevere, the number of souls whom I have brought to religious profession will be a total of 93 persons."[511] She keeps the copy of the holy Gospels, which he gave her with this brief dedication: "Here you have the teaching of your Spouse, Jesus, and of your Sanctifier, the Holy Spirit. Take it with you, read it, be satiated by it. Let it be your favorite book. Carry one of its sentences in your heart daily with affectionate love."[512]

....

507 D. DE FELIPE, 154.

508 FERMINA BRIONES, *C. Beatificationis - Declaraciones* II, 594.

509 Translator's note: Unciti is a town of 230 people in the province of Navarre.

510 TEODORA BELZUNEGUI, *C. Beatificationis - Declaraciones* III, 748-750.

511 JOSEFA NUIN, *C. Beatificationis - Declaraciones* II, 419.

512 J.J. GOROSTERRATZU, *Evangelios dedicados a Josefa Nuin* en: *C. Beatificationis - Escritos.*

The most eloquent testimonies about Fr. Javier's quality of director of souls, as we have already said, come from the religious women who had him as their confessor. They all confirm the view of Fr. Dionisio de Felipe and reveal, at the same time, his know-how in the artwork of grace and the Holy Spirit. Antonia León Viñal (Sr. María Margarita), who met Fr. Javier in Pamplona and had spiritual direction with him before professing vows in Burlada in 1927, affirmed: "He put all of his priestly spirit in the spiritual direction of souls and had a lively sense of faith." Fermina Briones Uriz (Sr. Javiera) had the same kind of experience with him. Her testimony recalls an eloquent and important part of the life of both of them, and sums up, in her bold ingenuousness, the aspects we've talked about before:

[I got to know him] from his having gone to preach in my town and heard my confession and I had spiritual direction with him before my becoming a religious sister. I went to confession and had direction with him in Burlada for nine years....He was all on fire for God and for neighbor, as much in his talks as in spiritual direction. He conducted himself with everyone as the most tender of Fathers, thus concerned with everyone as much in the spiritual as in the material....In my way of looking at it, his main virtue was the love of God and his best quality was that of confessor and spiritual director of souls....Fr. Gorosterratzu was most prudent, especially as spiritual director and confessor. Forgive me for saying it, but I have found no one equal to him.[513]

This apostolate of spiritual direction he also conducted by way of correspondence. Some samples are still in existence from his letters and are incorporated into the acts of the process.[514]

....

513 FERMINA BRIONES, *C. Beatificationis—Declaraciones* II, 592-594.

514 Two letters written from Cuenca to Sr.María Estela de Jesús are preserved (13-7-1933 / 7-12-1935), 10 to Margarita Irurzun (19-1-1933 / 16-7-1933 / 11-1933 / 1-1934 / 4-1934 / 31-12-1934 / 28-3-1935 / 25-6-1935 / 6-1935 /22-12-1935) and two to the Redemptoristine community in Burlada (J. J. GOROSTERRATZU, *Correspondencia* in: *Causa Beatificationis—Escritos*). [Translator's note: the European method for abbreviating dates is to order them day/month/year, as in contrast to the American method of month/day/year.]

One Facet of the Missionary: Researcher and Historian

We have seen Fr. Gorosterratzu as professor of Latin and of philosophy, and also as a self-sacrificing missionary. But his love for his little homeland, Navarre, and for Basque history and culture, his maternal language and culture, is fundamental for understanding his special dedication to history.[515]

The first and only original work published by Fr. Javier Gorosterratzu was a biography of the Navarrese D. Rodrigo Jiménez de Rada, a key person in medieval history. The second was a translation from Latin to Castilian of the classic work of the historian Arnaldo de Oyenart: *Noticia de las dos Vasconias,*[516] which we will later explain. He wrote a small biography of a woman religious Oblate of the Most Holy Redeemer. He worked on a fourth book, which had as its protagonist the Archbishop of Toledo Fray Bartolomé de Carranza, also a Navarrese. It was almost ready for publication when he was mowed down by death, one hot day in August in Cuenca.

Biography of Rodrigo Jiménez de Rada[517]

We are not able to verify in what year he began the historical investigation about Jiménez de Rada. In October 1922, the chronicler informs us, as a thing done in the past, that he was doing research at the provincial archive of Navarre.[518] Much more explicit is the entry for April 11 of the following year, since the chronicler offers us data from the archives and libraries which the author collected as resources for his work:

....

515 Because of his work in historical investigation he had a special relationship with the Center and Review for Basque Studies. He came to have a certain friendship with its creator, D. Julio de Urquijo. This was confirmed by three letters addressed from J. J. Gorosterratzu to Julio Urquijo with dates 26-12-1925, 5-2-1926 and 29-11-1929 (DIPUTACIÓN FORAL DE GUIPUZCOA, BIBLIOTECA KOLDO MITXELENA - San Sebastián, Sala de Fondos reservados).

516 Translator's note: "Report from the two Vasconias, the Iberian and Aquitaine"; the author is also known as Arnauld Oihenart and he lived 1592-1667.

517 X. Gorosterratzu, Redemptorist, D. Rodrigo Jiménez de Rada, great statesman, writer and prelate. A documented study of his life, of his forty years as Primate of the Church in Spain and of his Chancellorship in Castile; and, in particular, proof of his attendance at the Fourth Lateran Council, as debated as the controversy over the coming of St. James to Spain (Pamplona 1925).

518 October 8: "The day before yesterday, Fr. Gorosterratzu providentially ran into him (a Jesuit by the name of Escala, whom the chronicler had previously mentioned) in the provincial archive, talking about a document on the Jesuits" (*Crónica de Pamplona* II, 389).

A journey by Fr. Gorosterratzu for the purposes of science. Since R. Fr. Gorosterratzu needs to do certain investigations into data and one-of-a-kind documents about the life of D. Rodrigo Jiménez de Rada, Most Reverend Father provincial gave him permission to go about some cities of Spain where he could collect such details and information. In Madrid, he visited the National Library and the National Historical Archive and the Library of the Academy of History; in Toledo, the Archive and Library of the Cathedral; in Sigüenza, the Archive of the Cathedral; the libraries in Segovia and in Valladolid, and in Osma, the Archives and Library. He worked very intensely, employing many hours a day in the task, as he himself has said (up to ten hours a day).[519]

On April 12 of that year he arrived in Madrid "to finish preparations for a book he is thinking of publishing about the history of D. Rodrigo, Archbishop of Toledo." On April 26 the chronicler adds: "Fr. Gorosterratzu leaves Madrid to go to Segovia and Osma to collect data for a book he is thinking of writing; before this, he was in the Archives of Toledo."[520] The chronicle in Pamplona does not mention the date of his return but does say that he preached an in-house Triduum of May devotions from May 9 to May 11.[521]

---

519 *Crónica de Pamplona* III, 86.

520 *Crónica de Madrid-PS*, 1918, April. [Translator's note: "PS" in this case stands for *Perpetuo Socorro*, meaning "Perpetual Help," abbreviation for the community at the house of Our Lady of Perpetual Help in Madrid.]

521 *Crónica de Pamplona* III, 93.

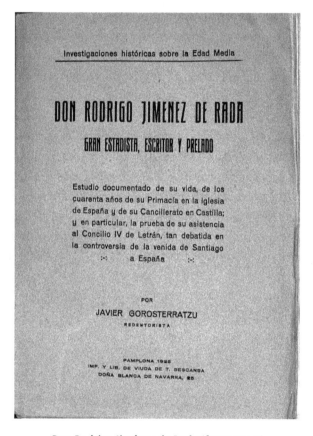

Don Rodrigo Jiménez de Rada (front cover)

In the section "Explanation to the Reader," Fr. Xavier Goroster-ratzu reveals the genesis and the process of his work *D. Rodrigo Jiménez de Rada*. While still a student in the Redemptorist major seminary in Astorga, he proposed to demonstrate the inconsistency of the thesis of Fr. Fidel Fita[522] which labeled as fable the attendance of the Archbishop of Toledo at the Fourth Lateran Council. According to Fr. Gorosterratzu, he was concealing a prejudice: "to maintain unscathed the glorious Spanish tradition of the coming of St. James to Spain which professor Duchesne[523] was rejecting, citing the testimony attributed to D. Rodrigo in the afore-mentioned Council. Denying that he was present at the Council, his words gathered from the alleged acts lacked a basis in fact, a theme too compli-cated to get into in his study."[524] This is the way there arose in him the restlessness for science which later led him to discover something that we had not imagined: the rich personality of Jiménez de Rada in fields as distinct as the religious, the political, and the cultural. From then on, he

....

[522] Translator's note: Fr. Fidel Fita (1835-1918) was a Spanish Jesuit who became director of the Royal Academy of Madrid; he was an archeologist and historian.

[523] Translator's note: Msgr. Louis Duchesne (1843-1922) was a French priest and critical historian who believed all the churches of the West, including that of Spain, owed their origins to St. Peter and his successors, not to St. James.

[524] X. GOROSTERRATZU, *D. Rodrigo Jiménez de Rada...*, XIII. In Chapter X, which is dedi-cated to this theme, he collects the "historical" words "of D. Rodrigo (or attributed to him) in a reply to the Compostelan," in the dispute over the primatial see: "*If he is alleging the first preaching of the divine word and the conversion of many to the faith of Christ in Spain by St. James, let those speak who know the Sacred Scriptures. I have read that he was given the power to preach in Spain: but while he was disseminating the divine law throughout Samaria and Judea, under Herod, his throat was slit in Jeru-salem, he breathed out his soul and gave it up to the Lord. So, how did he preach in Spain if he had not yet gone to Spain? Or by chance did the Lord convert them without preaching? I remember well to have heard in my first years from some holy nuns and pious widows that he converted very few to the faith through his preaching, and since little progress was made in the faith, he returned to his homeland, where he died, by the disposition of heaven.*" He added the note: "*I cite here the text of Loaísa because it was he who traveled around Europe and changed the opinion of the critics.*" (*Ib.*, 161).

felt himself fascinated by this key figure from the thirteenth century.[525]

When Javier Gorosterratzu was freed from teaching philosophy, he dedicated himself to the historical research in the various places we have already cited, while not giving up his apostolic work as itinerant missionary for parish missions, as we have seen. The result was a work with important primary documentary sources, while it was at the same time a passionate work. His Basque-Navarrese heart mixed together the strength of an investigator with his admiration for the archbishop from his native land.[526]

The book on D. Rodrigo had a good reception in the scientific world. On April 24, 1926, the chronicler in Pamplona writes:

In a telegram sent from Madrid, the Most Reverend Father provincial has communicated that Fr. Gorosterratzu has been awarded a prize for the talent he shows in the book on D. Rodrigo. As a result, Father Rector granted permission to speak during the meal.[527] The author of D. Rodrigo Jiménez de Rada again received the congratulations of his confreres in community and of many people from outside; to those

....

525 D. Rodrigo Jiménez de Rada had a hand in the victory of the Plains of Tolosa. [Translator's note: The Battle of Tolosa on July 16, 1212, fought by Christian troops from Castile, Aragon, Navarre and Portugal allied against the superior number of troops of the Muslim Caliph Muhammed An-Nasir. The Christian forces won and the victory became a turning point for the end of Muslim domination of Spain. The military action was advocated by Archbishop Jiménez de Rada.] D. Rodrigo was Chancellor of the Court of Castile. He defended the primacy of the See of Toledo and amplified it considerably. He took up the task of building the grandiose cathedral, contributed to the definitive union of Castile and León in the person of San Fernando. [Translator's note: King Ferdinand III (1201-1252) was canonized in 1671. He was son of King Alfonso IX of León and Berenguela of Castile. He united the two kingdoms. He also contributed greatly to the "Reconquest" of Spain by the Christians from the Muslims.] His works contributed to preparing the cultural ambient of the court of Alphonsus X the Wise. Finally, D. Rodrigo was pontifical legate with continuing relationships with Popes Innocent III, Honorius III, Gregory IX and Innocent IV.

526 For example, after pointing out many of his great works, he says: "The incomparable Chancellor, great minister and consummate politician of Castile during that era, the divine counselor, who transformed Alfonso VIII into a hero, Fernando III into a saint and Alfonso X into a wise man...the admirable luminary of the ecumenical councils of the Lateran and Lyon, the incessant oracle consulted by the Roman Pontiffs...the holy Pastor, the marvel of charity, zeal, wisdom and prudence who enlightened with his teaching the Church of God and sanctified his flock, the man of various and fruitful initiatives and enterprises in all areas of life which the middle ages offered." (J. J. GOROSTERRATZU, *D. Rodrigo Jiménez de Rada*, XIII).

527 Translator's note: In Redemptorist houses, generally there was silence during meals with one member reading aloud from a book. That permission was granted for conversation during the meal indicates an exceptional circumstance.

congratulations, I who write these lines wish to add my own very sincere ones.[528]

The prize mentioned was given by the Royal Academy of History.

Noticias de las Dos Vasconias[529] (*Report from the Two Vasconias*)

The second scientific contribution of Fr. Javier Gorosterratzu was the Castilian version of the Latin work by Arnaldo de Oyenart, *Report from the Two Vasconias*.[530] It was published for the first time in 1638 and republished in 1656. It was the work of a distinguished Basque born in 1592 in Mauleón. So, it dealt with a work that was difficult to find except in specialized libraries. The translator was an expert in the history of the Basque people. Fr. Javier had the know-how to discover the importance of the work and he took on the huge task of dedicating many hours to it so as to put it in the hands of the reading public who did not know Latin.

In the "Prologue of the Translator," the only part of the work that comes from the pen of Fr. Javier, we find the reasons that moved him to do this work. First of all, the intrinsic qualities of the work of Oyenart, "so solidly conceived and constructed and so universally consulted by the erudite in order to know the nature of the Basque people and their more important deeds in the passage of time, from the first historical vestiges until the days of the distinguished author." According to him, it was "the most universal source of information for those who have wanted to know the more relevant actions and other curious observations pertaining to the earliest and

....

528 *Crónica de Pamplona* III, 313-314.

529 Translator's note: *Report from the Two Vasconias*.

530 X.Gorosterratzu, Redemptorist, *Noticia de las dos Vasconias, la Ibérica y la Aquitana* ["Report of the Two Vasconias, of Iberia and Aquitaine".] *In it is described the situation of the region and other things worthy of knowing. It also contains the genealogy of the kings of Navarre, that of the princes of Gascony* [Translator's note: Gascony is the Basque-speaking area of southwestern France and northeastern Spain; it is a duchy rather than a kingdom] *and other families illustrious for their antiquity and nobility, as found in ancient authors. In addition, there are catalogs of the Prelates of Aquitaine Vasconia, more complete than those published until now. It was written by Arnaldo Oyenart of Mauleón.* [Translator's note: Mauleón is the eastern-most of three regions of French Vasconia.] *The second edition was corrected and was added to, translated into Spanish by him...* (San Sebastián, 1929). Before it appeared as a book, it was published in installments in *La Revista Internacional de los Estudios Vascos* [International Review of Basque Studies] of Eusko-Ikaskuntza, *included in the issues between April-June 1926, and January-March 1929.*

enigmatic Basque people."[531] Secondly, the limitations of "the only work of its kind that Vasconia possesses;" but "very imperfect, certainly, for the age in which we live, even though for that in which it was published...it merited the highest praise that has been given to it."[532] Those limitations are superficially noted in the prologue.

The work was translated in a politically complex epoch. The Basques began to divide themselves between those who supported a "communion" with Spain and those who wanted independence. We can find in the prologue his personal vision of the story of the Basque-Navarrese people.

These pages, in their brevity, reveal three dimensions of José Javier Gorosterratzu in the stage of his life when he was at his greatest human and intellectual capacity: his love for his land and for the Basque-Navarrese culture, the surmounting of all exclusive political partisanship, and finally, his passion for seeking knowledge and investigation which demand freedom of thought and opinion.[533] The following is a presentation of some of these ideas.

As a young man, Javier thought Pamplona was at the entry to Vasconia, not within Vasconia. His ample knowledge later made him modify that view. In the biography of D. Rodrigo, he points out that "Basque or Navarrese was, according to Sancho the Wise, the national language, since he calls it *lingua navarrorum*, Latin for 'language of the Navarrese.'" Also, "Navarre was nothing else but the most powerful and indomitable tribe of the Basques. In the most critical moment of its history it became a Christian kingdom in order to keep its liberty and religion as over and against the Franks and Arabs. These were harassing and battering Navarre from both sides of the Pyrenees in order to subject it, each one to its own empire."[534]

....

531 *Ib.,* V.

532 *Ib.,* VI.

533 One of the affirmations made by Oyenart is that the conquest of the Kingdom of Navarre was violent and unjust. Gorosterratzu prefers not to enter into the polemic which in his time gave rise to this question (J. GOROSTERRATZU, *Noticia de las dos Vasconias,* IX). And so, he ends up saying *"this question is neither nationalist nor anti-nationalist as has been suggested; it is antecedent to it. It came up already in the days of the conquest of Navarre and continues unresolved (...) They can put forth an opinion just the same in favor of its legitimacy or against the nationalists or anti-nationalists, without having the right to label them in the process as good or bad Navarrese, as good or bad Spaniards or patriots, under the pain of the labelers themselves deserving some hard description. The second thing that is certain, is the subsistent capacity to give an opinion in whatever sense of this sentence"* (*Ib.,* IX-X).

534 J.J. GOROSTERRATZU, *D. Rodrigo...,* 26.

In *Noticias de las Dos Vasconias* he writes that "the Basque people do not have another strictly national history of its own independent activity... the history of Navarre, which created its own completely independent life, from the beginning of the Reconquest[535] until the annexing of Navarre to the other kingdoms of Spain...Take away the period of the historical life of Navarre, and the Basques, divided into various tribes, seem to be without any activity of their own as a nation...Álava, Biscay, and Guipúskoa[536] present the etched features of a special tribe, a tribe whose life is also strong and vigorous, but they do not seem to have been given the attributes of a true nation, as absolute arbiters of their own destiny. Instead they are seen under the orbit alternately of one of the better constituted nations...Those tribes do not live in their own full independence, as Navarre does, nor do they create a national history of their own, as it is understood by De Oyenart."[537]

A Victim of Charity: Sr. Josefa de San Alfonso

Fr. Javier published this third work. It is much smaller and on a completely different kind of topic.[538] Only a few copies carry the author's name because he wanted the edition to be anonymous. In the book he intended "that this simple narration produce and revive in her sisters a holy emulation of greater virtue and sanctity, especially of fraternal charity, which, in the expression of the Apostle, is the bond of perfection."[539]

Josefa was born in Amezqueta (Gipuskoa) on February 14, 1884, "and

---

535 Translator's note: The reconquest of Spain began in 722 when the Christians of Asturias revolted against their Muslim lords over taxation. The Moorish Muslims had established a caliphate in Spain in 711 and ruled Spain for 300 years. The last area to be taken from Muslim rulers was Granada, which was conquered by King Ferdinand V of Aragón and Queen Isabela I of Castile in 1492.

536 Translator's note: Álava, also spelled "Araba," has the main political institutions of the Basque region in its capital city of Vitoria-Gasteiz, is the largest of the three in area and the smallest in population; Biscay has as its capital Bilbao and in the nineteenth and early twentieth century had become the most prosperous region of Spain; Gipuzkoa is the smallest of the three, situated on the Bay of Biscay in Northern Spain, between Biscay and the French border; these three provinces comprise the Basque Region of Spain.

537 J. J. GOROSTERRATZU, *Noticia de las dos Vasconias...*, VII-VIII.

538 J. J. GOROSTERRATZU, CSsR, *Una víctima de la caridad. Reseña biográfica de Sor Josefa de San Alfonso. Religiosa Oblata del Stmo. Redentor* (Zaragoza, 1927) 48. [Translation: A Victim of Charity. A Brief Biographical Sketch of Sr. Joseph of St. Alphonsus, Oblate Religious of the Most Holy Redeemer] (Zaragoza, 1927) 48.

539 *Ib.,* 7. [Translator's note: Colossians 3:14]

received in the bosom of her Christian and modest family an upbringing at once refined and Christian."[540] After being employed as a maidservant by a family with means for eight years in Irún,[541] she enrolled in 1910 in the Oblates of the Most Holy Redeemer of Saragossa. She was invested with the holy habit on August 8, 1911, and professed her religious vows on August 3, 1913. Her first and only assignment was San Sebastian.

"On the afternoon of September 28, 1926, she was making her daily visit to the Most Holy Sacrament of the altar when a sudden and frightening fire in the sacristy caught her attention and, terrified, she also heard the cries for help from the sister sacristan. Sr. Josefa ran fearlessly into the sinister scene." She attempted to put the fire out with a sheet dipped in water and this was her downfall. The fire surrounded her and set aflame her habit. A great part of her body was burned. Five days later, at six o'clock in the afternoon, she flew to the bosom of God after a very painful agony. She was forty-one years old.[542]

Fr. Javier knew Sr. Josefa very well from the time of her religious profession until the end of her life. He many times preached the spiritual exercises in the community and was her spiritual director. He wrote her biographical sketch, fascinated by three facts of which he was a privileged witness:

1. The vocation in the Church of the Oblates of the Most Holy Redeemer. He knew them very well and found in them one of the evangelical missions most dedicated to the liberation of poorer women: a mission to those exploited by prostitution in the age of liberalism and of industrialization.[543]

2. The fidelity of Sr. Josefa to her vocation of following Christ the Redeemer. Fr. Javier, expert director of consciences, writes about what motivated her to evangelical charity: prayer; spiri-

....

540 She was the daughter of Antonio Zabala and Josefa Echeverría (*Ib.*, 9).

541 Translator's note: Irún is a town of some 69,000 people in Gipuskoa.

542 *Ib.*, 37. 41.

543 "Sister Josefa is the name of one of the many...heroic souls" who belong to "the Congregation of the Religious Oblates of the Most Holy Redeemer: honor and adornment of the Spanish Church, which values having produced her, for the glory of the Divine Savior of the human race, in the midst of the pains and tribulations of the 19th century....How well known it is in Spain that the Oblates of the Most Holy Redeemer, faithful to their heroic vocation...rehabilitate each year thousands of those victims with deeds of burning zeal and marvelous abnegation" (*Ib.*, 6-7).

tual direction, and ongoing conversion through the sacrament of reconciliation; the Eucharist, lived daily since her early childhood; obedience and humility about her own opinions; all this after the example of Mary of Nazareth. These things allowed her to make a free oblation of total service to the kingdom and to the dignity of women.

3. The preparation of Sr. Josefa, because she was found to be "prepared to receive her Spouse with lamp lit" (see Luke 12:35-40) during those days in which she was crucified with Christ in interminable agony as a result of the burns to her body. She gave many evidences of this preparedness to those who visited her, including her elderly mother. But maybe the most sincere expression of this preparation was what she said to the chaplain, after the manner of Christ's prayer in the Garden: "Father, help me to become holy in these sufferings." Fr. Javier adds, "She rejoiced at the moment she went to the bosom of God."[544]

The Biography of Fray Bartolomé Carranza

The fourth work that Javier Gorosterratzu wrote had as its protagonist one of the most representative figures of the sixteenth century: the Archbishop of Toledo, Fray Bartolomé Carranza.[545]

Writing a biography of the controversial Bartolomé de Carranza meant Fr. Javier Gorosterratzu took on his shoulders an immense amount of work.

....

544 And he collects two testimonies from people who did not know her until this moment: Sr. Germana, superior of the hospital, explains, "I am still astonished at such patience. I do not recall anything similar. All the time she was here, she never complained about anything and she prayed a lot." The doctors who attended her were even more amazed and said, "This is the way saints act." (*Ib.*, 39).

545 He was born in the Navarrese town of Miranda de Arga in 1503 and did his studies in Salamanca, Alcalá, and Valladolid. He professed his vows in the Order of St. Dominic, was professor of theology and a consultant for the Inquisition. He shined with a light characteristic of him in the Council of Trent. He was named provincial of Castile in Spain and refused the bishopric of the Canary Islands because he preferred the simplicity of the cloister, evangelical poverty and the silence of his monastery cell. Philip II proposed him for archbishop of Toledo. He was consecrated as such in 1558. In this primatial see he developed ample pastoral and charitable activity. [Translator's note: The archdiocese of Toledo was a primatial see, meaning it had authority over all other dioceses in Spain. It came to be the richest diocese in the Church, after Rome itself.] On August 22, 1559, the Inquisition imprisoned him in Torrelaguna and initiated a process that endured for seventeen years.

We know about the steps that he took in its elaboration from the correspondence that he maintained from Cuenca with his friends.[546] In November 1933 he wrote: "In January I'm going to travel to Salamanca, Madrid, etc., in search of archives related to my book."[547] On January 1, 1934, he points out: "The morning after next I leave to do research in the Archives of Salamanca for my writing."[548] In a letter in April, he speaks about his missionary work in the territory of La Mancha, an area that differs so much from Navarre: "This place is extremely dry for an apostolic mission. It's not the worst thing that my writing absorbs my attention. It's moving along slowly...I had a fruitful stop in the Archives of Madrid, Salamanca, Simancas, and Valladolid."[549] On Christmas Eve 1935, he writes: "I am very far along with my work...I'm fine and the days flash by as quickly as lightning when I am working on my papers."[550]

The rest of the comments about the work come from two witnesses at the process of beatification years after the shooting in Cuenca. One of the nuns in Burlada (Navarre) declared: "I am sure that in April 1936, he came to say goodbye to us because he was thinking about going to Rome to give himself time to do research there." Fr. Isidro Posado, a member of the community in Cuenca, said: "I know the following: [in July 1936] he took his papers [to the seminary that was serving as a jail], to put together the index for the book which he was writing about Bartolomé de Carranza."[551]

In seems that in view of the difficulty of traveling to Rome, due to the political circumstances which Spain was going through, Fr. Gorosterratzu decided to give to the printer his study about Archbishop Carranza of Toledo. In the end, the work was never published. It disappeared after the death of the author.

....

546 This correspondence is included in the Acts of his Beatification Process (*Causa Beatificationis—Escritos*).

547 J. J. GOROSTERRATZU, *Letter written to Margarita Irurzun: Cuenca, November 1933: Ib.,* 4.

548 J. J. GOROSTERRATZU, *Letter written to Margarita Irurzun: January 1934: Ib.,* 1-2.

549 J. J. GOROSTERRATZU, *Letter written to Margarita Irurzun: Cuenca, January, 1934: Ib.,* 1-2.

550 J. J. GOROSTERRATZU, *Letter written to Margarita Irurzun: Cuenca, December 22, 1935: Ib.,* 3.

551 ISIDRO FDEZ. POSADO, C. *Beatificationis—Declaraciones* I, 147.

The Person that Fr. J. Gorosterratzu Became

The personality of Fr. Javier experienced a strong transformation when confronted with martyrdom as his fate. It was for him a rapid process of accepting the will of God that brought him to a confident surrender of his own life. The inhumanity of violence and the possibility of a violent death were incomprehensible for him in his natural character, as is reflected in various testimonies about him from the end of his life: "...I want to insist that when Fr. Gorosterratzu had took shelter in my house and thought about leaving in order to avoid dangers, he said that 'we could not be condemned as being suspicious people,' but that it was a matter of sectarianism and of genuine persecution. And so he was determined to leave."[552] A few days before he said: "I'm not ready for martyrdom."[553] Already in May he had described to his nephew the situation in Cuenca and concluded with these words: "What's waiting for us over the horizon is terrible."[554] And his niece Escolástica always remembered his goodbye, a very short time before the events: "Mine shall not be the lot of being a martyr." But that same witness assures us that little by little he came around to facing the situation.[555] Because of his nervous character, he had to have put forth considerable effort to find a supernatural meaning in the events that he was suffering, experiencing moments of great emotional intensity, and being subject to great nervousness.[556]

Sr. Remedios Acedo Maeztu, of the Mercedarian Order, was a witness to the last days of Fr. Javier. She writes:

> He comported himself as an untiring apostle, encouraging all of us with his words and his presence. He was until his last moment in control of all of his actions. He heard our confessions for the last time on August 9, around eleven o'clock in the morning. He was consoling us and encouraging us to give our life, if it were necessary, for our holy faith. All of his

---

552 M.ª CARMEN GARCÍA DE LA ROSA, C. Beatificationis—Declaraciones I, 120.

553 Ib., 111.

554 Cit. D. DE FELIPE, 160.

555 "He was very involved and enthusiastic about his writings and work; although, when they began to drop bombs on San Felipe, he then began to say that things were going badly, that the situation had become very serious" (Sr. Escolástica Nuin, C. Beatificationis Declaraciones I, 111).

556 M.ª NATIVIDAD CUENCA PÉREZ, C. Beatificationis—Declaraciones II, 409.

longing was that we would be saved, because the dangers that we faced could not be hidden. That same day, around nine o'clock in the evening, we had an interview with him, now for the purpose of saying goodbye because he had the intuition that it would be the last night he would spend on this earth. He wished us farewell until heaven. He asked us what we might wish from him there. We asked that he intercede for us so that our Lord would bring us there with Him.[557]

The human and spiritual loftiness, which Fr. Javier demonstrated at the end of his life, he did not acquire in one day, but it was the work and accomplishment of all of his lifetime. In the beginning, Fr. Javier forged his personality in the following of Jesus by proclaiming the good news as a Redemptorist missionary. The fount from which he fed his interior life was the sacrament of the Eucharist, center of his personal and community life according to the Rule and according to Redemptorist spirituality. It was concretized in three stages: preparation, celebration and thanksgiving in quiet and profound prayer at the beginning of the day.[558] Moreover, faithful to the tradition of St. Alphonsus, participation in the Eucharist was prolonged in the visit to the Most Blessed Sacrament at the end of the after-noon, which was the practice of having an affectionate conversation with the Friend, whose living presence is among us until the end of the world.

Every Redemptorist, formed in the spirituality of St. Alphonsus, lives devoted to Mary from his first steps in the Congregation. Javier had begun loving the Mother of the Lord, learning to do so from his grandfather, in the many rosaries they said together in the solitude of the valleys of Laba-

....

557 SOR REMEDIOS ACEDO, *Carta al Fr. Lucas Pérez, 26. IX. 1944,* cit. en D. DE FELIPE, 161. In her responses during the Process, she also says: "In the time in which I got to know Padre Gorosterratzu he demonstrated a great interior life; he heard the confessions of us religious, he gave us talks and in those critical moments he showed his Faith. From what he did for us, as a spiritual director, he was seen as a man of God; in those days he strengthened us and helped us a great deal, especially through his talks and in hearing confessions....Once the Revolutionary Committee became in charge of the seminary, we were not able to communicate among ourselves. During that time, Fr. Gorosterratzu lived a life dedicated to prayer: until the last day he celebrated the Holy Mass. During that period of time, he demonstrated a complete and absolute conformity to the Will of God as his characteristic virtue. ..." (SOR REMEDIOS ACEDO, *Declaración* en: *Causa Beatificationis. Acta Processus Ordinarii* II, 566-660).

558 "In preaching and celebrating the Holy Mass, especially in saying the words, 'Lord, I am not worthy'...it was evident that he was in possession of and penetrated by a profound spirit of faith." (MARÍA DEL CARMEN IGLESIAS, *C. Beatificationis—Declaraciones* II, 589).

yen,[559] watching the sheep. In the measure that he deepened his knowledge of theology and of the word of God, his understanding of the critical role of Mary in the history of salvation was enriched. We recall his Marian meditations with the people every Saturday, and his presentations to those same people on the mysteries of Mary and on the Magnificat, a biblical theme developed by Fr. Javier, which was scarcely treated in those days. In his Marian devotion there is a privileged place for Our Lady of Perpetual Help, the mother who accompanies him on popular missions.

Fr. Isidro Posado, one of the confreres in the community in Cuenca, reveals to us characteristics of Fr. Javier accessible only to someone who has shared with him what had come to maturity in Javier's life and the everyday aspects of religious life. Fr. Posado would have viewed these things free from any suspicion of heroism or mythification:

He was regarded as both knowledgeable and pious. He kept busy writing, being spiritual director for nuns, and preaching...No blame could be placed on him by any confrere in the Congregation in the way he related to them... He had a great deal of love for the religious habit,[560] he esteemed it very much. He was one enamored of St. Alphonsus, and I remember having heard him say many times, referring to the habit: "I want them to bury me in it"...I never saw him, never heard him complain about anything, even though he had his trials, and no small ones either. He never neglected his meditation ever, or the rosary, or his examen;[561] in short, he lived the life in community...I believe that he was never moved by any purely human motivation, but only by the divine. I never saw him miss the daily examen; he was a slave to his religious duties, and his duties to the community...He was very charitable with everyone. If, for example, he saw some confrere sad about something, he would give him a little word, advice or a "spiritual nosegay." It was the same with the people. He was very self-sacrificing, he had very much

---

559 Translator's note: the little town in Navarre where he grew up.

560 Translator's note: the phrase "love for the religious habit" here has the meaning "love for the religious life."

561 Translator's note: Until the 1960s, each Redemptorist community had a short period before the midday meal in which the members examined their conduct in view of points taken from the morning meditation.

patience. He was always taking care of the sick, seeing to it as much that they were receiving proper attention, as well as reading a meditation to them, etc....I have no recollection that he gave any preference to any persons. I never saw him at a loss for how to deal with a situation; he was well balanced. And this, in spite of the fact, that he was nervous, by temperament...He was very affable and kind. I never saw him raise his voice. Man of philosophy that he was, he defended his opinions heat-edly, but without having any sort of rancor at all, no quibbling over small points, and he always put himself forward to help the most in need of help...He hardly even ate. He didn't bother very much about his clothing, as a good scientist would not. The concept that all of us had about him was that he was no lazy bones. He practiced all the mortifi-cations and penances prescribed by the Order. I never heard anything to the contrary that he faithfully observed and fulfilled his vows.

And this confrere resumes his spiritual profile by responding: "I think that charity was of utmost importance to him."[562] To come to the point of having love so great that he would permit it to transform his life into an offering was possible for him only because of a process of growing spiritu-ally and personally. This was a process that he began years before. Fr. José Machiñena, a countryman of his and companion in community for many

....

562 A spiritual directee of Fr. Gorosterratzu, Fermina Briones (Sr. Javiera), offers us this panoramic view of the interior life of Javier: *He was enthusiastic about his religious habit. Many times he told us: 'I would like to have you understand what it is to be a Redemptorist, and I need to give you a retreat for the sole purpose of having you see what it means to live only for God.' It is true that the poor Padre was not able to see fulfilled this hope of his and of ours. Faith. In his talks he insisted a lot to us that it was necessary to live only from faith, and he did the same in the confessional. And we were convinced, all of us, that he said it with all his heart, because it came out from his soul and because he lived it. Hope. He was completely supernatural and everything he did was for love of God and with confidence in Him. In charity. As much in talks as in spiritual direction he was totally on fire for God, and with regard to neighbor he conducted himself with everyone as a most tender Father caring for everyone that way in the spiritual as well as in the material. Justice. Not only was he just, he was most just; in fact, in one talk in a retreat he emphasized the virtue of justice a great deal, and he distinguished himself in its practice. He would tell us that when things were going well in a community and according to how God would want them to be going, this should not be passed over in silence but it should be said so that everyone knows it. Forti-tude. Yes, sir! When he thought that something was for God's glory or for the good of souls, he was always strong about that. He was never sullen nor irritable, but affable and kind with everyone. Temperance. He not only accepted mortifications and penances, but he sought them out, and even though he had chronic health conditions, he never bothered very much about them. He was most zealous and most fervent about observing the vows just as he was in fulfilling their obligations.* (FERMINA BRIONES, C. *Beatifica-tionis—Declaraciones* II, 594-595).

years, records testimony of this in the report of a canonical \ [563] In this process he had to also confront critics and the lack of understan g of some confreres in community. His spiritual direction for persons of t opposite sex appears to not have been looked upon well.[564] But from love a pardon his process of surrender to the Most Holy Redeemer culminate on the night of August 10 with his martyrdom on the road to the cemetery s

As we have said, Fr. Javier in his apostolic activity as a Redem brist missionary worked in favor of peace and reconciliation. In losing hi life he was faced with a different situation. He was condemned to death, or no reason and without the slightest support from the juridic institutio s of the Second Republic. Moreover, he knew that various companions fron that same seminary building had been assassinated with identical lack of legality in the previous days. And the news reached him that all of Cuenca was whispering in trembling tones: the first priestly victims had been the Redemptorists Ciriaco Olarte and Miguel Goñi. They surrendered their life on behalf of their Friend under the implacable sun of July 31 at a quarry near the Jucar River. In those moments, Fr. Javier and Br. Victoriano responded to the violence by uniting themselves in prayer, with the community of Mercerdarian Sisters, to plead to the Father on behalf of all, including those who very soon would lead them off to their death because they were the only ones who were left.

....

563 [Translator's note: according to Church law, periodically, the general government and the provincial government in religious orders must make visits to each community of the order and make a report about the community and each of its members.] Fr. Machiñena, provincial superior at the time, says about the subject of our biography in the report from the Canonical Visitation for the year 1935: "R. Fr. Javier Gorosterratzu: talented, of a serious character, but at the same time harsh and inclined to favor his own opinion....In these last years, he has behaved himself well." (AHGR 30150002,0034, 1)

564 In the report previously mentioned of Fr. Machiñena, he writes in the area for comments: "Sometimes of a doubtful moral character." (*Ib.*)

565 According to his death certificate written on August 14, 1936, Javier Gorosterratzu "died in the early hours of August 10, on the right side of the road which leads from the Capital to the Municipal Cemetery, as a consequence of a wound to the head" (*Certificate of Death of the Servant of God Javier Gorosterratzu Jaunarena, d.c.*)

Ciriaco Olarte as a young missionary

CHAPTER FIVE

Ciriaco Olarte Pérez de Mendiguren

Birth and First Years

Ciriaco Olarte Pérez de Mendiguren was born in Gomecha, a small town that belongs to the municipality of Vitoria,[566] at 8:30 AM[567] on February 8, 1893, at number 13 on the only street in the town. On that same day, he was baptized.[568] His parents, simple farmers, were Saturnino Olarte Ortiz de Urbina from Ali (Álava) and María Pilar Pérez de Mendiguren Marinda, native of Sendadiano (Álava). The fruit of their marriage was a large family of ten

---

566 Gomecha belonged to the municipality of Vitoria (Álava). [Translator's note: Álava is a province in the Basque Country.] In the middle of the nineteenth century it had fourteen houses, "a temperate and healthful climate…. A little stream that comes down from the mountains washes it in its waters" (Fr. MADOZ, *Diccionario Geográfico-Estadístico-Histórico de España y sus posesiones de Ultramar*, Vol. VIII [Madrid, 1847] 439-440). [Translator's note: The title of this work in English is translated: *Geographical-Statistical-Historical Geography of Spain and its Overseas Possessions.*]

567 Cf. REG. CIVIL DE VITORIA (ÁLAVA), Sec. 1.ª, T. 50, 26.

568 PARROQUIA DE LA TRANSFIGURACIÓN DE GOMECHA (ÁLAVA), *Libro de Bautismos* n.º II, f. 187.

' Ciriaco was the third of the siblings and the first of the boys. He
.rmed at age six at the nearby parish of Ariñez (Álava) on May 7,
,uring the pastoral visit of the Bishop of Vitoria, D. Ramón Fernán-
e Piérola.[570]

He spent his childhood in Gomecha. Years later, Ciriaco would retain
poetic memory of his small town: "I came into the world on the eighth of
February, 1893. My town of Gomecha is a small but beautiful place situated five kilometers[571] from the capital, Álava. It is sheltered by jagged and
extremely high mountains. The numerous groves of trees in the springtime
offer their tall tops fitted out in green to the towns that rest in the valley.
From the mountain groves descend fresh breezes which the inhabitants of
the towns enjoy with such tranquility that nothing in this world is capable
of disturbing that peace."[572]

But if Ciriaco keeps vivid memories of his homeland, memories of the
faith in which he grew up during his childhood move his heart even more:

But if the breezes which descend from the heights of the mountains are
fresh and pure, more fresh and more pure still is the faith which is passed
on from the elders. The patriotic breasts of those neighbors still keep the
faith. They are always ready to lose the blood from their own veins to
defend priests. They love religion and because they love it, they respect
the clergy and defend them. They love religion and because they love it,
they are happy when the number of priests grows. They are most happy

....

569 There were ten siblings: Ciriaco was the oldest of the boys. Older than he were two
Carmelite Sisters: Sebastiana (Carmen) in Saragossa, and Vicenta, in Tarazona. Younger were:
Doroteo, married and living in Gomecha; Avelino married in Vitoria; Román and Fernando, priests
incardinated in the Diocese of Bilbao and living there; Pilar and Eusebia, both single and residents
of Bilbao; Blanca, married in Barcelona. Cf. VALENTÍN HERNÁNDEZ, *Letter sent to Fr. Lucas*
Pérez; Gomecha (Álava), 28 August 1944 in: C. Beatificationis—Escritos sobre C. Olarte).

570 PARISH OF THE TRANSFIGURATION OF GOMECHA (ÁLAVA), *Book of Confir-*
mations n.º I, f. 1.

571 Translator's note: 5 kilometers is 3.1 miles.

572 C. OLARTE, *Curriculum vitae; Nava del Rey 1910-1911*, 1 en: C. *Beatificationis—Escritos.*
We shall make use of this autobiographical narration to reconstruct his childhood.

to offer their own sons to be consecrated to God and to the service of the Church.[573]

Ciriaco also offers us a portrait of the family in which he shows us his religious formation and the encouragement of vocation, which was given to him in the bosom of his family:

My parents were models in this regard. They knew that priests are despised, persecuted, that they have to suffer a hundred persecutions, but they were not afraid. They know that Jesus Christ himself instituted the priesthood. They know that the work of a priest is the work of God. And what danger can deter the one who walks with God, the one who interests himself in working with God? Illuminated by their faith, they see in a flash the sublimity of the priesthood. With their minds so enlightened and with their hearts full of faith, they promise to consecrate to God the first son who would be born to them. For this reason, no sooner was I born than they closed off the tendencies of natural parental love, which seemed to insist to them in the depths of their souls not to deprive themselves of a son. Instead, they repeat their offering all anew. They think of nothing except to give me the kind of upbringing that would correspond to the plans, which they had formed for me.[574]

His Carmelite sister, Sr. Carmen de la Santísima Trinidad, also will record after his death how the seed of a vocation was cultivated in a special way from his childhood in little Ciriaco, the first boy in the family: "From the moment he came into this world it seems that our Lord had chosen him for himself. Since the first two of us were girls, when God gave us as the third child a boy, our parents experienced immense joy, and the even greater thing is, in the midst of all that joy, parents and uncles and aunts offered him to God to become a priest." And further: "And it seems to me my supremely good parents loved him best of all."[575]

....

573 *Ib.,* 1-2.

574 *Ib.,* 2-3.

575 S. CARMEN DE LA SMA. TRINIDAD, *Letter sent to Fr. Lucas Pérez: Zaragoza, 24.9.1944;* 2, in: *C. Beatificationis - Escritos.* Cit. in D. DE FELIPE, *Nuevos Redentores* (Madrid, 1962) 164.

But his parents did not induce this vocational call in him, since Ciriaco will tell us:

I still did not understand what they were telling me, since I learned to speak only with difficulty, yet my mother asked me a thousand and one times what it was that I wanted to be in the future. This she asked me because she knew beforehand what I was going to answer. She had taught me to answer in these situations that I would be a priest. Since this idea was placed in my soul from such a tender age, it never left me, and in fact it grew greater every time I was asked. From when I was very small, I had a great inclination toward what is good.[576]

While Ciriaco was still a child, he lived out this vocational call through the desire of helping at Mass. He himself describes with humor the struggles he had with the heavy and ancient Latin missal, before the council, which had to be moved from place to place when celebrating Mass with one's back to the people: "Before I was five years old, I thought I had enough strength to be able to serve alone at the altar and I succeeded in getting them to let me serve alone. That's what they did. But the many times that I dropped the missal on my own head obliged another server to come bring it to me, nevertheless letting me do everything else. I did not stop attending Mass and helping until I was ten years old."[577] His family also contributed to making sure the call of God was not stifled and they took care that he would faithfully fulfill his obligations as an acolyte.

Time passed and far from disappearing, this desire to be a priest only increased and became more specific: he wanted to be a missionary priest. Among the different possibilities that were available to him, he chose the Congregation of the Most Holy Redeemer because it brought together both

....

576 C. OLARTE, *Currículum...*, 3.
577 *Ib.*, 4.

conditions: priesthood and missionary.[578] For this decision, God made use of a man from the same region, Fr. Leoncio López de Armentia,[579] who at the time was a young student: "They asked me if I wanted to be like R. Fr.[580] Armentia (who is from my town). Without hesitation, I said yes because they had told me something about the Redemptorists, and when I found out that they were committed to preaching missions, I didn't want to know anything further. 'I'm going with them,' I said and from that day until the day that I entered all questions about what Redemptorists do, how they dress, if they practice a lot of penances, simply left my mind."[581]

If the desire to be a priest was urgent in his life, once he made the decision to be a Redemptorist, this desire increased his impatience until he could live the Redemptorist life. He himself gives proof of these sentiments: "Impatiently I awaited the day of my entrance in the juvenate, which finally arrived on September 21, 1904."[582]

But he still had to get through the final proof of his readiness for the juvenate: D. Saturnino, a very sensible man, wanted to test the liberty of his son in making his vocational choice, and "on the way (to El Espino) my father asked me, to try me, if I wanted to go back home; a question which mortified me not a little, because I did not even have the remotest thought like that."[583]

....

578 *It was when I was about to celebrate my eleventh birthday that they asked me in earnest if I wanted to be a priest and, as always, I answered in the affirmative; without waiting for me to explain where I wanted to go, they each wanted to take me to a different place. My teacher wanted to take me to the Franciscans, and had even gone so far as to have everything ready to take me there. Some relatives that I had in Vitoria did everything possible for me to enter the seminary there. And although none of this was upsetting to my parents, they were not very much interested in it. I, for my part, wanted to be a religious, although I had not decided upon which order, because the ones that I knew were not dedicated to parish missions and what I wanted was to preach. So it was I found a difficulty with each order: one I didn't like because of the way they were dressed; others, because they were dedicated to begging; others, because they walked around without shoes. Finally, someone talked to me about the Redemptorists (Ib., 5-6).*

579 Leoncio López de Armentia López de Murga was born in Gomecha on September 12, 1886, professed his vows on September 8, 1905, was ordained to the priesthood September 10, 1910, and died in Santa Fe (Granada) on December 30, 1974.

580 [Translator's note: R.Fr. = Reverendo Padre]

581 C. OLARTE, *Curriculum...,* 6.

582 *Ib.,* 7. Cf. APRM. *Book of Admissions for the Juvenate in El Espino, 1904.*

583 C. OLARTE, *Curriculum...,* 7.

Years of Apostolic Formation: El Espino, Nava del Rey, and Astorga

Things were not easy in El Espino. Ciriaco himself confesses that studies were difficult for him—especially Latin, which was so important in that epoch. The situation even got to the point that his formators thought seriously about sending him home. Nevertheless, in those days he found propitious help in one of his younger professors, Fr. Gregorio San Román,[584] who had been ordained the year before. Fr. San Román discovered in the boy great strength of will for bettering himself and especially oratorical skills, a decisive foundation for a future missionary. He believed in him, he fended off the boy's being dismissed from the school, and he stood by his side to strengthen Ciriaco in the effort that the difficult path of studies involved. His efforts met a generous response on the part of Ciriaco and together they began the slow work of improvement and progress. In spite of the difficulties, Ciriaco came out ahead in the first-year course and his ability to improve was recognized by all.[585]

He still had to finish one course of preparation in El Espino and Ciriaco, together with his eight companions, was sent to the novitiate. There was fear that otherwise he could be called up to military service. On August 8, 1910, they took the train from Miranda de Ebro[586] and arrived in

---

584 Dionisio de Felipe, who knew Fr. Ciriaco quite well, since he was two classes below him, also had Fr. San Román as a professor. He describes Fr. San Román this way: "...all the students loved him as a mother." And about the years in El Espino with Ciriaco: "He was not brilliant in studies, because he did not have great talent nor did he enjoy one of those great capacities for memory such as those capable of reciting from memory the Roman emperors or the Visigoth kings....Instead, he was pious, respectful and diligent: he could always be seen with his elbows on his desk and his head between his hands and he was moreover well-organized, tidy, curious and as sharp as a tack" (D. DE FELIPE, 165-166).

585 *In El Espino I encountered a fair amount of difficulty in studies, but I had the ability to give speeches well and this got Fr. San Román (my professor) enthused. It moved him to do all possible to get me successfully through the studies, a thing which he managed to do, thanks to his efforts and to the determination I had to respond to his encouragement. When Fr. San Román saw me later take the courses without difficulty, he called me his pearl; he told me many times that it was thanks to him that I was in the juvenate, and it is true, because if he had not seen in me that quality for public speaking, together with the excellent desire of following his advice, there would have been nothing in the way of those wishing to dismiss me. The remainder of the juvenate I finished happily on August 8, 1910, at which time they sent me to the novitiate. When that was finished, without mishap, on September 8, 1911, I left for studies in Astorga.* (C. OLARTE, *Curriculum...*, 7).

586 Translator's note: Miranda de Ebro is a city on the River Ebro in the province of Burgos.

Medina del Campo[587] on August 9; in Nava del Rey he was reunited with the five companions who had finished all the courses in El Espino and who had arrived a few days before with the intention of preparing themselves for the novitiate year.[588] Directing the novitiate as master was Fr. Nicanor Mutiloa Irurita, a man of rich human and religious personality, who carried out appointments of high responsibility in the Congregation of the Most Holy Redeemer and in the Church.[589] Ciriaco was invested in the Redemptorist habit on September 8, 1910, at the age of seventeen years and seven months.[590] As a synthesis of the year, we offer the report written by the Fr. Master, in which he left us a record of the human, intellectual, and religious profile of Ciriaco:

He began his studies in September of 1904 and finished them in July of 1910. On September 8 of that same year he was invested in the Redemptorist habit and a year later he made his religious profession. His studies of rhetoric are delayed until after the novitiate so that he can be exempted from military service. He has robust health. The basis for his vocation—according to the testimony of Brother Olarte—is the salvation of his soul and the commitment to proclaim salvation and sanctification to others. Good and bad qualities: he has good talent; he is arrogant, on occasions flippant, frivolous and not always sincere. Pious, obedient, and condescending enough; after three months in the novitiate, he dedicated himself, with a great deal of gain as a result, to the interior life. Behavior in the novitiate: He gave himself to studies with seriousness and with great effort and his admirable progress is evidence

....

587 Translator's note: Medina del Campo is a town in the province of Valladolid, in farming country.

588 APRM. *Book of Chorist and Lay Postulants* I, n.º 248.

589 CF. D. DE FELIPE, *De hojalatero a Obispo* (Madrid, 1945). [Translator's note: The name of the book is *From Tinsmith to Bishop*; it is the life of Fr. Nicanor Mulitao, who was born in Pamplona in 1874. He joined the Redemptorists at age twenty-three. He had important assignments as a Redemptorist, including holding the office of provincial superior for nine years. He created four foundations in Spain and increased the number of Redemptorist missionaries working in Mexico, South America and Central America. He sent the first Redemptorist missionaries to China. He was appointed bishop of Barbastro, Spain, by Pope Pius XI in 1921. Seven years later he became bishop of Tarazona, Spain. He died in 1946.]

590 APRM. *Liber primus inscriptionis vestium mutationis choristarum (1866-1934),* año 1910 n.º CCXXIV.

of it all. As can be deduced from what was said before, he was negligent in the modification of his interior and exterior life; in everything else, he was exemplary. Expectations for the future: Good religious and gives promise of being an excellent missionary.[591]

The year passed without anything shocking happening, and Ciriaco professed his religious vows on September 8, 1911.[592] With vows recently made, Br. Ciriaco Olarte and his companions were transferred from Nava del Rey to Astorga to begin higher studies previous to priesthood. As we said, Ciriaco began novitiate a year before normal to avoid military service;[593] for this reason, they had to do the course in rhetoric before philosophy.

The situation of the Redemptorist major seminary had changed with respect to the style implanted by the French founders, characterized by seriousness and by an iron discipline. The prefect of students, Fr. Victoriano

....

591 AHGR 30150009, 0451. The report concludes with a favorable vote from the master and the provincial.

592 *Ego, Ciriacus (Olarte), e pago Gomecha, provintia alavae, novitius Congregationis Ssmi. Redemptoris, hac die 8 septembris 1911, Nativitati B. Mariae Virgini sacra, in hoc collegio Sanctae Theresiae de Iesu, in civitate Navae Regis, inter manus multum R.Fr. Nicanoris Mutiloa, Magister Novitiorum, secundum Regulam nostram, et ad tenorem Privilegiorum nostrorum, sponte nuncupavi Vota simplicia Paupertatis, Castitatis et Obedientiae, una cum Voto et Juramento perseverantia ad mortem usque in praefata Congregatione, praesente tota Communitate, praesertim Patribus Salvatore Fernandez et Casto Calvo. Ego, Ciriacus Olarte, manu propia. Ego, Salvator Fernández, praesens adfui. Ego, Casto Calvo Rodrigo, praesens adfui. Ego, Nicanor Mutiloa, Novitiorum Magister ex facultate a Rectore.*

Majore mihi concessa, praefatum adolescentem ad oblationem admissi, in cujus fidem propia manu subscribo. Nicanor Mutiloa (signed and witnessed) (APRM. *Liber secundus inscriptionis Professionis Religiosae Perpetuae in Congregatione SS. Redemptoris of the Province of Madrid CSSR, in the year 1911*, n.º 195). [Translator's note: The above Latin inscription reads: "I, Ciriaco (Olarte), from the village of Gomecha, province of Álava, a novice in the Congregation of the Most Holy Redeemer, on this 8th day of September, 1911, on the feast of the Nativity of the Blessed Virgin Mary, in this formation community of St.Teresa of Jesus, in the city of Nava del Rey, under the guidance of R.Fr. Nicanor Mutiloa, Master of Novices, according to our Rule, and in line with our Privileges, I have taken of my own free will the simple Vows of Poverty, Chastity and Obedience, together with the Vow and Oath of Perseverance until death, in the aforesaid Congregation, in the presence of the whole Community, in particular before Frs. Salvador Fernández and Casto Calvo. I, Ciriaco Olarte, sign in my own hand. I, Salvador Fernández, attending. I, Nicanor Mutiloa, Master of Novices, by a faculty conceded to me by the Rector Major, have admitted to profession the aforesaid young man, of whose faithfulness I subscribe with my own hand. Nicanor Mutiloa"].

593 On September 9, 1912, the newly professed arrived in Astorga to follow their studies. "The thirteen of them formed two classes: The first six [Jerónimo, Díez, Benito, Posado, Bocos and Otero] are studying philosophy. The last seven Rhetoric [Olarte, Cudeiro, Munárriz, Caso, Villalunga, Cordero and Arbilla; they did not study this course in El Espino because of the law of Military Service. There was common recreation" (*Crónica de Astorga* III, 19).

Miguel Sánchez, describes the environment of the Studendate in a report sent to Rome in 1912: "Among them the spirit of the Congregation reigns—simplicity, piety, fraternal charity, the love of studies, and the observance of the Rule. A certain flippancy is to be noted and, in many of the students, an inclination to less serious and useful studies, especially in favor of reading literary works, although not dangerous ones."[594]

In the exams of 1912, Ciriaco received grades that can be expected of a person of not very bright intelligence, but driven by a determined will to overcome.[595] He suffered this difficulty in studies throughout his theology years. In spite of everything, his personality, characterized by openness, spontaneity, his great sense of humor, and his capacity for exaggeration—consciously put on as playful—gave him another kind of intelligence necessary for his missionary dedication, as were his social abilities. But these were not always understood by his formators, who interpreted them in a negative way, qualifying them as "flippant, frivolous, not always sincere and not very spiritual."[596] One of his companions, Fr. Dionisio de Felipe, offers us this profile of him:

> He became a deacon, a responsibility that he carried out with absolute competence and the complete confidence of his superiors. His personality was open, happy, and enthusiastic. He possessed a great power of attraction because of his friendliness and because of the nobility of his heart. He had a physical constitution like rubber: he enjoyed an agility and endurance without being in athletic competition. Nevertheless, his

....

594 AHGR 30150007, 0017-23.

595 The grades ranged from 10 to 20: Rhetoric, 17; Speech, 15; Grammar, 17; History, 17; Greek, 17; French, 19; Algebra, 16 (AHGR 30150007, 0017). In the philosophy courses, he never got higher than a 13; in Church history, 14; in dogmatic theology, "good"; in sacred Scripture and Hebrew language, "mediocre," as also in canon law, moral theology, and ascetical theology.

596 Fr. Nicanor Mulitao gives this view of Br. Ciriaco Olarte which, with slight differences, he maintained to the end: "He has little talent (mediocre); he does not seem very supernatural. He enjoys good health." The report from the following year, Ciriaco's first year of philosophy, is a little fuller and offers a positive vision for the future: "He has mediocre talent; but I think that he will be able to handle the whole course of studies, although with difficulty, and begin those leading to Holy Orders. Although he does not seem very spiritual, he is a good person and seems able, in his character, to carry out apostolic ministry effectively. He comes across as fairly sure in his vocation. He enjoys good health" (*Ib.*). Later reports remained along the same lines, with a few variations.

height was average: approximately 1.66 meters.[597] In spite of all that was said, at bottom he was serious, reflective, and pious. In high school, he won all the honors and had the best grades for behavior. Once beyond that level of education, those who were not able to gain such honors tend to have an Olympic-size disdain for those who do. He experienced happy moments as well as emotional setbacks...He had a spontaneous tendency toward exaggeration, so that it was not strange that when he resided in Andalusia[598] he wrote to his family that people there took him for Andalusian:[599] he threw out more unproven claims than they did, and in that sense, he said he had the audacity to speak two hours without uttering a single truth. Where he was more splendid was in his charity. When it came to chores, as much when he was a student as when he was a priest, he took on himself the more difficult ones and even assumed responsibility for part of the work of people less able. It would be said that he was made of steel: flexible and vibrant, without getting broken. On mountain excursions during the Studendate, he took on the heaviest baggage and even still he alleviated of our burden those of us who were weaker. This was done in such a natural and cordial way, that no one gave it any importance. He did not settle for practicing charity; he became elegant in his charity. And thus, he habituated himself in virtue: without posturing, almost covering it up.[600]

In July 1917, the culminating moment arrived of ordination to the priesthood. It was set for the July 25, the feast of St. James, but the bishop of Astorga, Msgr. Antonio Senso Lázaro, was in the middle of doing the pastoral visit of the diocese. The superior went to find him and arranged with the prelate the day and place most convenient for everyone. On July

....

597 Translator's note: this would be about 5 feet 5 inches, which was the average height of men in Spain in the 1920s.

598 Translator's note: Andalusia is the southernmost region of Spain, consisting of seven provinces.

599 Translator's note: Some anthropologists describe the tendency of Andalusian men to exaggerate their masculinity as "hypermasculinity," for one example of a supposed spontaneous exaggeration in Andalusians.

600 D. DE FELIPE, 166-167.

25 those who were going to be ordained left for Villafranca del Bierzo.[601] Fr. Rector, Fr. Gómez and Fr. Reoyo, professor of moral theology, accompanied them. The train arrived three hours late and Fr. Gómez returned to Astorga. In Villafranca they stayed at the one-of-a-kind monastery of the Vincentian Fathers, who took great care of them. On July 26, they received the subdiaconate; on the day following, the diaconate; and on Sunday, July 29, they were ordained priests in the Monastery of the Annunciation. The ceremony in its solemnity was so simple with such a family atmosphere about it that the house chronicle mentions it only in passing: "[July 25] The future second year moralists[602] left this morning for Villafranca, since our Prelate happens to be there, to be ordained subdeacons, deacons, and priests on the 26th, 27th, and 29th, respectively. On Sunday, July 29, the whole community went to the parlor at the end of evening recreation.[603] Every heart was full of holy joy. We had the happiness of congratulating the new priests and of receiving their first blessing."[604]

Ciriaco Olarte remained in Astorga one more year, along with his classmates, to finish his studies. On July 25, 1918, the community of Astorga prepared a farewell party for them, after which Ciriaco left for new missionary horizons.[605]

....

601 Translator's note: Villafranca del Bierzo is a Galician-speaking municipality in the province of León which began in the 700s as a rest stop on the Camino del Santiago.

602 Translator's note: The four years of theology were divided between two years of dogmatic theology and two years of moral theology. The moral theology was intended to prepare the seminarians for hearing confessions.

603 Translator's note: Evening recreation was a period of conversation following supper.

604 APRM. *Student Chronicle of Astorga* II, 49. Cf. *Chronicle of the house of Astorga* III, 112. On the 30th "*Frs. Olarte and Munárriz sang their First Mass; there was kissing of the hand. At 8:30 AM, exams continued. During dinner, we celebrated with readings and songs and toasts to the newly ordained.* [Translator's note: In Spain, dinner is traditionally at 2 PM, though it seems it must have started earlier in this case.] *At 2:30 PM, exams continued.*" (*Crónica de Astorga* III, 114).

605 *The farewell to the young Fathers* [Translator's note: in Redemptorist circles the newly ordained priests in their fourth year of theology studies are called "young Fathers." In this case, they have just finished that last year of theology] *took place in the refectory: two compositions in prose and one in verse, the song* "Vivat" [Translator's note: "*Vivat in eternum*" is a song traditionally sung in Redemptorist gatherings as a toast to someone being celebrated for something; the words mean, "may he live forever!"] *and a toast; there was common recreation. Young Fathers Olarte and Gottau (an Argentinian) gave speeches in the refectory.*" (*Ib.*, 125).

First Missionary Stage

On July 27, 1918, Ciriaco Olarte left Astorga on his way to the monastery of Our Lady of El Espino, where he arrived the next day. It was his first community as a young priest, and he was to remain in it only a short time, since on November 10 he was sent to Nava del Rey,[606] where he arrived with another priest who had been in the seminary with him, Fr. Isidro Fernández Posado.

Nava del Rey formed part of the first apostolic phase of the life of Ciriaco Olarte. On Saturday, the November 14, he preached his first sermon in the church in honor of Mary. The chronicler does not pass over in silence this important event in the life of a missionary: "he occupies the holy cátedra for the first time."[607]

---

606 APRM. *Crónica del Jovenado del Espino* II, 72. 84.

607 APRM. *Crónica de Nava* II, 495. [Translator's note: *catedra* is Latin for "seat." In medieval times, teachers taught from a seated position; *cathedral* comes from the notion that the bishop sat and taught his congregation from his chair in his main church.]

Ciriaco Olarte Pérez de Mendiguren

As a young priest, he scarcely was to preach again until he finished his second novitiate.[608] The chronicle only records another two Saturday sermons, and two more to the Associates of the Holy Family. All these sermons took place in the Redemptorist house. The first apostolic foray was to the nearby town of Sieteiglesias (Valladolid) on November 22 "to say Mass in the oratory of a particular person on the anniversary of death of the son of said family.[609] He also spent November 23 there, saying Mass both days in that town."[610]

Ciriaco was in the community of Nava del Rey on February 4, 1919, when the draft lottery for recruits took place. These men were to go to Africa.[611] The various relocations of young priests were the fruit of different strategies that they were following to free these young missionaries from military service. For example, those sent to Africa were not inducted because substitutes were found for them. Ciriaco was sent to La Coruña, and so he left Nava del Rey on February 3 and was due in Astorga, so that he could continue on February 7 to La Coruña with Fr. Guerra and the prefect of students "so that they could scout out the territory and see if they could be free from having to go into the army." Things didn't go as quickly as the superiors wished. On February 12, Father prefect returned, but left behind the two recruits "in the hospital—without being able to leave for any reason—until on February 28 they were to be examined."[612]

On March 7 Fr. Olarte concluded his brief stay in La Coruña and, free from military service, returned to Nava del Rey.[613] The chronicle records his arrival with affection and humor:

....

608 Translator's note: The second novitiate was a period of six months to a year in which the young priest under the guidance of a veteran preacher wrote the bulk of the sermons he was to preach.

609 Translator's note: It was the custom, especially of wealthier Spanish families, to have private chapels in the home. It was at one of these that Fr. Olarte celebrated a Mass.

610 *Ib.,* 495. 500. 501.

611 More precise details are found in the chronicle of Astorga because various students resided there who were eligible for the draft: Fr. Cipriano Zabalza had to go to Laracha [Translator's note: Laracha is a municipality of the Galician province of Coruña]; Fr. Miguel Reymóndez, Melilla [Translator's note: Melilla is a Spanish city on the north coast of Africa]; Frs. Gumersindo C. Guerra and Ciriaco Olarte remained in Spain.

612 APRM. *Crónica del Estudiantado de Astorga* II, 28.

613 *Ib.,* 79.

After thirty-four days of compulsory living in the barracks, which he did in La Coruña, R. Fr. Olarte has returned to the bosom of this community—anxious, as it should be, for his presence. The community finds itself finally satisfied with the result that the beloved Father has come out of the situation absolutely exempt from military service. Nevertheless, he has not gotten out of it completely. He ended up posting sentinel the entire night of his arrival here at this house, since it was impossible for him to get anyone's attention as he stood outside calling. The community had already retired for the night.[614]

With the problem of his military service resolved, he had to begin the last trial on his road to becoming a missionary. "On May 4," the chronicle records, "Frs. Posado, Olarte, and Munárriz left for second novitiate."[615] Their destination was the community in Cuenca. During the months that second novitiate continued, the young priests were initiated in missionary work accompanied by an experienced Father, and under his direction they wrote and learned from memory the sermons on the great themes of the Redemptorist popular mission. When this period was finished in October 1919, Fr. Ciriaco Olarte remained as a full community member of San Felipe de Cuenca and as a missionary for a period of a year.[616]

Missionary in Mexico

The young Spanish province (canonically erected in 1900)[617] very soon set sail for new foundations outside its borders: Puerto Rico in 1886, Portugal in 1903, and Mexico in 1908. Once the foundation in the Antilles[618] failed in 1900, the Redemptorists fixed their gaze on Mexico, sending Frs. Pedro Pérez and Baldomero del Pozo to found it. Very soon they opened commu-

....

614 APRM. *Crónica de Nava* II, 500.

615 *Ib.,* 501.

616 The disappearance of documents during the religious persecution prevents us from giving more details from this period, which lasted one year.

617 Translator's note: For a religious institute, such as a monastery or convent, to be officially recognized by the Church, canon law says it must meet certain requirements, such as having a superior that was legitimately appointed, the consent of the local bishop and they are to have a chapel on their premises. With those conditions met, it is recognized by Church law officially as a community.

618 Translator's note: Puerto Rico; Spain gave up its colonies in Cuba, Puerto Rico, and the Philippines as a result of its defeat in the Spanish-American War in 1898.

nities in Veracruz, Cuernavaca, and Mexico City, then in Monterrey, Oaxaca, and Puebla. But peace did not last very long. From 1911 through 1920 the thousand and one revolutions occurred.[619] The Constitution of 1917 was particularly hostile toward the Church: it prohibited religious from living a life in community and demanded that only Mexicans serve as priests. This put a stop to sending to Mexico new missionaries, and a few returned to Spain. Those who remained in Mexico changed their names, accepted the fact that they would work undercover, and slowly there was a return to a certain kind of normalcy.[620]

In this moment of apparent calm, the provincial, Fr. Nicanor Mutiloa, visited the vice-province of Mexico (1920) and "while still in the Mexican Republic Fr. Mutiloa prepared for the expedition of Fathers and Brothers who needed to reinforce that vice-province."[621] After his return to Spain, he communicated on October 6 that he sent thirteen new Fathers and Brothers. Among them was Fr. Ciriaco Olarte, who at the time was in the community in Cuenca. The chronicle in Madrid details that on October 16, 1920, "this month there is continual coming and going of the Fathers and Brothers assigned to Mexico. All come through this house and, God be praised, all are of good spirits and happy. They are finally going to work for

....

619 Translator's note: from 1911-1920 there were a series of skirmishes in which various leaders proclaimed themselves head of the Mexican government.

620 L. MIGUÉLEZ, *Los Redentoristas. Veinte lecturas sobre su historia* (México, 1986) 214. (Translator's note: the book's name is *The Redemptorists. Twenty readings on their history*)

621 *Anales* VII, 386-387. The provincial left from Mexico on August 2, 1920. *La Historia de los Redentoristas del Cono Norte de America Latina* [Translator's note: the name of the book in English is: *The History of the Redemptorists of the Northern Cone of Latin America*] gathers together more data about the arrival in Mexico of that large group of Redemptorists which came to support the persecuted vice-province of Mexico: "On his return to Spain Fr. Mutiloa prepared an abundant expedition of missionaries for Mexico. They came in three groups: the first, on November 16, was made up of Frs. Lesmes Miguel Palacios, Valentín García Vilorio, Gregorio Arboleda and Antonio Rey plus Brs. Donato Estarrona and Mateo Alcalde. The second group, on the 12th of December, 1920, consisted of Frs. José Pardo, Félix Ruiz de Samaniego, Francisco Padilla, Benito González Pérez, Ciriaco Olarte and Gumersindo Cerdeiriña Guerra. On December 26, Frs. Teodomiro González Ronda, Eulogio Cocina Peláez and Antonio Fuertes, plus Brs. Tomás Megas and Julian Sagüez arrived. If in the year 1919 the vice-province had lost seventeen confreres through death, through their return to Europe or for some other cause, in December 1920 they quickly replaced them: (J. COLÓN-R. BOLAÑOS, *Historia de los Misioneros Redentoristas en el Cono Norte de América Latina y el Caribe* [Santafé de Bogotá, 1995] 225-226).

God and the good of souls in other lands! We honor them as best as we can and it is for this purpose that those from the other residence come here."[622]

Because it was a big group and because of the difficult political situation in Mexico, they took a great deal of time to prepare their passports and obtain their new secular clothes.[623] Nor did it seem like a good idea that all would go together. Departures were arranged from three different seaports. Fr. Ciriaco Olarte and his five companions left Madrid on October 22 to embark from Valencia on the October 26. The confreres in the capital city on the Turia River[624] received them with open arms. The Oblate Sisters of the Most Holy Redeemer also went out of their way for the departure and saw to the detail of offering a beautiful Valencian paella[625] to the community and to the missionaries being sent to Mexico.

From the day they arrived until October 26, when they embarked from Grao[626] there was recreation at table and great feasting. We went with them everywhere, even to a town in the district of La Huerta, because various ones of them on a number of occasions wanted to go to Godella to visit the Oblates (of the Most Holy Redeemer) and to see the environs of Valencia. And the superior spared no expense nor skimped in honoring them...On October 26 all the Fathers from the house went to wish them farewell onboard the ship Monserrat...All the travelers left Valencia very pleased and happy.[627]

....

622 *Crónica de Madrid-PS*, Año 1918, 104.

623 Translator's note: The Mexican constitution of 1917 was extremely anticlerical, including prohibiting the wearing of clerical garb outside a church.

624 Translator's note: Valencia.

625 Translator's note: Paella is a traditional dish in Valencia. It consists of chicken or seafood on a bed of rice, resembling something like a pizza.

626 Translator's note: Grao is a maritime district in the city of Valencia.

627 APRM. *Crónica de Valencia* I, 144.

C. Olarte in Mexico

Those who were sent forth went content to finally fulfill their missionary dreams. Father provincial wrote to Rome about the departure of the three missionary groups and added: "They are all content to be on their way. Blessed be God! Since they have to go incognito it has been very difficult to make all the arrangements; but the evident providential care of the good God has been clear. We shall see if there yet may be something that comes up."[628] Fr. Ciriaco shared in those same missionary sentiments and said so in a letter addressed to his sister, Sr. Carmen de la Trinidad, two days before leaving:

> *Valencia, October 24, 1920*
> *My dear sister:*
>
> *I only have a few minutes; I want to make use of them to communicate with you what perhaps you already know from the family. I have been designated for assignment to Mexico. I am going most willingly because I know that God calls me and he wants me to work in the Mexican region for his glory. I stopped in at home: our parents are feeling my departure very strongly. I consoled them as best as possible and they told me that they remain committed to the will of God.*
>
> *You well know the obedience which we religious ought to practice, and you need to continue encouraging them and consoling them. Never tell them you are sad about this news because that would serve no purpose except to heighten their pain.*
>
> *It has pained me a lot to not be able to say goodbye to you; but it wasn't possible. You can't imagine the cartwheels I've had to do in Madrid to arrange for my passport...If I had had a free day, I would have visited you, my two sisters, as it was my hope. Offer to God the pain my leaving is causing you and don't fail to pray for me.*
>
> *It is an honor for me that the superiors have chosen me for the mission in Mexico, and even though I have deep feelings about leaving Spain, I thank God for this opportunity.*
>
> *I have been in Valencia since Friday in order to leave on the 26th. Here the consul has been favorable to us. There are fifteen of us going out from various points of departure.*

---

628 AHGR 30150001, 1546.

As far as my address, I can't tell you that just yet, because I don't know which house I am being sent to: I will let you know from there. I shall be fine there; say so to our parents and don't lose hope for seeing me again in Spain.

Goodbye, then, until God wishes, and if God wishes until heaven, goodbye until heaven.

Ciriaco Olarte

Fr.S.—I offer my greetings to your community and I ask their most fervent prayers. Especially I tell my chaplain[629] *that she needs to be that now more than ever before.*[630]

There is not much data remaining about the apostolic work of Fr. Ciriaco Olarte in Mexico. From the letters sent to his family we can put together a map of his assignments. In 1922 he is in Oaxaca, from where he writes his sister on May 1, 1923,[631] and tells her about the situation of religious persecution they are are experiencing, though he comforts her by telling her that he is happy. In January 1924, he is listed among the members of the community in Puebla,[632] and in September 1925 he is sent to Monterrey. On December 12, 1925, he writes to his sister, telling her about the intense work that community has, as much in preaching as in the confessional.[633] Although we have little facts about Ciriaco, "for six years, whether from Oaxaca or Puebla or Monterrey he dedicated himself, body and soul, to the Mexican religious field. There was no sermon in which he did not make the people burst into tears, a companion on the mission testified."[634] On June 22, 1926, he writes again explaining that the work is overwhelming, with

----

629 Translator's note: It is not very clear who this "chaplain" is, except that the form of the word is feminine, indicating one of the sisters.

630 C. OLARTE, *Letter to his sister, Carmen: Valencia, 24-10-1920*, in: *C. Beatificationis - Escritos.*

631 Cf. C. OLARTE, *Letter sent to his sister, Carmen: Oaxaca, 1-5-1923*, in: *Ib.*

632 D. DE FELIPE, 167.

633 Cf. C. OLARTE, *Letter to his sister, Carmen: Monterrey, 12-12-1925*, in: *C. Beatificationis —Escritos.*

634 D. RUIZ, *De camino 3, 7* (APRM. Mártires 0400124).

preaching, retreats, and confessions. Also, he informs them that a systematic religious persecution against the Church in Mexico has begun.

The persecution became more violent, reaching its zenith between 1926 and 1929, when President Plutarco E. Calles applied with rigor the antireligious legislation of 1917.[635] As a result, the revolution of Calles obliged him to leave Mexico in August 1926, together with eight companions, who embarked for Spain from Veracruz.[636] The last time that he ascended a pulpit in Mexico was in the community in Monterrey, parish of Los Dolores. Fr. José Campos records it in his book *Por un México mejor*:[637]

Among the sacred services of that difficult year 1926, I remember the novena of Dolores, which Fr. Olarte preached. The Mass of the novena was celebrated at seven in which numerous faithful went to Communion. But the moment in which enthusiasm exceeded all limits was during the evening. By four [the parish church of] Dolores was jam-packed and the service did not start until six. The service consisted of a sung rosary, novena, sermon, and benediction with the Most Blessed Sacrament. It's true that the church of Dolores, at maximum, could not hold more than a thousand persons, but one has to count those who saw it necessary to attend in the vestibule and in the doorways.

It was a splendid feast day. A "flood" of people came to Dolores. If at any time this metaphor [flood] is clearly applicable, it certainly was this time. The last event ended with singing a solemn Salve Regina in Spanish.[638] People left the church with the indescribable nostalgia that great memories bring. Obedience sent Fr. Olarte to his mother country as a precaution. The superiors did not know that they were having him flee from Herod, only to fall into the hands of Pilate. There he would die a martyr during the civil war. None of us who remained in Mexico lost our lives; but he, what could he do? He was told to go, so he went.[639]

....

635 Cf. J. CAMPOS, *Por un México mejor. Cincuenta Años de Historia Redentorista* (México, 1959) -unedited-.

636 J. COLÓN-R. BOLAÑOS, *o. c.*, 266. The part of this history referring to the province of Mexico was produced by Fr. Lauerentino Miguélez.

637 Translator's note: The title in English is "Toward a Better Mexico."

638 Translator's note: the Salve, Regina is a prayer directed to Mary.

639 Testimony of Fr. Antonio R. Cabello, superior of Monterrey: cit. J. CAMPOS, *o. c.*, 36.

On September 12, 1926, he disembarked in La Coruña together with Fr. Cándido Fernández Peña. Four days later, on September 16, he again wrote his sister giving her the news about his arrival: "I came, as the majority of Spanish priests have done, because the situation there is impossible. The president does not give in in any way in his campaign against religion and we were living in private homes, since churches have been declared property of the nation and since July 30 no priest ministers in public. Since things are in that state, it seemed more prudent that we come back, thinking a time will come for returning."[640]

Missionary in Galicia: La Coruña (1926-1928)

The community in La Coruña received the deported missionaries from Mexico and immediately incorporated them in community life: "September 12, Frs. Ciriaco Olarte and Cándido (Fernández) Peña were assigned to this community. They have come from Mexico because of the religious persecution."[641]

The community in La Coruña was very new since it had been in existence for only one year when Fr. Olarte became a member. The founders of the community had arrived in January 1925. There was neither house nor church. The first chapel was inaugurated on the feast of the Assumption in 1926. Fr. Olarte did not get to know the church during his stay in Galicia.[642] From the first, the community in La Coruña made missionary evangelization in rural Galicia a priority. This was in total faithfulness to the charism of the Congregation founded by St. Alphonsus. There Fr. Ciriaco would have very intense missionary activity.

He had his debut in the ministry of preaching eight days after joining the community. He gave a sermon in Culleredo (La Coruña).[643] On October 4, he began his first mission in San Miguel de Reinante[644] and from

....

640 C. OLARTE, *Letter to his sister,: Coruña, 16-9-1926*, in: C. *Beatificationis—Escritos*.

641 *Crónica de La Coruña* I, 21.

642 R. TELLERÍA, *Un instituto misionero* (Madrid, 1932) 422-423. [Translator's note: before going to Mexico.]

643 Translator's note: Culleredo is a bedroom community of La Coruña in northwestern Spain. Its population mostly works in the service industry, so it is made up of the working poor.

644 Translator's note: a city known for its white-sand beaches in the province of Lugo.

the November 2 to November 13 he gave a mission in Escairón (Lugo).[645] March was an intensely missionary month.[646] Because Fr. Olarte himself is the chronicler for the community, we get from the chronicle a greater amount of detail about the apostolic work of this time. Crossing over into the year 1927, we find Fr. Olarte again in Lugo, in Santiago de Reinante, beginning on March 6 a seven-day preaching event to prepare the people to fulfill their Easter obligation, which then became a mission. Everyone in the town attended.[647] In the company of Fr. Nuin, he returned to San Miguel de Reinante for the renewal of a mission that had been preached there earlier.[648] Fr. Ciriaco continued on by himself preaching in San Pedro de Benquerencia[649] and in San Cosme de Barreiros (Lugo).[650] There was total success in the attendance. The chronicler records the results in his favor: "Only when they[651] saw that Fr. Olarte was carrying out the work of three

....

645 Translator's note: Escairón is a small town in the province of Lugo, consisting of under a thousand people. They celebrate a fiesta on the eighth and nineteenth of every month.

646 He started it with a renewal in San Miguel de Reinante (Lugo). [Translator's note: While a number of religious orders and congregations give parish missions, the "renewal" was an innovation of St. Alphonsus, the founder of the Redemptorists. Missionaries who had preached a mission would return to the town after a period of time to renew the spirit of conversion brought about by their first visit.] He ended March with the novena of the Seven Sorrows in Melide (La Coruña). [Translator's note: Melinda is a town going back to the tenth century and is along *el Camino de Santiago*.] On April 14, he went to Mugardos (La Coruña) to preach during Holy Week. [Translator's note: Mugardos is a city on the Atlantic Ocean known for its specialty dish, octopus.] Ten days later, he was in Montemayor doing a mission renewal (*Crónica de La Coruña I, 30 and 33*).

647 Fr. Nicasio Nuin accompanied Fr. Olarte on a number of the following apostolic works. Since Fr. Nuin was younger, Fr. Olarte was appointed superior for the mission. The population consisted of 925 inhabitants. About 650 went to Communion, and they set up in the parish the Apostolate of Prayer at the request of the pastor (*Ib., 36*).

648 "A very large number of people came, from the first day on. The eternal truths were preached, divided into two distinct days: 'The gates of hell,' covered the many ways in which the people in this parish could be lost. They did a renewal of baptismal promises and on two days they prayed the Way of the Cross. Las Damas de Perpetual Socorro were persevering. [Translator's note: "the Ladies of Perpetual Help" was a lay association for women.] It was an association started during the mission and new ladies joined up. At the end of this mission renewal, the Fathers were called to Mondoñedo by the Bishop and were honored with a banquet. [Translator's note: Mondoñedo is the cathedral city of this diocese, where the bishop lives.] He showed himself very pleased with our work and desirous that we continue working in his diocese" (*Ib., 37*).

649 Translator's note: San Pedro de Benquerencia is one of eight civil "parishes" which comprise the municipality of Benquerencia, a coastal town.

650 Translator's note: San Cosme is another civil parish in the city of Barreiros, province of Lugo, in the region of Galicia, along the Atlantic coast.

651 Translator's note: the members of his Redemptorist community.

missionaries...did others wish to join in, and they telegraphed the house for the superior to give those orders." It wasn't possible, however, for others to join him since the superior had accepted other work. The missionary remained very content with the work he had done and the response in both towns. About San Cosme he writes: "The people en masse accompanied the Father calling him 'our missionary.' The preaching, as in the previous assignment, was a commentary each day on 'the deeds of a Christian.'"[652] In April, we find him preaching in Montemayor (La Coruña) and in May he did so in Rodís (Lugo), where the pastor of Soján (La Coruña) called the Redemptorists "to preach a Triduum in honor of the Sacred Heart of Jesus, and a retreat for thirty-two students that he has in his school."[653] In May and June, Olarte and his other companions went to preach the Mission in Curtis and Baños de Curtis (La Coruña). In these places, the atmosphere was difficult because the influence of the new ideologies was notable.[654]

On August 25 he and Fr. Lorenzo began the mission in Canduas (La Coruña): "It came out fairly well, against all the prognostications that had been made against it....At our welcome, there were, after we had waited a long time, only thirteen children, four women, and a man who was walking along the highway and then walked with us. On the first two days there were no sermons, because of the lack of people. On the following days, things were more encouraging."[655] In October, the same missionaries

....

652 In San Pedro, with 800 inhabitants, the event began March 20 and continued for three days: "In that time he was able to do the work of a mission in the preparation of children and preaching to older people," as special groups. Some 1,200 Communions were distributed, which means that people from other nearby parishes attended. San Cosme had 1,500 inhabitants. That event began on the afternoon of the 23rd; 2,125 Communions were distributed. "The Pastor remained enthusiastic and perhaps was convinced to have a mission the following October" (*Ib.*, 38).

653 Without saying the number of inhabitants of Montemayor, they distributed 1,200 Communions. From May 1-7, Olarte and Nuin were in Rodís. As in the previous case, they only mention the 3,000 Communions. In Soján, the feast day was the eleventh, and there were Masses from six o'clock in the morning until noon, with help from other priests, and they distributed 1,311 Communions. The missionary chronicler describes himself as happy (*Ib.,40*).

654 "None of its effects are knowable. The renewal was a waste of time, since there were neither confessions nor General Communions, with the exception of some 120 children. Field work had something to do with it" (*Ib.,43*).

655 The mission went from August 25 to September 6, 1927. The place was in the diocese of Santiago, with 140 households. "185 children went to Communion and 1020 adults." Although some went to Communion several times, it is evident that a number of different townships took part (*Ib.,47*).

arrived in Guitíriz (Lugo). The mission was well presented, but did not have good results, because of the work that had to be done in the fields, such as the harvest, among other reasons. The farmers could not attend, though they regretted it. At the end of October, they gave a mission in the parish of Castrofeito (La Coruña): "The people were free from their business and the whole parish showed up."[656] The month of November, especially in Galicia, is reserved for the dead. For this reason, all the missionaries of the community dedicated themselves to this reality, as much in the house chapel as outside. Fr. Olarte preached various sermons on the souls of the dead outside of the house from November 21 to November 23. In the first days of January 1928, he preached the renewal in Barreiros, and without interruption, the seven-day renewal in Benquerencia (Lugo). Attendance was small and the men very reluctant to go to confession.[657] The first days of February he gave a mission in San Isidro de Montes (Pontevedra): "It is a parish of faith which loves the Church, but it is very neglected by its pastor. They came morning and night with real enthusiasm."[658] From March 4 to March 11 he preached the seven-day renewal in San Miguel. This was the last during his stay in Galicia. From then on, until he was transferred to Madrid, he did apostolic work of a lesser intensity in diverse provinces.[659]

Besides the missions, Fr. Olarte took part in the house chores in the community and in the work in the small chapel that the Redemptorists maintained, and which little by little became more frequented. By 1928, the community and the chapel had acquired a certain popularity. One Sunday a month, they had devotions to the Virgin of Perpetual Help. All the priests

....

656 Olarte the Chronicler realistically writes: "The mission was beneficial for a hundred summer vacationers and for forty households of the village" (Ib.,50).

657 Ib., 59.

658 February 8-11. 800 Inhabitants. 600 Communions were distributed (Ib., 62).

659 Holy Week in Mugardos; Triduum in honor of the Sacred Heart in Area and in San José in the city. In May, the Novena to Mary Auxiliadora for the Salesians and a sermon in Oliveira for the Daughters of Mary; he returned in June to give a sermon on the Sacred Heart. In the same month of June the chronicle records that he gave seven more sermons in various places, including the city [Translator's note: "The city" refers to Madrid.] July is a month that is not very conducive to preaching popular missions, due to the harvest. Fr. Olarte went off to Santiago to preach a sermon on St. Mary Magdalene and another on St. Martha in a residence for the elderly in La Coruña. On August 2, the feast of St. Alphonsus, he preached a sermon in honor of the saint. On September 9, he preached a sermon on the rosary in Camouco [Translator's note: a town in Lugo, Galicia.] (cf. Ib., 66. 69. 71. 72).

in the community took turns in leading them.[660] In the month of November, a ten-day event in honor of the deceased was celebrated.[661] By March 1928, they organized for the first time a retreat for workers and servants, which had a good turnout. In the distribution of community services in 1927, Fr. Olarte was assigned the task of hospitality and welcome to visitors, and also the writing of the chronicle. In 1928, Fr. Olarte had the duties of prefect of the sick[662] and continued as chronicler.

An audience which he discovered at this time, and which he would continue to care for frequently in his apostolic ministry, was the girls in residence with the Oblate Sisters of the Most Holy Redeemer. He preached to them on numerous occasions. This was difficult work because these young ladies mostly came out of a world of prostitution and marginalization. Fr. Olarte was one of those who learned to understand the option for the poor as a core belief, in clear response to the call of the Lord to bring freedom to the oppressed: "tax collectors and prostitutes are entering the kingdom of God before you."[663] He could identify with Fr. Javier Gorosterratzu in this evangelical refinement. Both understood the words of Antonia de la Misericordia[664] when she said, "These girls are the grace of God."[665]

....

660 The chronicle gives the detail that in February 1927 Fr. Olarte preached in the community chapel on the Sunday dedicated to the archconfraternity of Perpetual Help (*Ib.,* 29).

661 *Ib.,* 51.

662 Translator's note: his job was to take care of ailing members of the Redemptorist community in the house.

663 Translator's note: this refers to the words of the Lord in Matthew 21:31.

664 Translator's note: Venerable Antonia María de Oviedo y Schönthal was born in Lausanne, Switzerland, to Antonio de Oviedo and Susan Schönthal on March 16, 1822. She became the governess for the daughters of the reigning Queen Maria Christine de Bourbon and served in this capacity from 1848 through 1860. Archbishop José Benito Serra of Madrid was dedicated to the Hospital de San Juan de Dios, which saw to the needs of sick prostitutes. He attempted to recruit Antonia for this work but met resistance from her. He invited her to go with him to a location in the park where these women frequently met. From this experience, beginning in 1863, she committed herself to working with the prostitutes. She had as her motto in dealing with them the expression: "If you find all the doors closed to you, I will open one for you." In 1870, she founded the Congregation of the Oblate Sisters of the Most Holy Redeemer, which today has spread throughout various countries. She also founded a school in Argentina (Colegio Schönthal), which trains its students to fight human trafficking. Madre Antonia died in 1898 in Madrid.

665 M. ANTONIA DE LA MISERICORDIA, *Carta dirigida a Mª de la Presentación, Oblata: Madrid, 28-11-1874,* in: OBLATAS DEL SANTÍSIMO REDENTOR, *Biblioteca Histórica OSR I* (Madrid, 1981) 298.

On to La Villa y Corte (1929-1932) [666]
with a Stop in Cuenca (1928-1929)

On September 17, "Fr. Olarte left with a ticket for Madrid. Transferred"[667] with the community in Cuenca as his destination. He knew the city and the missionary field entrusted to that community, since he spent time there when he was to be sent to Mexico. In the time that he has in this city of La Mancha[668] he preaches missions with Fr. Casto Calvo, assigned to the community of Madrid, Perpetual Socorro.[669]

From November 28 until December 8, Frs. Calvo and Olarte gave missions in Vigastro (Alicante),[670] the diocese of Orihuela: "Enthusiasm describes the mood during this mission from the very first moments and without diminishment until its conclusion; to encapsulate everything that could be said or pondered in extensive pages: the inner disposition of the people were echoed in their outward expressions, with scarcely a single soul who did not fulfill the obligation of going to confession, taking advantage of the fervor in the many and wonderful general Communions and in the final procession with the cross."[671] On the next day, they began the mission in Molins (Alicante).[672]

We have no more information about his stay in Cuenca. On September 4, 1929,[673] he arrived at his destination, the community of Perpetuo Socorro in Madrid. He will stay there until August 15, 1932. During his stay in la Villa y Corte, he will engage in intense missionary activity which will send him all over the peninsula of Spain. This time could be considered the golden age of his apostolic life, although the appearance of the Second

....

666 Translator's note: This nickname for Madrid was learned by every school child in Madrid. It harkens back to the historical fact that King Felipe II in 1561 transferred the royal court to Madrid, which had the effect of building up the city into the capital of the country, which it is today.

667 *Ib.,* 75.

668 Translator's note: La Mancha is the geographical area from south of Madrid to the hills of Cuenca.

669 Translator's note: the community of Perpetuo Socorro in Madrid.

670 Translator's note: Vigastro, also written "Bigastro," is a small community in the province of Alicante in the southeastern region of Valencia.

671 *Crónica de Madrid-PS,* año 1928, 407.

672 Diocese of Orihuela. The mission was "so much like the previous one that it could be said it was the same in the response it got and the fruit it bore" (*Ib.*)

673 *Ib.,* 444.

Republic frustrated his apostolic projects. It made the giving of popular missions impossible and obliged him to seek asylum for a while in Nava del Rey.

But until political events turned totally hostile, Fr. Olarte gave himself completely to the apostolic life. From November 9-20, 1929, Frs. Ortiz and Olarte preached a mission in the civil parish of San Juan,[674] in the diocese of Orihuela and the province of Alicante. On November 20, they began a new mission in the civil parish of Aguas de Busot,[675] in the same diocese and province: "The mission was excellent, from every point of view. The church was full every day and the city officials were there, giving a good example. There were conversions of people who had not been to confession for twenty years, according to what people said." And without stopping, the two missionaries began a mission in Busot: "The maximum turnout: complete attendance in the morning and evening. Beautiful procession of children and the Hijas de María.[676] More men went to confession than in previous missions."[677]

After the Christmas break, from February to April 1930, he took up the missionary work again in the diocese of Orihuela with his new companion in the work, Fr. Crescencio Ortiz. They began in Formentera,[678] where they had "good attendance." He considered it "a pious parish. There were 896 Communions (something rare for here), 200 just of men." Also in February they brought the mission to Almoradí.[679] The chronicle is more concise: "Great mission."[680] They gave a mission in March in Hondón de los Frailes (Alicante):[681] "A parish cold to the faith in extreme. The men go off to work

....

674 Translator's note: a beach city, today loaded with resorts.

675 Translator's note: this town is now simply called "Aguas," since Busot is another city nearby.

676 Translator's note: the *Hijas de María*, or "Daughters of Mary," is an association of young laywomen dedicated to honoring Mary, following her example and evangelizing their own families.

677 *Ib.,* 455-456. 458.

678 Translator's note: Formentera is a beautiful island in the Mediterranean belonging to the Spanish autonomous region of the Balearic Islands.

679 Translator's note: a town in the province of Alicante on Spain's famous Costa Blanca.

680 *Ib.,* 479.

681 Translator's note: The name of the town distinguishes it from nearby Hondón de las Balsas and Hondón de las Nieves. The name *de los frailes* indicates a monastery was located in the area at one time.

in Orán[682] and France, where they leave the faith and bring home the practice of using contraceptives, among other things they smuggle in. We placed a big mission cross on the hill. There were some 350 Communions." The mission in Aspe[683] was considered "good: with days of excellent attendance. We placed a big mission cross on the mountain. 2,900 Communions." On March 25, they brought the mission to Petrel,[684] qualified as "medium. The immense majority are socialists. 700 Communions."[685] The missionaries are beginning to notice the political tensions, and on April 3 they return to Madrid because it was not possible to preach a mission in Elda[686] "because of the disturbances caused by the labor strike."[687]

Again, on the April 23, Frs. Ortiz and Olarte went off to give a mission in Yecla,[688] accompanied by Fr. Calvo, since the town had 32,000 inhabitants. One of the missionaries wrote the letter which the chronicle records, in which the situation of an increasingly confrontational Spain reveals itself, a year before the founding of the Republic:

The mission is having excellent results. We were welcomed by a river of people who, between nudging each other and trampling one another, swept us along into the immense parish church with its three spacious naves. To judge only by the number of scapulars ordered, there were more than 2,000 children and teachers. Attendance is overwhelming. We preach four times a day, and meet with the various associations. There have been not a few difficulties: there is a center for workers, whom

....

682 Translator's note: a city in northwest Algeria, ruled from the sixteenth to eighteenth centuries by the Spanish.

683 Translator's note: Aspe is a town about twenty-five kilometers from the city of Alicante. Aspe is famous for growing grapes, which traditionally are eaten all across Spain at the stroke of midnight each New Year's Eve. As the clock strikes twelve, one grape is eaten for each strike of the clock.

684 Translator's note: this town of the province of Alicante is called "Petrer" in the Valencian dialect. It hosts one of the region's many "Moors and Christians" festivals each year, a commemoration of how the Muslims conquered the town and later Christians took it back.

685 *Hondón de los Frailes*, 900 inhabitants, 300 confessions. *Aspe*, 10,000 inhabitants y 2,000 confessions. *Petrel*, 4,000 inhabitants, 400 confessions (*Ib.*, 479-480).

686 Translator's note: companion town to Petrel. The two form one urban area.

687 Translator's note: Elda has a long history of labor and student strikes.

688 Translator's note: Yecla is a town in the autonomous region of Murcia in southeastern Spain. It has three important industries: raising goats and producing lumber and wine.

*the bishop prohibits from calling themselves by the title of "Catholic";
moreover, there are 5,000 socialists who throw their weight a great deal
on the opposite side. They have written and voiced a lot and promise
demonstrations and debates. There were 20,000 Communions.*[689]

While great social tension increased in Madrid, Frs. Martínez and
Olarte returned to their parish missions. They began the one in Cazalilla
(Jaén)[690] on October 22, where the whole town turned out to welcome
them.[691] On November 10, they changed locations and began a mission in
Collado Villalba (Madrid).[692] The numbers for attendance and participa-
tion in this mission were very poor.[693]

The partial or total collapse of this last mission was viewed as made
up for by the apostolic joys which the same missionaries experienced in
the province and diocese of León.[694] On November 21, 1930, they began
the mission in the little town of Matadeón.[695] Not only did all the townspeople participate, but many people also from neighboring towns, "as they
came to hear about the uncommon zeal and eloquence of the missionaries.

....

689 *Ib.,* 480.

690 Translator's note: Cazalilla is a very small town in south-central Spain, in the province of
Jaén, region of Andalusia.

691 "Attendance, fairly good. There were good confessions. The young people gave the unexpected good example of all coming forward to go to confession and Communion. The fruit of it all,
given the reality of the town, has to be considered very good. The Lord Bishop attended on the last
day, had Confirmations and presided over the procession with the Holy Cross" (*Ib.,* 500-501).

692 Translator's note: Collado Villalba is a community about 39 kilometers (twenty-four
miles) from central Madrid.

693 "People, indifferent. Other than the dozen people in town for summer vacation, only
another dozen townspeople came to the morning event. Attendance in the evening was about 150
people. Adult men were conspicuous in their absence; about 20 young people went to confession.
And yet this place has the reputation of being the best town in the surrounding area...and even in
the province! Ordinarily two men fulfill their Easter obligation, and these are foreigners" (*Ib.,* 501).

694 Translator's note: The province of León in the northwest of Spain has a long history in
which Fernando III, King of Castille, became King also of León in the 1200s.

695 Translator's note: Matadeón de los Oteros is a very small town of less than 400 inhabitants.

1,620 Communions."[696] The same thing happened in Valdesaz de los Oteros, where the mission began on December 1 and where the inhabitants from nearby towns also came to attend.[697] The cycle of missions in León concluded in Gusendos de los Oteros, whose population, the chronicle says, "are people of faith, moderate...and all this without a doubt because they are a town far from any center of corruption."[698] Ciriaco wrote in a letter to his sister, Carmen, about his experience of missions in Jaén, Madrid, and León. In the letter, he decried the lack of faith in certain areas of Spain, and especially emphasized the tie between prayer and the mission, which he was constantly asking for and desiring:

On the morning of December 23, I found myself in Madrid, after almost two months on the missions. In this series of missions it was my lot to experience a variety of climates, both in the sense of weather and also in the sense of "spirit." I began on October 20 in the province of Jaén, mild climate, but cold spirits; nevertheless, considering how things usually are there, I dare call what came about as almost a triumph. The authorities and five officers of the Civil Guard were out in front for the general Communion. In the middle of November, I gave a mission in a town near Madrid. Very little was accomplished; but I tell you because you know these people. Last year the Jesuits wanted to give a mission in another nearby town and they could not even get the chil-

....

696 The chronicle takes these phrases from a letter from the pastor, D. Antidio Villafañe: "The four towns of Matadeón, Santa María, San Pedro, and Fontanil came out to welcome the missionary priests outside the town of Matadeón, with the children waving their little flags and the people cheering the padres. The four towns and also many from Matallana and Santa Cristina de Valmadrigal attended each event of the mission with total punctuality. Each day there was a greater influx of people from outside of town as they came to hear about the uncommon zeal and eloquence of the missionaries. Inhabitants, 380. Days, 10. Confessions, 340" (*Ib.*, 501).

697 "The nearby towns came to this mission: Quintanilla and Fuentes, this last one with full participation with its pastor at the head in the mornings and afternoons in that the events were at 8:30 in the morning and 3:30 in the afternoon. Complete attendance and devotion, everyone went to confession. Inhabitants, 350. Days, 10. Confessions, 320" (*Ib.*, 501).

698 "People came from neighboring towns. There was not a single person who had not gone to confession. These are people of faith, moderate...and all this without a doubt because they are a town far from any center of corruption. The town council and the Daughters of Mary lauded the Fathers. The parish priests from the neighboring towns all came to the mission. The parish priest gave words of thanks to everyone on the day of the departure of the missionaries with an ágape of brotherhood. [Translator's note: a reception with "finger food."] His toast left everyone with the taste of sincere charity. Inhabitants, 250. Days, 10. Confessions, 320" (*Ib.*, 502).

dren to come together. They came to the conclusion they would have to abandon the mission. On the November 20 we went on to the province of León, where the situation was reversed. The climate is very cold, but souls are warmer. The work done ended up being consoling. In all the missions in this part of León only two remain to be given. So you see something works. But more than anything else, prayer is needed. It is the watering without which the plant withers. I hope that a beneficent shower of prayers is never lacking to my work. Such prayer comes from the fervor of your holy community. All the women, but especially those who were my former chaplains and the one for the new year, can see that there is a great deal of untilled ground which can only loosen up with a great torrent of prayer. I commend myself, then, to the prayers of your community. Without those, there will be no fruit coming from my work.[699]

During his stay in Madrid Fr. Ciriaco Olarte, besides his work as a mission preacher, took part in service to the Redemptorist community by being the librarian for the house library and helped with the services in the church connected to the community as well as doing sporadic preaching.[700]

In 1931, tensions began. On February 14, "the political unrest is deep-

....

699 C. OLARTE, *Letter to his sister,*: s. f., in: *C. Beatificationis—Escritos*. Although the letter has no date, by its content it pertains to Christmas 1930.

700 The chronicle records the various sermons that he preached in the shrine of Perpetual Help, in the capital Madrid as well as outside of it: in Ciempozuelos, to the girls in residence with the Oblates of the Most Holy Redeemer [Translator's note: these were girls who were rescued from a life of prostitution.] From May 9 to 14, 1930, he preached at the shrine of Our Lady of Estíbaliz, his home area. On the twenty-fifth he left for the Zamoran town of Aldea del Fresno for the talk on fulfilling the Easter duty.

ening to the point that Governor Berenguer[701] resigned."[702] Curiously, during this time, Fr. Olarte spent very few days in Madrid. From February 9 through February 18, he gave a retreat to the young women residents of the Oblates of Vitoria;[703] from February 21 to March 2, he preached a mission in Totanes (Toledo);[704] from March 13 to 23 he gave a mission in the parish of Santiago[705] in Valladolid.[706] When this mission was finished, he went to the farm, which is located in El Plantío, Heredia Espínola, an enclave in Madrid, to prepare its sixty inhabitants for the reception of the sacraments during the Easter celebration.[707]

....

701 Translator's note: Dámaso Berenguer y Fuste was a Cuban-born general who was appointed by King Alfonso XIII to form a government after the forced resignation of the dictator Rafael Sanchez-Guerra in 1930.

702 The reason, according to the chronicler, was the ostensive motive that the liberals, republicans and socialists on the left had withdrawn from the elections to the Cortes Generales set for the first of March. [Translator's note: The Cortes Generales was the legislature of the government of Spain at the time.] "Such is the guarantee of a great revolution, so they say (and it is seen that way in some quarters) that the convents and churches are designated on their exteriors with red or black marks to indicate which have to be attacked and which have to be attacked and burned." April 16: "Sánchez Guerra, who was given the responsibility of forming a new government, went to the jail where leaders of past revolts were (A. Zamora, M. Maura, L. Caballero, etc.) to ask them to join him as his new cabinet." [Translator's note: Rafael Sánchez-Guerra was president of the Second Republic throughout the Civil War in Spain; Niceto Alcalá-Zamora y Torrez served briefly as the first prime minister of the Second Spanish Republic and then became its president from 1931 to 1936; Miguel Maura Gamazo was Minister of the Interior in the Second Spanish Republic, who failed to take action against mobs who were burning churches and convents; Francisco Largo Caballero was a union leader and activist for socialism.] April 17:) "Failure for S.Guerra in his attempt to form a cabinet from the monarchists, republicans and socialists." The chronicler does not mention the declaration of the republic on April 14. He does so on April 15: "We removed the main objects of value from the house and put into effect an order received previously from the provincial, that is, to wear secular clothing. Since yesterday, with the declaration of the Republic, we are living through a time of terror: disorder, insolence, and shots out in the streets, the wave of the revolution!" April 16: "A tailor is coming to take measurements for our suits. Our 'somatenistas' are being told to disarm and to hand in their weapons" (Crónica de Madrid-PS, for the year 1931, 508). [Translator's note: the *somatanistas* were a Catalonian para-police force. They were a band of civilians who had grouped together for self-protection and for the protection of Catalonia. Under the dictatorship of General Miguel Primo de Rivera (1923-1930) this group was spread throughout Spain. It was dissolved in 1931 under the Second Republic, except in rural Catalonia.]

703 Translator's note: capital and seat of government of the autonomous Basque region; the Oblates of the Most Holy Redeemer had a house for former prostitutes there.

704 "They had not had a mission for fifty years. Many of the men had not been to confession for seventeen to twenty years. They eagerly welcomed the mission and responded well" (*Ib.*, 521).

705 Translator's note: St. James.

706 He preached this mission with Fr. Esprit. "An isolated, Gypsy neighborhood. The Church has difficulty making headway here."

707 *Ib.*, 521.

The proclamation of the Second Republic on April 14, 1931, happened as Fr. Olarte was preaching the word of God to the people of Mascaraque (Toledo). Although news of the proclamation reached them and the atmosphere became tense, the circumstances did not have an impact on the celebration of the events of the mission.[708] In the following weeks, there were anticlerical demonstrations.[709] On May 11, the provincial called together all the members of Madrid-Perpetuo Socorro and gave them orders to dress in secular garb and to go underground in homes of friends "because of the risk we could run if the Communist rabble, boys aided by girls, continue to burn the monasteries and convents, a hellish work begun in midmorning at la Flor (the Jesuits)[710] and continued on....The day before, the Communists assigned the intentions of the friars to those of *ABC*.[711] They tried to attack the edition of May 10 under the pretext of the first Monarchic Assembly presided over by Luca de Tena![712] Indeed, a mutiny against the assembly exploded on Calle de Alcalá."[713]

....

708 Fr. Luis Fernández de Retana, companion to Fr. Olarte and superior of the mission to Mascaraque, tells us about it: "The people are indifferent to their faith and rude, and they have forgotten their religious duties. Not even fifty men and women have fulfilled their Easter duties. Yet the whole population of the place attended the mission en masse. In the middle of the mission, the Second Republic was proclaimed. The mission peacefully continued its agenda of processions and talks, in spite of the disorder produced everywhere. There were some overdue confessions: one of sixty years; many since the people had married; and a very great many from the last mission (eighteen years ago). Everyone was happy with it. One night, anticipating possible disorders by people who came from the outside against the priests, the men and boys came to the church armed with clubs and truncheons" (*Ib.*, 512).

709 From May 11 to 13, there were demonstrations of an anticlerical type "with attacks, sackings, and burning of churches, monasteries and convents, which the public law enforcement did not care to fend off because both the Civil Guard and the fire-fighters stood off in the distance. More than a hundred religious buildings were totally or partially destroyed" (V. CÁRCEL ORTÍ, *La persecución religiosa en España durante la Segunda República (1931-1939)* [Madrid, 1990] 107-108). [Translator's note: *The Religious Persecution in Spain during the Second Republic (1931-1939)*.]

710 Translator's note: the Jesuit house was located on Calle La Flor in Madrid and was burned down by a mob on May 10, 1931.

711 Translator's note: *ABC* is a major national daily newspaper in Spain that has conservative leanings.

712 Translator's note: A group of young right-wing monarchists assembled in an apartment on Calle Alcalá in Madrid on May 10, 1931, and called themselves the Independent Monarchist Circle. They played the *Marcha Real*, the national anthem associated with the monarchy, over a gramophone out the window. The monarchy had been defeated by the Second Republic and many people in nearby Retiro Park heard the provocative anthem and rushed as a mob against the offices of the newspaper *ABC*, published by Juan Luca de Tena. They blamed him for the provocation.

713 *Crónica de Madrid-PS,* año 1931, 513-514.

The chronicle of the community of Perpetuo Socorro gives an account of the events that they lived through in Madrid during those days of agitation and tension on the streets. For May 12 the chronicler writes:

They continue to burn monasteries and convents; the troops bivouacked on the streets have orders to let them do it. Religious men and women, more or less dressed in secular clothing, are fleeing the cloisters. And our church remains closed to services. [For May 13 we read:] Since as of this afternoon an alert has been going around that a decree of expulsion and dissolution of religious orders has been given, it has made us rush back to the house to collect as much as we can of our things and to carry them to private homes. The alarm and shock are worse than on May 11! [The next day, May 14:] Fugitives from our communities in Granada and Carmona have arrived.

In view of the insecurity of the situation, the refugees from these communities and other members of Perpetuo Socorro in Madrid began to flee to more secure places.

Fr. Ciriaco Olarte, who had been preaching the novena to Our Lady of Perpetual Help to the Oblates in Vitoria since May 9, went on to the community in El Espino on May 18. He did not return to Madrid until June 8. The chronicle gives these details: "He was caught by the events of May while he was preaching the novena in Vitoria. He took refuge in El Espino, where he made a retreat. Then he went back to Vitoria to preach at a first Mass."[714] The elections for the legislature were set for June 28, 1931. Previously, on June 21, he concluded the novena to Our Lady of Perpetual Help "with a completely full church. Because of the political circumstances and the rain, the procession with the Virgin took place inside the church." On June 26, news was more dramatic: "Because of the probable disturbances by the mobs who are plotting attacks against the persons of religious and attacks of vandalism against the monasteries and convents, father provincial has decided...to remove part of the personnel from Madrid. And so,

....

714 *Ib.,* 514-516.

last night, Frs. Bayón and Olarte left for Nava del Rey."[715]

Ciriaco returned to Madrid again on August 4, 1931. He took care of the ministry in the church shrine, and preached various Saturday worship services and Masses on Sundays. On September 23, Fr. Olarte once again preached a retreat to the young women residents of the Oblates (Ciempozuelos).

On October 13, 1931, discussion of the famous Article 24 of the proposed Constitution began in the Congress of Deputies. It was known as "the religious question," and occasioned a great debate. The point that was most discussed and which raised the most passions was that with reference to the expulsion of religious orders and the confiscation of their property, especially as to how it applied to the Jesuits. Besides the three vows common to all religious orders, they had another vow—obedience to a foreign authority.[716] The churches and convents had to be guarded by patrols of Catholics from possible violence. On October 14, the chronicle indicates that "the famous Article 24" was approved "in a mild form. An atheistic demonstration against religious. Beatings, fright, running through the streets. The compatriots Sánchez and Alonso go to the city center to observe what is happening. At night, with the same motive, Olarte and Bayón go out between ten o'clock and midnight. Everything is tranquil."[717]

Because of the political circumstances, Fr. Ciriaco Olarte preached little outside of the house through the end of 1931: a sermon on Christ the King for the Visitation Sisters, three days of retreat for the students of the Marists, a sermon on the Virgin Mary in the parish of Santa Rita (Carabanchel Bajo),[718] and a Triduum on defense of the faith in Valladolid.

....

715 "Fr. Hermosilla and Brs. Francisco and Estanislao to El Espino; Santamaría to Pamplona; Esprit to Ciemposuelos (to the Oblates). On the 27th, Fr. Abelda and Br. Santos go to Torrelodones, to a farm that belongs to Srs. Font and Serra, friends of Most Reverend Fr. Gil. There they will gather, along with three Fathers from the community of San Miguel, under the leadership of Fr. Gil" (*Ib.*, 517). The chronicle of Nava del Rey (II, 202) records how, on June 27, Frs. Bayón and Olarte arrived to form part of the community for now.

716 Translator's note: The Jesuits take the vows of poverty, chastity and obedience, which are common to all religious orders. They also take a vow of obedience to the pope.

717 *Chronicle of Madrid-PS, for the year* 1931, 517. In both cases, the chronicler gives only the last name of the members of the community who go out to observe the situation, without mentioning that they are priests.

718 Translator's note: Carabanchel Bajo is a district in the southwestern suburbs of Madrid where this parish is located. There is also a reform school by that name in the same district.

In 1932, the name of Fr. Ciriaco Olarte appears in the list of members of the community of Madrid-Perpetuo Socorro, with his well-known services of being missionary and librarian. For some months, he helped especially in the religious services at the shrine. Outside of the house, he went to preach that or the other sermon or retreats for the Oblates and their young women refugees.[719] The number of missions was to diminish greatly. Missions were preached only in Garganta de los Montes and its district El Cuadrón[720] (province of Madrid).[721] He preached some services at which parishioners could fulfill their Easter obligations in the townships of el Plantío,[722] Villalba, and Valdaracete.[723]

In June 1932, more than a year had passed since the proclamation of the Republic. In spite of the problems which we have mentioned above, the chronicle records on June 3 this data which in itself shows how the Christian people accepted the Republic and the insertion of its supreme symbol[724] in the normality of daily life and the expression of faith: "The Heart of Jesus. In the streets unusual energy produced by the never-before-seen spectacle of banners hung on almost every balcony; and also there were those with

....

719 In the month of January, the chronicle only notes a sermon on la Virgen del Pilar and the usual retreat for the young women of the Oblates of Ciempozuelos. [Translator's note: "The Virgin of el Pilar" is the name given to the Blessed Virgin who, tradition taught, had appeared to the apostle James in Saragossa, Spain. Mary is the patroness of Spain under this title.] In February it does not mention any extraordinary activity, which means he limited himself to working in the library and to long hours in the confessional. In March he preached one Sunday and several Saturday services in the church, plus six Lenten talks to the Congregation of the Immaculate in Martínez Campos; he shared with Fr. Alonso the preaching of the mission-novena of St. Joseph (cf. *Ib.*, 539).

720 Translator's note: El Cuadrón is a small area with thirty inhabitants located in the city of Garganta de los Montes in a valley in the north of the civil province of Madrid.

721 "People of the sierra; cold morally and physically. It seems they are becoming more and more indifferent to their faith. When we asked two good men who had attended the mission why they did not want to go to confession, they answered, 'We will do whatever you want, but as to confession...no.' In El Cuadrón, almost everyone is illiterate; children learn doctrine from their parents or grandparents. These are two towns that are connected to each other." He preached the mission with Fr. Renuncio (*Ib.*, 546). The two conjoined towns where they gave the mission had 500 inhabitants. The mission lasted ten days; 195 people went to confession (*Ib.*, 547).

722 April 20-25, 1932. Sixty-seven people took part; there was an equal number of confessions (*Ib.*, 547).

723 200 people attended in Valdaracete and there were 150 confessions (*Ib.*, 547). [Translator's note: the three places mentioned—El Plantío, Villalba, and Valdarecete—are all municipalities in the civil province of Madrid.]

724 Translator's note: the flag of the Second Republic.

the flag of the Republic and the Sacred Heart at its center. The church is completely full, with confessions and Communions without number."[725]

On August 15, 1932, Fr. Ciriaco Olarte was assigned to Granada, closing this period of his life that he had spent in Madrid.

In the Lands of Andalusia: Granada (August 1932 to July 1933)

Fr. Olarte arrived in the city of the Alhambra on August 16, 1932. The atmosphere was very tense politically because of the pronouncement in Seville of General Sanjurjo on the night of August 10.[726] The workers responded with a general strike. As a precaution in view of these threats, in Granada the community had to sleep away from the house for a number of nights.[727] Nevertheless, they maintained services in the Church with caution; one of so many such paradoxical situations of the time.[728]

In 1932, the community in Granada was very reduced in personnel, due to the circumstances. This being the case, the superior, Fr. Miguel García Alonso, welcomed Ciriaco Olarte. Fr. Olarte began preaching in the southern lands on September 4: "Fr. Olarte made his passionate debut with the devotion to the Eucharistic Heart of Jesus; some 170 persons attended."[729]

....

725 *Ib.*, 543.

726 Translator's note: José Sanjurjo y Sacanell was a Lieutenant General and commander of the Spanish Civil Guard; he with other monarchists declared a rebellion against the Second Spanish Republic on August 10, 1932.

727 "The events of August 10 (1932) obliged the religious to sleep away from the house several nights. The churches of San Nicolás (the jewel of the Sixteenth Century) and the convent of La Divina Infantita in the Calle de San Antón were set afire and there were attempts to burn down Santa Paula and San Luís" (L. PÉREZ, *Los redentoristas en Granada 1879-1979. Historia corta de cien años largos*, 76) [Translator's Note: *The Redemptorists in Granada 1879-1979. A Short History of One-Hundred Long Years.*]

728 In August 1932, they distributed 6,000 Communions in the church, a number which kept growing in the following months until, in December, there were 6,940. In the first part of 1933, Communions increased considerably, reaching 9,750 in the month of June, the last month of June, the last month of Fr. Olarte's stay in Granada (cf. *Crónica de Granada* III, 470).

729 From the time of the arrival of Fr. Olarte the chronicle gives this summary: "We slept away from the house. On the 17th a new governor arrived, Mariano Joven, from Salamanca, founder of the Partido Radical Socialista and he went as Delegate to Cordova. [Translator's note: The Radical Socialist Party; Mariano Joven was a moderate Socialist concerned with the welfare of the poor, but the party he founded was intensely anticlerical] They agreed to stop the strike but would renew it on the 22nd if the prisoners were not released. We slept away from the house. At the last minute, they set free the Count of Guadiana. June 21, third Sunday, good attendance, maybe from 250 to 300 people. June 22nd, we spent the night in the house for only the third time since the night of June 10-11. There was no strike. But they announced it for the 24th. It did not happen then, either" (*Ib.*, 470).

As the review says, he remained faithful to his apostolic style of living and acting, a style well-known to all the Redemptorists of Spain and Mexico: passionate, ardent, dedicated, as if he had been born to preach to the masses, as his missionary trajectory now would testify.

They entrusted to him two tasks for the internal life of the community: he was responsible for welcoming guests and was substitute for the administrator of the community. He made ten days of retreat in the house, as the Rule prescribed to be done annually. Outside, he preached a week of retreat for the Sisters of the Pious Schools; in Bujalance (Cordova), a Triduum in honor of Christ the King; an homage to San Francisco in the church of La Encarnación; and two days of a novena in honor of Santa Teresa for the Discalced Carmelites, the sisters dear to him because of so many ties of affection.[730]

His journey to Cordova was his first contact with the atmosphere of Andalusia. On October 19, 1932, he wrote from Granada to his parents, brothers and sisters, and nephews and nieces in the Basque country. He described in the letter the new sensations and news he had about his missionary apostolate with reference to the scarcity of work due to the political situation:

It happens that I have come to the extremity of Spain...Everything here is very beautiful, though fairly ill-affected due to the times in which we live...In September, I spent ten days preaching a retreat in the province of Cordova. In my travels, I have been able to appreciate the immense riches, which these Andalusian territories produce. Olives are their principal harvest; and the oil, which it produces, would be sufficient to fill a river like the Zadorra.[731] This year the olives are full of oil, and even though they may lose some, nevertheless they hope for the best harvest known for many years. The wheat harvest also was most abundant, but I don't believe that the sale of the harvest was favorable to them. Also, the owners here are in a very bad way, having had to abandon their lands. The climate is spring-like, even though the nearby Sierra Nevada mountains are always covered with snow and tend to greet us

....

730 *Ib.,* 474.

731 Translator's note: The Zadorra is a tributary of the Ebro River in Basque Country.

with a little wind which reminds us of where it came from. The people are not bad, except for those who wish to be so and... (it is certain that they are many). On the fourteenth of this month I finished my retreat of ten days; and on the fifteenth and sixteenth I preached in the convent of the Discalced Carmelites of this city. From the twenty-eighth to the thirtieth I will preach a Triduum in our church for the feast of Christ the King. This house in Granada always has had plenty of work, but now it is not possible to do so much. Let us hope for better times.[732]

November was a cold month in Granada and there was political agitation in the city with gunshots, bombs, and firecrackers.[733] In December he participated in the eight-day event in honor of the Child Jesus in the shrine in Granada, and he also preached the novena in honor of the Immaculate Conception in the parishes of Santa Escolástica and San Cecilio, where he took the place of Fr. García Alonso on December 7-8. On the second Friday of December he did the same in Las Angustias[734] and finally he preached a retreat to the Carmelites in the *Granja*[735] *de María Luisa*, Armilla, Granada.[736]

On the December 16, 1932, Fr. Olarte wrote to his "unforgettable sister, Carmen." The year had been difficult because of the new political situation, so that the Redemptorist missionaries saw themselves obligated to limit their evangelization activities in the parish missions. The community of Granada was one of those that suffered the consequences of the political

....

732 C. OLARTE, *Letter to his family: Granada, 19-10-1932*, in: *C. Beatificationis—Escritos*.

733 "During this month we have had nights of shots, bombs and firecrackers, due to a strike connected with the revolution. They staged one strike in Santa Paula [Translator's note: was a sixteenth century convent that was turned into a hotel in the twentieth century] and another at [the convent of the nuns] of Zafra [Translator's note: the Convent of Santa Caterina de Siena of Zafra, originally built in the sixteenth century by the widow of Hernando de Zafra, secretary to King Ferdinand and Queen Isabela], among others, and for the second time at the same site at the home of the Count of Padul [Translator's note: The Count of Padul from 1924 through 1935 was Isidoro Pérez de Herrasti y Pérez de Herrasti, whose palace was located in the municipality of Padul in the civil province of Granada]" (*Crónica de Granada* III, 474).

734 Translator's note: Our Lady of Sorrows is the patroness of Granada; there is a basilica there with this title.

735 Translator's note: A *granja* is a working farm. This one was located in the Andalusian municipality of Armilla. "María Luisa" was a queen consort of Spain, married to Charles IV of Spain, from 1788 to 1808.

736 *Ib.*, 476.

situation more, as the statistics about missions and retreats reflect.[737] In spite of this, Fr. Olarte felt happy in Andalusia. There is no trace of nostalgia for having left Madrid and he gave himself to the apostolic work that was possible for him then: retreats and preaching in various churches and monasteries. In the letter not even the least hint of anger is to be found, not even a criticism of the circumstances. On the contrary, it overflows with confidence in the nearness and friendship of the presence of Christ, Christian hope in a future guided by Providence, the invitation for peace in the context of Christmas, tranquility and "holy joy even in the midst of major trials":

I believe that this year the Child Jesus will come with his hands full of goodies in order to relieve us from the bitter taste of past frights; so, it is necessary to go out to meet him well prepared and to ask for these gifts with a great deal of insistence and confidence. We need to recognize, nonetheless, that Jesus has not distanced himself from our side even for an instant. And for this reason, it is a lack of confidence and an offense to Jesus to become too frightened and lose confidence before the storm that has been let loose and surrounds us. If he is at our side, we shall not drown. I have had the opportunity to speak about this with different classes of women religious. Some have edified me greatly, because they have not spent even one single day worrying about what is happening. And when I told them that the next day they were going to kick them out, they replied calmly: on the one day that we still have, we are going to live out the Rule better than ever. And the day of that sad announcement has not come yet and it is to be hoped that it will never come. Others, on the other hand, have not had such serenity and have suffered a lot of anxiety for no reason, because the evil they were fearing has

---

737 Granada was always a missionary community. The number of missions varied according to the number of priests assigned to the community. In 1930, they preached thirty missions and twelve retreats; in 1931, 12-12; in 1932, 5-9; in 1933, 10-8; the number goes up for the next two years: 1934, 27-14; 1935, 23-19; and went down again during the war: 1936, 0-6; 1937, 9-6; 1938, 13-7; 1939, 26-21. Lucas Pérez (*Los redentoristas en Granada [1879 a 1979]*) [Translator's note: *The Redemptorists in Granada (1879-1979)*] notes in 1931: "The years of the Second Republic were difficult ones: 1931-1936; in 1931, the house and the shrine remained closed from May 11 to September 16 (Ib., 107, nota 1). In 1936, the year of the National Uprising, a great part of this zone remained in the hands of the Reds" (*Ib.*, 107, *nota* 2). [Translator's note: The National Uprising was the coup d'etat against the Second Republic which took place on July 17-18, 1936. It led into the Civil War.]

not happened and, unfortunately, they lost much of the recollection that they should have had instead of those worries....Will these cases be of some benefit to you? Think about the first, and...viva holy joy, even in the midst of the worst trials! I am preaching a retreat to the Discalced Carmelites in a village near Granada. I enjoy dealing with them, because all are most fervent and they don't think of anything except growing in holiness. In the two years that we have been bearing with persecution, they have not wanted to know about anything, saying that if they fulfill the will of God, God will watch over them. I have also dealt with the Carmelites of Granada and they have the same spirit of fervor. If I have to tell you the truth, I feel genuine satisfaction in dealing with the Carmelites, because everywhere I find them in the same spirit of fervor inherited from the Holy Mother.[738] I don't have a moment's rest. After preaching several series of retreats in the city and outside the city, I preached two novenas in honor of the Immaculate Conception, both at the same time, in two parishes of this city; after that, some sermons; and at present the aforementioned retreat to the Carmelites; then, the eight-day event in honor of the Child Jesus, from the twenty-fifth on. Things go very well for me in this land of the Andalusians. I have found myself in sympathy with their character and they tell me I am more Andalusian than they are.[739]

In 1933, Fr. Olarte was given the same services in the Redemptorist community. From January 16 to 22, he was in Almería[740] preaching a seven-day service. He returned to Granada on January 23, and the chronicle tells us something we did not know: "He returns from Almería in lamentable condition because of his asthma."[741] His vigorous health began experiencing problems, which obliged him to leave Andalusia in the summer that same year. In a few brief weeks he recuperated.

....

738 Translator's note: this probably refers to their foundress, St. Teresa of Ávila, or perhaps to Mary under the title of Our Lady of Mt. Carmel.

739 C. OLARTE, *Letter to his Carmelite sister: Granada, 16-12-1932*, in: C. *Beatificationis-Escritos*.

740 Translator's note: one of the provinces of Andalusia; very likely he was in the municipality of Almería in the province by the same name.

741 *Crónica de Granada* IV, 3.

In the political chronicles the discussion continued in the Cámara[742] about the so-called "religious question." At the beginning of February[743] the community agreed to pray "the litany of the saints while the discussion went on about the proposed law on confessions and religious congregations in Parliament."[744]

From February 10 to 11, he preached the novena in honor of Perpetual Help in Novelda (Alicante).[745] He began March with apostolic energy: March 1-12, he went to Murcia to preach a mission and a five-day preaching event in the parish of San Lorenzo.[746] Without a rest, from March 12-19, he preached a seven-day preaching event in Lorca (Murcia) in honor of Perpetual Help and a retreat for ladies. He finished the month taking one more step forward in his missionary prestige: On March 26, he began in the cathedral of Granada "the mission for the Associations of Men; more or less in last year's form, although it looked like there was less attendance...Microphones were installed in the cathedral in order to hear better."[747] In the first days of April, from April 3-11, he preached a mission in Padul (Granada) and immediately preached for Holy Week in the same place.[748] On April 16, he left to preach a sermon in Santa Fe and Belicena (Granada),[749]

....

742 Translator's note: During the Second Republic, the two *Cámaras* of parliamentary government in Spain were united in one, *la Diputación Permanente*.

743 Translator's note: 1933.

744 *Ib.,* 4. [Translator's note: The law, first introduced in Parliament in October 1932, demanded universal public education without the involvement of the Church; confiscation of all Church property, so that the Church had to rent the property it formerly owned; clergy and religious were prohibited from engaging in commerce, industry and education; government subsidy to the Church was to end, the Church was to be taxed on its income; and the government had the right to veto appointments of Church hierarchy.]

745 And also: "This year they did not have the usual Triduum of Carnival at the Shrine since solemn worship has been banned in all churches of the City, except the cathedral, where services were held with all solemnity. For three days from 10 AM until 5 PM they held holy hours in the parishes. In the afternoon from 3,000 to 5,000 people came" (*Ib.,* 5).

746 *Ib.,* 6. 34-35. Fr. Dionizio de Felipe accompanied him.

747 In the cathedral of Granada (March 26 through April 2) he had as his companion the superior of the community, Fr. Miguel García Alonso (*Ib., 6-29-31*).

748 *Ib.,* 31-34.

749 Translator's note: the distance between the city of Santa Fe, Granada, and the small town of Belicena is about 3.5 kilometers, or a little more than two miles. It can be walked in forty-five minutes or driven in about eight minutes.

respectively.[750] May was not a tranquil month politically. May devotions seemingly took place as usual in the church, but this was not true. On May 9, "because of threats of public disturbances a couple Civil Guard officers for the first time offered and came. They spent the night in our house. Perhaps more because they had nowhere else to lodge (the Civil Guard is concentrated in Granada), than for any other reason. May 10: ninety to 100 persons attended May devotions. Tonight, 1,500 in attendance and three of the guard."[751]

Away from the house, he preached the novena in honor of Perpetual Help in Málaga and the "Little mission of El Marqués."[752] June was the last month that Fr. Olarte spent in Granada. Although it was summer and was not the season for mission-preaching, he was in Porcuna (Jaén)[753] from June 22 to July 3 preaching the novena in honor of the Sacred Heart. He left Granada the following day, July 4, en route to Perpetual Help in Madrid because in Granada his asthma was killing him.

....

750 *Ib.*, 8.

751 Fr. Olarte preached on May 5-6 (cf. *Ib.*, 10).

752 The novena was May 20-28; May 29 was the twenty-fifth anniversary of the Defense of the Faith. El Marquéz was a farmhouse in Albolote (Granada), where from May 29 to 31 he substituted for the preacher, who had lost his voice (cf. *Ib.*, 10 and 34).

753 Translator's note: Porcuna in the province of Jaén is about fifty kilometers from Córdoba. Its main employment is growing olives.

Community of Perpetuo Socorro, Madrid:
C. Olarte, first on the left, second row

He Returns to the Capital of the Republic, Madrid (1933-1935)

On July 5, he arrived again in Madrid, in the community of Perpetual Help. Fr. Ciriaco Olarte's purpose was to recuperate his health.[754] In the first part of 1933, he did not slacken in his efforts and, as much as he could, he volunteered to take part in preaching missions, insofar as his health problems permitted him to do. In July and August the chronicle of Madrid offers this data: Fr. Olarte preached in-house on Sunday, July 30, and on the first Sunday of August. Outside the house, he preached a sermon for the silver jubilee for the Little Sisters of the Poor on Calle Almagro. We do not have a lot of data for this period due to pages being missing from the chronicle.[755] We know that on June 30, 1934, he gave a retreat to the Scapularian Sisters of Carabanchel.[756] Before that, and we do not know the exact date, he had given missions in the parishes of his brother priests[757] in Álava, Spain. He did not give further details to his sister, Carmen, in his letter because she had received those earlier. We know, as well, that he was in Terrer, near Saragossa,[758] and in Calatayud,[759] where he preached on Holy Thursday. He added: "It was the fifth sermon which I preached that day, and in places fairly distant one from another; but for cars there are no distances."[760] Even so, he could not come to Saragossa to visit his dear sister, Carmen. We let him do the talking to tell us about new apostolic wanderings that he records in the same letter:

....

754 The community of Perpetual Help in Madrid was an ample one in July 1933: sixteen priests and seven brothers. There were only three who were officially designated as mission preachers, but practically-speaking all were mission preachers, as the chronicle itself confirms.

755 We enter the last three years of the life of Fr. Ciriaco Olarte. Unfortunately, there is less and less news of him until the days of his martyrdom. The chronicle of Madrid ends on August 12, 1934. But an intermediate notebook is missing, as is demonstrated in the jump in page numbering and threads from the binding being cut. We will attempt to make up for the missing information by using family correspondence.

756 C. OLARTE, *Letter to his sister, Carmen: Granada, 14-7-1934*, in: C. *Beatificationis—Escritos.*

757 Translator's note: Ciriaco had two brothers who were priests: Román and Fernando.

758 Translator's note: Terrer is a very small town in the province of Aragon.

759 Translator's note: Calatayud is the second largest city in the province, after Saragossa. It was given the title "The very noble, loyal, always august and most faithful City of Calatayud." After democratic elections were permitted in 1977, it held elections a day sooner than the rest of Spain.

760 *Ib.*

On June 21, I went with the children from catechism class on pilgrimage to el Cerro de los Ángeles,[761] *where I preached to them twice; once in front of the monument to the Sacred Heart, the other time in the church of the Carmelite Sisters. On June 24, I came back to the same place with the pilgrimage of Perpetual Help, having with me more than five hundred members of the archconfraternity. Once again, I preached to them in front of the monument. On June 26, I began a series of retreats for the Brothers of the Christian Schools,*[762] *with their provincial superior in attendance. Pray for me so that these and the many other activities be for the glory of God.*[763]

A few days later he wrote to his sister, Asunción, to congratulate her on her feast day. He was not able to do it later because on the following day he began his own retreat of ten days, prescribed by the Rule. He adds: "Once I finish my retreat, other series of work await me and, after that, the missions. As you can see, in every season of the year requests for work come pouring in."[764]

At the end of December 1933, he sends Christmas greetings to his sister, Carmen. He appears to say little about his apostolic work, but a great deal about its intensity, as we have pointed out before: "An abundance of work is available, perhaps more than can be done." The year 1934 was complicated

....

761 Translator's note: The Hill of the Angels is a hill 670 meters high (2,200 feet) about 10 kilometers (6 miles) from Madrid near the town of Getafe. It claims to be the geographical center of Spain. (The town of Pinto makes the same claim.) On the Hill of the Angels there are two baroque buildings from the seventeenth century: the hermitage of Our Lady of the Angels and the Convent of the Discalced Carmelites. Also, a white-stone tower called the Monument to the Sacred Heart, built by public subscriptions in 1919, stood there at the time when Fr. Olarte brought the children there. Later, in 1936, the Republican army dynamited the monument to the Sacred Heart.

762 Translator's note: these were the FSC, La Salle Christian Brothers, founded by Jean-Baptiste de La Salle, rather than the Irish Christian Brothers, CFC, founded by Edmund Rice.

763 *Ib.*

764 C. OLARTE, *Letter to his sister, Asunción: Madrid, 5-8-1934,* in: *Ib.*

by protests, strikes, and revolutions.[765] Fr. Olarte echoes all of this in the letter quoted before to his sister, Carmen:

We all have a great deal of thanks to render to God for his protection which he has given us in the midst of the difficult times such as we have experienced. We can only hope that this same protection will not fail us in the times ahead. That is what I will ask the Baby Jesus and it is the Christmas bonus that I am sending you through the Holy Family of Nazareth. I have your news, and although there has been no lack of scares for your Community, nothing disagreeable has happened to it. I ask the Divine Child that he continue protecting you always.[766]

In these words, not only is there an absence of partisan elements or political references—he speaks of difficult times—but they also express with elegance a total openness to Providence and intense prayer before the celebration of Christmas. In these same words, we are able to perceive with

....

765 The right and the center won the elections of November 1933. Future governments were headed by Alejandro Lerroux (December 16, 1933), Ricardo Samper (April 28, 1934), and again by Lerroux (November 4, 1934). In the first two governments, the president and the great majority of ministers belonged to the *Partido Republicano Radical* [Translator's note: Radical Republican Party.] In the third government, three ministers from CEDA were seated, whose leader was Gil Robles. This gave pretext to the Revolutionaries on the left to give the first blow to the jugular vein of the Second Spanish Republic, "especially through socialist directors obsessed with European parallels" (R. CARR, *Historia de España, 12. La República y la Guerra civil* [Madrid, 1999] 46). For revolutionary socialism and other extremist groups, it was necessary to eliminate a Republic of the bourgeoisie and install a revolutionary government of *the proletariat class*. The gravest consequence was the Revolution in Asturias with its resulting destruction and burning of churches, and what is even more serious, the assassination of priests, religious and lay believers for the sole *crime* of being priests, religious or lay believers. A number of them have now been canonized, as, for instance, the martyrs of Turón (one Passionist and eight Brothers of the Christian Schools). [Translator's note: The eight Christian Brothers taught at Nuestra Señora de Covadonga, high school. The school was financed by Altos Hornos de Vizcaya, a mining business, which was the chief employer of the area. The Passionist priest was Fr. Inocencio de la Inmaculada. He saw to the religious needs of everyone in the community. A number of the company's directors and engineers also were killed.] The legitimate government acted with harshness and within a few days ended the revolution which called itself "'the red army' when it was all finished, the country was divided between those who favored the repression of the revolution and those who did not....Asturias was the source of division in Europe as much as in Spain: the accusations of atrocities committed by both sides stirred the consciences of the right and of the left and were exposed in the European press" (*Ib.*, 49). D.Niceto Alcalá Zamora was president of the Republic.

766 C. OLARTE, *Letter to his sister, Carmen: Madrid, 19-12-1934*, in: *C. Beatificationis - Escritos.*

clarity the manner in which many of the Christians who suffered persecution, and even martyrdom in later years, rejected an already unstoppable violence and took upon themselves the testimony to their faith, independent of political, social, or ideological questions.

The last letter which we preserve from his stay in Madrid—mentioning his apostolic works—also is addressed to his sister, Carmen to wish her a happy Easter: "Last Tuesday I arrived from Bilbao after I finished my mission work and Holy Week...The missions were stupendous...with prospects for returning there. On Friday, the twenty-sixth, I leave again for the area of Plasencia."[767] In May 1935, Ciriaco was on his way to Cuenca.[768] His purpose was, on one hand, to support the mission work of that community and, on the other hand, to recuperate from asthma in a drier and healthier climate than that of Madrid.

Cuenca (1935, *Cursus Perficio*)[769]

Fr. Olarte left Madrid on May 8, 1935, en route to his new and final community, Cuenca.[770] In order to reconstruct his life in Cuenca[771] we make use of two letters to his sister, Carmen. The first, December 1935, offers ample information about his apostolic commitments already in progress that year and about the program planned for the following year. He informed her of his missionary plans up through April 1936, a few months before his self-offering as a martyr:

The last months I have spent, almost incessantly, outside the house. There has been a little of everything in the missions I have given, but more bad abounds than good. In one place with more than 10,000 inhabitants there was a great deal of enthusiasm and openness to the

....

767 C. OLARTE, *Letter to his sister, Carmen: Madrid, 24-4-1935*, in: *Ib.* [Translator's note: Plasencia is a town in Extramadura, in Western Spain.]

768 The destination is published in the BPE, 3 (May 1935) 1.

769 Translator's note: the Latin phrase means "Race completed." This is a reference to St. Paul's declaration when he was facing the end of his own life: "I have competed well; I have finished the race; I have kept the faith" (2 Timothy 4:7). It is applied to the final moment of the life of Fr. Olarte.

770 Cf. *Anales* X, 306.

771 The chronicle of Cuenca was totally destroyed in the religious persecution of 1936.

sermons, but everything failed in trying to get a rendering of accounts in the confessional. I had another case in which not even the young girls came forward to fulfill their religious obligations. Not everything was that way. In one town where resentments ruled and they did not know the way of the Church, the result was public reconciliations and almost the whole town went to confession. As you can see, there is a great deal of work to be done with prayer and with preaching the word and we have to help one another.

Yesterday on the twentieth of May, I returned to preach a retreat to the Oblates of the Most Holy Redeemer and for the perpetual profession of some of them. The ceremony they use is very solemn. I received their vows. The service lasted more than two hours.

I will leave after the feast of the Three Kings[772] for almost uninterrupted work until the middle of March. I have to take care of various sets of Lenten retreats for men in our church.[773]

The second letter is very short and is in reality a greeting card for the feast day of Carmen:[774] "wishing you all the protection[775] of our dear Mother, and the same for the Community." There were four days left before the military uprising. The situation was very difficult. He doesn't mention it, but he prays "that the feast of Mt. Carmel be a sign of peace for your Community." He adds: "Nothing new here, although without work outside the house."[776]

Days later, Fr. Ciriaco Olarte will give his life for Christ. Once the community is dispersed to go underground in different homes, Ciriaco Olarte was welcomed along with his companion, Miguel Goñi, by D. Enrique García, a priest of Cuenca in the cathedral of Almería.[777] Recognizing the danger, Ciriaco commented to his companions on one occasion: "We will be spending the feast of St. Alphonsus in heaven." And so it was.

....

772 Translator's note: this is the feast of the Epiphany, then on January 6.

773 C. OLARTE, *Letter to his sister, Carmen: Cuenca, 21-12-1935*, in: *C. Beatificationis-Escritos*.

774 Translator's note: Our Lady of Mt. Carmel is celebrated on July 16.

775 Translator's note: in Spanish it is clear that *all* refers to "protection."

776 C. OLARTE, *Letter to his sister, Carmen: Cuenca, 14-7-1936*, in: *Ib.*

777 Translator's note: The Cathedral of the Incarnation is in the Andalusian city of Almería.

On July 31, 1936, after the Redemptorists had celebrated Eucharist, some militiamen showed up at the house to make a search; the Redemptorists had an intuition of the destiny awaiting them. They said goodbye to D. Enrique, telling him: "Until heaven."[778] Fr. Olarte was shot together with Fr. Goñi on an embankment near the hermitage of Our Lady of Sorrows. He was shot in the chest.[779]

The image, which Fr. Ciriaco Olarte has left among the Redemptorists, is that of a missionary who is a tireless worker, easy to get along with, sociable.[780] His best calling card was his friendliness, which along with his special gifts for social relationships, his easy and agreeable manner, his musical abilities, and his talent in oratory, made him a great missionary who consecrated his life to the preaching of the gospel on both sides of the Atlantic.

---

778 Cf. Cap. III. Grupo de la casa de D. Enrique M.ª Gómez Jiménez: Ciriaco Olarte y Miguel Goñi. [Translator's note: Group in the house of D.Enrique M.ª Gómez Jiménez: Ciriaco Olarte and Miguel Goñi.]

779 *Acta de defunción de Ciriaco Olarte Pérez de Mendiguren*: REG. CIVIL DE CUENCA, Sec. 3.ª, T. 42, F. 304, n.º 603. [Translator's note: Death Certificate of Ciriaco Olarte Pérez de Mendiguren.]

780 AHGR 30150002,0034, 1. The previous words are incomplete without a postscript: "*but it is not certain with regards to his moral conduct.*" That presents a difficulty. But there is no further data for us to know what it means. It probably has to do with his expansive personality.

Julián Pozo as a young priest

CHAPTER SIX

Julián Pozo Ruiz de Samaniego

In Payueta, a Little Town of Álava[781]

On February 12, 1898, there was a fiesta in the little town of Payueta, in the province of Álava. In the parish church of San Juan Bautista were joined in matrimony "D. [Toribio] Marcelino[782] Pozo Fernández, single, native of Villabuena (Álava), seventeen years old, miller by profession...and Doña Micaela Ruiz de Samaniego Viana, single, twenty-four years of age, native of Payueta."[783] The couple established the family home in Villabuena, where the father had his work. At the end of the year, they welcomed into their home the first daughter from the marriage, Elisa.[784]

Four years later on January 7, 1903, at five o'clock in the afternoon, the

------

781 Translator's note: Álava is the name of the province, in the Basque area in northern Spain.

782 On the matrimony certificate the name of the groom is Marcelino; but on the birth certificate of the same person (Villabuena, April 27, 1880) the name that is given is that of Marcelino Toribio (cf. AHDV-GEAH 2645-2 *Baptismal Records Villabuena. 1833-1891*, f. 279 r-v).

783 Parish of SAN JUAN BAUTISTA DE PAYUETA (ÁLAVA), *Matrimony Records. 1886-1965*, f. 6 r-v.

784 Elisa del Pozo Ruiz de Samaniego (de la Visitación) was born in Villabuena (Álava) on December 5, 1898. She joined the Congregation of the Sister Oblates of the Most Holy Redeemer on September 17, 1918; she professed her vows on March 19, 1921, and made her final vows on March 19, 1926. She died on April 13, 1992, in Benicasim (Castellón) (cf. *Archives of the Secretary General of the Sister Oblates of the Most Holy Redeemer*).

second child from the marriage was born—the one they called Julián.[785] Although the couple lived in Villabuena, when Micaela was to give birth to her child, she went to the home of her parents. Therefore, the child was born in Payueta. On January 9, the child was brought to church and the parish priest gave him the name Julián. His grandparents were natives of the province of Álava. His paternal grandparents were Pedro Pozo, of Villabuena, and Feliciana Fernández, of Baroja; and the maternal grandparents were Julián Ruiz, also of Payueta, and Caya Viana, of Berganzo.[786]

When his father got married, he worked as a miller; and on the baptismal certificate for Julián, the father's profession is listed as farmer. Soon because of an infirmity of the mind suffered by Julián's father,[787] Julián had to go to live in Payueta at the house of his maternal grandparents. It is there that he spends his infancy and receives the necessary formation.

In December 1903, the same year in which Julián was born, two Redemptorists preached a parish mission. They had come from El Espino. The chronicle offers us this impression of Payueta and of the Samaniego family, thus giving us a description of the surroundings in which Julián grew up:

Payueta (Álava), 54 vecinos. Fairly good people; the youth a little worse than in the other towns. Among the men blasphemy reigns and among the women the custom of going to wash clothes on Sundays. The fault lies principally with the pastor who never preaches and who opposed as much as possible having the mission. He went to bed on the second day so as not to go to the mission, according to his reputation and what everyone was saying. The local government is divided and, as a result, enmities, hatreds, etc., have arisen. The mission had very good results. People came together and reestablished peace. There were important restitutions. Attendance was very good and everyone, but four people, went to confession. The archconfraternity of Our Lady of Perpetual

....

785 Cf. Juzgado de Paz (Translator's note: Justice of the peace) of PEÑACERRADA (ÁLAVA), Sec. 1.ª, T. X, n.º 53.

786 Cf. SAN JUAN BAUTISTA DE PAYUETA (ÁLAVA), Baptismal Records 3, f. 47.

787 In the book of admittance to the postulancy it appears as one of the fears for the vocation of Julian that his father died in a state of insanity and that Julian might inherit the illness (cf. APRM. *Book of Chorist and Lay Postulants,* I, n.º 349).

Help was established. The people were very content, especially in seeing the unity of the town, and two months later it was said that not even one blasphemy has been heard since the mission. The mission was held in great part because of Señor Julián Ruiz Samaniego, father of the juvenist Félix Samaniego. The missionaries were given free lodging in the house of Señor Julián during the mission.[788]

The environment in the home of Julián and Caya was profoundly faith-filled and, as is seen, was favorable toward fostering a vocation. One of their children was at the time of the mission in El Espino: the future Fr. Félix Ruiz de Samaniego Viana. In this environment Julián finished his Christian Initiation with catechesis, First Communion and the sacrament of confirmation, which he received in Peñacerrada (Álava)[789] on April 19, 1912, from diocesan Bishop Msgr. D. José Cadena y Eleta.[790] Later the subject of our biography will see in these first years the origin of his religious and missionary vocation: "Already from my tenderest years I notice in myself a well-marked inclination toward the religious state; I was asked many times by my parents about what I wanted to do in the future and I always answered that I wanted to be a religious."[791]

While Elisa and Julián were still children, they were orphaned as far as their father goes. Julián makes no reference to his father's death in his curriculum vitae, which means it must have occurred before he was old enough to know about it. His mother, now a widow, entered a second marriage with the schoolteacher of Payueta, D. Sixto González Boix,[792] on

....

788 Frs. Pedro del Palacio and Pedro Larrañeta preached the mission from December 1 to 10, 1903. Señor Julián, host for the missionaries, was the grandfather of our Julián Pozo and, thus, father of Fr. Félix Ruiz de Samaniego Viana and of Doña Micaela (*Chronicle of El Espino* III, year 1903, December; the third volume is missing pagination; the references have to be looked for at the date or month mentioned).

789 Translator's note: The distance between these two towns is 2.2 kilometers (1.3 miles), about a twenty-five-minute walk.

790 Cf. Parish of SAN JUAN BAUTISTA DE PAYUETA (ÁLAVA), *Book of Baptisms* 3, f. 60.

791 J. POZO, *Curriculum vitae*: Nava de Rey, 1920, 1 in: *C. Beatificationis—Escritos*.

792 Sixto González Boix was born in Barcelona on October 8, 1882. His first assignment as school teacher was Payueta (February 1908-August 1908); after that he was in Antoñana (until April 1910), Albaina (until May 1911), Lagrán (until January 1912), again in Payueta (until September, 1912), in Nájera and Armentia (Cf. *Service Sheet of Sixto González Boix* in: AGA. *Record of political-social clearance for Sixto González Boix*, Sig. (05)001.030, Caja 32/12428, Exp. 38).

October 31, 1908.[793] Sixto became a true father to Julián. In a letter sent to his family from Astorga on December 24, 1922, he wrote: "Grandmother Isabel is not indifferent to me...on the contrary, I well remember her and the affection that she showed Elisa and me thirteen years ago."[794] Without being able to identify precisely who this grandmother is, it does reveal the attention that they received after being orphaned. Julián, in that case, would have been little more than six years old.

In spite of the fact that Sixto was not his father, he always treated him as such and professed great filial affection for him. Later, Julián expresses that in this way in his letters: "I want to know about mother whom I love and respect so much; about father whom I esteem so much and in whom I glory."[795] From the new marriage of his mother to Sixto there were born other brothers and sisters: Joaquín, Fernanda, José Luís, and Félix Francisco.[796] Julián always maintained with them a very close, affectionate relationship: "my little brothers and sisters Joaquín, Fernandita, José Luís, and Félix, to whom I give lots of kisses."[797]

Julián offers us little more data about his childhood. His brother, Félix Francisco González Ruiz de Samaniego,[798] although he did not know him

....

793 AHDV. Parish of SAN MIGUEL DE VITORIA, *Marriage Records* VII, f. 374.

794 J. POZO, *Letter addressed to his parents: Astorga (León), 24-12-1922*, 2, in: *C. Beatificationis—Escritos*.

795 J. POZO, *Letter sent to his parents: Astorga (León), 16-08-1922*, 2, in: *C. Beatificationis—Escritos*.

796 Cf. D. DE FELIPE, *Nuevos Redentores* (Madrid, 1962) 181. The will which Julian ecomposed during the novitiate and approved on February 2, 1926 (J. POZO, *Testament: Nava de Rey, 8-8-1919*, in: *C. Beatificationis - Escritos*) speaks about his brothers and sisters Elisa, Joaquín, Fernanda and José Luís, but does not mention Félix Francisco, who was born in 1922.

797 J. POZO, *Letter sent to his parents: Astorga (León), 16-08-1922*, 2, in: *C. Beatificationis—Escritos*.

798 Félix Francisco González Ruiz de Samaniego, Marianist [Translator's note: This is the Society of Mary founded by William Joseph de Chaminade in 1817. Its initials are S.M. In Spanish, the term *Sociedad* is not used for religious orders, so in Spain the group is known as "*la Compañía de María*"], was born on January 29, 1922, in Nájera (La Rioja), professed vows in the Society of Mary in 1939 and died on February 27, 2002 (cf. PARROQUIA DE SANTA CRUZ DE NÁJERA [LA RIOJA], *Baptismal Book* 25, f. 264, n.° 672; Archivo de la Secretaría de la Provincia Marianista de Madrid). In 1954 he wrote down the memories of his family for the process of beatification of Julian and asserts that "*I have no direct recollection of Julian since he was in the monastery when I came into this world*" (F. GONZÁLEZ, *Letter addressed to Ricardo Colmenares: San Sebastián (Guipúzcoa), 8-1-1954*, 2, in: *C. Beatificationis, Written testaments about Julián Pozo*).

in Payueta, offers us recollections from childhood about his martyr-brother, who was always held up to him as a model of conduct:

If I was reluctant to go to Mass, I would get a sermon about the love which Julián had for the Mass. If I fell asleep during the rosary, which we said as a family, I would get a reprimand in which the piety of Julián was extolled. If I did not at first obey, I was saddled with a sermon praising the blind obedience of Julián. If I didn't want to study, Julián was placed before me as the model of how to apply oneself. In sum, I always thought of my brother as a child who was the model of goodness, of purity, of self-application, docility, and piety as proper for a saint.[799]

In the minds of his parents, Julián was considered the model son: pious, obedient, hard-working, joyful, playful, respectful. As his brother, Francisco, tells us, "In our house I heard him being praised as the model child, like a permanent musical soundtrack."[800] And in that model child, little by little, a desire to be a religious was growing. "When I reached ten years of age, little by little I saw through the vanity of the world and into the joy, peace, and genuine happiness of the cloister. Short meditations contributed very greatly to this, but what exercised great power over my soul was meditation on the pains of hell, the brevity of life, the unhappy death of the worldly person, and the blessed end of the religious."[801]

This capacity for introspection that was growing in Julián will forge of him in the future a man who is reflective, sententious, with a tendency to give advice, to express himself in refrains and proverbs. Dionisio de Felipe, who knew him personally, describes him that way: "It was his strong distinguishing mark to be reflective and to give advice."[802] This strong personal spirituality was nourished fundamentally in his custom of meditating on the eternal truths: hell, heaven, the vanity of earthly things, the judgment

....

799 *Ib.*, 2.

800 *Ib.*

801 J. POZO, *Curriculum...*, 2.

802 D. DE FELIPE, 182.

of God, all "a catalog of ideas taken from Rosignoli,[803] from Nieremberg,[804] or from St. Alphonsus María de Liguori in his books[805] about the four last things."[806]

Years of Discernment: Paradise in El Espino, Trial in Cuenca

As we have said, Julián had the desire to be a religious since he was small. His daily prayer fed this desire. His mother, Micaela, cultivated the seed of his vocation with her recollections from her visits which she had had various times with her brother, Félix, when he was studying at the old Benedictine monastery, converted into a Redemptorist seminary: "She tried to feed this fire with recollections which she had of El Espino. She had visited there several years prior."[807] And "Divine Providence, which employs so many and such diverse means to guide souls toward their end, was guiding [the] steps [of Julián] along the path of childhood to open the gates of the Congregation for me with his own[808] hand."[809]

The opportunity presented itself in April 1913, with the visit of his Uncle Félix to Payueta[810] on the death of Caya, the mother of the Redemptorist and the grandmother of Julián. After celebrating the Mass of Christian burial, he remained in the town a few days to more quickly take care of some household matters. At that time Fr. Félix got to know his nephew Julián and learned of his desire to be a religious. Since Julián was too young, Uncle Félix was inclined to take to El Espino another nephew a bit older,

....

803 Translator's note: Carlo Gregorio Rosignoli was a Jesuit preacher and writer from the seventeenth century. One of his several works was on the Eternal Truths, arranged for use during retreats.

804 Translator's note: Juan Eusebio Nieremberg lived in the first half of the seventeenth century. Though his parents were German, he lived out his life in Madrid as a Jesuit, teaching scripture in the Jesuit seminary. He wrote *Of Time and Eternity*, which recommended fixing the will on the eternal truths and doing the will of God.

805 Translator's note: among Alphonsus' writings on death, judgment, heaven, and hell, is particularly his work called *Preparation for Death*. Alphonsus wrote at least sixty-five meditations on the eternal truths.

806 *Ib.*

807 J. POZO, *Curriculum...*, 2

808 Translator's note: referring to God.

809 *Ib.*, 1-2.

810 *Ib.*, 3-4; *Chronicle of El Espino* IV, 227. Fr.Félix Samaniego went back to Payueta "to take care of some family matters" (*Ib.*, 242).

but when the moment to leave had come, that nephew decided to stay home and to drop the idea of a vocation. Julián saw in that fact the provident hand of God "who does what he wills and allows no obstacle to his will." He felt called, without a trace of doubt, and for that reason left in writing the following: "So then, without further thought regarding my young age, my uncle seconded the plans of heaven. I coldly took leave of my relatives and enrolled in El Espino on August 30 (Sunday), 1913."[811] There he got to know for the first time Miguel Goñi, with whom he would share the years of formation, apostolic life, and finally martyrdom in Cuenca.

His time in El Espino, Julián says, "slipped by rapidly. They were happy years in the juvenate, filled sometimes with interior sadness and exterior setbacks."[812] The gray tone with which he tints these years of adolescence perhaps have to do with the loss of his father, left out of the curriculum vitae, but which seems to be present in certain neurotic signs not proper to boys of ten to twelve years of age, such as the cold farewell to his family on enrolling in El Espino and the recurring meditation on "the vanity of the world, the brevity of life, unhappy death of the worldly and the blessed end of the religious."[813]

At the beginning of February 1915, work was begun on rehabbing the old monastery of San Pablo in Cuenca as the Redemptorist minor seminary—the juvenate, properly speaking. On February 22, the new rector and director, Fr. Bernardo Fernández, arrived from El Espino. In April 1915, the juvenate of El Espino was split up so that thirty-four juvenists were transferred to San Pablo in Cuenca to begin formation in that new center. Among them were Julián Pozo and Miguel Goñi.[814]

"The sixth of April dawned, the day on which, after a moving farewell, Frs. Barredo and Monroy, accompanied by thirty-four juvenists, were on their way to Pancorbo. A special train car was arranged for them on which

....

811 J. POZO, *Curriculum...*, 4. He had to have registered at night time because in the registration book he put down as the date of his entrance August 31, 1913 (cf. APRM. *Book of Registrations for the Juvenate, El Espino* I, year 1913) and *The Chronicle of El Espino* IV, 244 says: "August 31. Fr. Samaniego returned, bringing with him his nephew who offered himself as a juvenist."

812 J. POZO, *Curriculum...*, 4.

813 *Ib.*

814 Cf. APRM. *Book of Registrations of the Juvenate of El Espino* I.

they traveled commodiously to Madrid. At one or the other station[815] they had at their disposal a local train so that the boys went from that of 'El Norte' to that of 'Mediodía,'[816] where there was a train car waiting for them which took them to Cuenca so as to arrive at four o'clock in the afternoon of Wednesday, April 7."[817]

On the following day they enjoyed for the first time the surprising land-scape which surrounded them: "The juvenists took their first walk along the gorges of the Huecar River. They were very satisfied with the loveliness of the scenery, with the freshness of the springs, with how steep, picturesque, and dangerous were the rocks which, like giant walls, ran along the whole valley."[818]

The monastary of San Pablo was built in 1553. It was inhabited by Dominican friars until the confiscation of 1835, and until the arrival of the Redemptorists it had had a variety of uses: "It is to be found in a picturesque spot outside the city walls of Cuenca; it is connected to the city at present by a daring metal bridge of 100 meters in length and fifty in height crossing over the River Huécar....The monastery and the church are cemented in living rock,[819] at the edge of imposing precipices and shaded by the granite blocks which wall the hillsides of the Socorro."[820, 821]

On April 14, school life began. The kinds of things were lacking which usually are lacking when any new foundation is begun and when there

....

815 Translator's note: Even today the train route runs from Pancorbo in the north through two stops to Madrid.

816 Translator's note: The train line between Pancorbo and Madrid belonged to *la Compañia de los Caminos de Hierro del Norte de España*, which means "the Railroad Company of Northern Spain" and was known simply as "*el Norte*"; the first railroad station built in Madrid was called "*la Estación de Mediodía*." Perhaps the train was named after the station from which it proceeded.

817 *Anales* VI, 229.

818 APRM. *Chronicle of Cuenca - San Pablo*, 20.

819 Translator's note: "Living rock" refers to rock which has not been cut or quarried.

820 Translator's note: The Socorro is the hill across the River Huécar Gorge from the old town of Cuenca.

821 R. TELLERÍA, *Un instituto misionero* (Madrid, 1932) 400. [Translator's note: The title of the book by Raimundo Tellería, CSsR, is *A Missionary Institute* and is about the Redemptorists] Federico Muelas, poet and writer from Cuenca, sees "the convent of S. Pablo, a true monastery that appears crystalized—so clean are its arris [Translator's note: In architecture, an "arris" is a sharp edge formed by the intersection of two surfaces] —over a gigantic stump of rock" sticking out of the Gorge of the Huécar (F. MUELAS, *Cuenca.* "*Tierras de sorpresa y encantamientos*" [Translator's note: the title of the book is "*Lands of Surprises and Enchantment*"] [León, 1983] 27).

is a need to adapt from a rural setting, from which they had come, to an urban setting, to which they had arrived. As a curious fact in this process of adaptation, on April 17 the seminarians were obliged to abandon the old and showy uniforms that they had brought with them from El Espino. The reason was that "the style of clothes which they wore was not very elegant. It was of such a design that the students even gave a bad impression in the city, simply because of the clothing they wore." On April 25 they celebrated the inauguration of the juvenate in Cuenca, although the weather spoiled the party: "The severity of that very cold morning was such that only some fifty people came to visit and even these at a cost to themselves of no little sacrifice for being so devoted to the Congregation." In spite of everything, Father provincial celebrated the Solemn Mass with the presence of the Fathers and Brothers of the community of San Felipe.[822]

The life of the young men who had come from the lands of Burgos was not easy for them. The old Dominican monastery of San Pablo offered difficulties due to lack of space. How unhappy they were can be deciphered in the words of Julián himself. In the pages of his autobiography he tells us: "I let down my guard as far as fervor goes."[823] In spite of everything, his comportment and his grades were fairly good during his four years in San Pablo.[824]

At the end of his period of formation in the high school in Cuenca, Julián received an unexpected invitation which would profoundly mark his personality. He called it "the great test" and it happened on the eve of the retreat for taking his habit, August 9, 1919. The superiors sent him home with the following explanation, which Julián himself received and which he left in writing later: "Seeing my pallid complexion, they judged it necessary that I go to spend a large amount of time in the warmth of my mother's home."[825] In reality, the real cause was more serious: they threw him out of

---

822 APRM. *Crónica de Cuenca - San Pablo*, 20.

823 J. POZO, *Curriculum...*, 4.

824 Cf. APRM. *Libro de notas del Jovenado de San Pablo.* [Translator's note: "Gradebook from the Juvenate of San Pablo."] Julián always appears as one of the students who stood out more. Dionisio de Felipe says of him, *"... having done well in his studies and being one of the students who was best behaved"* (D. DE FELIPE, 182).

825 J. POZO, *Curriculum...*, 4-5. An interesting detail, the original looks like it was crossed out with "father's" replaced by "mother's."

the seminary because they did not consider him an apt candidate to begin the novitiate. The book of postulants records the fear of the formators regarding Julián's future: "This young man was dismissed from the juvenate in Cuenca, on the point of making his retreat for the reception of the habit. The reason was that his father died in insanity, and we noted in Julián some peculiarities that are perhaps rooted principally in the circumstance of the insanity of his father."[826]

These were, perhaps, the most difficult moments in the life of Julián, who was thrilled with his Redemptorist religious vocation. He would later write: "This news came like a complete surprise to me....I pleaded, I promised, but everything was in vain." Although confused and pained with this news, Julián lived this difficult experience from a religious perspective, negotiating it as a moment of personal purification: It was "the great test that Providence demanded of me...like a touchstone on which is discovered whether my vocation and love for the Congregation was made of gold or glitter....I made the resolution to not give up in the matter, thanking God for the vocation that I felt and conforming myself to his holy will."[827]

On August 9, he left Cuenca on his way to Payueta, at the age of sixteen years. The journey in the slow trains of those days was intense. The psychological battle grew inside him. The long meditation in the solitude of the train brought Julián to reaffirm his desire to be a Redemptorist. The moment was difficult, but his hope strengthened during the long night of his test: "On the journey I saw clearly and openly the loving action of Providence in a thousand and a thousand prods."[828] In those moments Mary, the mother, appears in his *Notes*, a key figure in Julián's spirituality and in that of every Redemptorist formed in the spirituality of St. Alphonsus Maria de Liguori:

On the first night that I arrived home, I prayed with my arms extended in the form of a cross, as best I could, three Hail Mary's to my mother. I put myself under her protection and I asked her that she deliver letters of negotiation on my behalf. And, lo and behold, it was on the fourteenth of that same month, in the evening, that I received the most gratifying

---

826 APRM. *Book of Chorist and Lay Postulants* I, n.º 349.

827 J. POZO, *Curriculum*..., 4-5.

828 *Ib.,* 5.

news of my return. What had happened? It was Mary's hand, it was the loving providence of God. Without my knowing it, I was dismissed; without my involvement, I was again admitted. I left the monastery on August 9 and I entered the monastery on August 16. O, Mary, thank you! O, God, let your holy will always be done in me![829]

Julián spent five days in Payueta when he received "the most gratifying news" that he should go to Nava del Rey to begin the novitiate. He himself wondered what had happened. He attributed the response solely to the protection of Mary, to whom he had so often prayed. Throughout his whole life he would always maintain a confidence, affection and special devotion to the Most Holy Virgin, as some people who knew him would attest.[830]

He arrived at the novitiate in Nava del Rey (Valladolid) on August 16, as the book of postulants records. There the reason for his readmittance is added:

When he returned home, he was examined by a doctor, who said that there was nothing abnormal to be noted in him and that he could become a religious without any difficulty. So, Most Reverend Father provincial, considering this, and considering the requests and reasons which Frs. Gil y Samaniego put forward, admitted him again. Three days after he had left the postulancy, he came to this house to take the habit on August 16, 1919....In the three days that he was out he showed great love for his vocation. He himself put forth a lot of effort so that they would again admit him. Most Reverend Father provincial gave his OK for him to stay in his town to be there for the fiesta that was to take place the following day, but Julián did not want to wait. For the present, there is no particular difficulty with him and everything is going well.[831]

....

829 *Ib.*, 5-6.

830 Fr. Isidro Fernández Posado affirmed in the Process of Beatification that Fr. Pozo "had a great deal of devotion to the Most Holy Virgin. He showed it always, in every place and at all times, and mortified himself especially on Festival days of the Virgin, although, because he was ill, he was dispensed from mortification..." (I. FDEZ. POSADO, *C. Beatificationis - Declarationes* I, 161). Patricinio Moya Martínez said something similar: "...and you could see that he was very devoted to the Virgin and always inculcated in us his love for her, saying that 'without a mother could you be either on earth or in heaven?'" (PATROCINIO MOYA, *Ib.*, II, 444).

831 APRM. *Book of Chorist and Lay Postulants* I, n.º 349.

In the novitiate house he waited for his large group of fellow disciples, who were busy finishing off the month of preparation in Cuenca. They were reunited on August 24, and the next day they celebrated the taking of the Redemptorist habit. The ceremony was presided over by Fr. Rafael Cavero, the novice master.[832] Thus it was he began the novitiate, the intense time of preparation to consecrate his life to Christ the Redeemer following the missionary charism of St. Alphonsus de Liguori.[833]

The Years of Formation for a Redemptorist Missionary *Sui Generis*[834]

Br. Julián remained at Nava del Rey during his novitiate year in the silence of that sober house situated on the infinite Castilian plain. In this land-scape, so beloved of San Juan de la Cruz, there matured in their vocation to the religious life Julián, Miguel Goñi, and Brs. Victoriano and Gabriel, the four martyred in 1936, as is written at the end of the record of investiture for the four, where is added: *occisus* 1936.[835]

Fr. Cavero pointed out at the beginning of the novitiate that Julián was "of an open and jovial character; but somewhat of a boy yet; he has a slightly weak head, shows good will, piety, and a delicate conscience."[836] A special joviality and joy characterized him throughout his whole life, expressed with a constant smile, even when he was suffering from illness, a habitual companion in his life. For this reason, we intuit that he lived his novitiate with the intensity and joy that characterized him. During this time, he contracted the so-called Spanish influenza, which wreaked havoc on the

---

832 *Anales* VII, 151 y 153.

833 *Julianus Pozo Ruiz. Die 25 augusti, feria secunda 1919, in hac domo Seraphicae Theresiae de Jesu in civitate Navae Regis prov. Vallisoletana a R. Raphaele Cavero, Novitiorum magistro in novitiatu admissus est adolenscens Julianus Pozo Ruiz e pago Payueta prov. Alavense, dioc. Vitoriense, natus die 7 Januarii anno 1903,annos 16 et menses 7* (APRM. *Liber Primus Inscriptionis Vestium mutationis Choristarum. Noviciado, Coristas*, Año 1919, n.° CCCXVI). The Latin means: "Julián Pozo Ruiz, on Monday, August 25, 1919, in this house of the Seraphic Teresa de Jesús in the city of Nava del Rey, province of Valladolid, was admitted to the novitiate by Reverend Rafael Cavero, Master of Novices. The teenager Julián Pozo Ruiz from the town of Payueta in the province of Álava, the diocese of Vitoria, was born on January 7, 1903, and is 16 years, 7 months, of age." (APRM. *Liber Primus Inscriptionis Vestium mutationis Choristarum. Noviciado, Coristas*, Año 1919, n.° CCCXVI).

834 Translator's note: the Latin phrase *Sui generis* means literally "of his own kind" or "unique." It conveys the idea that Fr. Julián was to have a style of giving missions which was completely his own, not like that of others.

835 Translator's note: the Latin word *occisus* means "slain."

836 APRM. *Book of Chorist and Lay Postulants* I, n.° 349.

population in those years.[837] Although he managed to overcome it, it left him with a damaged lung for the rest of his life.[838]

In order to admit anyone to profession of vows, the master of novices had to send to Rome required reports on Br. Julián and his companions.[839] Among the reports, there was the assertion that his health was fairly good, in spite of the infirmity of his father for which they had sent him home. He was out of danger. With regard to his qualities and defects, the master of novices emphasized, "He had a fairly good mind and talent. On occasions, he suffered from anxiety and, for this reason, from bad humor; he is a bit of a boy, inclined to contradict and censure everybody else. He esteems his vocation, he is respectful, very religious and pious, upright, open, agreeable." And he adds with regard to his comportment in the novitiate that "except for a few light faults committed in the beginning of the novitiate, generally he behaves in an excellent way. He worked daily, and with great results, to acquire virtues and to overcome his defects." With regard to expectations for the future, Fr. Cavero believed that Julián would be a very good religious, a good professor, and missionary. Therefore, the vote of the master of novices was positive.

At the end of novitiate, Br. Julián made his profession of vows on August 26, 1920, through which he consecrated his life to following Christ—poor, chaste, and obedient—and according to the charism of the missionary Congregation of St. Alphonsus, to announce the good news to the poorest people, according to the example of Jesus Christ. He added the name of

....

837 Translator's note: The Spanish flu epidemic killed around 30 million people worldwide in 1918-1919 and is the worst epidemic in history.

838 "The flu somewhat disturbed the novitiate, especially Br. Pozo, who was able to recover, although his weak constitution did not promise anything much for the future" (Anales VII, 405).

839 AHGR 30150009, 0503.

Mary to his own name, writing it as Julián María Pozo.[840] Father rector of the community, Fr. Leoncio Domínguez Yañez, received the vows of the whole class. Julián had the good fortune to have present with him at his profession his uncle, the missionary, Fr. Féliz Ruiz de Samaniego, who served in the capacity of witness.

At the end of August 1920, once he was professed, he along with the rest of his classmates went to Astorga (León) to begin his studies of philosophy and moral theology as preparation for priesthood. A new era began in his life. If the period of the juvenate was centered on working out the difficulties he had in fulfilling the desires which God placed in his heart of being a religious, his life as a Redemptorist student was to be centered on overcoming the chronic illness which would make an apostolic life as a missionary difficult for him. It was the desire he had from the first. In the novitiate he had had problems with the flu. In the Maragata capital[841] he contracted tuberculosis in the autumn of 1921 and his right lung remained

....

840 *Ego, Julianus Maria Pozo R. de Samaniego e pago Payueta Provinciae Alavensis, Novitius Congregationis Sanctissimi Redemptoris, hac die 26 Augusti 1920 Sancti Zepherini sacro in Collegio Sanctae Theresiae in civitate Navae Regis inter manus admodum Rdi. Patris Leontii D. Yañez Rectoris hujius domus, secundum Regulam nostram et ad tenorem sacrorum cononum et privilegiorum nostrorum, sponte nuncupari vota temporalia ad trienium valitura, Paupertatis, Castitatis et Obedientiae, praesente tota communitate, praesertim Patribus Felix R. de Samaniego et Theodomiro G. Ronda. Ego: Julianus Maria Pozo* [Translator's note: the Latin means "I, Julián María Pozo R. de Samaniego, from the town of Payueta, province of Álava, a Novice of the Congregation of the Most Holy Redeemer, on this day, the 26th of August, 1920, the feast day of St.Zephyrinus, in the holy house of St.Teresa in the city of Nava del Rey, in the hands of Very Reverend Fr. Leoncio Domínguez Yáñez, Rector of this house, according to our Rule and in accord with Canon Law and with our privileges, I have pronounced of my own free will temporary vows for a period of three years of Poverty, Chastity and Obedience, with the whole community present, especially Fr. Felix R.de Samaniego and Theodomiro G.Ronda. I sign this: Julán María Pozo"] [Signatures of the Rector and the two named witnesses] (APRM. *Liber secundus inscriptionis Professionis Religiosae Perpetuae in Congregatione SS. Redemptoris de la Provincia de Madrid CSSR,* año 1920, n.º XXVII / 273). In Astorga he renewed temporary profession a number of times until he reached 21 years of age (APRM. *Actus Authentici Renovationum 1921-1953 Professionis Temporariae. Estudiantado Astorga,* 42). [Translator's note: in 1920, canon law specified that a candidate to a religious order had to be a minimum of twenty-one years old to profess final vows. Until that time, candidates in vows would keep repeating a temporary profession of vows.]

841 Translator's note: Maragatería is a region of central León. The capital city of the region is Astorga, where the Redemptorist major seminary was located.

affected.[842] Looking for a healthier climate and the benefits from taking in the native airs, Father provincial permitted him to go home to Payueta for a while to recuperate. On November 26, he wrote a letter to his parents[843] telling them about his arrival on December 1, but trying not to alarm them into thinking that his leave was definitive. Julián calmed them by saying: "Don't worry about anything, and least of all about my illness." The prefect of students, Fr. Carlos Otero, added in his own handwriting in the same letter: "He is going for a period of time; he is coming as a Redemptorist and he will remain a Redemptorist as long as he wishes." He wrote from Payueta to his parents, who at the time were residing in Najera, where Sixto was teaching school, and told them about his state of health, the journey, and his desire to see them.[844]

After a week in Payueta, he left on December 7 in the afternoon for El Espino to spend the feast of the Immaculate Conception among his confreres. He stayed there until December 16, when he finally left for Nájera (La Rioja)[845] where he spent Christmas with his parents. He returned to El Espino on January 8, 1922.[846] In fact, he experienced a notable improvement in his health. Once the harsh winter of Astorga had passed and the treatments for tuberculosis were finished, Julián returned to Astorga on February 27[847] to take exams. With a great deal of effort on his part, he managed to catch up with his companions in his studies and earned very good grades. In a letter he told his family about the results of his exams

....

842 Tuberculosis was an almost "endemic" illness in the Convent of San Francisco in Astorga, the theologate of the Redemptorists. The hard winter cold and the poor ventilation of the convent backed up against the city walls assured that many of those who resided there would be infected by the Koch bacillus. [Translator's note: Robert Koch was a German physician and researchist who discovered the bacillus that causes turberculosis.] A great number of religious died of tuberculosis. In the case of Fr. Julián Pozo, it degenerated into a chronic infirmity. With the exhumation and identification of his remains in 2008 a rheumatic process was diagnosed of notable seriousness, which is known as Bechterew's disease, which produces ankylosis (stiffness) of some of the segments of the spinal column and in advanced cases, aside from the limitation of mobility of the trunk, it causes shortness of breath. This problem degenerated into a chronic tuberculosis (cf. *Informe médico-pericial de los restos. Madrid 2008* en: *Actas de la recognición y traslado*, 55-56).

843 J. POZO, *Letter addressed to his parents: Astorga (León), 26-11-1921*, in: *C. Beatificationis —Escritos.*

844 J. POZO, *Letter addressed to his parents: Payueta (Álava), 6-12-1921*, in: *Ib.*

845 Translator's note: La Rioja is the province in which Nájera is located.

846 Cf. *Crónica de El Espino* V, 101. 114.

847 Cf. *Anales* VIII, 13; *Crónica de El Espino* V, 115.

and let them know about his state of health: "I'm satisfied and content; everything turned out as well as could be, although to catch up with my fellow students cost me some effort (...) I have not lost the good health that I gained there, and every day I am getting better, thanks be to God."[848]

The effort left him exhausted and he began to experience a condition of continuous debility, which contrasted with his happy, optimistic, and contented spirit. At the end of the year, he again wrote: "I am continuing my studies completely happy. As far as everything else goes, I am always in good humor, joyful, optimistic and happy."[849] His optimism, Fr. Dionisio de Felipe will later say, was serene and let itself be known through his perennial smile, even in the presence of trials and reverses.

The exams of March 1923 again debilitated him. In a letter to his parents in April 1923, he commented to them about symptoms of his illness: "I feel weak and my pulse runs fast and my lungs get tired whenever I attempt anything active; the outside temperature (also) quickly affects my health."[850] And although he showed optimistic expectations, the effort it took to take the summer exams ended up wearing out his fragile health. On August 15, 1923, he had a hemorrhage that lasted four days: "On the day of Assumption, the solemn feast day...I was immobilized, confined to bed, spewing out my life in painful mouthfuls of blood....This contrast[851] anchored me even more to my vocation..."[852] A medical examination prescribed that he leave off of studies and recuperate through rest. As he was not improving, in November 1923, it was decided that he should suspend his studies of theology and have him pass the winter in the community at Nava del Rey in hope of a healthier climate for him. He again wrote his family to let them know.[853] Father provincial made the decision to send him to Nava del Rey in the years following from December through April.[854]

On September 17, 1924, he made his profession of perpetual vows in

848 J. POZO, *Letter to his family: Astorga (León), 6-4-1922*, in: *Causa Beatificationis—Escritos.*

849 J. POZO, *Letter to his family: Astorga (León), 24-12-1922*, in: *Ib.*

850 J. POZO, *Letter to his parents: Astorga (León), 3-4-1923*, in: *Ib.*

851 Translator's note: between the joy of the feast day and the desperation of his health.

852 J. POZO, *Letter to his parents: Astorga (León), 27-9-1923*, in: *Ib.*

853 J. POZO, *Letter to his family: Nava de Rey (Valladolid), 12-11-1923*, in: *Ib.*

854 Cf. *Anales* VIII, 99 y 167; *Anales* IX, 26.

Astorga before the provincial, Fr. Nicanor Mutiloa, promising and taking an oath to die in the Congregation of the Most Holy Redeemer.[855] With perpetual vows, the door to Holy Orders was open for him. On June 14, 1925, he received the subdiaconate from the hands of the Bishop of Astorga, Msgr. Antonio Senso Lázaro, and after receiving the diaconate was consecrated a priest on September 27, 1925, at which time he began the study of his last course in moral theology. Ordained, but without finishing his final course, Julián received his first assignment as a priest—Granada, where he was sent because of his illness.

....

855 *Ego, Julianus Pozo R. de Samaniego e pago Payueta, Provincia Alavensi (Alava), Professus a votis temporariis congregationis Sanctissimi Redemptoris, hac die 17 septembris anni 1924, in hoc Collegio ad Beatae Mariae de Perpetuo Succursu, in civitate Asturica, inter manus Plurimum Reverendi Patris Nicanoris Mutiloa, sponte nuncupair vota simplicia et perpetua Paupertatis, Castitatis et Obedientiae, una cum voto et juramento perseverandi ad mortem usque in praefacta Congregatione, praesentatibus Patribus Carolo Otero et Joanne Prado. Ego Julianus Pozo R. de Samaniego, manu propia* (APRM. Actus Authentici Professionum a Votis Perpetuis I, 46, n.º 29). [Translator's note: the Latin reads, "I, Julián Pozo R. de Samaniego, from the town of Payueta, province of Álava, professed with temporary vows in the Congregation of the Most Holy Redeemer, on this day, the seventeenth of September in the year 1924, in this house of the Blessed Mary of Perpetual Help, in the city of Astorga, freely have taken in the hands of the Most Reverend Fr. Nicanor Mutiloa, the simple and perpetual vows of Poverty, Chastity and Obedience, together with the vow and oath of perseverance until death in the aforementioned Congregation, with Frs. Carlos Otero and Juan Prado present. I, Julián Pozo R. de Samaniego, sign this in my own hand."]

Julián Pozo Ruiz de Samaniego

The years he lived in Astorga were years of formation, not only in theology but in what pertains to the personal and the spiritual. He had to find a way to deal with both his studies and his illness, and thus there grew in him the ability to accept his limitations, as well as joy and optimism; he always had a smile on his face. Through the letters, which he wrote to his family, we see how not only did he love people but he also had cultivated a unique capacity for communicating that affection.

One of his companions, Fr. Antonio Armada, with whom he spent practically all of his years of formation (1913-1924), recalls him as a very normal, pious, simple and hard-working confrere.[856] He developed during those years the capacity to listen and to give counsel. Dionisio de Felipe, who knew him in Cuenca, is convinced that "the reflective nature of Julián showed itself from childhood, and was accentuated later to the point of making of him the sententious man, ready to give advice, which all of us recognized in Fr. Pozo, even when he was a young priest, and even before he was ordained. It was his strong distinguishing character to be reflective and to give advice...Fr. Pozo was in possession of sensible and safe opinions; from that came the abundance of his advice...."[857]

....

856 A. ARMADA, *C. Beatificationis - Declaraciones* I, 136.

857 D. DE FELIPE, 182. 185.

Community in Granada. J. Pozo, top row, third from the right

Apostolic Life of Fr. Julián María:
Suffering, Approachability, Listening, Smiling[858]

On December 3, 1925, Fr. Julián Pozo arrived in Granada "for reasons of health" according to the chronicle,[859] although "he is a priest now and will be able to help in that community." This is the life that Fr. Julián is going to have in Granada: put up with his suffering and help with the apostolic tasks of that community which took care of a shrine dedicated to Perpetual Help. It had been inaugurated twelve years prior and, by the time Fr. Julián arrived, it had been converted into a center of apostolic work which radiated throughout the city.

Fr. Tomás Vega, superior of Granada, entrusted to Fr. Pozo those apostolic works of the shrine that did not demand a great deal of physical exertion or strain on the voice. These would have included spiritual direction, sacramental reconciliation, the celebration of the Eucharist, and a few little occasions for preaching; because of his fragile health, he could not be sent out to preach parish missions.[860] He helped in the community by being the chronicler. Further, he would spend some months in Granada with his classmate and future companion in martyrdom, Miguel Goñi, who arrived in the community on March 2, 1927.

Among the responsibilities given to Fr. Julián by the superior was one of helping the servant of God Conchita Barrecheguren[861] in her last days. She was under the direction of Fr. Vega. Dionisio de Felipe, the biographer

....

858 This title was inspired by the statement of Fr.José María Machiñena, in which he said "the apostolate of suffering was his apostolate." (*C. Beatificationis—Declaraciones* I, 99).

859 *Anales* IX, 27 y 44.

860 That is what one of his companions who resided there with him said, Fr. José María Ibarrola: "He was sick and could not commit himself to ministries of preaching but to functions of worship and events in the church of the Convent." (C. Beatificationis - Declaraciones I, 99).

861 Servant of God María Concepción Barrecheguren García was born in Granada in 1905 and died in the same city in 1927. She lived for twenty-two years marked by suffering and characterized by a strong experience of God, which helped her to endure that sickness. With her reputation for sanctity, her process of canonization was begun, which continues in Rome. Her father was Servant of God Francisco Barrecheguren Montagut, who was born in Lérida in 1881 and died in Granada in 1957. Married to Concepción Garcia in 1904, they had one daughter, Conchita. Because of her illness, he was her father and her teacher. After his daughter died, he had to accompany his wife in her illness. She died in 1937. He professed vows as a Redemptorist afterward in 1947 and was ordained to the priesthood in 1949. He died in Granada in 1957. His process of canonization was begun and continues in Rome.

and vicepostulator[862] for both, assures us that Fr. Julián told him during a walk that "more than once, he went to visit the convent of the Carmelites of San Valentín (later known as the Carmelite Convent of the Martyrs) to console that holy soul, Conchita Barrecheguren, with his words and with the Holy Sacrifice of the Mass and holy Communion...He had the consolation of helping her in the last moments of her life and hearing her confession for the last time in the absence of her regular confessor, Fr. Tomás Vega."[863] Both young people, united in suffering from the same illness and with identical aspirations for holiness, entered almost immediately into a profound spiritual harmony. Conchita died on May 13, 1927. Using a privilege of the associates of *Las Marías de los Sagrarios*[864] of celebrating the Eucharist each week at the bedside of an ill member, Fr. Julián went some six times to where the infirm woman was confined. Her last days had to have impressed him so much that he has left us in writing what happened:[865]

I went to say Mass on the ninth [of May]. Her mother was in a room, which adjoined the half-open room of Conchita.

Her mother said openly, time and again: "What a calamity has fallen upon us! What a calamity!" Conchita heard her, but was peaceful and serene. In the wee hours of the night, the nuns brought Doña Concha to the infirmary....

Later, I returned to celebrate Mass and give Communion [to the ill woman], on May 11. I remember well....After Mass I stayed to make my thanksgiving,[866] in front of the bed of the infirm woman; afterwards,

---

862 Translator's note: The vicepostulator prepares the paperwork for a candidate for canonization.

863 D. DE FELIPE, 185. Fr. De Felipe, besides being biographer for both, was vicepostulator in both processes.

864 Translator's note: A spiritual association founded by Jesuit Fr. José María Rubio in 1911 in Madrid has as its purpose to accompany Jesus in the Blessed Sacrament. The name means literally "The Marías of the Tabernacles." They were granted the privilege of arranging to have Mass celebrated at the homes of the homebound.

865 D. DE FELIPE, *Flor de Granada. Historia documentada de Conchita Barrecheguren* (Madrid, 1935) 229. [Translator's note: the name of the book translates as *Flower of Granada: The Documented Story of Conchita Barrecheguren*.]

866 Translator's note: it was a practice of Redemptorists to spend at least fifteen minutes in prayers of thanksgiving after saying or attending Mass.

I asked her how she was doing, and whether she wanted to go to heaven with Jesus: she told me that she did and that she wanted it very much. I added to what she said, for her consolation, that soon she would be in heaven and that she was suffering with patience for the love of God, that she would not be going through purgatory. Afterwards, I took break-fast....There were moments of silence....During one of them I said that the sick woman was admirable and that she wanted to go to heaven, and that I told her that soon she would go there.

This very much offended her father, and to calm him I promised to speak to his daughter and to remedy the effect (which he believed was depressive). I went in alone, and it was not necessary to rectify anything; she had heard everything...and it was all ratified by her desire to go to heaven.

For me what was a source of pain for her...was her anxiousness for heaven, clashing against the vehement, and very human, desire of her parents and relatives for a cure through a miracle by St. Teresita, achieving it through her prayers.

On Thursday, the twelfth, at ten o'clock in the morning, I was sent expressly by Fr. Vega. I went to see how she was doing. Since her confessor heard her confession frequently, I took care of her confession in four minutes and I gave her final absolution. For her part, she was anxious for heaven. No other priest saw her. I left her still smiling with the hope of soon going to heaven.[867]

Another important event which Fr. Julián himself experienced in Granada was the pontifical coronation of the icon of Our Lady of Perpetual Help, venerated in the shrine of that city. It took place on June 12, 1927, and the Redemptorist superior general, Most Reverend Fr. Patrick Murray, was present. Acting as pontifical delegate was the archbishop of Granada, Cardinal Vicente Casanova Marzol. The auxil-iary bishop, who also would become a martyr, Blessed Manuel Medina

---

867 J. POZO, *Relación sobre los últimos días de Conchita Barrecheguren*: cit. D. de Felipe, *Ib.*, 229-230; cited in part by T. VEGA, *Historia de otra alma* (Madrid, 19443) 272-273. [Translator's note: the first book is named *The Narrative of the Last Days of Conchita Barrecheguren*; the second book is named *The Story of Another Soul*, this last having a subtle reference to *The Story of a Soul* by St. Therese of Lisieux, especially popular in the first decades of the twentieth century.]

Olmos, assisted him. It was a moment of popular enthusiasm in honor of the venerated icon.[868]

Fr. Julián would remain in the city of the Alhambra[869] until October 30, 1927, when he was on the road to Cuenca,[870] where he would continue practically until his death, living the same kind of life that he led in Granada. There, besides resting and walking, he would help with confessions, spiritual direction, reciting the rosary and giving care to the sick. One of his companions, Fr. Isidro Fernández Posado, remembers him thus: "Yes, I knew of his infirmity, of his poor state of health; but he worked as much as he could; in spite of his infirmity he was known as a hard worker, insofar as he could. And he always showed himself to be a man of ready cooperation and, because of that, resigned to the ailments or infirmities and his difficulties. I heard nothing from anyone against his good dispositions and cooperation, his acceptance of his situation. His cooperation was constant in him; everyone saw him as happy, with an interior and exterior joy."[871]

Although physically, the change to Cuenca came as something good for him, his illness once more played a dirty trick on him. His state of chronic weakness introduced a new element in the otherwise consistent picture of his health, a type of typhoid that put him on the verge of death.[872] On October 7, 1928, early in the morning, the superior of San Felipe, Fr.

----

868 *Anales* IX, 160.

869 Translator's note: The Alhambra is a well-known Moorish palace in the city of Granada that attracts visitors from all over the world.

870 *Ib.*, 160.

871 I. FDEZ. POSADO, *C. Beatificationis—Declaraciones* I, 160. Also, María García Moya recalls that he was dedicated to these tasks (*Ib.*, I, 75-76).

872 Fr. Chaubel describes it to his parents in these terms: "His illness is not irritation in the chest, it is a different thing; it consists of gastric fevers whose origin is unknown." [Translator's note: Typhoid fever is characterized by high fever, abdominal pains, constipation, headaches, and a rash. It is caused by ingesting contaminated substances, such as drinking unsanitary water. Vaccination for typhus became available in the period between the two World Wars and antibiotics were first developed during the Second World War.] "He is always registering between 38 and 39 degrees." [Translator's note: In Europe, Celsius is used for thermometer readings, while in the U.S. body temperatures are measured in Fahrenheit degrees. The normal body temperature is 98.4 degrees Fahrenheit, 37 degrees Celsius. 38 degrees Celsius would measure as 100.4 Fahrenheit; 39 degrees Celsius would be 102.2. High-grade fevers would be considered those in the 103- to 104-degree range; dangerous fevers are 104 to 107.] "... In short, it is a benign typhoid. His body is little developed, as you know, his bones weak, all in all...his general state is what makes us cautious with the gastric fever and for that reason the care we give him is extreme" (E. CHAUBEL, *Letter to Sixto González: Cuenca, 7-10-1928*, in: *C. Beatificationis—Escritos sobre Julián Pozo*).

Enrique Esprit Chaubel, saw that the fever was not going down and thought that he was dying. He gave him extreme unction[873] and wrote to the family of Fr. Pozo to tell them that he had done so: "I don't think that it is anything imminent, but I think that it is necessary that I advise you of it. Our good Father is a saint. I believe he is wishing to die; that is what chosen souls do. He himself has requested all the sacraments and I did not want to deny him them. I finished giving them to him at 3:30 in the morning and he received them with great devotion."[874] His hour had not yet come and Fr. Pozo recovered slowly from his stomach maladies, to the point of taking up the apostolate of the confessional, to which he dedicated himself with true supernatural spirit.

In 1930 another person in ill health was sent to Cuenca to recuperate, Fr. Dionisio de Felipe. Together they spent time walking through the beautiful town enjoying its out-of-the-way spots, the Castilian sun, and the conversation they shared. Later, when he wrote Fr. Pozo's biography, his companion would record for us his pleasant memories: "...the frequent walks that we took, like two souls in pain with a plan for repairing our physical damage through visiting those rugged spots of unhewn Cuenca. Seldom is there not some painter there intoxicating his inspiration with light and scene. Uphill and downhill, in the shade of the gorges, through the gate of San Juan, along the descent to Las Angustias, along the banks of the rivers, on fresh mornings of summer, throwing our cares to the wind and the water."[875]

During his stay in Cuenca, his capacity for listening and his marvelous gift for giving advice, which he possessed, resulted in the fact that many people, both lay and professed religious, sought him out for spiritual direction and for the sacrament of reconciliation, which he was always ready to give. There were a lot of people looking to go to confession to him.[876] Mrs. Patrocinio Mora Martínez, his penitent in the Church of San Felipe in Cuenca, recalls:

....

873 Translator's note: Extreme Unction was the name commonly given to the sacrament of the sick before Vatican II and was generally administered in the last moments of a person's life.

874 E. CHAUBEL, *Letter to Sixto González: Cuenca, 12-10-1928*, in: *Ib.*

875 D. DE FELIPE, 185.

876 Felicia Martínez Andrés maintains that "he spent a lot of time in the confessional; he had many people coming to him for confession; he had a lot of penitents" (*C. Beatificationis—Declaraciones* I, 225).

I considered him a very good person and I can assert that he always listened to us with much kindness and patience, although certainly many times he did not feel like it since he was in poor health. And it could be seen that he was very devoted to the Virgin....The good way in which he conducted himself in the monastery was well known and people were drawn to go to confession to him because of his virtue, and that in spite of everyone knowing about the chest problems he had; we were a little pained that we made him work so hard and that we would bother him when he was sick. But because he was so good, we just could not leave him alone, and when we would tell him that we could, that we should change confessors—in order to not make him work so much—he said no, that if we were okay with his service, that we should continue, that he was consecrated to the service of God in order to serve his faithful, to spend his life doing so, that we should not worry, that we should just keep coming.[877]

Likewise, Leopoldo Rivera, a layman who went to him for confession and was under his direction, chose him for his "spirit of prayer":

He could always be found in the chapel, and always very recollected, always meditating. And so, because of that, my opinion of him was that he was a saint; regarding the rest, the community of religious and the faithful, I think they all regarded him as a good person, and I never heard anything against him, neither from his community nor from the faithful. As I say, although I never heard him say so about himself, he was sick and no doubt could not engage in other activities, but, despite his infirmity, he dedicated himself to the confessional, and had a great deal of confession work.[878]

The change of regime and the advent of the Second Republic caught him by surprise in Cuenca. Despite being a sick man, involved in active ministry within the Church of San Felipe, he did not remain aloof from political reality. That is what we read in a letter sent to his family:

877 *Ib.*, II, 444.
878 *Ib.*, I, 239.

If we can believe the newspapers (I read only El Debate),[879] *the social question in our dear country is a desperate one; the speech by Miguelito Maura (the son of Antonio Maura is Gabriel),*[880] *with the additional aggravation that the deputies of the Esquerra Republican Party*[881] *were not brought to a halt, amounts to a crushing blow. It is a dilemma that with the logic of a pair of pliers is garroting the young Republic. If Maciá*[882] *protects the CNT the government will be inhibited, as any would be with a Morrocan boat,*[883] *and now we have Catalonia in the arms of the Communists; if Maciá hits the CNT hard, then.... he will humiliate M. Anido.*[884] *Oh, the irony of events! Every insanity has its straightjacket: the republic is straightjacketed by those who just yesterday praised it. Things will get immensely worse; the news sotto boche*[885] *is that he wants to set the Republic against religion.*[886]

....

879 Translator's note: *El Debate* was a Catholic daily newspaper published in Spain between 1910 and 1936. Its last publication was in July 1936, when at the beginning of the Civil War, the Second Republic ordered its offices closed and confiscated. At the end of the war it had one short revival, but since it was not approved by the Franco regime, it ended soon after.

880 Translator's note: Antonio Maura Montaner was prime minister of Spain on five separate occasions. He entered politics with a reform agenda but veered to the conservative side. His eldest child was Gabriel Maura y Gamazo, who was Labor Minister in the government of King Alfonso XIII; Miguel Maura y Gamazo was his younger brother, who became Minister of Security in the Second Republic.

881 Translator's note: The Esquerra Republicana of Catalonia was a political party founded in Barcelona in 1931. It played an important role in the politics of Catalonia during the Second Republic.

882 Translator's note: Francesc Macià i Llusà was the 122nd president of Catalonia, in office from December 14, 1932, until December 25, 1933. He declared the Free Catalonian Republic in Barcelona in 1932.

883 Translator's note: From the context it can be guessed that this idiom means that, as boats from Morroco had a reputation of not being very safe, the new Republic is constrained by political ties to the radical left.

884 Translator's note: Severiano Martínez Anido was civil governor of Catalonia between 1919 and 1922. He became Subsecretary of the Ministry of Government in 1923 under dictator Primo Rivera and fostered the formation of a workers' union under government control, as opposed to the CNT, which was forced to go underground. When Primo Rivera was deposed in 1930, he was sent into exile. He opposed the legalization of workers' unions in Catalonia. He returned to Spain to fight on behalf of Franco in the Spanish Civil War in 1936 and became Minister of Public Order. He had a reputation for cruelty, making use of *los pistolares*, assassins of political figures.

885 Translator's note: He may mean *sotto voce*, Italian meaning "in a soft voice" or "whispered."

886 J. POZO, *Letter to his family: Cuenca, 7-8-1931*, in: *Causa Beatificationis - Escritos*.

Fr. Pozo was perfectly informed about the events in the young Republic, and shared with many of his contemporaries worries for the future of the Republic regarding positions that were against the faith, promoted by more rationalist ideologies and the pressure of Marxist political parties.

In 1933 he was sent to El Espino as confessor to the juvenists.[887] He arrived on July 27 and soon succumbed once again to his infirmity. The humidity of that valley near the Ebro River aggravated his pulmonary infection with a strong hemoptysis.[888] He was prohibited from having any contact with the teens in order to avoid spreading the contagion. With the impossibility of continuing in that task, once he had again recuperated his health, he returned to Cuenca on October 4, 1934.[889]

One interesting aspect of the life of Fr. Pozo was the propaganda that he created among his acquaintances on behalf of good reading. This was the pulpit from which he promoted the following of Jesus: "He was seen pushing propaganda on behalf of good books among trusted persons."[890] He was devoted to and an admirer of St. Alphonsus. It was Alphonsus' books, preferably, which he recommended to be read or which he gave his acquaintances. He wrote to his sister Fernanda on March 25, 1936:

Let me know if you have read The Glories of Mary and whether you like it. I would be very happy if you promoted this book among friendly families. Oh, my sister! Blessed will you be if you manage to win one soul to true devotion to Mary; you will have won it for heaven. I don't know if you are active like Martha or contemplative like Mary, keen on filling your concha[891] and fattening your spirit at the feet of Jesus; for this reason, I sent you a packet of most useful books for reading at home. I am personally interested in and work on behalf of that cause. Good books have to be brought into the home! The devil and his cohorts

....

887 Translator's note: Juvenists were the students at the juvenate, or high school seminary.

888 Translator's note: Hemoptysis is the coughing up of blood associated with tuberculosis or other bronchial diseases.

889 *Anales* IX, 190. 192. 243-244.

890 CLOTILDE NOTARIO, C. *Beatificationis—Declaraciones* I, 358.

891 Translator's note: The *concha* is a scallop shell. It was used by pilgrims, especially on the Way to Santiago, to eat from or to drink from.

bring bad ones in."[892] *He also wrote to his mother, recommending to her St. Alphonsus' Visits to the Blessed Sacrament and to the Virgin Mary: "It is my daily spiritual fodder and, for that reason, when you read the day each month*[893] *you can truly tell yourself: My son is saying this same thing today to our Father Jesus.*[894]

In Cuenca he was preparing himself for martyrdom in his personal fragility. In view of the illness he suffered, one year before leaving this life, he wrote to his parents: "Oh, let us live for Jesus here, in order to live in tight embrace in the beautiful heaven which I hope is near!"[895]

The spirit of a martyr was not something unprepared for. His life story was leading him along the way of virtue. Those who lived with him shared the idea that he was a man of God. Fr. José Machiñena lived with him for several years in Granada, and later was his provincial superior. He said that "he was a saint; he never complained about his illness, although he was sick and never could do anything other than suffer, but he suffered offering his suffering for souls, and that already came from the religiosity of his family."[896] Fr. José María Ibarrola, also a companion of his in his years in Granada, points out to us "in general, everyone took him for a good person, a very good person; lots of camaraderie, lots of charity; and he put up with his health problems very well, in that he always gave off that he was in good spirits. People who were not members of the Congregation [of the Redemptorists] also appreciated him a great deal, having high opinions of him."[897] And Fr. Isidro Fernández Posado, with whom he was first in Granada and later in Cuenca, remembers that he was "very charitable with his neighbor, with his Brothers; he never bothered anyone, and he especially showed charity to the sick, sparing them as much as possible work or things that might bother them."[898] If any defect were seen in him, it would only be his

....

892 J. POZO, *Letter to his family: Cuenca, 25-3-1936*, in: *C. Beatificationis—Escritos.*

893 Translator's note: *The Visits to the Blessed Sacrament and to the Blessed Virgin Mary* by St. Alphonsus Liguori offers a prayer for each day of the month.

894 J. POZO, *Letter to his family: Cuenca, 27-6-1936*, in: *Ib.*

895 J. POZO, *Letter to his family: Cuenca, 9-9-1935*, in: *Ib.*

896 J. MACHIÑENA, *C. Beatificationis—Declaraciones* I, 99.

897 J. M. IBARROLA, *Ib.,* 271.

898 I. FDEZ. POSADO, *Ib.,* 161.

great naiveté and candidness. That is how Fr. José Machiñena, who knew him well, described him: "He was intelligent, but with an innocence and childlike simplicity. He had the simplicity of a child of eight years of age. What he thought and what he felt, he always said out loud."[899]

Also among the laypeople who knew him in Cuenca he left the reputation of being an angelic person, without any defect. In the declarations of the canonization process all emphasized about him that he was an authentic saint. That's what Patrocinio Moya Martínez believed about him. He said that Julián "was a very caring Father, always wearing a smile on his lips in spite of the fact that he was sick, and always prompt for when he was called to the confessional for the little girls who were to make their First Communion."[900] María del Carmen García de la Rosa, who had quite a bit to do with him, remembers that "he was very kind, very pious, a great interior peace was reflected in him. He was ill and, from what you could see, I suppose and I believe that he bore it with much patience, much peace, much spirit of sacrifice."[901] Emiliana López also noted his piety and kindness, which caused him to be loved by all.[902] Clotilde Notario noted his charity: "You could see in him that he had a great deal of love for neighbor, he dealt with souls with a lot of affection, and nothing else, except that he had, as I have already said, the reputation of being good, very good in general; welcoming souls, I repeat, with much care and charity."[903] Concepción Sanz Gabaldón summarizes the impression of Julián among the People of God in Cuenca, declaring that "he was total goodness, complete gentleness; very patient and very charitable."[904]

Martyr in Doing the Will of God

A day before the Spanish Civil War began and the religious persecution which developed with it, Julián wrote these words to his sister Elisa, who had just recovered from an illness: "Dear sister, these last days have been for

---

899 J. M. IBARROLA, *Ib.*, 99.

900 PATROCINIO MOYA MARTÍNEZ, *Ib.*, 76.

901 M.ª DEL CARMEN GARCÍA, *Ib.*, 115.

902 Emiliana López says: *"He seemed to me to be of a kind character, and very pious....He was much appreciated in Cuenca"* (*Ib.*, II, 535).

903 CLOTILDE NOTARIO, *Ib.*, 538.

904 CONCEPCIÓN SANZ GABALDÓN, *Ib.*, 459.

you 'a sachet of myrrh,'[905] since you have shared the chalice of the sufferings of Jesus...Jesus has had the courtesy of asking a gift of you, and we should sing: What happiness to suffer for the Beloved!....To do his will is our work, as his was in his mortal life."[906]

This is the last letter that Julián wrote. In it he shows his total conformity to doing the will of God. When he writes this, he is not remote from the antireligious storm that is brewing around him. On July 1, 1936, he had written to his family, giving them a description of the social tension that was taking place in the city:

> *Here essentially nothing new: yesterday there was a demonstration by women demanding back pay for their husbands. (Through an initiative of CNT and UGT they have been working on a highway, and now they want the management of City Hall to pay.) They also want them to increase the daily wage and to lessen the hours. They come across as aggressive and not very well educated....Since they are not getting their salary, business is not giving credit. Business also needs money. Now they are sowing the seeds of hatred and threats. Soon the storm will break loose. On the other side, the people of the so-called right wing are people of order and propiety, but they care nothing about practicing religion, which is the basis for mutual respect and justice.*[907]

On July 24, 1936, under order from the superior to seek asylum in the home of friendly persons, he and Br. Victoriano Calvo fled to the house of the Misses Muñoz. Joaquina, one of the sisters who gave him refuge, describes for us the exemplary life that he led and his preparation for martyrdom: "He spent the day praying and, according to what my sister (Eugenia Muñoz) told me, Fr. Pozo sighed after martyrdom and said, 'We do not have martyrs; let's see if we will be the first.' This demonstrates that he was ready for martyrdom and that he sensed it coming."[908]

....

905 Translator's note: This is a quote from the Song of Songs 1:13: "My lover is to me a sachet of myrrh." A sachet was a small perfumed bag used to scent clothing. The meaning is that his sister's recovery was an experience of relief for her in otherwise trying circumstances.

906 J. POZO, *Letter to his family: Cuenca, 17-7-1936*, en: *C. Beatificationis—Escritos.*

907 J.POZO, *Letter to his family: Cuenca, 1-7-1936*, in: *Ib.*

908 JOAQUINA MUÑOZ, *C. Beatificationis—Declaraciones* II, 502.

His readiness for giving his life for Christ, for abundant redemption, was total and passionate. Among the six Redemptorist witnesses to Christ in Cuenca, it seems that he was the one who had the greatest consciousness of martyrdom.

When the imminent danger presented itself in a search of the house where they were staying, they moved to the seminary, where a witness, D. Camilo Fernández de Lelis, tells us "you could see he was peaceful, pious, and compliant with the will of God."[909] Sr. Remedios Acedo saw him pass hours and hours before the Blessed Sacrament.[910]

At midnight on August 9, in company of some other priests, among whom was D. Juan Crisóstomo Escribano, he was taken to the highway to Tragacete. On that road he was killed.[911] "He died as he had lived, in the posture of the classical martyr: on his knees and praying the rosary... Certainly he smiled at the executioners and at the bullets. He had always smiled at everyone and everything, so it is a sure thing that he did not lose his smile until he had lost his life."[912]

Julián was the youngest of the witnesses to the faith who so generously gave their life in the Redemptorist community in Cuenca. He was thirty-three years old. His was an intense interior light which broke forth through having to live with sickness, tuberculosis, which he contracted a little after his religious profession and which never left him. In this way, his life was joined closely to that of Christ: in his yes to religious consecration, in his openness to the mystery of the cross in sickness, in the voluntary offering of his life to be slowly consumed in pain, joyfully accepted through intense prayer,[913] in the daily celebration of the Eucharist and in the sacrament of reconciliation; and finally, by means of offering his life in martyrdom.

....

909 CAMILO FERNÁNDEZ DE LELIS, *Ib.*, I, 286.

910 Cf. REMEDIOS ACEDO, *Ib.*, II, 667.

911 *Death certificate of Julián Pozo Ruiz de Samaniego*: REG. CIVIL DE CUENCA, Sec.3.ª, T. 42, F. 324, N.º 642.

912 D. DE FELIPE, 188.

913 ELOY GÓMEZ JORGE, who was a Redemptorist who lived with Julián Pozo in Cuenca. He declared: "*He was dedicated to the contemplative life, dedicating long hours to being in the chapel in prayer....He was very resigned to it when he said, 'I am not good for anything other than prayer'*" (C. Beatificationis—*Declaraciones* II, 688).

Miguel Goñi Áriz

CHAPTER SEVEN

Miguel Goñi Áriz

Miguel's Little Town, Imarcoain,

Miguel was born on April 27, 1902, in Imarcoain,[914] a little town of Navarre, near Pamplona. His parents were Domingo Goñi Gaztelu and María Áriz Biurrun. The next day he was baptized in the parish church of San Martín.[915] "Two years later," he writes in the notes in the novitiate, "on May 3, 1904, the Most Illustrious Lord Doctor Friar José López de Mendoza, bishop at that time of the Diocese of Pamplona, gave me the sacrament of confirmation."[916]

....

914 REG. CIVIL DEL VALLE DE OLORZ (NAVARRA) Sec. 1.ª, T. 10, f. 126.

915 According to the baptismal records entry "legitimate son and of the lawful marriage of Domingo Goñi, native of Imarcoain, and María Áriz, native of Beriain, both residents of Imarcoain.... Paternal grandparents: Dionisio Goñi, native and resident of Imarcoain, and Felisa Gaztelu, native of Otano, now deceased. Maternal grandparents: Pedro José Áriz, native of Beriain, now deceased, and Josefa Biurrun, native of Biurrun and resident of Beriain. Miguel Eslava, native and resident of Lerruz, was his godfather" (AD. PAMPLONA, *Book of Baptisms of the Parish of San Martín in Imarcoain* I, f. 160 vto. n.º 4).

916 M. GOÑI, *Curriculum vitae: Nava de Rey (Valladolid), 1920, 1*, in: *Causa Beatificationis - Escritos*. In the note in the margin of the Baptismal Register it says: "Miguel Goñi y Áriz. Received the Sacrament of Confirmation in the Parish of Torres on May 3, 1904, as the book of Confirmation attests, page 26" (Parish of SAN MARTÍN in IMARCOAIN, *Book of Baptisms*, I, f. 160 see Marginal Note).

Imarcoain had a dwindling population very similar to what Fr. Madoz[917] described at mid-nineteenth century. It formed part of the district of Elorz, at two-and-a-half leagues from Pamplona,[918] "partly on the plain, partly in the hills, by the highway from Pamplona to Tafalla and Sangüesa[919] .... It had thirteen houses constructed of masonry stone," comprising one lone street. "The land is of good quality; the Elorz River fertilizes it, which goes off to its right, a short distance. There is a hill without trees, but which offers great views in every direction and a grove to the north with good pastures for cattle of every kind."[920]

Miguel also left us a description of Imarcoain during his Castilian stay in Nava del Rey, very far from Navarre. It is a romantic vision of his town, written from the imagination of a boy of eighteen who dreamed of utopian worlds wrapped in nostalgia. Miguel writes in his Notes: "...situated on the side of Mount Aralar of such culminating importance in the thread of Basque tradition and whose glorious summit was sanctified so many times with the appearances of the Archangel Michael."[921] Although in reality Imarcoain is not on the side of Mount Aralar, Miguel liked to see it that way, illuminated by the presence of its angel protector. A desire that he would maintain throughout his life was to see his hometown in the context

....

917 Translator's note: Pascual Madoz wrote a sixteen-volume dictionary of the geography, statistics, and history of Spain and its overseas territories, which was published between 1846 and 1850.

918 Translator's note: this would be 7.5 miles.

919 Translator's note: Tafalla is a municipality and a town in the province of Navarre twenty-one miles (thirty-three kilometers) south of Pamplona with an industrial and agricultural base. Sangüesa is a town on the Aragon River in Navarre that is dotted with many medieval buildings and is twenty-seven miles (forty-four kilometers) from Pamplona.

920 Fr. MADOZ, *Diccionario Geográfico-Estadístico-Histórico de España y sus posesiones de Ultramar* (Madrid, 1845-1850), IX, 423-424. [Translator's note: the title is *Geography-Statistics-History of Spain and its Overseas Possessions*]

921 M. GOÑI, *Curriculum...*, 1. Miguel's curriculum vitae is replete in details, for which reason we shall follow it fairly closely in presenting his infancy and adolescence. [Translator's note: Mount Aralar was the site of a shrine to St. Michael. The eleventh-century Romanesque chapel was built by the Lord of Goñi. The legend is that a knight accidentally killed his own parents. As a penance, he chained himself to the wall of the chapel. St. Michael the Archangel appeared to him and released him from his penance and his chains. A statue of St. Michael was left behind by the archangel to commemorate his visit. A Basque tradition centered on carrying the miraculous statue of St. Michael from town to town.]

of Basque culture, language, and tradition. It was an idea that would stay with him until the moment of his death.[922]

The Notes of Fr. Miguel also show us the family formed by Domingo and María as a privileged place for living out an experience of the faith. In the language of the Second Vatican Council, we would call it a "domestic church." "From my tenderest years my pious parents tried to carefully instruct me in the rudiments of Christian doctrine. They saw their efforts rewarded in how incarnate innocence was deposited in my soul in my First Holy Communion when I was scarcely seven years old. That day was so memorable and so exuberant with consoling recollections for my soul. From that day on, I helped every day at Mass and I prayed the rosary sheltered under the roof of our home."[923]

Miguel's childhood transpired in the normal way in the family setting with his five siblings.[924] Later he would remember in a letter that his oldest brother, Santos, gave him some "slaps on the neck."[925] Even though he was a boy who frequented church a lot, he was not particularly noted for his piety. He was just one more boy from the town. He writes in his Notes that he only went to school for some intervals in his childhood "because of the critical circumstances that surrounded the teacher in the town; the little bit

....

922 In a letter written to his family in the month before his death, he said: "Fr. Gorosterratzu showed me in the last few days a copy of the *Diario de Navarra* which could just as well have been from Cáceres or Albacete, so I was no great fan of it. [Translator's note: *Diario de Navarra* is "The Navarre Daily" newspaper; Cáceres is a city in the autonomous country of Extremadura; Albacete is a city in the autonomous country of Castille-La Mancha. Fr. Miguel Goñi, an ardent Basque, seems to be lamenting the notion that the local Basque newspaper in Navarre is not Basque-oriented and could have been published anywhere else in the country for the little attention it gives to the Basque culture. He even says it tries to destroy Basque culture.] "It had no other interest than to 'un-Basque' Navarre. In it I saw an article accompanied by a photo of Ángel Goñi Navarcorena" [Translator's note: Ángel Goñi Navarcorena was a combatant in the Civil War and was from Imarcoain, so was probably known to Miguel Goñi.]

923 M. GOÑI, *Curriculum…*, 1-2.

924 The Goñi-Áriz family was composed of three boys and two girls (*cf. AD. PAMPLONA, Book I of Baptisms and Confirmations*): Santos (1888), married to Juana Lecumberri; Ángela Josefa (1890), nun in Estella [Translator's note: Estella is a town in Navarre, southwest of Pamplona]; Salustiano Tomás (1892), died at four months old; Severiano (1893), married to Elena Beaumont; Máximo Rosario (1896), married to Felisa Arree; Teresa (1898-1907); and Paula Primitiva (1906-1920). (cf. *Necrology card*; J. ERICE, *Letter to Lucas Pérez about Miguel Goñi: Imarcoain 15-9-1944*, in: *C. Beatificationis - Writings about Miguel Goñi*).

925 M. GOÑI, *Letter to his family*, in: *d. c.*, 1.

I learned, I picked up as a hobby at home."[926] We imagine that the situation of the teacher had something to do with sickness or age. At any rate, home became the place where Miguel would be initiated not only in religious training but also in the first rudiments of reading.

In that situation, his parents were thinking of taking Miguel to a school in Pamplona. In all seriousness, he writes in his Notes: "…so that, after I had studied the fundamentals, I would choose the career that I most liked."[927] It didn't happen, for a reason which today would seem strange and which the novice Miguel saw as providential. We prefer to reproduce his narrative here because it reveals some key characteristics of the extremely sensitive personality of young Miguel, as well as his closeness to his mother and her decisive influence over him:

> *The idea would have been carried out if an unforeseen[928] event had not stifled it. It was the first stage of the road that God had laid out for me and which seemed clear and precise in the eyes of my pious mother. Indeed, one day in Lent—it is engraved in indelible letters in my memory and I remember it as if it happened today—I was crying bitter tears in the solitude of my room. I was scarcely nine years old, and the cause of my tears was the cumulative effect of the dramatic words our pastor had aimed at us, his parishioners, about the pains of hell. They had permeated my faith during my childhood. My mother had heard the sound of my sobs and asked me what the reason was for such strange sighs. I remember I answered her: I'm afraid of going to hell. She tried to console me and among her tender words she suggested to me an idea that came from her maturity and from what she preferred for me. She suggested that I should study for the priesthood.[929]*

---

926 *Ib.*, 2. This lack of a cultural base would become a hindrance in his later academic preparation.

927 M. GOÑI, *Curriculum…*, 2.

928 Translator's note: In Spanish, the word *sic* appears here. It is a Latin word meaning "thus," and is used to point out that what precedes it may appear erroneous, but it is exactly as the author had writtern it. The reference here is to the word *improvisto* ("unforeseen") in Spanish. The correct spelling would have been *imprevisto*.

929 *Ib.*, 2-3.

Miguel said that he liked the idea from the start and they began to think about enrolling him in the seminary as soon as possible. A few months later, in the middle of October 1909, the Redemptorists Laureano Navarro Lizarraga and José Villoslada Villoslada arrived in the town of Imarcoain[930] to preach a parish mission there as well as for the surrounding towns. Miguel confessed that he felt excited with the missionaries from the beginning, and he was attracted to their way of life in an irresistible manner. We come across new data in this context which we know only from his Notes: "I knew about the Redemptorists because I had gone many times to their residence in Pamplona."[931] His enthusiasm was for being a missionary rather than for being a priest.

Miguel mixes a strong dosage of divine Providence into the events that led to his desiring to be a missionary instead of a priest. D. Francisco, his father, died at the age of forty-nine on November 3, 1909,[932] "victim of pneumonia. Without doubt, God used these means to put into action his divine plans; just the same, God prepared a happier future for me and one which embodied for me a more exquisite love."[933]

Stages of Becoming a Missionary

As has happened so many times, the missionary vocation of many Redemptorists had its origin in missions and in contact with the missionaries. That's what happened with Miguel Goñi. Doña María knew the attraction her son had to the missionaries "and putting the matter in the hands of Fr. Navarro

....

930 The chronicle of the mission contains the following notes: "Imarcoain together with the neighboring town of Oriz counts thirty people altogether; Frs. Villoslada and Navarro preached a mission from the seventeenth to the twenty-fifth of October. People came from seven villages to attend. In the mornings we preached in the parish and in the additional place, and every afternoon we made the Visits to the Blessed Sacrament with no scarcity of attendance. We gave out 500 certificates, which indicated that a great number of outsiders and that many of the parishioners had repeatedly gone to Communion. As a means of perseverance, we established the daily visit to the Most Blessed Sacrament. Five people promised to read it aloud in turns for one week each. We also established the work of the Conservation of the Faith with seven people signing up" (*Crónica de Pamplona* I, 322). Fr. R. Sarabia preached several missions with Fr.Villoslada around that time. He described Fr. Villoslada as a native of Granada "somewhat grave but kind" and a great missionary.

931 M. GOÑI, *Curriculum...*, 4.

932 Cf. AD. PAMPLONA *Death Records Imarcoain* I, 84, n.º 6. Although Miguel places the death of his father before the mission, facts show it was the contrary.

933 M. GOÑI, *Curriculum...*, 4.

it was determined that he would be in El Espino at the beginning of the academic year."[934] Four boys left Imarcoain for the minor seminary in El Espino, where they arrived on September 16, 1913.[935] He wrote in his notes: "Two lost their vocations and the third had a saintly death in the juvenate of San Pablo (Cuenca)."[936] In El Espino he came to know Julián Pozo, who entered in the same year as he, and their two lives ran parallel paths.

Miguel began his studies with the difficulties that are usual to one having to adapt to new circumstances and to the lifestyle of a boarding school. He confessed "after the first onslaught of discouragement was over, I went on joyful and content until April 1915. At that time the new juvenate in the city of Cuenca was begun. God wanted to send me there along with my schoolmates."[937] The Redemptorist who accompanied him in these years of formation as director was Fr. Bernardo Fernández Martínez, who left a profound mark on him.[938]

On April 7, 1915, together with Julián Pozo and another thirty-two students coming from the juvenate in Burgos, he arrived at the old monastery of San Pablo in Cuenca. There, atop the gorge and in front of the hanging houses, Miguel Goñi and his fellow students spent their years of formation leading up to novitiate. For him, they were years of change, of passing from adolescence to young manhood, of finding a world of relationship more open than that of El Espino. That, together with his especially sensi-

---

934 *Ib.*, 4.

935 Cf. APRM. *Book of Registrations in the Juvenate of El Espino, year 1913.* The September 6 date, which appears in the Book of Registrations, seems more reliable to us, although Miguel in his curriculum vitae places his date of registration at El Espino as September 8 (M. GOÑI, *Curriculum...*, 5). Of the four boys who registered at the time, only Miguel is from Imarcoain. The other three natives of Navarre are from nearby towns. Their names are brothers Pedro and Abilio Irujo Irure (Salinas de Pamplona) and Seguro Aranguren Áriz (Berain). [Translator's note: Pedro and Abilio Irujo are blood brothers. They are from Salinas de Pamplona, which is a town about 3.9 kilometers (2.4 miles) to the northwest of Imarcoain. Berain is not found on a contemporary map of Spain, but Beriáin is about 4.2 kilometers (2.6 miles) from Imarcoain. It is probably this town that is meant.]

936 M. GOÑI, *Curriculum...*, 5. The four boys from Navarre (Miguel, Pedro, Abilio and Segundo) left from El Espino for the juvenate of San Pablo in Cuenca (cf. APRM *Book of Registrations in the Juvenate in El Espino, year 1913*) and from there Abilio left in 1915 and Segundo in 1916 as a result of not having a vocation. And Pedro *died a saintly death on July 1, 1918* (APRM. *Book of Registrations for the Juvenate in San Pablo-Cuenca, year 1915*, 10-11 y 14-15).

937 M. GOÑI, *Curriculum...*, 5.

938 *Ib.*, 6.

tive character, created difficulties for him in discerning his Redemptorist vocation, when others opted to return home. The lines that we reproduce here from his Notes have accents of sorrow and of a dark night, illuminated only by the security of the closeness of the enveloping and hidden presence of Holy Mary of Perpetual Help, one of his great loves, which he knows is mutual:

There (San Pablo) the years of being a juvenist slipped by, permeated by a thousand twists and turns which many times swept my vocation along and in which I surely would have shipwrecked, if the Virgin of Perpetual Help had not lent me manly courage to keep moving ahead.

How many times was I without an ounce of energy, my soul desolate, without a ray of hope, my heart bleeding and, adding to the contrast and bringing me closer to the abyss, my imagination presenting me with the thought of happy days, of fanciful reveries—I was at the point of abandoning my Mother in heaven![939]

One of the problems that Miguel ran into was his studies.[940] We see that his grades fell during his first academic years in Cuenca and that he was given some failing grades. But little by little he overcame the low grades and ended up being among the best in his class. In that, he saw the hand of Mary. Overcoming his difficulties, he went flying toward his goal: "But she loved me a great deal and many times I clearly and palpably saw her protection and help. She wanted me to be a promoter of her glories and she made sure I would be clothed in the Redemptorist habit."[941]

The last paragraph has clear Alphonsian connotations and helps one discover that one of the veins of Marian devotion in every Redemptorist is *The Glories of Mary*, one of the more universally known works of St. Alphonsus Liguori, the founder of the Redemptorists.

---

939 M. GOÑI, *Curriculum...*, 5-6.

940 Cf. APRM. *Grade Book from the Juvenate of San Pablo.*

941 M. GOÑI, *Curriculum...*, 6.

Juvenists of San Pablo, 1919: M. Goñi,
first on the right, last row

The fact of two minor seminaries raised the number of aspirants to the novitiate. Confronted with this difficulty, Father provincial decided that they would begin a postulancy—a step previous to novitiate—at the same San Pablo, Cuenca. To prepare them, he sent from Astorga Fr. Agustín Pedrosa, a warm-hearted soul from Zamora,[942] who left his mark on generations of Redemptorists and who, we shall see, was the superior of the community in Cuenca at the moment of martyrdom. The postulancy lasted for a month. On the August 23 they left Cuenca to arrive in Nava del Rey (Valladolid) the next day, and received the holy Redemptorist habit on the following day.[943] This information helps us to better understand Miguel's Notes: "I began my postulancy on July 23, 1919, and on August 24 I left for Nava del Rey, receiving the habit of St. Alphonsus on the twenty-fifth. I hope, with the help of God and of Mary, that it will be my shroud of glory."[944] That was his way of saying that his desire was to persevere until death as a Redemptorist. With the change from secular clothing into the Redemptorist habit he began the novitiate under the tutelage of Fr. Rafael Cavero.

In his report on the occasion of this celebration which began the novitiate, the novice master writes down the origin of Miguel's Redemptorist vocation, the parish mission in his town, and gives his judgment about Miguel: "He seems to have love for his vocation and to be a serious man. He seems a little rustic and to have some difficulty in pronunciation because of the configuration of his teeth."[945] At the end of the novitiate the same novice

....

942 Translator's note: Zamora is the capital city in the province by the same name and part of the autonomous region of Castile and Leon.

943 Cf. *Anales* VII, 151-152. 153-154.

944 M. GOÑI, *Curriculum...*, 6. The record of receiving the habit says: *Michael Goñi Ariz. Die 25 Augusti, feria secunda, 1919 in hac domo Seraphicae Theresiae de Jesu in civitate Navae Regis prov. Vallisoletana a R. Raphaele Cavero, Novitiorum magistro in novitiatu admissus est adolenscens Michael Goñi Ariz e pago Imarcoain prov. Navarrensis et dioc. Pampilonensi, natus dies 21 Aprilis, anno 1902, annos 17 et menses* (APRM. *Liber Primus Inscriptionis Vestium mutationis Choristarum. Chorist novices, year* 1919, n.º CCCXVII). [Translator's note: "Miguel Goñi Áriz. On Monday, August 25, 1919, in this house of the Seraphic Teresa de Jesús in the city of Nava del Rey, province of Valladolid, was admitted to the novitiate by Reverend Rafael Cavero, master of novices. The teenager Miguel Goñi Áriz from the town of Imarcoain in the province of Navarre, the diocese of Pamplona, was born on April 21, 1902, and is 17 years and months of age."] (APRM. *Liber Primus Inscriptionis Vestium mutationis Choristarum. Novitiate, Chorists,* Year 1919, n.º CCCXVII).

945 APRM. *Book of Chorist and Lay Postulants* I, n.º 350.

master sent to Rome the obligatory report, giving the reasons for having him profess his vows.[946] In the section "good and bad qualities" he writes: "He has a fair amount of wit and judgment. He is by nature proud, haughty, and irritable."[947] "Sometimes harsh, easily correcting others, a little rustic." On the positive side of the scale, he says: "He is serious, upright, prudent, and fairly pious." About Miguel's behavior in the novitiate: "Sufficiently good; however, he could take greater care to overcome his defects. On occasion he shows himself domineering and a good deal haughty among his companions." Regarding the future, he thinks that "he is able to be a good religious, magnificent missionary, professor, and a good fit for any other ministry in the Congregation," so that in spite of the contradictions in the opinion of Fr. Cavero, the novice master's vote was affirmative.

Miguel Goñi, together with his companions, made his first profession of vows in Nava del Rey on August 26, 1920, signing the document with the name "Miguel María,"[948] which significantly expresses his devotion to Mary. With his profession of vows, he started a new stage in Astorga (León) where he did his studies in philosophy and theology, necessary for priestly ordination.

In the history of Astorga, the major seminary of the Redemptorists received the large class of Brs. Miguel Goñi and Julián Pozo at the end of August with important construction modifications: a new building designed to accommodate the students of philosophy and theology. It was

....

946 AHGR 30150009, 0287.

947 The report says:...*ac imperiosus stomachosus*, without a comma, which we have inserted into the translation.

948 *Ego Michael Goñi Ariz e pago Imarcoain Provintiae Navarrensis, Novitius Congregationis SSmi. Redemptoris hac die 26 Augusti 1920 Sancti Zephirini, sacro in Collegio Sanctae Theresiae in civitate Navae Regis, inter manus admodum Rdi. Patris Leontii D. Jañez, Rectoris hujus domus, secundum regulam nostram et ad tenorem sacrorum et privilegiorum nostrorum sponte nuncupari vota temporalia ad trienium valitura, Paupertatis, Castitatis et Obedientiae, presente tota communitate,praesertim Patribus Felice R. de Samaniego et Theodomiro G. Ronda. Ego Michael Mª Goñi Ariz* [Translator's note: The Latin means, "I, Miguel Goñi Áriz, from the town of Imarcoain, province of Navarre, a Novice of the Congregation of the Most Holy Redeemer, on this day, the 26ᵗʰ of August, 1920, the feast day of St.Zephyrinus, in the holy house of St.Teresa in the city of Nava del Rey, in the hands of Very Reverend Fr. Leoncio Domínguez Yáñez, Rector of this house, according to our Rule and in accord with Canon Law and with our privileges, I have pronounced of my own free will temporary vows for a period of three years of Poverty, Chastity and Obedience, with the whole community present, especially Fr. Felix R.de Samaniego and Theodomiro G.Ronda. I sign this: Miguel María Goñi Ariz."] (APRM. *Liber secundus inscriptionis Professionis Religiosae Perpetuae in Congregatione SS. Redemptoris of the Province of Madrid CSSR, year 1920*, n.ºXXVIII / 274).

inaugurated on April 12, 1921: "It measures seventy meters[949] in length by eighteen[950]in height, the whole thing designed for rooms for the students and a splendid gallery. The prelate of the diocese, Most Excellent Bishop Senso Lázaro, gave it a solemn blessing."[951] The Cathedral chapter and the clergy of the city attended. The event inspired an air of optimism in the young Redemptorist students. No doubt Miguel Goñi and his fellow student, Julián Pozo, shared in the feeling.

We have preserved all the academic grades that Br. Goñi received during his courses of philosophy and theology in Astorga. With rare exceptions, he maintained between a seven and an eight[952]; that is to say, a high passing grade.[953] In the middle of the routine of vacation time in Astorga,[954] Miguel Goñi received the difficult news in August 1922, that his mother was gravely ill. He went to Imarcoain, but arrived after the death of his mother, which occurred on August 18,[955] as the chronicle of Pamplona informs us: "Rev. Br. Goñi returned from Imarcoain. Today, the twenty-eighth, the afore-mentioned Reverend Br. returned from such town where he had precipitously gone from Astorga to be present at the death of his dear mother.

....

949 Translator's note: almost 230 feet.

950 Translator's note: 59 feet.

951 A. SOTÉS, *El convento de San Francisco de Astorga* (Madrid, 1934) 135. The chronicle of the studendate of Astorga tells us: "The great day of the inauguration of the new building dawns triumphantly. A day which will be one of the greatest in the history of the Congregation in our country. And not precisely for what the inauguration is in itself, but for what it means, because it is an indication of the vigor of the Congregation in Spain, in that now the old ways are not enough. It is necessary to broaden them. And it can even be perceived that one day they will be insufficient to contain the overflow of energy that continues to develop. *Gloria Patri!*" [Translator's note: These last two words are Latin, meaning "Glory be to the Father," the first words of the prayer called the "Glory Be."] (APRM. *Chronicle of the Studendate in Astorga* II, 142).

952 Translator's note: Spain has a 10-point grading system for elementary and high schools. 9.0-10 is the highest possible grade; 5-5.9 is the lowest possible passing grade.

953 "Year 1921: Philosophy, 7-7; Sciences, 7-8; History, 7-8. Year 1922: Philosophy, 6-7; Sciences, 8-7; History, 10-8. Year 1923: Dogma, 8-7; Hermeneutics, 8-7; Hebrew, 6-6; Sacred Scripture, 7-7. Year 1924: Theology, 8-7; Sacred Scripture, 8-8. Year 1925: Moral, 7; Canon Law, 7-8. Year 1926: Moral, 7; Patrology, 7; Canon Law, 6-7; Pastoral Theology, 7" (*APRM, Book of Student Grades. Astorga 1901-1951*). This objective data explains the opinion of Fr. Dionisio de Felipe: "He was not brilliant in his studies; he remained average. He did not have extraordinary talent." (D. DE FELIPE, *Nuevos Redentores* [Madrid, 1962] 177).

954 Translator's note: At the time, Redemptorist novices and students in vows did not go home for vacation with their families. Instead, a relaxed schedule was provided for them at the seminary or some other place where they remained together throughout the time.

955 Cf. AD. PAMPLONA, *Death Records Imarcoain* I, 97 vto. n.º 1.

Unfortunately, he arrived late and when they had already buried her; today, the twenty-ninth, after he had spent a few days in his native home, he left for Estella accompanied by his sisters to visit his religious sister and this morning, September 1, he returned to the studendate in Astorga."[956]

....

956 *Crónica de Pamplona* III, 135. [Translator's note: The annals entry appears to have been pieced together over a series of days.]

Family of M. Goñi

After three years of temporary profession, the time came for perpetual profession. The reports sent to Rome by the prefect and the provincial superior asking perpetual profession for Br. Goñi and his classmates were as short as they were positive: "He is adorned with very good qualities and seems to be a good religious."[957] The certificate is signed by Br. Miguel María Goñi Áriz in Astorga, September 15, 1923, with the formula established by the constitutions.[958]

On September 19, 1925, Miguel Goñi received the subdiaconate with three other classmates; the next day the chronicler describes it: "With everyone in the class now suitably prepared, the eighteen students of moral theology in their second year received together the holy order of deacon, which filled the hearts of all of us with joy."[959] September 27 was the great day of his priestly ordination together with the rest of his classmates, among them Fr. Julián Pozo. Although we lack correspondence or personal notes, which would allow us to know the spiritual intensity he experienced in these moments, we possess a significant reference by the chronicler in Astorga celebrating the fact of having eighteen new priests. If we read carefully, realizing we are dealing with a student chronicler, we can approximate the feelings of rejoicing in the group and in each and every one of the particular individuals:

Alleluia! Alleluia!, the angels sang around the sanctuary and we, behind the sacred tabernacle, repeated: Alleluia! Alleluia! The Divine Prisoner, the Eucharistic Redeemer, has chosen a new and numerous group of ministers of his Most Holy Body and of his Most Holy Blood! Our hearts were full of holy joy and happiness to receive on our knees today the first blessing of these new priests, who, eighteen in number, ascended the steps to the holy altar. What a great consolation to think that eighteen new priests together joined the ranks of the missionaries

....

957 The prefect of students in Astorga, Fr. Carlos Otero, and the provincial, Nicanor Mutiloa, recommended them for profession (Astorga, 29.8.1923; AHGR 30150007, 0027). The affirmative response of the general government to Fr. Mutiloa is dated in Rome 30.VIII.1923 [Translator's note: This follows the European custom of writing numeric dates with day/month/year] (AHGR 30150001, 1626).

958 APRM. *Actus Authentici Professionum a Votis Perpetuis* I, p. 41, n.º 20. [Translator's note: This Latin title translates "Official Acts of Profession to Perpetual Vows"]

959 *Crónica de estudiantado de Astorga* III, 27.

*of the Redeemer! The next day they all said their first Mass, forming
an interminable series.*[960] *In the refectory*[961] *the customary homages of
song and compositions were made to them.*[962]

In this previous passage we can discover the spirituality in which Miguel
and Julián were living at those moments. It was a spirituality centered, by
preference, on the priesthood as a calling to a sublime ministry through the
Eucharist and the missionary charism.

The large group continued on in Astorga until they had finished their
second academic year of moral theology. On July 25, 1926, Fr. Miguel
Goñi and fifteen other classmates moved to Nava del Rey (Valladolid) to
begin second novitiate. During this long time of prayer and reflection—
under the direction of the expert teacher of mission preaching, Fr. Antonio
Girón[963]—they dedicated themselves to tempering the spirit, to the study
of the method and contents for the parish mission, and to prepare sermons
to be delivered in the spirit of St. Alphonsus de Liguori.[964]

Physically and intellectually, Fr. Miguel Goñi had good qualities for
preaching. Thirty-five sermons of his remain, many of them written during
these months. Dionisio Ruiz, acting as critic, considers that "the oratorical
pieces which he wrote with the idea of later preaching them, and which have
been preserved, do not offend by coming up too short either in content or in
delivery. Especially in his apologetical works and his homages to the cross,
the Eucharist, and the Virgin, he hits notably high notes. Also striking is his
talk for the wedding of one of his brothers."[965] With his sermons composed,
Miguel was ready for the missionary life.

The First Missionary Stage: Granada (1927-1928)

With the period of his formation as a missionary concluded, Fr. Goñi was

....

960 Translator's note: At the time, concelebrated Masses were not permitted, and all Masses
were finished by midday. So these eighteen new priests had to say Masses quickly one after another
so that they all could say their first Mass in the seminary.

961 Translator's note: dining room.

962 *Ib.,* 27-28.

963 Antonio Girón González (cf. Appendix 2).

964 *Crónica de Nava* III, 92.

965 D. RUIZ, *De camino* 3, 8 (APRM. Mártires 0400124).

sent to the community in Granada on February 27, 1927. The chronicle of his new house welcomed him this way: "On March 2, Fr. Miguel Goñi and Francisco Rodríguez Robles arrived to become part of this community. They had finished their second novitiate in Nava del Rey. With them the community numbers twelve priests, a number which, I think, it had never reached before."[966] There Fr. Goñi was with Fr. Julián Pozo, who had come to the city of the Alhambra in 1925. The two schoolmates were again reunited.

In those years young priests spent a long period of active waiting. They could not do much apostolically, especially in a large community, because the Rule limited their preaching and prohibited them from hearing confessions for the first five years after ordination—especially confessions of women. It is understandable that in that situation the apostolic activity in which young Miguel Goñi was engaged in Granada was minimal. The superior of the house—in this case, the great missionary from Zamora, Tomás Vega—distributed the missions and apostolic commitments to the older Fathers, beginning with himself. Throughout these months the community in Granada was enjoying the hope and enthusiasm engendered by the pontifical coronation of the icon of Perpetual Help, which the superior was promoting and which took place on June 12, 1927.

Miguel Goñi initiated his preaching with two sermons for Lent in Santa Fe and Albolote, two towns on the Granadian plain. He also gave two sermons for special occasions, one on St. Anthony and the other on the passion of Christ, also in Santa Fe. Up until November he preached four more sermons.[967] His first pastoral assignment of any importance was the novena in honor of the Immaculate Conception in Castro del Río, in the province of Córdoba. It seems he made a very good impression because three years later he was invited again to preach there when he was

....

966 *Crónica de Granada* III, 311.

967 *Ib.*, 312. 314. 317-318. 344. When assignments within the community were made in May 1927, the two young priests, Goñi and Robles, did not receive any.

living in Santander.[968] In January 1928, he preached the mission in Agrón (Granada)[969] with Fr. José Daquinta Nieto. Although it was the first mission that he preached, he seems to have been quite satisfied with it:

Mission in Agrón (9 to 18 of January). Agrón, a poor town with more than 900 souls, province and diocese of Granada, regular in religious practice. Good welcome. A great deal of attendance in the evening. The majority of men and almost every woman went to confession. Frs. Nieto and Goñi gave the mission. The mayor was most attentive: he even clarified Church teaching one day. Fr. Goñi went to the rural residence of the friars of D. José Casinello, preaching and hearing confessions.[970] There were 800 Communions.[971]

It was the first and last mission of his time in Granada. We find only three more sermons preached by him up to the time when he left the city: two of the sermons were in May and one in June.[972]

On July 3, 1928, Fr. Miguel left the city of the Alhambra and went on route to Barcelona. The impression left by the chronicler is that the chronicler did not regret Fr. Goñi's departure too much: "May everything go well there for Fr. Goñi, and good journey." And since various priests and brothers left the community during these changes in personnel, the chronicler concludes: "With this fact the community can now begin to breathe... even though there still is a lot of cloth remaining to be cut."[973] By way of this

....

968 *Ib.*, 344. We read in the chronicle of Madrid for November 27, 1930: *"Fr. Goñi arrived in Santander, for a brief stay, in order to preach the Novena in Castro del Río (Córdoba)."* He rested a bit and on the twenty-ninth continued his journey. On "December 10, Fr. Goñi arrived in his residence in Santander after his Novena in Castro del Río. On December 11, Fr. Goñi left for Santander" (Chronicle of Madrid-PS, the year 1930, 495, 497). It is confirmation that he was well remembered for his short stay in the Andalusian lands.

969 *Crónica de Granada* III, 349.

970 Translator's note: José Casinello-Barroeta and his brother Andrés were devoted to the Dominican Friars at the Monastery of San Domingo el Real, which was in Madrid. They themselves were laymen, but members of the Third Order. During the Spanish Civil War they were both martyred for their faith. D. Andrés was beatified on March 25, 2017. D. José apparently hosted the preaching event at his rural residence.

971 *Ib.*, 354.

972 *Ib.*, 353.

973 *Ib.*, 360.

comment, uneasiness can be detected in the community of Granada. More than the difference in age and mentality with the chronicler, Fr. Agapito Carpintero, ordained in 1893, discomfort with the size of the community, the presence of young priests, and the lack of work for everyone is hidden in the words.

Member of a Newborn Community: Barcelona (1928-1929)

The Redemptorist community in Barcelona began its journey in August 1926.[974] Frs. Ramón Sarabia, Domingo Saa, and Matías Martínez were sent along with Brs. Alfredo Gómez and Rafael Martínez to found that house. They were provisionally housed in a chalet along the Méndez Vigo alley-way.[975] They fixed up the living room to serve as their chapel. They lived squeezed together there until August 1929 when the new church on Calle Balmes was blessed.[976] These were difficult years in which their fundamental work was to achieve being a religious community in the "Ciudad Condal"[977] where they were to be simply "available." The main work of the community in Barcelona was worship in the house chapel first of all and in the church after that, the promotion of eucharistic Thursdays[978] and the spread of devotion to the icon of Perpetual Help.

Even though Miguel is not mentioned in Barcelona, we know that on the same day that he left Granada, July 3, 1928, the chronicle in Madrid records that Fr. Goñi arrived in the house of Perpetuo Socorro and left

....

974 The chronicle of Barcelona began in 1939 since the earlier chronicle had been destroyed in the religious persecution. The annals for those years were written after the religious persecution, and were written from later sources. To put these years in Barcelona in context, we shall use the following bibliography: R. TELLERÍA, *Un instituto misionero* (Madrid, 1932) 430-434; D. RUIZ, *50 años en Barcelona*: BPE. XV, 104 (1977) 112-157; T. CEPEDAL, *Barcelona (1936...)*: BPE. XXVII, 81-82.

975 Translator's note: this narrow street or alley in Barcelona connects in midblock the larger streets of Carrer d'Aragó and Carrer del Consell de Cent.

976 Translator's note: The new church was built about an eight-minute walk to the southwest of where they were living on Passatge de Méndez Vigo. It was called the Shrine of Our Lady of Perpetual Help.

977 Translator's note: Barcelona is often referred to as *la Ciudad Condal*, meaning "City-County," because in the past its demarcations included it as a county and a city.

978 Translator's note: "Eucharistic Thursdays" are a form of devotion to the Blessed Sacrament, on Thursday in particular since it is associated with the Last Supper.

Madrid on July 6 for Barcelona.[979] The great missionary and catechist, Ramón Sarabia,[980] continued as superior of the community. It happened that he lived, even though provisionally, in the little house and the chapel on Calle Méndez Vigo while waiting to move to the permanent location. "The flow of people to the simple and pious chapel increased to the point that for novenas of the Virgin of Perpetual Help and other solemnities it was necessary to assign people turns for coming into the chapel."[981] They also geared their apostolate toward religious boarding schools.

Miguel Goñi was able to experience the move to the permanent residence in Barcelona. Once they had bought a building, the community moved to Pasaje Mercader and rehabbed a garage as a church with the entrance on Calle Balmes. Once it was in shape, the newly ordained Redemptorist Bishop Nicanor Mutiloa blessed it on August 10, 1929. "All the associations of ladies and gentlemen which had been created in the chapel and part of the nocturnal adoration group formed long lines, mostly made up of men who had candles in their hands and who were accompanying the Blessed Sacrament. The Señor Comandante of the Marina, representing city government, D. Manuel Luengo,[982] director of the royal palace of Pedralves[983] and other distinguished persons presided...."[984] While the excitement of the event was still palpable, Fr. Miguel was sent to Santander in September 1929. He was in Barcelona a little more than a year. We have very little detail about his time there.

Missionary out of Santander (1929-1932)

Fr. Goñi arrived in Santander on September 17, 1929.[985] The community

---

979 *Crónica de Madrid-PS*, year 1928, 382.

980 In his *Memorias*, he does not mention Fr. Miguel. That has its explanation. Fundamentally, they are missionaries and it is certain they were not companions in giving missions (R. SARABIA, d. c. X, 1-101).

981 R. TELLERÍA, *o. c.*, 431.

982 Translator's note: This may be D. Manuel Luengo who was wounded in battle in Morroco in the first half of the 1920s and became commander of a company of Civil Guard in 1930 fighting on behalf of the Nationalist troops.

983 Translator's note: The Palau Reial de Pedralbes, as it is called in Catalán, is in a large garden area in Barcelona. It was the residence of the Royal Family from 1919 until 1931.

984 *Ib.*, 431.

985 *Anales*, IX, 299.

had been founded in 1920.[986] The residence and church were finished in 1928. Even though there was still work to be done on it, the church was consecrated by Redemptorist bishop Nicanor Mutiloa on December 14, 1928.

The provincial chronicle[987] for 1930 includes Fr. Miguel Goñi in the list of personnel and with the office of librarian. In April 1930, Fr. Donato Jiménez was named superior. In 1931, Fr. Miguel is listed as zelator for the community, guest prefect,[988] and librarian. In 1932, he is listed only as guest prefect. In spite of his youth, the work entrusted to him in the community reveals the moral prestige that he had there.

In 1931, with the establishment of the Republic, the community in Santander was terrorized with the burning of monasteries and convents. On May 13, all the religious went to sleep in homes of friends. Once the scare was over, they lived out "the rest of the year without threats or social convulsions, in a climate of relative peace." The chroniclers point out that, "happily, the people of Santander are more sensible than people in other places."[989] In spite of the strained mood in the first year of the Republic, the work of the missions not only did not suffer any decrease, but in fact intensified. They preached twenty-five missions in Cantabria, Vizcaya, Orense, Salamanca, and Burgos. Fr. Miguel Goñi also participated in this apostolic activity, working with the veteran missionary, Fr. Manuel Vélez. "The team Vélez-Goñi became deeply involved in the territories of Orense—diocese of Astorga—and preached in Jagoaza, Castelo, Cascallana, Cobas, Santa María de Arones, Freijido de Arriba, and Freijido de Abajo."[990]

....

986 R. TELLERÍA, *o. c.,* 411-417.

987 *Anales* X, 45. 98. 152.

988 Translator's note: The job of the guest prefect was to welcome and see to the needs of any guest who came to stay in the community.

989 *Ib.,* 98.

990 *Ib.,* 99.

Fr. Miguel Goñi Áriz

Compared with the intensity of the missionary activity, religious services in the church of the community were poorly attended. The geographical situation of the church—up on a hill—and the infrequent participation of the people of Santander in organized religious activities outside of the Mass, meant that the usual services (sermons, instructions, novenas, seven-day prayer events, for example) had rare participation by the faithful.[991] Fr. Miguel would participate in many of them, but the chronicler does not mention names.

The last year that Fr. Miguel spent in Santander was 1932, and not the full year—just until September. The lack of details in the chronicle keeps us from being more precise about the missionary activities of Fr. Miguel and of the others. In spite of the sparse details, the departure of Frs. Retana and Goñi stands out with this detail: "good workers in the vineyard of the Lord." This allows us to be sure that Fr. Miguel participated in various missions, renewals, novenas, and very "many individual sermons" that the chronicler mentions.[992]

Vigo: Generous Self-Surrender to the Poor (1932-1935)

The Redemptorists founded the community of Vigo[993] a little before Fr. Miguel Goñi arrived, which also was his situation in previous assignments. In

....

991 "In the house," says the chronicler, "they had worked hard, but without any humanly satisfying results, nor hope of anything possibly better. First, the number of participants is small, even in the solemn functions. There was an occasion in which they had preached a sermon to fifteen people. Second, one has to battle against the extremely bad acoustical conditions of the church, a situation that is worth studying to see what solution there may be. Third, the interior of the church is completely dark so that as a result the preacher does not see his congregation, nor does the congregation connect with the preacher, because they don't see him. He may as well save himself all the gestures he makes in the pulpit. Fourth, there is not in Santander the custom of listening to sermons. It is a common sight that a group of people will walk in when the preacher is speaking, and even preaching something interesting. They make their visit and are out again in two minutes. There are whole families very addicted to staying home. They attend Mass every day in our church and are considered serious and pious. And yet perhaps they have not heard a single sermon in our church during an evening solemn function. Regarding the viability of the Associations, our chronicler says, 'they drag out a languid and neglected life. For instance, for the weekly meetings of Perpetual Help and Eucharistic Heart, with difficulty perhaps sixty people might attend at maximum. Eucharistic Thursdays are more viable, but aren't enough'."

992 "The year 1932. External Ministry: Missions, 13; Renewals, 5; short Missions, 4; Novenas, 6; Tridua, 23; Holy Week sermons, 4; retreats, 8; individual sermons...very many" (*Ib.*, 153-154).

993 Translator's note: Vigo is a city in the northwest of Spain, on the coast of the Atlantic.

July 1925 they rented an apartment on the highway to Baiona[994] and they set aside a room as the chapel. It was a humble and poor beginning. However, from the start its principal activity was the parish missions. At the end of 1927, they began work on the provisional house and chapel, which were inaugurated the following May. From the beginning it became the spiritual focus of "people of the area, generally humble and dedicated to the work of fishing...and, especially on feast days, they hurried to come to the four Masses of the morning and to adore Jesus in the Blessed Sacrament."[995]

Miguel Goñi arrived in Vigo on September 17, 1932,[996] freshly in the priesthood and with his missionary charism open to simple people of a fishing area. He heard the cries for revolution in the city and in the town during his process of changing assignments and he invested himself, as a preacher of parish missions, in the sweet, fog-filled lands of deep Galicia.[997] It was the apostolic stage of his life, which is the most ample and the best known.

Galicia lived in the tension of the time between being a rural environment, anchored in immobility,[998] and the world of the awareness of the proletariat, which was making advances in industrial zones. This clash is discernible in the mission chronicles, in which are heard the voices and groups of the left, radical and anticlerical, with another vision of the future and of the Spanish problematic. The community of Vigo, and in particular Fr. Miguel, will become privileged witnesses of this change in Galician society.

Moreover, with the beginning of 1932 and confronted with the diffi-

....

994 Translator's note: Baiona, Pontevedra, is another municipality in Vigo Bay.

995 R. TELLERÍA, *o. c.*, 427-428.

996 *Ib.*, 175.

997 Translator's note: Galicia is an autonomous community of northwest Spain that in ancient times was inhabited by Celts.

998 Around this time Juan Ramón Jiménez gave a pained view of Galicia—poor, in mourning, "with its beautiful soul hemmed in and isolated," as suggested in the poetry of Rosalía de Castro (J. RAMÓN JIMÉNEZ, *Españoles de tres mundos (1914-1940)* [Madrid 1969] 90). [Translator's note: Juan Ramón Jiménez Mantecón was a Spanish poet who won the Nobel Prize in Literature in 1956 for his poetry. He died in 1958. María Rosalía Rita de Castro was a Spanish poet who wrote in Gallego, the language of Galicia. She was an important figure of the Galician Romantic movement. She died in 1885.]

culty of preaching missions, the provincial government[999] made the decision that missions would be preached free of charge almost in their totality. The chronicler considered it "a big mistake in Galicia where they still regard highly our missions and up to the present they are well-compensated." And he offers this reason: "From now on there will hardly be a pastor who will want a mission if it is not free because the word that it can be gotten for free will have run the course of the four provinces[1000] with lightning speed."[1001]

Disputes aside, his apostolic activity soon commenced. In November, he gave the first mission with Fr. Aniceto Orive in San Martín de Barreiros, a little town of Pontevedra and of the diocese of Tuy. It is worthwhile listening to the chronicler to situate ourselves, from the start, in the missionary environment of Fr. Miguel and in the political climate in which it unfolded: "This parish is made up of 118 household; more than a third of the men are in America. The beginning was good, morning and afternoon. 489 Communions were distributed; 185 to 200 people went to confession; of the three somewhat small neighborhoods scarcely one person came because there was a Communist preacher who was dissuading them from doing so. Devotion to the Sacred Heart of Jesus received a boost."[1002]

From there they went to Parderrubias, a larger parish, in the same diocese. In this case, attendance at the holy mission was very good. In a population of 900 souls "thirty-five people remain who have not gone to confession, in the majority men perverted by the antireligious ideas which saturate the social ambience."[1003] They returned to Vigo on December 22, 1932, and, for the first time, the whole community was able to get together to joyfully celebrate the mystery of the Nativity in a brotherly environment.

Fr. Miguel began the first half of 1933 with great apostolic activity.

....

999 Translator's note: of the Redemptorists.

1000 Translator's note: Galicia is divided into four provinces: A Coruña, Lugo, Ourense, and Pontevedra.

1001 APRM, *Crónica de Vigo* I, 182.

1002 *Ib.*, 178.

1003 "1,620 Communions were distributed and the Apostolate of Prayer was given a strong push" (*Ib.*, 179).

The chronicle only mentions his preaching dates.[1004] It neglects to add the hidden dimension to which he dedicated the greater time: the sacrament of reconciliation. So, once the Christmas liturgical celebrations were over he went with Fr. Orive to San Pedro de Cea, province of Pontevedra,[1005] to begin a new mission. The town of 235 households was difficult:

Scarcely sixty people went to Mass on Sunday. We reached an audi-ence of fifty to sixty people with the morning talks, of whom eight or ten were men. In the evening, some 300 persons came in the last days. 517 Communions were distributed and confessions were heard for 350 people. Because of the coldness to religion there were neighborhoods, some even close to the church, from which not even ten people came. On the other hand, the good people were left with such a hunger for the Word of God that they continued sometimes to attend the mission in Bayón, at a distance of an hour and a half.[1006]

It was planned for the same Fathers to preach the aforementioned mission in Bayón,[1007] but Fr. Miguel could not "because of indisposition" and was replaced by a confrere from the community. We don't know exactly what happened to Fr. Miguel. By way of the details that the chronicle goes on to give, we are inclined to think that it dealt with the first symptoms of the bronchial illness that will keep him from continuing in the wet climate of Galicia with its lack of sunshine. In March and April, Fr. Miguel preached

....

1004 January: 7-18 mission in Cea; 28, retreat to the Little Sisters of the Poor; 22, talk. February: 2, Holy Hour; 5-12, talks and commentary on the Exercises to servant women; 17-1, mission in Previdiños. March: 5-7, talk in Pradende on fulfilling the Easter Obligation; 8-10, the same in Destériz; 14-19, retreat for the Little Sisters for the Abandoned Elderly; 19, sermon in Rosál; 26, the same. April: 1-7, seven-day prayer service for the Seven Sorrows in La Guardia; 14-15, two sermons for Holy Week in Arbo; 25-27, Triduum for the Oblate Sisters of the Holy Spirit (Institute of Santa Zita). May: 6-17, mission in Chapela; 20-21, Triduum in honor of St. Rita for the Little Sisters; 28, Daughters of Mary in Viceso. June: 4, Daughters of Mary in Barcela; 21-23, Sacred Heart in Vilar; 25, the same in Ramalleza (San Pedro de); 27-29, Perpetual Help in Bouzas (Cf. *Ib.* 181).

1005 Translator's note: San Pedro de Cea, Pontevedra, is a civil parish in the municipality of Villagarcía de Arosa in the province of Pontevedra; it has a small, diminishing population.

1006 *Ib.*, 183.

1007 Translator's note: San Xoán de Baión (in Galician) is a civil parish situated in the munic-ipality of Villanueva de Arosa, province of Pontevedra. The church of San Juan de Bayón is from the twelfth century.

a variety of retreats, services for fulfilling the Easter obligation, and Holy Week sermons.

The third mission was in Chapela.[1008] Its environment was not propitious for the mission either. The chronicler gives two reasons: "Masonic propaganda against the mission...and the scandal which came from the administrator of the parish": the priest had fallen in love with a girl from the place and "ended up marrying her civilly"; moreover, in spite of being settled in Orense, the couple came back "from time to time to give public scandal with their cynical displays and their lack of concern." With these things in the background, "in the morning some twenty-five older people came and in the evening some sixty and a hundred children in the first days...135 souls went to confession and 280 Communions were distributed. The 100 seamen who were on strike could easily have attended, but not a single one did. In spite of the disaster that the mission was, the few who attended requested a renewal for the end of October and it is hoped that the situation will improve and the results may be different."[1009]

In the second half of 1933 Fr. Miguel had less outside activities, which makes us believe that his health had weakened. In reality, only two novenas, a few Tridua, and sermons for special occasions.[1010]

In 1934 Fr. Miguel seemed to feel better and resumed the missionary apostolate in the province of Orense. His companion and the superior of the missions was Fr. Angel Alonso, who probably passed on to the chronicler the information that has been preserved. In January they preached a renewal in Barja: "Complete attendance...Renewal with very good results. Everyone or almost everyone went to confession and Communion."[1011] In

---

1008 Translator's note: Chapela is a beautiful seaside town on the Ría de Vigo, an estuary of the Atlantic. Its deep waters make it ideal for sailing.

1009 The mission was given May 6-17. The town consisted of 750 households. It belonged to the Diocese of Tuy, the province of Pontevedra (*Ib.*, 186-187).

1010 "Novena of Perpetual Help in Mugía. Sermon in honor of the Virgin of Mt. Carmel in Arbo. Some 'fervorinos' and a Holy Hour in the house." [Translator's note: "fervorinos" tend to be short, pious talks, usually made up on the spot.] "One First Sunday in the house" [Translator's note: this was probably a sermon that he preached for his own community and which the members would have taken turns in giving.] "Triduum in honor of Christ the King in Cambados. Triduum in honor of the Holy Souls in Purgatory in Boiro. Sermon on Christ the King in Valladares. The same in honor of the Virgin in Cangas. The same in honor of Sta. Cecilia in Santiago de Vigo. The same in honor of Mary most Pure in Cangas. The same in honor of the Holy Souls in Purgatory in Cirán" (*Ib.* 199).

1011 "A town of 185 households, approximately 1,000 souls." (*Ib.*, 204).

February the missionaries went to Torno.[1012] Success did not smile upon them: "Missionwise, one of the Fathers says, it was a real disaster. Not a single extraordinary confession, no sign at all to do credit to the outcome of the mission. Rather, this could be considered a compliment: they came, but not all, and only to pass by." The chronicler gets more exact: "It seems, however, that the harshness and severity of these words need to be somewhat toned down."[1013] They went through something similar in the mission in Gález to judge by the descriptions the chronicler gives us of the town and the period.[1014] In March, both Fathers gave the mission in Lobios, a town "very divided by political parties, and governed by a priest with very little zeal" who did not announce the mission until the day it began. The terrain was "fertilized very little for the seed of the holy mission....The fruit was, and it necessarily had to be, very little. Scarcely half attended until the end of the mission, and that poorly."[1015] Once the mission ended, Fr. Miguel preached in Trino "a sermon to prepare the people for fulfilling their Easter duty." In April, a Triduum to Perpetual Help in Santa María de Gándara and a sermon on St. Joseph in the boarding school in Vigo. In June, two more: in honor of the Sacred Heart in Cangas and in honor of Perpetual Help in Bouzas. In August, novena of Perpetual Help in Moraime.[1016]

From July 10 through 22, 1934, the superior general Fr. Murray and the

----

1012 Translator's note: Torno is a small civil parish in the province of Orense.

1013 *Ib.*, 201.

1014 Province and diocese of Orense. Population, 120-130 households, "...approximately 700 souls. Focus of socialists and Communists. It was a mission very similar to the one in Coya, as previously described. [Translator's note: we do not have a description of that mission.] The result was very consoling, although to judge by the externals it was not showy for its solemnity or the kind of pomp you find in towns of great faith. All the men, except forty, went to confession; of the women, only two did not go to confession. The children helped a great deal with their enthusiasm to set the scene for a success. It was an enthusiasm that then spread to the adults. It is especially to be noted about this mission that not only the children, but also the adults, went to their homes each night singing the words of the hymns of the mission; and this without any fear of the opposition and war with the socialists and Communists threatening from their dingy places. [Translator's note: the Spanish word used, *antros*, translated here as "dingy places," has the colloquial sense of a "dump."] Nothing came of the loud-mouthed threats" (*Ib.*, 206).

1015 Alonso y Goñi. province and diocese of Orense. "Town of 150 households, around 800 inhabitants" (*Ib.*, 208).

1016 *Ib.*, 211. 212. 225.

consultor Sordet[1017] made a canonical visit to Vigo. They left in writing their impression of the young community in Vigo, made up at that time of nine priests and three Brothers: "The work in the provisional church was not interrupted by the Revolution and has good attendance, especially during the summer, and always for the Tridua, novenas, festivals, and so on. They have offers for outside work, which they cannot accept, and many missions. The people are generous, care a great deal about our men, and encourage them to build the new church. The new house and the little garden are pleasant and their position above the port very pretty."[1018]

The superior, Fr. Tomás Vega, received this assessment from them: "Good preacher, enthusiastic, and with good judgment. He is spiritual and leads the community well, so that as a result there is a good deal of fraternal union among them all." And the assessment that the visitors made about Miguel Goñi is the following: "His health is a little weak, is of good character, and a good preacher and missionary; but not too supernatural, and vain; he enjoys being in the parlor and has an inclination toward sex; but he has been warned and seems to be doing better."[1019]

We will pause briefly to consider this assessment. First, we note the explicit reference to his health: "a little weak." Secondly, Father general gives a positive assessment about the missionary charism of Fr. Miguel and says the same about his "good character," an important aspect for pastoral ministry and for community life. Thirdly, the report makes a critical reference to his inadequate interior life: "not too spiritual," a note which will be repeated in the provincial canonical visitation the following year, which also takes place in Vigo.[1020] It is clear that we are dealing with an opinion shared by the major superiors in Rome and Madrid. Fr. Miguel's open disposition

....

1017 Translator's note: Irish Redemptorist Most Reverend Patrick Murray was elected superior general and rector major of the Redemptorists in 1909. He resigned his office in 1947. Rev. Auguste Sordet, CSsR, was a French Redemptorist who was consultor general to superior general Murray from 1915 to 1947. A consultor general is an assistant to the superior general.

1018 AHGR 30150002, 0033.

1019 *R. Michele Goñi. Di salute un po' debole, buon carattere e buon predicatore e buon Misionario, ma poco sopranaturale, e vanitoso, ama il parlatorio ed è inchinato al sesso, ma ne è stato ripreso e sembra andare meglio. (Ib.).*

1020 "Reverend Miguel Goñi: Sickly, of a disposition and facility for preaching but lacking in a supernatural spirit. It is a defect which affects his preaching and his ability to get along with others; just the same, there was no serious complaint about this latter point" (AHGR 30150002, 0034).

and his youth lead him to sin through imprudence and to go up against the stereotypes of the time in the issue of understanding the relationship of a religious with persons of the opposite sex.

For the last ten days in October, Miguel went to Caleiro[1021] for the novena for the Poor Souls. He could not finish it, "impeded by a deep cough and something of a fever."[1022] On October 25, Fr. Ferrero came to take his place. The bronchial-pulmonary infirmity, always lurking in him, struck him each time with increasing force. He began November with various talks in different places and a Triduum for the Carmelites of Vigo. However, each time he could give fewer consecutive days to preaching.[1023]

The year 1935, even though not to be completed, was the last for his stay in Vigo. The chronicler does not record any journeys away from the house for him. His weak health had become a serious problem. The "good preacher and missionary," as Father general called him, had to accept the idea that this phase of his life was coming to a close for him and he had to choose another form of announcing and giving testimony to the gospel: to take up his cross and carry it with Redemptorist elegance on the paschal road. During this long time of apparent inactivity in outside things, Fr. Miguel Goñi lived out his dark night. He certainly must have gone out on walks, on the days and in the hours prescribed by the Rule, to breathe into his wounded lungs the smell of iodine and sea salt that wafted from the estuary.

On September 18, 1935, a letter from Father provincial transferred Fr. Miguel Goñi to the community of Nava del Rey. The explanation of the chronicler is very clear and we give a glimpse of it: "His acute bronchitis health problem does not allow him to continue to endure the humid climate of the port."[1024]

Nava del Rey: Pain Accepted (1935)

The chronicler of Nava del Rey wrote on September 25: "Fr. Miguel Goñi Áriz arrived to be part of this community."[1025] It was his third stay in the

---

1021 Translator's note: a town in Villanueva de Arosa, Pontevedra, Galicia.

1022 *Crónica de Vigo* I, 230.

1023 Summary of the second half of 1934: Novenas, 1; Tridua, 2; Sermons, 9; Talks, 6 (*Ib.*, 233. 237).

1024 *Ib.*, 271.

1025 *Crónica de Nava* III, 343.

little city of Castile. During his first stay he interiorized the call to follow Christ the Redeemer according to the charism of St. Alphonsus Liguori: to proclaim the good news to the poor. During his second stay, as a young priest, with his hands still fresh with the oils of the priestly anointing, he worked hard to become a sower of that word in barren, rocky fields, as well as those which were receptive and fertile. He said yes when he received in his shaking hands, the Christ of the missionary proclamation: "For the Greeks...and for the redeemed, the power of God." Now on his third stay, ill with tuberculosis, which was destroying his bronchial tubes, keeping him from announcing the word, he still had hardly begun his missionary life. And Miguel began again to stammer his yes to following Christ the Redeemer, now crucified in his own flesh.

The "change of air," as they called it back then, did not improve his health. Miguel knew it. On November 3 the chronicler wrote: "By doctor's orders Fr. Goñi stays in bed all the time because of his infirmity."[1026] At that time medicine could do little in cases like that of Fr. Goñi. Rest, a dry climate, good ventilation...Nava del Rey had all of that in abundance, spread out as it is over the clean Castilian mesa. Although the infirmity did not worsen, Miguel did not improve either. When he was a little better, he appears from time to time in the chronicle preaching in the church the Saturday service, which the Redemptorists dedicated each Saturday to the Mother of the Lord.

We don't know anything more about his public activities, since surely there were none. But it is important to see him completing his walk of following Jesus at the side of Mary, almost in total silence, learning from her to say yes with her at the cross, to be standing there with her, to be faithful in the moment of deep pain, of giving himself up to the will of the Father, as St. Alphonsus taught in one of his gems of spirituality.[1027] Thus was he training himself for the total offering in Cuenca.

Starting now Fr. Miguel knew himself to be wounded unto death for the missionary proclamation. The suspected outcome gradually became the hard reality. He attempted to rise above it all by being faithful to the Redemptorist charism but the illness ended up imposing itself upon him.

1026 *Ib.*

1027 St. Alphonsus Maria de Liguori, *Conformity to the Will of God.*

Little by little, he accepted it as one more dimension of the abundant redemption that the Lord Jesus offered for him to bring to completion in his own body. For this reason, he did not see it as a deprivation. On the contrary he accepted it as a new opportunity to make visible the paschal light in the mystery of priestly suffering lived out. Once he had recovered, he left Nava del Rey on January 13 for his new assignment in Cuenca,[1028] where he will give the final surrender of his life.

Cuenca: The Descent to Las Angustias (1936)

Cuenca has three great Marian devotions: The Virgin of Light, Our Lady of the Shrine, and Our Lady of Sorrows (Las Angustias).[1029] Miguel, as all the Redemptorists who lived in the community of Cuenca, knew the tortuous path that went down among rocks and ivy. It pauses at the hermitage and continues on down to the Júcar...It was their favorite walk, and the favorite of many men and women of Cuenca. All the Redemptorists, and the others as well, took it in order to stop off in the appealing silence of the hidden hermitage, before the Dolorous Mother, to remain a while longer in gratifying and grateful prayer, as if they were together with the Mother who had remained standing near the cross giving herself and giving us to her Son, mystery of clarity and welcoming. This descent is going to be an analogy for what the life of Miguel will be in Cuenca. And what he never imagined is that it would be the way, which, together with Fr. Ciriaco Olarte, he would take with his hands tied behind his back, hearing blasphemies, receiving shoves and blows with rusty rifles, along the road to the Júcar, in order to be shot....No, he could not imagine it. But yes, he asked many times from the Mother of Sorrows the generosity to remain at the feet of Jesus, together

....

1028 Cf. *Crónica de Nava* III, 343.

1029 The Devotion to Our Lady of Light "...is based on a legend...Patron of the city, she appeared—small, dark, stony—near the river, in the niche which the waters had cut through for her. Nobody brought her, she came on her own. [Translator's note: the author is describing a miraculous statue of Our Lady of Light.] Our Lady of the Shrine is based on history. [Translator's note: Our Lady of he Shrine is found in the cathedral of Cuenca.] It arrived with Alfonso VIII, bearing in her womb the Blessed Sacrament. Our Lady of Sorrows is, simply, a devotion. There one goes to speak to her more than to pray to her, to tell one's story to her more than to recite to her. Her hermitage is hidden among the rocks, guarded by rare giants of stone, colossal sentinels bundled up in ivy a thousand years old. She, all clarity, humbles herself in shadows within the placid corner which shady elms cover....The Júcar River, many meters below, prays to her its dark litany" (F. MUELAS, *Cuenca."Tierras de sorpresa y encantamientos"* [León, 1983] 68).

with him, as she did, in the difficult moments which everyone experiences.

Fr. Miguel Goñi arrived in Cuenca in mid-January 1936.[1030] He, who was called to proclaim the good news, saw himself obliged to do it in a new way, in silence. With his delicate health he dedicated himself to internal ministry instead of through a missionary life, which had been his motivation for his vocation. Until the moment he was martyred in Cuenca he gave himself to the sacrament of reconciliation, which is another dimension of the proclamation of the kingdom—profound mercy—very dear to St. Alphonsus. "He was suffering from tuberculosis and he bore it with patience. He dedicated himself to celebrating the Holy Mass and a few times to the confessional."[1031]

Insofar as he got a little better and recovered, besides "his internal ministry...within the church itself," he had "an occasional particular preaching date in some town or in some church in the city."[1032] He also tried to preach the novena in honor of Perpetual Help, but he barely got through three days.[1033] And embracing this situation he was preparing himself for martyrdom. His infirmity was his novitiate for martyrdom. That is what another companion in Cuenca, Fr. Isídro Fernández Posado, suggested, convinced that "he always saw it as conforming to the will of God, and thus demonstrating love for God....As to the neighbor...he always showed himself attentive and diligent in seeing to the needs of others. He always bore his illness with the kind of acceptance that a martyr would have. 'If they have to kill us, let them kill us,' were his words which reflect his disposition of spirit and his courage. The truth is, in view of his illness, he already had a martyrdom because of it, and through it he showed well his fortitude and mettle."[1034] This conformity to the will of God in a joyful way is what he manifested to his family in the letter written on June 30, 1936:[1035] "I have spent two years that way, with more than 200 injections administered to my body, and without being able to do absolutely anything. It is evident that

....

1030 Cf. *Anales*, XI, 60.

1031 E. GÓMEZ JORGE, C. *Beatificationis - Declaraciones* II, 686. The laypeople hardly got to know him in the short time he was in Cuenca.

1032 D. DE FELIPE, 177.

1033 M. GOÑI, *Letter, d. c.,* 4.

1034 I. FDEZ. POSADO, C. *Beatificationis—Declaraciones* I, 158.

1035 M. GOÑI, *Letter, d. c.,* 1-3.

God wants me that way, at least for a part of my life. I myself am surprised by my good mood, in spite of my infirmity. With the hope that I had to work in the vineyard of the Lord." [1036]

On this journey of martyrdom, he experienced religious persecution in his own flesh in May: together with Br. Benjamin he offered hospitality to the Vincentian Fathers and he was chased by the demonstrators. Telling his family about it in the letter cited before, he shows a clear consciousness that it was "by a miracle that we saved our precious lives." He openly talked about the persecution of the Church:

The first suspicions regarding us began near San Pablo where a crowd had gathered to attack the monastery and to beat the Vincentians. At first, I managed to convince some of them that we were from Madrid and that we had arrived on the evening before the elections. That day every unfamiliar face seemed to them to be a Vincentian. At the insistence of some of them, I let loose some coarse phrases, which had good results. But that my companion was a monk, no one could get out of their head. "You are not a monk, but this other guy is," they repeated incessantly. At this, the Assault Guard [1037] arrived and they made them search us. This was our downfall. Seeing us without weapons and the possibility that I may be an undercover policeman, they pounced on us. Completely by instinct we acted as if we were going to draw a pistol, they all took off for a moment, enough time for us to take advantage to run into the first house we saw. There we found protection for two hours, with the hope that finally some force would come to our aid. We could escape by the back door, but they closed it on us. Two doors were knocked to the ground, reduced to splinters.

With clairvoyance, he makes his family understand that Navarre is very different in this, since in the south the social situation is very chaotic and an authentic revolution is getting organized:

....

1036 *Ib.,* 4.

1037 Translator's note: The *Guardias de Asalto* (Assault Guard) were the special blue-uniformed police force created in 1931 by the Second Spanish Republic to control urban violence.

And to be sure, Cuenca is the best province in Castilla la Nueva.[1038] *In the others and in Andalusia and in Valencia the Soviet has practically been established for some time. The socialist and Communist militias give orders dressed in uniforms and with weapons on the highways and are those who control the life of the towns. In Murcia, Alicante, etc., there is scarcely any church and the priests have had to leave from almost every village. There, where you are, you are not able to pick up on it, and even less with the censorship of the press, regarding how it is in Spain from Madrid on down...*

As we perceive in his letter, Miguel was aware of the situation and could intuit what would be the eventual outcome.

Alarmed by the circumstances, he left with Fr. Ciriaco Olarte on July 20, 1936, and concealed himself in the home of the priest D. Acisclo Domínguez. After a few days, they realized that they were the center of attention of the militias who patrolled the streets, and went to hide in the house of the old priest D. Enrique García, in the Calle Pilares. On July 31, after celebrating the Eucharist, they received a visit from the militia who tied them up and took them away. They walked through Cuenca to the descent of Las Angustias. In the proximity of the hermitage, on a slope near the electrical station of the fulling mill[1039] they were riddled with bullets. After a long agony in which his cries of pain could be heard, Miguel died "after twenty hours as a result of hemorrhage and destruction of the brain."[1040]

We can conclude that Fr. Miguel Goñi went through a process of personal and spiritual growth. The missions, contact with simple people, and illness helped him identify little by little with Christ until he died a martyr's death.

....

1038 Translator's note: New Castile is the historic region of Castile, located in its south.

1039 Translator's note: In medieval times, water mills were used for part of the process of making clothing from wool. Perhaps this reference is to one that remained as a historic oddity in the vicinity of Cuenca.

1040 *Death Certificate of Miguel Goñi Áriz*: REG. CIVIL DE CUENCA, Sec. 3.ª, T. 42, F. 305, N.º 604; written on August 3, 1936.

Victoriano Calvo Lozano

CHAPTER EIGHT

Victoriano Calvo Lozano

A Boy with the Vocation of a Monk

Victor Calvo Lozano was born on December 23, 1896, in Horche, a town of the province of Guadalajara[1041] and at that time in the diocese of Toledo.[1042] He was baptized that following Christmas Day (December 25) at the parish church of la Asunción de Nuestra Señora.[1043] His parents were Christians of a profound Catholic faith and they wished to raise their children in that faith. His father was a farmer, Juan Calvo Martínez, and his mother was a housewife, María Candelas Lozano Monge.

....

1041 In the middle of the nineteenth century, Horche appeared as "a village with a town council, in the province and judicial district of Guadalajara, territorial court of Madrid...diocese of Toledo. GEOGRAPHICAL LOCATION: in a valley and protected from north and west winds; it enjoys a temperate and healthy CLIMATE, with unusal infirmities being unknown there, such as gastric-bilious fever. [Translator's note: Gastric-billious fever is a disease related to malaria.] It has 420 HOUSES; a town council with a jail, one building [Translator's note: probably meaning one government building], granary silos; a school for primary education, attended by 110 students, under the care of one teacher whose salary is 2,500 reales plus the compensation provided by their students [Translator's note: In 1898 four reales made up a peseta, and one peseta was worth $7 US in terms of 2017 money. The average teacher's salary was 2,500 reales, paid by the local town government. This would have meant a yearly stipend from the town government of $4,375 in terms of US dollars in 2017.]; two founts with three faucets each and their trough to provide water for the cattle, and in one of them a beautiful basin made of stone; a monastery which belonged to the Friars Minor; at the end of town, a parish church (the Assumption of Our Lady), served by 1 pastor and 1 associate; the public cemetery is found at the west of town, at a distance of 100 paces [Translator's note: the "pace" is an informal unit of measurement, meaning either the distance that one places one foot in front of another when walking (.75 meters = 2.5 feet) or the distance of a complete step with one foot, then the other (1.5 meters = 4 ft., 11 in.).].... four hermitages (La Soledad, San Roque, San Sebastián, and San Isidro) and various springs which serve to water some vegetable gardens. TERRAIN: in general it is fertile and of good quality; the Tajuña River fertilizes it...and the Hungría River ...; there are two hills with oak and dwarf oaks...PRODUCTION: wheat, barley, rye, oats, olive oil, wine, and vegetables; wool-bearing livestock, goats, cattle and swine are raised; hunting of partridge, hares and rabbits, and in the Hungría River some fish and eels are caught. INDUSTRY: farming, production of ordinary cloth, two flour mills, two olive presses, one hydraulic press and 1 fulling mill. COMMERCE: export of surplus fruit and import of consumer articles as needed; there are five merchandise stores: by royal order of June 23, 1842, the village of Horche was given one festival and one farmers' market; the first is celebrated on October 10, 11, 12, 13, and 14; its principal trade is in wool-bearing livestock, cattle, mules, and pigs, although to date only in small quantities; Sundays were set for the farmers' market, but it has been discontinued due to lack of business. POPULATION: 475 households, 1,884 souls" (Fr. MADOZ, Diccionario Geográfico-Estadístico-Histórico de España y sus posesiones de Ultramar [Madrid, 1845-1850], IX, 227-228).

1042 Cf. REG. CIVIL DE HORCHE (GUADALAJARA), Sec. 1.ª, T. 9, f. 135, n.º 69.

1043 PARROQUIA DE LA ASUNCIÓN DE NTRA. SRA. DE HORCHE (GUADALAJARA), *Baptismal Records* 17, f. 274 vto. [Translator's note: in English, the name of the parish is "Assumption of Our Lady."]

Victor was the youngest of four children of the marriage.[1044] According to what his autobiography[1045] tells us later on, his father was "a man of good intentions" and his mother was "a woman who feared God, desiring to fulfill her obligations, of a delicate conscience and zealous for the upbringing of her children." The mother was the one responsible for the handing on of the faith and for the life of piety, which culminated with confirmation. Victor was confirmed at the hands of the auxiliary bishop of Toledo, Msgr. D. J. José Laguarda Fenollera on May 22, 1901.[1046] Besides a Christian upbringing, María Candela initiated Victor in the practice of prayer, examination of conscience, and the celebration and veneration of the Eucharist.[1047]

The natural disposition of Victor for spiritual things bonded to the commitment of his mother. He was receptive, given to reflection and silence. With the passage of time this inclination became a marked tendency toward self-absorption. At age seven or eight he received his first Communion. Consistent with the custom of the times, he would approach the Eucharist once annually. He grew and socialized through play. Together with the leisure that a child experiences, he continued cultivating his life of piety with the catechism, instruction, and friendship with a seminarian; he himself tells us:

The years passed and I grew in the use of reason, now gaining friends, with whom many times I spent hours of recreation building altars and statues of cardboard or clay, sometimes of our Lord, other times of the Most Holy Virgin or of other saints, according to the time in which we found ourselves and the feasts which we were celebrating. So sweetly did we spend the time occupied in these activities and in others like them, such as making little carts, etc., that it made us forget the hour to eat or go home...Piety was my main inclination; to hear sermons, the expla-

1044 Four children were born of the marriage: Basilia, who died while small (1890-1893); two twin brothers born in 1892, Faustino and Pilar; and Victor (Cf. *Baptismal Records* 17, ff. 160, 200, 201; *Death Records* 17, f. 205).

1045 V. CALVO, *Curriculum vitae; Nava de Rey 21-10-1920,* 1, in: *C. Beatificationis—Escritos.* This autobiography of Victoriano will serve as our principal source for his life before his entry into the Congregation of the Most Holy Redeemer.

1046 Parish of LA ASUNCIÓN DE NTRA. SRA. DE HORCHE (GUADALAJARA), *Baptismal Records* 18, f. 63 vto., n° 126.

1047 Cf. V. CALVO, *Curriculum...,* 2-3. 4.

nation of the catechism or to attend other religious functions, especially in Lent and Holy Week, were more pleasant to me than all my games. Other occasions offered me the opportunity to feed my piety through my dealings and recreation that I had with a seminarian who was a neighbor (at present, a priest). He enjoyed teaching religious songs to the children.[1048]

Besides being initiated into a life of piety, Victor was also introduced to his first academic studies. Although we know little about his intellectual formation, he tells us that he attended the primary school in his town. As was proper for the children of his time, he soon abandoned school and was initiated in farm work.[1049] At age twelve, he gave himself to reading pious books and meditating, which permitted him to acquire a self-taught education in the field of asceticism and mysticism.[1050]

Victor would go on maturing and would become an adolescent, and with adolescence he would enter a period of trial and a desert in his spiritual life.[1051] This was caused by a life of labor in the field, contact with other youth who lived with their backs turned on a life of devotion, the dream of personal freedom in the face of the norms of his parents, and social pressure, which has such power over people in their adolescence. "So as not to seem a strange or stupid individual in front of my peers, I could not resolve to be less than them," he wrote.[1052] In the midst of this desert he began to feel in his heart a great emptiness.

Without knowing very well how it happened, he applied himself to reading books on spirituality. Among the books that fell into his hands was an 1876 edition of *The Rule of St. Benedict*, father of Western monas-

....

1048 *Ib.*, 5. The seminarian probably was Manuel de la Fuente Cortés, who was born in Horche in 1893; he was ordained in Toledo in 1917; he was canon of the primatial cathedral and died in Toledo in 1973. [Translator's note: The Archbishop of Toledo is the Primate of Spain, his cathedral being considered the primatial cathedral. It is given first place of honor among the churches of Spain.]

1049 Cf. *Ib.*, 6.

1050 Cf. *Ib.*, 8.

1051 Cf. *Ib.*, 7-10.

1052 *Ib.*, 7.

ticism. His reading impassioned him so much, that the book never left his hands; and while his siblings and the children of the neighborhood played and roughhoused through the streets of the town, he dedicated himself to reading his book. These readings led him to a certain type of eremitical life, giving himself to times of solitude, and with the complicity of the hiddenness of the field, to penances and prayers. But along with his arrival at sixteen and seventeen years of age, there came as well the ghost of human respect, which caused in him a coldness once again, tempting him with the idea of living a normal life and not complicating his life. He forgot about the life of prayer, left off participating in the Sunday Eucharist under the pretext that he had to work, and, "I felt a thirst for pleasures, for happiness, for joy...I wanted to talk with my friends with some freedom."[1053] But instead of feeling better, the sensation of interior emptiness increased in the depths of his heart.[1054]

Youth and the Difficulties of Vocational Discernment

While in this interior emptiness, his heart perceived the call of God. The root and cause of this vocational process we can find in his ascetic readings and activities. He felt himself called to things higher than a life in the gutter.[1055]

On November 24, 1913,[1056] when he was almost seventeen years old, his mother died. It was a real blow to him, as there was also a growing sense of emptiness in his own life. The sudden death of María Candelas made him reconsider and understand how transitory is human life. In a moment of conversion, he returned to the practices of piety, which he had abandoned. But he did it with such intensity that he spent hours and days praying the

....

1053 *Ib.,* 10.

1054 "I don't know what told me that that was not my path. My nature asked for something else. This would not possibly fill the emptiness that I felt in my heart. What was it that the world was offering me? Nothing. In the hours of dissipation, a knife wounded my conscience and, together with it, my soul, and afterwards left me in the most bitter desperation, and, thankfully, it invited in me remorse!" (*Ib.,* 9-10).

1055 Cf. *Ib.,* 11ss.

1056 Parish of LA ASUNCIÓN DE NTRA. SRA. DE HORCHE (GUADALAJARA), *Death Records* 18, f. 197 vto., n.º 45.

rosary, even in the midst of the rough labor of the field. It was then that there again surged in his heart the desire to be a monk, a Trappist, or Benedictine.[1057]

And God offered him a reply to that call. The occasion presented itself some few months later in January 1914, and came at the hands of the Redemptorist missionaries Frs. Hipólito García and Casto Calvo, who arrived in Horche to preach a mission.[1058] At first, Victoriano resisted taking part in the mission, but when encouraged by his sister, he decided to go and participated actively.[1059] When the missionaries left, Victoriano "decided to start a new life" and asked "the grace to live in such a way as to make amends to our Lord during as many years as I still have left."[1060] Even though he had no other choice than to conform to the society in which he lived, he decided to live a spiritual life in private.

As a fruit of the mission, he began to pray the rosary every day and to practice other devotions. With this cultivation of the spiritual, in the

....

1057 With his mother's death "Our Lord decided to knock for the first time on the door of my heart, even though I did not understand his voice then. With this knock, which was so urgent and unexpected, in some way the vanities and illusions which enwrapped my spirit disappeared; on the other hand, I recognized the obligation of commending her soul to God, as I had learned from her to do. With this motivation I resumed the custom of praying every day, in the morning, at night and during the day, and especially when the clock struck the hour. Now by reason of mourning, I was also removed from diversions and worldly disorder, and, because of that, ready to renew my dealings with God, which was until then sadly interrupted; now I could not accompany my friends in their diversions, for which reason, that time which I would have spent with them, I used instead at home reading some pious book" (V. CALVO, *Curriculum...*, 12-13).

1058 This mission was preached by Frs. Hipólito García and Casto Calvo, from the community of San Miguel in Madrid. The chronicle of the community disappeared during the religious persecution. Nevertheless, in the *Boletín de la Obra de la Defensa de la Fe en España* (XX, 1915, 331-332) [Translator's note: "Bulletin of the Work of the Defense of the Faith in Spain"] a report has been kept for us: "Horche (Guadalajara). - A town corrupted by politics, although with more faith and religious practice than those around it. The mission produced results and extraordinary fruit in the children, in a sufficient number of women, but little for some of the men. The cause of the distancing from the mission in the young and adult men and in the women was not hidden from the missionaries, but it was not in their hands to be able to avoid it. Indeed, besides there being a preceding cause, there will also be a consequent result. This is the reason for the fruit being completely and extremely consoling in the children, who are not aware of the local situation. -Frs. García and Calvo."

1059 "Those energetic explanations about sin, judgment, hell, etc....could not do less than move my heart and make me enter within myself. They provided me with materials which were more than sufficient for me to recognize the truth that I so much desired. Those pious talks and exhortations that followed the Holy Mass were fodder sufficient for nurturing my piety" (V. CALVO, *Curriculum...*, 14).

1060 *Ib.*, 15.

following years there would awaken in him a search for his vocation. It was fed[1061] by prayer, spiritual reading, and the personal accompaniment of the local pastor, D. Juan Antonio Cortés Moral.[1062] Victoriano subscribed to the magazine *El Perpetuo Socorro*[1063] and he read various works by St. Alphonsus, such as *The Practice of the Love of Jesus Christ* and *The Religious Vocation*. In spite of his simple, agricultural life, the measures he took to cultivate his vocation led him to live according to God's will. He searched for more than quantity. He looked at the quality of his prayer. His way of living fostered in his heart a strong desire for the religious life. When the fear of returning to a coldness in his life of faith came to mind, Victor told himself something which would later prove prophetic: "With the grace of God, I see the palm of victory in my hand."[1064]

In a small farming town like Horche, a young man with such inquietudes was considered a strange person. There was no short supply of nicknames being given to him, like *santurrón, beato*,[1065] and other less manly monikers. One of the obstacles he had to make his way around was his own family.[1066] They did not want him to leave since they did not want to lose any hands that could help with farm work. They could not understand Victor's behavior. He was a good worker, but very quiet, prayed all the time, a tremendous reader in a town of illiterate people, and he refused the kinds of fun considered appropriate for his age group. Secretly, Victor dreamed of dedicating himself to the study of theology, but now he was very old for this. And on the other hand, his family was very poor, needed his economic help, and could not pay for his studies in a seminary.

He directed his vocational search toward the Congregation of the sons of St. Alphonsus, whom he now considered his spiritual father. The parish priest wrote to the Father provincial to introduce Victor and the priest.

....

1061 Cf. *Ib.*, 15-19.

1062 Antonio Cortés Moral, pastor of Horche (cf. Appendix 3).

1063 Translator's note: The magazine *Perpetual Help* was founded in 1899 by Spanish Redemptorists, specifically to foster devotion to Mary under that title.

1064 V. CALVO, *Curriculum…*, 15.

1065 Translator's note: *Santurrón* means literally "big saint" and has the pejorative sense of "sanctimonious." *Beato* literally means "blessed" and also has a denigrating connotation of being a "holy Joe."

1066 Cf. *Ib.*, 19-26.

Victor settled in to wait for an answer. While waiting for this to happen, the parish priest gave some guidance to Victor, who opened his heart to his father. But his father, together with his uncles, tried to dissuade Victor from such strange ideas and behaviors. One of the brothers of his deceased mother threatened him with burning his books, which Victor jealously kept. Some of them he had inherited from his mother. With holy indignation, Victor responded to the one who was threatening him with a reverse *auto de fe*.[1067] He said that they would have to burn him before he would allow them to burn a single page of his books, some of which "were a holy remembrance of his mother." His life became a martyrdom.

When the time came for his military service, although he remained free, he had to go to military training for three months,[1068] and to fulfill this obligation Victor had to be quartered in Madrid. On September 4, 1918, he left Horche for the capital. The destination cheered him because he knew that the Redemptorists were on Calle Manuel Silvela but, although on occasions he tried, he could not work up the courage to explain to some priest or Brother his vocational searching: "On various occasions he wanted to go to the Redemptorist house to consult them about his situation, but did not manage to do so; finally one day, he armed himself with valor and he went to the Redemptorists of Manuel Silvela in order to consult them about his situation; but his natural bashfulness and his fearfulness tied his hands and when he was about to ring the doorbell he changed his mind and withdrew."[1069]

His companions in military service frequently made him the object of mockery and jokes of poor taste.[1070] One afternoon, after they went to a movie, some of them invited him to go for a walk. Victor gladly accepted the invitation. They arrived at a house, there in the barrio of San Bernardo. But when they were climbing the stairs, our Brother noticed that it was a joke by his friend, since the place was a brothel. Full of indignation, he said to them,

----

1067 Translator's note: An *auto de fe* was the punishment given to heretics or apostates by the Inquisition. The most severe sentence was death by burning.

1068 Cf. *Ib.*, 26-27. [Translator's note: Compulsory military service was introduced in Spain by King Carlos III in 1770 and remained in place for 230 years until it was revoked in 2001. During the First World War, Spain maintained neutrality.]

1069 D. DE FELIPE, *Nuevos Redentores* (Madrid, 1962) 193.

1070 Cf. V. CALVO, *Curriculum*..., 26-28.

"Go in, if you want, but I'm not going in." He turned around, sad and with lowered head, and got lost amid the barrios of Madrid.

When the period of his military conscription had come to an end, he returned to his village with the sadness of not having gotten to clarify the business about his religious vocation. He did have a greater desire for becoming a coadjutor[1071] Redemptorist Brother.[1072] In spite of his resolution, the opposition of his family would again be the major obstacle to him in taking this step. The only one who understood him and encouraged him was the priest. For some time now, understanding the dead-end that his parishioner had found himself in, he wrote to the Redemptorists recommending Victor for his good conduct and Christian piety, and he asked that Victor be admitted to the Congregation. The answer from Father Master arrived on January 20, 1919[1073] when Victor was now twenty-two years old. By way of this letter from Nava del Rey (Valladolid) it was communicated to Victor that he had been admitted as a coadjutor Brother and it was suggested to him that he present himself in that same city as soon as possible.

Without saying anything to anyone, counting only on the moral support of the parish priest, he set about preparing his things, putting his affairs in order, and at dawn on March 31 he fled his home for that place where God was awaiting him: Nava del Rey.[1074] He left on the writing table a letter in which he explained his motives for his running away and asked pardon for himself if, on that account, he had hurt any of them. Victor Calvo Lozano, as Gerard Majella had done,[1075] went off with determination to make himself a saint:

....

1071 Translator's note: The term *coadjutor* means "assistant." In clerical institutes of the Church, such as the Redemptorists, the coadjutor was seen as assisting in a supportive way those whose role was to carry out the main focus of the apostolate, such as preaching.

1072 Cf. *Ib.,* 28-29.

1073 Cf. *Ib.,* 30.

1074 Cf. *Ib.,* 31.

1075 Translator's note: St. Gerard Majella was a contemporary of the founder of the Redemptorists, St. Alphonsus Liguori, and was a Brother in the Congregation. He, too, fled his home to join the Redemptorists, slipping out a window because his mother had locked the door of his bedroom, thinking that thus he would not be able to follow the Redemptorists who had come to preach a mission in his town.

After various prayers before the crucifix, I took the money, which I thought necessary...and, closing my eyes to every natural affection, I left the house...en route to Nava del Rey, leaving on the table a letter to give some peace to my family. It was necessary to do it that way because I was fearing another delay, under any pretext and now I was fed up with "delays"; on the other hand, with or without the consent of my family, I had to fulfill my commitments to God and the Congregation, and especially to my own soul.[1076]

The Life of a Monk among Redemptorist Missionaries

Victor arrived at the monastery of the Redemptorists of Nava del Rey on March 31, 1919. He had with him "Money: fifteen pesetas with twenty-five céntimos.[1077] Books: *Glories of Mary, Practice of the Love of Jesus Christ, Advice about Vocations.*[1078] Clothes: he does not detail."[1079] He began as a postulant on April 2, was given the office of gardener,[1080] and was placed under the direction of Br. Luís so that Luís might initiate Victor in the work appropriate to Redemptorist gardening. In the *Book of Registration* to the postulancy, the Father Master wrote a brief report about Victor's vocational search:

Victor Calvo Lozano (Lay Brother): He arrived at this novitiate house on March 31, 1919. He is a native of Horche, province of Guadalajara, and the diocese of Toledo. He was born on December 23, 1896. His parents Juan and María Candelas.[1081] *This young man felt himself*

1076 *Ib.*, 31.

1077 Translator's note: A peseta in 1919 was worth 3.57 Euros by 2015 standards, $4.26 US. A céntimo was worth 1/100th of a peseta; this would have given him about 53.79 Euros or 64.01 US dollars in 2015 values.

1078 Translator's note: the first two of these were written by St. Alphonsus Liguori; perhaps the third was also by him, but known under some other title in English, probably *The Choice of a State of Life: The Vocation to the Religious State.*

1079 APRM. *Record of the objects brought by the subject upon arrival in the Novitiate 1885-1933. Espino, Astorga, Nava del Rey*, Year 1919. N.345. Victor Calvo Lozano (Lay Brother).

1080 Cf. V. CALVO, *Curriculum...,* 31-32.

1081 Translator's note: only the mother's last name is given here with the supposition that the reader knows the father's last name was Calvo Lozano. In Spain, the surnames of both parents are used, the father's first surname, then the mother's first surname.

called to a holier life from the mission, which our Fathers preached in his town five years ago. Afterwards he was inclined to the religious life through reading articles, which R. Fr. Sarabia was publishing in Perpetual Help magazine. Some obstacles were placed in his path on the part of his relatives, but he learned how to overcome them all. Finally, he left home without saying anything, leaving a letter on a table. He is reflective and seems led by the best dispositions.[1082]

After seven months in Nava del Rey among novices and postulants—a time in which he was instructed about life in a community, the practices of piety, and the task of being a gardener—on November 12 he received the Redemptorist habit and began the novitiate receiving the name Victoriano.[1083] That same day together with Victoriano, Br. Gabriel Sainz Gutiérrez, martyred in Madrid on July 20, 1936, received his habit. Also, the chorists Julián Pozo and Miguel Goñi, who had begun this stage of formation on the previous August 24, were together with them in the novitiate.[1084] The four witnesses to the Redeemer (three of Cuenca) began their following of Christ together.

The novitiate, which Fr. Rafael Cavero directed as master, was a very intense stage of prayerful discernment, of formation for the religious life and vocational choice. In accord with his personality, Victoriano took this time very seriously, so that at the end of the year he was found suitable for taking temporary vows in the Redemptorist Congregation. On November 13, 1920, he professed temporary vows of poverty, chastity, and obedience

....

1082 APRM. *Book of Chorist and Lay Postulants*, I, n.345.

1083 *Victor (Victoriano) Calvo Lozano. Die 12 novembris 1919, Sancto Martino, sacro in hoc Collegio Seraphicae Theresiae de Jesu in civitate Navae Regis, Prov. Vallisolletana, a Rev. Patre Raphaele Cavero, Novitiorum Magistro, admisus est adolescens Victorianus Calvo Lozano e pago Horche, Prov. Guadalaxarae, Archidioccesis Toledanae. Natus est 23 Decemb. 1896- a. 23. Ejus parentes: Juan Calvo y Candelas Lozano* (APRM. *Liber primus inscriptionis vestium mutationis laicorum*, año1919, n.º CL). The Latin means: "Victor (Victoriano) Calvo Lozano. On November 12, 1919, the Feast of St. Martin, in this sacred house of the Seraphic Teresa de Jesús in the city of Nava del Rey, province of Valladolid, the youth Victoriano Calvo Lozano from the town of Horche, province of Guadalajara, Archdiocese of Toledo, was admitted to the novitiate by Reverend Fr. Rafael Cavero, Master of Novices. He was born on December 23, 1896, and is twenty-three years of age. His parents: Juan Calvo and Candelas Lozano." (APRM. *Liber primus inscriptionis vestium mutationis laicorum*, año 1919, n.º CL).

1084 Cf. *Anales* VII, 154-155.

in the Congregation with the hope that "the Lord...give Holy Perseverance to all."[1085]

I, Victor (Victoriano) Calvo, native of Horche, province of Guadala-jara, diocese of Toledo, of the Congregation of the Most Holy Redeemer, on November 13, 1920, feast of St. Stanislaus, in the Monastery of Nava del Rey at the hands of Rev. Fr. Rafael Cavero, master of novices, according to our rules and in accordance with the sacred canons and our privileges, have freely made temporary vows for three years of poverty, chastity, and obedience, being present the whole community and espe-cially Reverend Frs. Manuel Taboada and Urbano Rodríguez. I, Victor (Victoriano) Calvo, sign with my own hand. Manuel Taboada: I was present. Urbano Rodríguez: I was present. I, Rafael Cavero, master of novices, by the faculty, which was conceded to me by the Most Reverend Rector Major, have admitted to temporary profession for three years the above referenced young man. And as good faith of this. Rafael Cavero, CSsR.[1086]

1085 V. CALVO, *Curriculum...*, 32.

1086 APRM. *Book of Chorist and Lay Postulants*, I, n.º 345.

Br. Victoriano Calvo

The Brothers dedicated themselves to the service of the community. Their consecrated life passed almost completely in the interior of the religious house, basically as cooks, tailors, sacristans, carpenters, and so on.[1087] Victoriano remained for a time in the novitiate house, working as the gardener: "From the start he inspired absolute confidence and moreover was trained and skilled in everything. He did not falter in his ideal of arriving at the practice of solid virtue. Since he was quiet by temperament, he did not waste his work time on conversation...he was a new version of San Juan Silenciario."[1088]

His first assignment was to the community of San Ignacio in Pamplona. He arrived there on January 17, 1921, where he remained until September, at which time he was sent to Astorga. During these months he was entrusted with the service of sacristan.[1089] On September 10, he arrived in the community of Astorga (León) with Br. Baltasar.[1090] He continued at Astorga until September 24, 1923, when he was transferred to El Espino in order to prepare himself for perpetual profession.[1091] We do not know very well what assignment he was given in Astorga since the chronicles do not give us notice of it. He reunited with Brs. Santos Cavero, Celso Alonso, and Juan Lorenzo Díez in the monastery of Our Lady of El Espino (Burgos) under the direction of Fr. José Chavatte so as to prepare for his definitive consecration.[1092] The four of them made their perpetual profession and vow

----

1087 Writing about the life of a missionary priest is easier because it is full of external activities and of other kinds of apostolates, which are recorded in the chronicles. But the life of a coadjutor Brother is difficult to write about because his life is totally lived on the interior of the community, dedicated to the tasks and more discreet efforts within the house. For this reason, we find few facts about their daily life.

1088 D. DE FELIPE, 194. [Translator's note: St. John the Silent was born in Armenia in 454. At age eighteen, he established a monastery in his hometown of Nicopolis, Armenia. He was appointed bishop of Colonia in Armenia at age twenty-eight, then after nine years he resigned his office and became a hermit in Jerusalem. In response to a vision, he joined the monastery of St. Sabas near Jerusalem, where he lived in solitude for seventy-five years.]

1089 *Crónica de Pamplona* III, 14.

1090 "September 10 [1921]. - Brothers Baltasar and Victoriano arrived from Pamplona, assigned to this community" (Crónica de Astorga III, 169).

1091 "*September 24 [1923]*. - Brothers Celso and Victoriano are going to El Espino to make the second novitiate in preparation for Perpetual Profession" (*Ib.*, 176. 191).

1092 Cf. *Anales* VIII, 122. 191-192.

and oath of perseverance on March 25, 1924.[1093] Victoriano wrote in his own hand on a sheet of paper with the seal of the community of El Espino:

I, Br. Victor (Victoriano) Calvo Lozano, native of Horche, province of Guadalajara, Novice of the Congregation of the Most Holy Redeemer, on this twenty-fifth day of March, 1924, feast of the Annunciation of Our Lady, and in this Monastery of Our Lady of El Espino, town of Gadea del Cid, at the hands of Rev. Fr. Pablo Vadillo, according to our rules and in accordance with our privileges, have freely made simple vows of poverty, chastity, and obedience, with the vow and oath of perseverance, until death, in said Congregation, being present the community and especially Reverend Frs. José Chavatte and Jerónimo Martínez. I, Victor (Victoriano), sign in my name.[1094]

He lived more than a month in El Espino after his profession. On April 28, 1924, Br. Victoriano took the train for Madrid, and from there another train with the destination of Cuenca. He arrived in Cuenca on May 1[1095] to become sacristan of San Felipe Neri. He left Cuenca on February 15, 1927, for Astorga, where he remained until the following April 21. He was then transferred to Nava del Rey, where he resided until October 3.[1096] On October 5 he returned again to Cuenca and in that city he would experience the reality of his oath of perseverance. He was there until his death, carrying out in particular the duty of sacristan and, for some time, that of receptionist as well.

....

1093 Cf. *Ib.,* 166. Of the four who at the time made perpetual profession and the vow of perseverance, Br. Santos died in China in 5-8-1932 [Translator's note: May 8, 1932] with a reputation for sanctity (Cf. L. F. DE RETANA, *Aún hay santos!* [Madrid 1935]) [Translator's note: The title of the book is translated: "There Still Are Saints!"] and Br. Celso Alonso also died as a martyr in Valencia on September 28, 1936.

1094 APRM. *Second Book of Perpetual Profession of Lay Brothers,* 1924, 122, n.90.

1095 Cf. *Crónica de El Espino* V, 176; *Anales* VIII, 193; V. CALVO, *Una hija de Mª del Perpetuo S. Autobiografía íntima de Paulina Muñoz* [Translator's note: the book's title is translated "A Daughter of Mary of Perpetual Help: Intimate Autobiography of Paulina Muñoz"]; 17-10-1933, 156, in: *Causa Beatificationis—Escritos.*

1096 Cf. V. CALVO, *Favores-Cuenca*: El Perpetuo Socorro XXX, nº 355 (enero 1928), 32-33; *Anales* IX, 133.167.

What did Br. Victoriano do throughout those twelve years in Cuenca? Possibly nothing extraordinary, at least nothing that would make him stand out from the rest of his brothers in the community. But he knew how to make of his ordinary life a path of spiritual growth, which led him to live out such a great and generous love that martyrdom presented itself to him as the best culmination of his life. As with any religious, he spent his time between prayer, devotions, work, tasks entrusted to him, and community activities. One of the altar servers of the church of San Felipe, Ángel Rodrigo, who because of his ministry had a special relationship with him, recalls about the Brother:

> He was tremendously serious; he didn't speak; only when we were ratting around a lot did he take appropriate measures, of quieting us down, but always speaking the least possible....As a religious, we held him in high regard, very high; he always carried his rosary in his hand, and, of course, he was praying it.[1097] Victoriano practically lived the life of a monk: Man of much action, but few words, not given to storytelling but much to prayer. He carried out with a great deal of diligence every manual duty that was given him in the community. That is what those who lived with him testify about him. He did not hold his body back from work....And in that comes out what is extraordinary about him....[1098]

Consecrated life was, for Victoriano Calvo, a true school of virtue, in which he gained a great maturity. His companion in the community, Fr. Isidro Fernández Posado, who spent several years in Cuenca with him, offers us a portrait of his character:

> In him, in his life, can be seen a very great zeal for the salvation of souls. It showed itself in the diligence with which he would call upon the Fathers when they were requested to hear confessions and in everything that has to do with worship—preparation of the altars, work in

----

1097 ÁNGEL RODRIGO, C. *Beatificationis—Declaraciones* II, 520.
1098 D. RUIZ, *De camino*, 3, 12 (APRM. Mártires 0400124).

preparation for the feasts—and the fact of what I have said about the direction of that young lady.

...*During the time that I knew him, faith showed itself in everything that has to do with worship*—care, diligence, cleanliness, genuflections—*he did it with great spirit, with much faith. He always went about the sacristy, the church, with dedication.*

...*Never ever did I see or hear that he was influenced by personal motives, only by higher motives, for God; human motives never persuaded him.*

...*He had great love for God, we can say*—as I have already indicated—*he was always in the church or in the sacristy; he helped with almost every Mass. A great charity, sacrificial charity, for his neighbor. His attention to and diligence for the sick was something exceptional*—*in spite of the fact that the patient may emit a terrible odor! That is how he cared for Br. Clemente, who was suffering the beginning of gangrene in the foot. He was very charitable toward everyone, those in the house and those outside.*

...*In all his actions he showed prudence; never was it seen or heard about him that he committed any imprudence, or any sort of foolishness, as much with those in the house as with the people outside.*

...*He was fair with everyone; and we have already been able to see, in what I have been saying, how he behaved with rectitude and being very just and balanced in everything, in all his actions.*

...*I have already said*—with regards to his courage—*that business about caring for Br. Clemente; I can add here the instance of his admirable composure with which he endured the removal of a cyst which he suffered; a cyst which was removed without injections or anesthetics, and in fact by a doctor who was a bit old and who could make the procedure more difficult with his tendency to shake; the courage with which Br. Víctor endured everything left everyone astonished.*

...*He was very regulated and did not like divergences from the norm. As far as penance goes, he did more than required; he loved mortification a great deal.*

... *He was very observant in obeying the Rule; he was always putting forth a real effort to keep very carefully all his obligations as a religious.*

...[His most outstanding virtues were] mortification, self-abnegation, charity, sacrifice.[1099]

The memories that Victoriano left among laypeople in his work as sacristan and receptionist could not have been better. He was a hard worker, he delighted in decorating the church, he had a good knowledge of the liturgy and rubrics. In giving welcome to others, he was affable and carried out his duties with promptness and patience:[1100]

Certainly, he was very pious, he had the assignment of being sacristan, very much focusing on the arrangement of the altar, that of the Most Blessed Sacrament, and of the Virgin especially. His fervor was noted in his genuflections that he made so many times in passing in front of the altar and he always did them very well. He was very helpful and agreeable, in spite of his dry character; and a worker, an extraordinary thing. Although he was attentive to everything that was deemed necessary, in dealing with him there was no place for conversations which would permit other displays of his inner soul...If I had to draw up a summary, I would say, or what would stand out, would be his work ethic and his eucharistic fervor; to me, he was worthy of the judgment of being, simply, a good religious....In Cuenca everyone regarded him as a good Brother, a good religious....He was patient, as manifested in the forbearance which he had when time came to have to shut the church and some person was reluctant to leave. And if it was asked of him that he open up the church before the designated time, he would try to do so in every way that he could.[1101]

....

1099 I. FDEZ. POSADO, *C. Beatificationis—Declaraciones* I, 163-165.

1100 His confrere in the community, Fr. Isidro Posado, declares that he was "always attentive to his business, in his work proper to a Sacristan. His work was silent and especially pious and, on account of it, he was always involved in things relating to God." And another companion, Br. Benjamin, points out: "Regarding virtue, [there stands out] especially humility; and he was a very observant religious; he was very devoted to the Virgin" (*Ib.*, I, 166). A lady witness says of him in the beatification process that "he was serious, very serious; a worker and pious" (*Ib.*, I, 117.226). Other ladies recall "that he was good, a very good Religious. He had a lot of patience with us little girls, when we were coming to pay a visit; he was serious...very observant and very much at service, very good" (*Ib.*II, 461.487).

1101 CAMILO FERNÁNDEZ DE LELIS, *Ib.*, I, 282-283.

Besides manual work and prayer, we know the fondness Br. Victoriano had for reading books on spirituality since the time he was a farmer in his town. During his religious life he found spaces and moments in the midst of his other activities to cultivate his spiritual life and for reading, so that his formation in this area was solid and ample. This formation he took advantage of not only for himself, but also to share with others who came to him. In the report that the provincial made in 1935, he left in writing about Victoriano a reference as to his reading and that knowledge of asceticism that the Brother had. However, as a result of the notion that was current about Brothers at the time, it doesn't seem he liked it: "good, helpful, pious, but reserved to an excess, and it seems too full of himself, of his ascetical-mystical knowledge. He is fond of those kinds of books."[1102] We intuit that Victoriano must have had to suffer misunderstanding on the part of some confreres because of his desire for formation and his search for the spiritual. In their minds these things should have been reserved to those who had studied theology.

As the provincial pointed out, he certainly was reserved. Interpersonal relations were difficult for him because of his naturally timid character, especially with people who were outside his community. To these people he could seem a bit indifferent and even harsh. But once one got past those appearances, they discovered a person quite dear, with a great interior richness and profoundly sensitive to the needs of others. Everything depended on taking the first step and getting to know him.

Master of Spirituality

The sensitivity for things of the spirit which Victoriano had from childhood, together with the formation he received as a Redemptorist and his self-taught apprenticeship through reading, all favored not only his spiritual growth, but also made him a master. Through his assignment in the community of Cuenca he had a great deal to do with laypeople, especially those women who took responsibility for the decoration of the altars, such

....

1102 AHGR. 30150002,0034, 1. Behind these words of the provincial, one sees a certain resistance to the spiritual reading of the Brother.

as the "Camareras de la Virgen."[1103] In this regard, many of the ladies found a good advisor in him. One of them, Bienvenida Millán, tells us: "He was very serious—very formal—good, very kind. And I considered him a good religious—a lot, a lot. He was always seen to give very good advice; very good."[1104]

Not only the women, but children found in him a master for beginning the Christian life. The community put him in charge of instructing children in Christian formation and the way of piety, since the priests themselves recommended that parents put their children under his care. And parents who knew him entrusted their small children to go for a walk with him. Joaquina Muñoz offers us this data about Br. Victoriano:

> He was very pious and very good; and everyone in Cuenca thought of him that way. That is how his superiors regarded him. They recommended to me that my children go with him for a walk, and children went very happily with him, in spite of the fact that he talked little; and it is curious, since he did not have permission, he did not come into the home when he went to look for the children, but he called them through the grille on the window, and nothing more.[1105]

Well, then, in reading the depositions about Br. Victoriano, in all of them one finds repetition about the spiritual accompaniment he gave to a young woman, Paulina, the sister of Eugenia Muñoz Girón. The two sisters were very pious, lived in Cuenca, and were "handmaidens of the Virgin of Perpetual Help." Through his work as sacristan Victoriano had the necessity of being in contact with them. His initial reservations gave way to a

....

1103 Translator's note: this group would have been an association of laywomen who are dedicated to helping in the church; the title of their association could be translated "Handmaidens of the Virgin."

1104 BIENVENIDA MILLÁN, *C. Beatificationis—Declaraciones* I, 332.

1105 JOAQUINA MUÑOZ, *Ib.*, II, 503. [Translator's note: Religious at the time were forbidden to enter the homes of laypeople without explicit permission from their superior.]

true friendship with both Muñoz sisters. But with Paulina,[1106] beyond a friendship, there arose a spiritual empathy, which with the passage of time became an extraordinary spiritual friendship and finally resulted in accompaniment.

....

1106 Paulina Muñoz Girón was born in Casasimarro (Cuenca) on June 25, 1889; her parents were Ricardo Muñoz and Luisa Girón. From childhood she felt an inclination toward religious life. In 1899 she went to Cuenca with an uncle and aunt and enrolled in the school of the Daughters of St. Joseph to study. While she was in the school, she began to frequent the Redemptorist church of San Felipe. She became a postulant in Ciempozuelos (Madrid) with the Oblates of the Most Holy Redeemer on November 5, 1916; in December she had to return home on account of tuberculosis, with the belief that death was imminent. She continued living on in Cuenca a number of years, although for the rest of her life she remained in precarious health; she lived at home as a "consecrated virgin." She was accompanied by several Redemptorist spiritual directors and came to know Br. Victoriano in 1924. She shared an intense spiritual friendship with him, in which she entrusted herself to his direction beginning in February 1929. At the beginning of 1933 the pulmonary disease again set in and she died on February 3, 1933. (Cf. V. CALVO, *Una hija de María del Perpetuo Socorro. Autobiografía íntima de Paulina Muñoz Girón. 1889-1933* (Cuenca, 1933). [Translator's note: the title of the book is translated, "A Daughter of Mary of Perpetual Help. Intimate Autobiography of Paulina Muñoz Girón, 1889-1933"]

Church of San Felipe, Cuenca, decorated for the Novena

Paulina had a great desire for perfection. She had been in the postulancy of the Oblate Sisters [of the Most Holy Redeemer], but she had had to leave because of the fragility of her health. While she could not live a vocation to the consecrated life, she always held a desire to respond radically to God. For this reason, "the ordinary Christian life does not satisfy the one who desires 'to be a religious;'" But because she could not be such because of her illness, "the life of a good Christian woman alone did not satisfy her, nor could it satisfy her." A director "was for her a necessity so that she could progress in virtue, so that she could develop the precious energies that enveloped her will."[1107] She was without a spiritual director for eight years, a fact that caused her to suffer a great deal, being without someone who would orient her along the paths of holiness. Formerly she had had various Redemptorists as directors, but with the change of priests she did not find one in whom she could find a word of help or guidance. She was suffering martyrdom from her fear of sin and judgment, and all of this produced in her much anxiety and guilt. Pauline said that without a director, "I am at a standstill and I can do nothing. Because I don't see, I do not know how to look and so I do not dare take a step for fear of making a mistake." She went on saying she needed a director "who understands me and wants to attend to me, one in whom I can comfortably confide and with whom I can place total confidence."[1108]

Victoriano understood the situation in which she was and what her needs were: "With her soul worn out with this continual battle, she shrank down into a certain state of timidity, in spite of her lively and resolute nature with regards to human things. She became incapable of taking a single step in the spiritual life without a director who could understand her, and she looked forward to putting before him what she wanted to and needed to... At the same time, she needed this guide to moderate her excessive fears and to undo her repeated scruples."[1109]

She continued having the Redemptorist superiors as her confessors, but the spiritual relationship with them did not go beyond the confessional. When she came to perceive the spiritual depth and virtue of Br. Victo-

....

1107 *Ib.*, 377.

1108 *Ib.*, 377.

1109 *Ib.*

riano, she decided to choose him as director (1929). He also accepted the charge she was offering him, but not without first asking permission from his superior, Fr. Leoz.[1110] The superior, who appreciated the Brother and knew Paulina, thought that Victoriano could help her. Joaquina, Paulina's sister, tells us: "And proof of the regard in which his superiors held him is that in fact they allowed him to help spiritually a sister of mine—my sister Paulina—who was sick much of the time and now has passed away; and my sister confided to me that Br. Calvo did her a lot of good. Fr. Leoz—who was superior of the house and who heard my sister's confessions—of course allowed him to do so."[1111]

Although they had the necessary permissions, many "tore their garments"[1112] in finding out that Paulina had Br. Victoriano as her spiritual director—a lay Brother! First among those was Eugenia, her sister, who broke off her friendship for many years with the poor lay Brother. In a Church which understands spiritual direction as tied to priestly orders, it is normal that there be that kind of reaction.[1113]

The fruit of the precision spiritual direction that Br. Victoriano gave the sensitive Paulina Muñoz was that she advanced rapidly along the road of perfection. God had given our Br. Victoriano Calvo the gift of counsel. Paulina confided to her sister Joaquina, who had been very opposed at first, "that Br. Calvo did her a lot of good."[1114]

When asking him about his spiritual accompaniment, Br. Victoriano tells us how he judged "advisable to find the root of those fears, because he saw that without destroying those first, he would only with difficulty situate her on the foundation of confidence and love of God, so that she would practice virtue from the motivation of divine love and not constrained by fear of

....

1110 Fr. Inocencio Tirapu Leoz was spiritual director for Paulina from 1921 until 1927 (cf. Appendix 2)

1111 JOAQUINA MUÑOZ, *C. Beatificationis—Declaraciones* II, 504.

1112 Translator's note: Tearing one's garments is a traditional biblical gesture to indicate rage (Mathew 26:65). The implication here is that those who took offense at the closeness of Br. Victoriano to his directee Paulina were as hypocritical as the offense that the Pharisees and scribes took to the actions of Jesus.

1113 In the history of the Church there had been priests who have been spiritual directors and have led people by the path of holiness; but there have been as well laypeople who have been magnificent spiritual directors, such as St. Catherine of Siena or St. Gerard Majella, a Redemptorist Brother.

1114 JOAQUINA MUÑOZ, *C. Beatificationis - Declaraciones* II, 504.

the judgment of God and his punishment, or the fear of being condemned, which, however good it may be, love is better for arriving at sanctity. The beginning, middle and end of sanctity is divine love."[1115] To walk the way of accompaniment, he asked her that she open her heart, even though it cost her. After getting to know her well and to discern the reason for her fears, he gave her motives for trusting in God. The path that they could walk together calmed the heart of Paulina of her fears that were constraining her and she tasted the joy of salvation. She herself expressed it this way: "V. has now convinced me. Blessed tears, those which it cost me to make my confession to him. It has produced in me such an intimate and great peace, such as I have never experienced! Were it only that my previous directors had worked thus with me!"[1116] For this Victoriano offers us a page from the spiritual pedagogy that he used with her:

> It was necessary to open her soul to unlimited, daughterly confidence in God and in the Most Holy Virgin. To do so, I began by inspiring her with absolute confidence in myself, conducting myself with her as would the best flesh and blood brother. Now in the beginning, there was nothing in me which could instill that kind of respect in her. I found myself able to consider and deal with her absolutely as my equal. Nor did she have reason to suppose I had other motives. I always treated her with the respect and dignity she was owed and that her condition and sex demanded, and which was proper to my religious state. And by her frank and communicative nature and even more by her great desire to speak of the aspirations of her soul, repressed now for some years, she did not find difficulty in growing in confidence. She well knew what it is was that she wanted from her director, since she is just and good. She gave that trust, and knew also that it was useless to explore her aspirations if she did not have an attitude of trust. She would not consent to what was simply capricious or even more to what was prejudicial to her soul, no matter how little it was...Once she had given such absolute and noble confidence to the spiritual director, it was not difficult to cultivate her confidence in God. And to make it happen, she

----

1115 V. CALVO, *Una hija de María del Perpetuo Socorro…*, 380.
1116 *Ib.*, 381.

was grateful to stop and think about the charity with which she was being treated by her director, to deduce from that what must be the love that God had for her. From the confidence that her director inspired in her, she deduced what must be the confidence that she was able and should be able to have in God. And from the compassion and kindness with which her director met her efforts, not demanding anything more than her efforts, she learnt how much must be the divine kindness and mercy in pardoning and forgetting our weaknesses and sins....Through this method she progressed admirably along the path of daughterly and loving confidence in God, and in perfect self-surrender, also daughterly and loving, to the will of God. In that she was singularly devoted. The desired success in overcoming her past fears finally was obtained. Her faith, which also was unbreakable, was affirmed and intensified all the more with this confidence. She delighted in contemplating Jesus in the Blessed Sacrament and the image of the Most Holy Virgin of Perpetual Help...."[1117]

Fr. Dionisio de Felipe dedicated abundant pages to studying the director-directee relationship between Victoriano and Paulina. In reading through his study, the impression one gets is that both ended up being enriched spiritually through this encounter.[1118] The spiritual life of people who live an ordinary life normally goes unnoticed. Occasionally, we can get some hint, we can see the tip of the iceberg, but for the rest remains hidden from others' eyes forever. The interior life of Br. Victoriano will remain unknown to us forever, although we can see it projected onto his directee Paulina Muñoz. In some of his writings, he called her "Theophila," that is, "beloved of God."[1119]

But the spiritual mastery of Victoriano does not remain uniquely in the intimacy of his personal growth or in his spiritual relationship with those who lived with him or whom he accompanied. His spiritual mastery was also at work in his spiritual direction in written communications. These are

....

1117 *Ib.,* 381-383.

1118 Cf. D. DE FELIPE, 195-200.

1119 Translator's note: *Theophila* is Greek; the same term was used by St. Francis de Sales when he put into writing his advice to his directee whom he called Theophila. That document became his book *Introduction to the Devout Life.*

reflected in various manuscripts. He wrote retreats, reflections, and other works for Paulina. They have come down to us and are authentic pieces of spiritual literature. Javier Elizari has us note, in his theological report that he did about these writings, how striking this is the case:

> *And this is the first striking phenomenon in this servant of God. With no more literary preparation than he acquired during his childhood in the country school of his town and without more theological preparation than what he received in conferences given him during his formation and some reading he did—and this would not have been much in the case of a coadjutor Brother, as was his case—he managed to write six books. They have not been published, but they perfectly well could be. They are not only free from theological error but also are full of the best ascetical-mystical teaching of his time. He reflects very well the currents of spirituality of that time (the first part of the twentieth century): holy abandonment to the will of God, union with Jesus Christ as a victim, association with the Virgin Mary, the presence of St. Teresa of the Child Jesus...Including that when he comments on St. Teresa or St. John of the Cross or on his founder, St. Alphonsus Maria de Liguori, he expresses himself with admirable precision.*[1120]

We present in the following each of these writings:[1121]

My Mother: Meditations on the love of the Most Holy Virgin, 1930, 183 pages

Manuscript in notebook form. It contains reflections from the first retreat, which Victoriano prepared for Paulina. It is divided into three parts:

1. *Meditations on the Virgin Mary,* pp.1-106. It contains twenty-two meditations on the life of the Virgin Mary, following the various mysteries of her life.

1120 F. J. ELIZARI, *Siervo de Dios Victoriano Calvo* in: *Causa Beatificationis, Informes Comisión Teológica.* [Translator's note: The title of this work, which was part of the beatification process for Victoriano, is "Servant of God Victoriano Calvo" in "Cause for Beatification, Report of the Theological Commission."]

1121 V. CALVO, *Causa Beatificationis—Escritos.*

2. *Reflections on the Gospel*, pp.107-114. It contains two meditations on the obligation involved in her being chosen by God.

3. *Retreat on my total abandonment to God*, pp.115-178. It contains
sixteen meditations on themes that have to do with the asceticism of the time, such as abandonment to God, reparation, loving God for who he is, and those who don't love him needing
to love him.

The style of the reflections is reflective, profound, dialogic, expressed in
feminine form, as if the protagonist were the soul.

Spiritual Retreat, 1931, 104 pages

A 104-page notebook contains meditations for an eight-day retreat, organized probably as spiritual exercises. These days of exercises were composed around the question which Jesus made to the one who arrested him:
"Whom do you seek? Jesus of Nazareth."[1122] And Victoriano asks his directee if she also seeks Jesus, including in the most holy things, and if she
seeks herself. Each day he offers two considerations for meditation and
some readings from Fray Luís de Granada,[1123] Fr. José Tissot,[1124] and Fray
Ambrosio de Valencina.[1125]

Collection of Retreats: 1. About the life of a victim; 2. About the
mystical life; 3. About abandonment and the truths of the faith;
Ember Days,[1126] 1932, 76 pages

This deals with a collection of retreats that are only partially preserved.
They were written on loose sheets of notebook paper, each page numbered,

---

1122 Translator's note: c.f., John 18:4-5.

1123 Translator's note: Fray Luís de Granada, OP, was a theologian and spiritual writer, whose
cause is up for canonization.

1124 Translator's note: This was perhaps Joseph Tissot (1840-1894), a Frenchman who edited
The Interior Life: Simplified and Reduced to Its Fundamental Principle by a Carthusian monk.

1125 Translator's note: Fray Ambrosio de Valencina (1859-1914), a Capuchin priest, wrote a
number of works, including *Edifying Legends, Soliloquies*, and *The Salve Regina Explained*.

1126 Translator's note: Ember Days were traditionally observed by the Church four times
a year, at the beginning of each season; it was an attempt to sanctify what was already a practice
among Roman pagans, of celebrating the changes of seasons. These were observed by Catholics as
days of fasting and abstinence. They are no longer obligatory.

with some missing. We still have: 104-109, 133-144, 147-157, 162-208. The index lists eight meditations, of which three are preserved, two in partial form ("about the life of a victim," six pages; "about the mystical life," twenty-four pages), and the last one which is completely preserved. The only date that we find is the one for the Ember Days of 1932 in the third retreat. He continues with the previous themes, in the style of a spiritual father, taking on certain methods that a teacher would use. In the first retreat the change is made from the Latin *Cor Jesu victima peccatorum* to the Spanish *Corazón de Jesús, víctima de amor por nuestros pecados.*[1127]

Continuation of the Reflections on Holy Abandonment, no date given, 200 pages

Written in a notebook of 200 pages, all handwritten. The writing is divided into two parts: the first, numbered as the third part and called "Abandonment in the Spiritual Life"; the second, numbered as the fourth part and called "Abandonment in the Mystical Life." By the numeration of the parts, it can be supposed that there were two previous parts, which could very well have been the meditation about holy abandonment in the previous writings. If that is so, these meditations were written toward the end of 1932 or in January 1933. The first part is divided into ten meditations and the second part into six meditations. They add up to a total of sixteen meditations which could be appropriate to some spiritual exercises of eight days. Following Fr. Valencina, the woman for whom the writing was intended is called Theophila, and it continues with the theme of the basis for reparation. It is worthwhile to point out how in the experience of God accompanying the soul, God is going to invite her to a glimpse of the martyrdom on the horizon in those years of difficulty for living the faith. Victoriano tells us on pages 109-110: "They can take our temporal life from us, not the life of the soul, that is, the life of grace...Humans can do nothing to us...which God does not have work to the accomplishment of his mysterious designs... The example for this we have in the martyrs."

....

1127 Translator's note: The phrase in both languages means, "Heart of Jesus, victim of love for our sins."

A Daughter of Mary of Perpetual Help: An Intimate Autobiography of Paulina Muñoz Girón, 1889-1933, Cuenca 17-11-1933, 402 pages[1128]
A4-size paper;[1129] the writing is divided into two parts with sixteen chapters each. Properly speaking the document is an autobiography of Paulina, written under the direction of Br. Victoriano, as his own curriculum vitae had been written by him during his novitiate. Only the introduction and the final chapter, titled "From Exile to the Homeland" is entirely from the hand of Br. Victoriano. The rest is from Paulina, whose writings Victoriano had, and he transcribed and edited them for publication later. Paulina died in February, and the text was composed around October 17. In eight months Br. Victoriano did the work of transcription and gave form to the material from his directee; and this without neglecting his community commitments. Beyond the biography of Paulina, through the pages of this work we can see into the friendship and spiritual accompaniment that Victoriano had formed with her. The manuscript ends on page 402 with some notations from the Brother indicating the *nihil obstat* of the provincial[1130] for its publication: "Sent for examination by the most reverend Father provincial and, since there was nothing substantially obstructing its publication, he authorized that it be done after some time with the prudent precautions which he demanded, with the hope that it would do good for the souls who would read it. Cuenca, October 17, 1933."

Appendix to the Autobiography of Paulina Muñoz: Her Virtues, Cuenca 18-3-1934, 150 pages
Manuscript in notebook form. It is conceived as the third part of the autobiography. In it, Br. Victoriano offers us what he calls "her physiognomy:" a portrait of Paulina from the viewpoint of her virtues and defects. What he accomplishes is the redaction of a new biography of Paulina, read from the point of view of the close association of the author with her. At the end, the interior and exterior sufferings of the subject of the biography

----

1128 Translator's note: in the European style of writing dates, this signifies November 17, 1933.

1129 Translator's note: European A4-size paper is 11.69" x 8.27" in US reckoning.

1130 Translator's note: The *nihil obstat* was required by Church law of any work published claiming to be Catholic writing, in this case, the publication of a manuscript by a religious. The superior would have had it reviewed for theological error.

are understood from that viewpoint as the distinguishing characteristics that marked her life as a "victim of love." In the manuscript there are many echoes of the autobiography of St. Thérèse of Lisieux, *The Story of a Soul*. At the same time, Victoriano also offers us, through Paulina, a manual for growing in spirituality and in the virtues by means of spiritual direction and accompaniment.

After presenting the spiritual friendship of Br. Victoriano and Paulina and the retreats that he put together for her, we can certify that both were seen enriched by this relationship. Both learned how to make of that friendship, guided as they were by prayer and the Holy Spirit, a road to human and spiritual growth. Let the following detail be sufficient for illustrating the point: In a moment in his writing in which he was unable to contain his emotion, Br. Victoriano says: "You [Paulina] who now contemplate him, and also our Mother, as I fervently believe, pray for me and obtain for me that love for Jesus in the Eucharist, and from your holy abandonment to the divine will which made you a true victim, and that filial and confident love for our Mother which I need in order to soon see the arrival of the day of my own entering into the celestial dwelling place of the eternal and divine love. There, as a prize for patient love in this exile, one receives joyful love."[1131] The expression of the author remains pure and holy even in the great human and spiritual affection he felt for her.

When Dying Is a Gain: He Receives the Palm of Victory

Victoriano wrote in his curriculum vitae that, after participating in the Redemptorist mission in his town in 1915, with the fear of returning to a life of coldness, he thought: "With God's grace I see the palm of victory in my hand."[1132] It seems everything like a prophecy that was fulfilled on August 10, 1936, when he received the palm of martyrdom. But he was preparing himself for the self-surrender of a martyr throughout his life by means of his mortification, silence, sacrifice, prayer, and service. His seeking to do the will of God and the practice of holy abandonment brought him to offer himself to go on the recently established mission in China in 1928. It is not exceptional for him that he was prepared for his final moment of martyr-

....

1131 V. CALVO, *Una hija de María del Perpetuo Socorro...*, 400.

1132 V. CALVO, *Curriculum...*, 15.

dom. When the religious were about to leave the monastery of San Felipe in Cuenca, his confrere Isidro Fernández Posado heard him say, "Let us save what we have hidden (we had the Blessed Sacrament hidden away) and let us save ourselves, but always conducting ourselves as good religious."[1133]

When the religious persecution broke out, he and Fr. Julián Pozo, who was sick, went together to hide in the house of Eugenia Muñoz, sister of Paulina. She lived on Calle Andrés Cabrera, 22. There they were in continual prayer and recollection. Joaquina Muñoz Girón remembers those tremendous events:

> When they had to abandon the monastery, Br. Victoriano hid in our house, along with Fr. Pozo. He lived a life of very great piety in our home, although, since he was so quiet, he never spoke about martyrdom or the rest. I have already talked about how he left my house and went to the Seminario de San Julián[1134] and the reasons for this....And I say the same, then, in respect to the motives and causes for them killing him, killing this Brother; that is, the persecution that reigned then—they killed him only because he was a religious. The fact is, especially because he was so quiet, he could never have given them any motive for doing so, except for the sole reason that it was a religious persecution. I don't have anything else to add, nothing more, nothing more.[1135]

When they got word of the death of Frs. Olarte and Goñi, they realized the situation of risk they were in. Not wanting to put their charitable hostess in danger and at the command of the superior, they went to the diocesan seminary. The days Victoriano spent there—as we have previously pointed out—he was using to prepare himself for martyrdom. He was taken from there by the militiamen, in the company of Fr. José Javier Gorosterratzu, in early morning on August 10, 1936, and was martyred along with his brother

------

1133 I. FDEZ. POSADO, *C. Beatificationis-Declaraciones* I, 167.

1134 Translator's note: St. Julian's Seminary, the seminary for the diocese of Cuenca, which became for all practical purposes the jail of the priests and religious of the diocese under the Second Republic.

1135 JOAQUINA MUÑOZ, *C. Beatificationis—Declaraciones* I, 296.

from the community along the road to the cemetery.[1136] From a study of the remains it has been able to be proven that he received the impact on the thoracic region[1137] and a *coup de grâce* to the skull.[1138]

For Victoriano, being a Redemptorist missionary and martyr were one and the same thing. The two aspects were united in Christ. His journey of configuration to Christ was brought to completion with martyrdom. It was a journey that never was easy, in that all of his life he had to confront difficulties. The perseverance he professed on the day of his perpetual vows became martyrdom on the day of his assassination. All his life, Victoriano was conscious that it all was pure grace on the part of God. In novitiate, he wrote: "I received my habit in the Congregation of the SsR.[1139] without meriting it, five years and eleven months after the first stirrings of the grace of my vocation. May the Lord give us all holy perseverance in this vocation."[1140] To the grace of his vocation, which would enable him to attain perseverance as a Redemptorist, he responded with his life of prayer, service, configuration to Christ, and spiritual accompaniment.

....

1136 *Certificate of Death of Victoriano Calvo Lozano*: REG. CIVIL DE CUENCA, Sec. 3.ª, T. 42, F. 326, N.º 647.

1137 Translator's note: The thorax is the chest.

1138 Cf. *Expert Medical Report on the Remains* in: *Records of Identification and Transfer,*40-42.

1139 Translator's note: CSsR = *Congregatio Santissimo Redemptoris* (Congregation of the Most Holy Redeemer). Since he has spelled out in full the word "Congregation," Victoriano goes on to use only the remaining three letters of the Latin abbreviation, SsR.

1140 V. CALVO, *Curriculum...*, 32.

Pedro Romero Espejo

CHAPTER NINE

Pedro Romero Espejo

Pedro Romero Espejo did not die a violent death, so that he does not completely or strictly fit the definition of a martyr. He does not figure among the victims bloodied by persecution.[1141] For this reason, one of his biographers, Dionisio de Felipe, found it difficult to catalog him among the martyrs. De Felipe wrote up Fr. Romero's life and described his martyrdom in a final appendix to his book *Nuevos Redentores*, an appendix titled: "Those who fell without shedding their blood."[1142] But Fr. Romero was always considered a martyr among the Redemptorists. The witnesses who gave testimony in the beatification process also agreed that he was a martyr: "In the Diocesan process (1962) the witnesses themselves unanimously agreed in favor of the title of martyr for him. One of them went so far as to create a maxim for him: He was more of a martyr than any of the rest."[1143] And that is how the Church has recognized him in the decree of martyrdom.

....

1141 D. DE FELIPE, *Nuevos Redentores* (Madrid, 1962) 215.

1142 *Ib.*, 219-229.

1143 D. RUIZ, *De camino* 2, 12 (APRM. Mártires 0400124).

A Boy with a Difficult Childhood[1144]

Pancorbo,[1145] a town of the province of Burgos that's surrounded by impressive gorges and guarded by high mountains, is the place where Providence wished Pedro Romero Espejo to be born on April 28, 1871, at 16:30[1146] hours.[1147] His parents were Cirilo Romero and Paula Espejo. Cirilo was from a little town near Briviesca (Burgos) called Vileña.[1148] His work was as a herder of pigs. Paula was a native to Pancorbo and worked full-time in household tasks. Both were very Christian.

On the day after the birth of the child, his parents brought him to the church so that he could receive the waters of baptism.[1149] They gave him the name of Pedro, and the priest gave him San Prudencio as his protector.

The Romero Espejo family had the reputation in the village of being welcoming and generous, even though they were poor.[1150] It was recounted that his father was so charitable that he would give lodging in his house to any transient or pilgrim who was passing through Pancorbo and who did not have a place to stay. For that reason, when some passerby needed a roof under which to spend the night or a plate of hot food to stem his hunger, they would tell him to go to the house of Cirilo, that certainly there they would give him a hand.

....

1144 We shall use as our principal source his written autobiography from during his novitiate (Fr. ROMERO, *Curriculum vitae; Nava de Rey [Valladolid, 1890]*, in: *C. Beatificationis—Escritos*).

1145 Pancorbo was visited by the Redemptorists in 1880. They left in writing a report that there were some 1,400 inhabitants, and several priests were at their service; that "the people of Pancorbo have a well-deserved reputation for being bad: the majority of the population are blasphemers, people who make Sunday profane. Moreover, there are among them those who have the accursed custom of the modern close dance. Each Sunday unchaperoned youth of various ages and both sexes meet...ages twelve to fifteen, fifteen to eighteen and eighteen to twenty-five. Thus unsupervised and close in on one another, they give themselves to these diversions and to sin and to the devil. These dances are preceded by what they call meriendas, in which they eat and drink to excess." (*Crónica del Espino* I, 91). [Translator's note: a *merienda* is a picnic or a light snack.]

1146 Translator's note: 4:30 PM. In Spain, as in Europe in general, the twenty-four-hour clock may be used more frequently than it is in the United States, especially when recording time must be exact, such as on flight or train schedules, birth or death certificates.

1147 REG. CIVIL DE PANCORBO (BURGOS), Sec. 1.ª, T. 1, F. 15 vto. N.º 24.

1148 Translator's note: Briviesca is about fifty-two kilometers (about thirty-two miles) northeast of Burgos, the province capital. Vileña is eight kilometers (four miles) south of Briviesca.

1149 PARISH OF SAN NICOLÁS Y SANTIAGO DE PANCORBO (BURGOS), *Baptismal records*, XVI, f. 129.

1150 Cf. Fr. ROMERO, *Curriculum...*, 1-3.

Pedro grew up in that home in which he also learned to share with the poor, though he did not always do it happily. Things were not easy for him, since he had to overcome a number of difficulties during his childhood. He himself recognized it when he wrote: "I suffered a lot during my life and it began already in my childhood."[1151] The first of his trials was ill health. His health was very fragile during his childhood and he suffered many ailments. No one thought he would reach adulthood.[1152] Another test was being ostracized when he was scarcely four years old. Even though the family had the reputation of being good Christians, magnanimously charitable, they had problems with their neighbors for political reasons.[1153] One son of Cirilo and Paula publicly declared himself to be a Carlist in front of their neighbors in Pancorbo, who were aligned with the liberals. Apparently, it is an action that does not have much importance, except in those years there was a great deal of political effervescence and a high degree of partisan virulence. This tension forced the Romero Espejo family to abandon their home for a number of months, fleeing to Basque Country. It had to have been hard on Pedro, as he tells us: "My parents and I were exiled. I was more or less four years old. We suffered this exile because I had a brother among the Carlists. We spent seven months in the Basque Provinces. What were not our labors and alarms in seeing ourselves many times surrounded by soldiers who fought or traded shots with their enemies!"[1154]

When the Carlist Wars ended, the family could return to live in Pancorbo without problems in 1877. At age six he began going to school, and it seems he had a facility for learning. Although he was mischievous and a bit of a rascal, he applied himself to studies, doctrine, and a life of piety.[1155] On September 9 or 10, 1877, he received the sacrament of confirmation in his parish church of San Nicolás de Bari in Pancorbo from the

----

1151 *Ib.,* 4.

1152 Cf. *Ib.,* 4 y 5.

1153 This has to do with the Third Carlist War (1872-1876). With the abdication of Isabel II, the partisans of Carlos de Borbón, Duque of Madrid, as pretender to the Spanish throne, rose up in arms against the governments of Savoy, the First Republic and Alfonso XII.

1154 Fr. ROMERO, *Curriculum...,* 4-5.

1155 Cf. *Ib.,* 6-7.

Archbishop of Burgos, D. Anastasio Rodrigo Justo.[1156] He began to feel very much inclined toward piety: "I enjoyed going to church to learn the things the pastor or other priest decided to teach the children."[1157] He made first Communion at age nine or ten. From then on he would go to confession four or five times a year, and he was delighted to help at Mass every day.

In February 1880, a group of Redemptorists who had established a foundation at Nuestra Señora de El Espino a few months previously came to Pancorbo to preach a mission.[1158] The group of preachers was made up of Frs. Pedro López, Luis Kent, and Arturo Payen. Pedro, who was eight at the time, was so impressed that a strong desire to some day be a missionary like them took root in his heart. It was not the first time he felt a desire for the ecclesiastical life, but the contact with the missionaries increased those desires and oriented him toward religious life—more precisely, toward being a Redemptorist.

Nevertheless, things weren't going to be easy because some difficulties imposed themselves between his desires and his ability to see them through. The poverty of his family[1159] was the main obstacle, since his father could not pay the tuition for the seminary. Between the pastor and Pedro's father, a decision was made for Pedro to do the shortened course, which was cheaper, or to enter a monastery. When the two consulted Pedro, he favored the monastery, motivated by his timidity and scruples: "I had a certain inclination for the cloister for various reasons...First, a certain interior disquiet and remorse afflicted me at certain times. I felt I would be free of them by entering a monastery. Also, I had a certain timidity and sorrow whenever I thought about death, which happened frequently. Moreover, I saw that if I took up a life in the world, it would to a great extent be difficult to see what I should do to gain my salvation."[1160]

1156 Parish of SAN NICOLÁS Y SANTIAGO DE PANCORBO (BURGOS), *Baptismal Register* XVI, f. 315ss.

1157 Fr. ROMERO, *Curriculum...*, 7.

1158 The mission took place from February 11-26 and was so successful that the whole town went to confession, 800 people took Communion and they promised to go to Mass, fight against blasphemy, and the youth organized their fiestas to take place in the plaza and in view of their elders (cf. *Anales* I, 134-135; *Crónica del Espino* I, 91).

1159 Cf. Fr. ROMERO, *Curriculum...*, 8.

1160 *Ib.*, 10.

That being the case, Cirilo set about looking for a religious order which would accept his son: [1161] the Sacred Hearts in Miranda de Ebro (Burgos); the Jesuits in Oña (Burgos), other religious. But everywhere there were obstacles. The father almost gave up as he saw his son being rejected over and over, although it seemed there might be one door still open. He had Pedro study with an ex-seminarian in town named D. Damián, who was able to offer a price that was closer to the economic possibilities of the family. In that small boarding school, Pedro studied for some two years. He learned a little Latin and was initiated into the adventures of the young people of the town.[1162]

But Pedro felt called to the religious life. Driven by his repulsion at the bad character, which from time to time manifested itself in his father, he decided to leave home. Meanwhile, Cirilo, seeing the state of things and the determination of his son to be a religious, made one last try and this time he managed to resolve all the difficulties. He went personally to El Espino, the minor seminary which the Redemptorists had opened just a few years before in the nearby town of Santa Gadea del Cid, and where there were some other young men from Pancorbo. He convinced Fr. Pablo Charrot, the director of the center, to accept his son in the middle of the school year. By that time, Pedro was a youth of fifteen, and because he had not had rudimentary Latin he would not ordinarily have been admitted for being "too old."[1163]

The day after receiving the positive response from the director of El Espino, Sunday, February 21, 1886,[1164] Pedro went to see the priest of the town, whose help had been effective in getting him admitted. There he made a general confession "in order to enter the threshold of the house of God, as is the house of religious who observe their Rule."[1165] After that, father and son set out and traversed on foot approximately three leagues[1166] between Pancorbo and the ancient Benedictine monastery.

....

1161 *Ib.,* 14-15.

1162 *Ib.,* 9.

1163 *Ib.,* 19-20.

1164 Cf. APRM. *Book of Admissions to El Espino I,* year 1886.

1165 Fr. ROMERO, *Curriculum...,* 23.

1166 Translator's note: nine miles.

Years of Missionary Formation

The juvenate, or minor seminary, of El Espino had been founded on July 16, 1882, so that Pedro was joining in its first years. He noted the clear emphasis on discipline that the French Redemptorists brought to the place. "Thanks to the Latin he had learned, they admitted him to the second-year course. He had average intelligence and a strong will. He was able to handle the classes in Latin, Spanish, French, history, geography, and algebra. And all the rest."[1167] Regarding academics, Pedro had serious problems in passing mathematics, especially since algebra was a torture for him. He stood out in his efforts, but did not fare very well in those studies. Nevertheless, his behavior and piety were outstanding, with some moments better and some worse. "I was the average juvenist. I obeyed the Rule perfectly enough, but at the same time I was not a model in every way....There were times of fervor for me, and I also had moments when in which temptations abounded in my head. The most common of these militated against my vocation."[1168]

His character was perhaps excessively retiring, and he himself described himself as a timid person. It cost him to reveal his interior experiences to the director, and his scruples were rooting themselves within him, causing him great interior suffering.[1169] These scruples "cast a shadow over his soul. On the occasion of a retreat, he made another general confession and felt better."[1170] The novice master, in his report written at the beginning of novitiate, perceived in him a tendency toward discouragement, although he had hope that Pedro would overcome it through his own efforts: "This young man by his nature gets easily discouraged. Just the same, sufficient good will was noted in him to hope that he will triumph over this defect."[1171]

On August 22, 1889, the future novices left El Espino for Nava del Rey. After a time of adaptation and retreat, the novitiate was begun on September

---

1167 D. RUIZ, *De camino* 4, 3.

1168 Fr. ROMERO, *Curriculum...*, 26.

1169 *Ib.*, 27.

1170 D. RUIZ, *De camino* 4, 3.

1171 APRM. *Book of clerical and lay postulants*, I, n.º 54.

22 with the ceremony of receiving the habit,[1172] under the direction of Fr. José Chavatte as novice master. Fr. Chavatte was a French Redemptorist who had the honor of having been a pontifical Zouave.[1173]

The novice brother Pedro Romero tended to be very serious in his undertakings and put a great deal of emotional intensity into whatever he did. For this reason, his scruples, which already had made their appearance in the juvenate, sharpened during the novitiate, because of the limited psychological horizon, which this canonical requirement demanded, and because of the particular demands of the master.[1174] Nevertheless, Fr. Chavatte was a man of great experience in the spiritual field. He helped Brother Pedro to overcome his scruples through the medicines of obedience to his superiors and faithful observance of the norms of the institute. Pedro noted in his autobiography what his master said to him with insistence: "The Rule is the fence around the vineyard of the soul."[1175] The novice took in the precept of the master so well that it served as a lesson for him throughout the whole of his life, even to his death as a martyr. Occasionally, this way of understanding religious life made him a bit intolerant of what he considered the faults of others. It was during this year that he raised the four pillars over which he constructed his missionary life: to live in the presence of God, a life of prayer, devotion to the Most Blessed Sacrament, and love for the Most Holy Virgin Mary.

....

1172 *"Petrus Romero Espejo. Dominica Dolorum B.M.V. die 22 Septembris 1889, in hac domo B. Theresiae Virginis, in civitate Navae Regis, a R.Fr. J. Chavatte, Novitiorum Magistro, in Novitiatum admissus est adolescens Petrus Romero y Espejo, laicus, e civitate Pancorbo, diocese et provincia Burgensi, natus 28 aprilis anni 1871: nempe annos 18, menses 4, dies 25. Ad oblatione admisus, die 24 septembris 1890"* (APRM. *Liber Primus Inscriptionis Vestium mutationis Choristarum. Novitiate, Chorists,* year 1889, n.º LI).). [Translator's note: the Latin means: "Pedro Romero Espejo, on the Sunday of the Sorrows of the B.V.M., on September 22, 1889, in this house of the Blessed Virgin Teresa in the city of Nava del Rey, the youth Pedro Romero y Espejo was admitted to the novitiate by Reverend Fr. J. Chavatte, Master of Novices. Pedro is a layman, from the city of Pancorbo, Diocese and province of Burgos, and was born on April 28, 1871; he is eighteen years, four months, and twenty-five days of age. He was admitted to vows, on September 24, 1890."]

1173 For a profile of Fr. José Chavatte, cf. J. CAMPOS, *Grandes del Apostolado* (Madrid, 1965) 73-94. [Translator's note: The translation of the title of the book is *Great Men of the Apostolate*.] [Translator's note: The papal Zouaves were an international infantry force made up of unmarried Catholic young men, formed in 1861 to defend Pope Pius IX and the Papal States against the armies of Giuseppe Garibaldi, who was seeking to unify Italy as a republic.]

1174 Fr. ROMERO, *Curriculum...*, 27-28.

1175 *Ib.,* 28.

At the end of his novitiate year, he made his religious profession of perpetual vows on September 24, 1890, when he was nineteen years old.[1176] Together with the vows of poverty, chastity, and obedience, he took the vow and oath of perseverance in the Congregation of the Most Holy Redeemer until death. As we shall see in the unfolding of his life, perseverance had a special meaning in him.

Once he had made his vows, he was assigned to Astorga (León) with his classmates to do his theological studies. They were years of many changes with regards to formation and professors, under the direction of Fr. Eduardo Bührel, also a Frenchman. These years in the studendate in Astorga, "years of higher studies went by with the same note of Pedro being an average student in his grades and excellent in the observance of the Rule and in the spirit of the religious life."[1177]

On September 20, 1891, while he was still a student of philosophy, he received the tonsure and the four minor orders.[1178] At age twenty-four, when he was in his final course of ecclesiastical studies, he received ordination to the priesthood on February 29, 1896, at the hands of the bishop of Astorga, Bishop Vicente Alonso y Salgado.[1179]

With his studies finished, he was appointed to Nava del Rey (Valladolid) in September 1896, but in October he had to go to Madrid—Perpetuo Socorro to switch places with the newly ordained priest Fr. Vicente

....

1176 *"Ego Petrus Romero e pago Pancorbo, Provincia Burgensi, Novitius Congragationis Sanctissimi Redemptoris, hac die 24 septembris 1890, Beata Virginis Maria de Mercede sacra, in hoc collegio sanctae Theresiae in civitate Navae Regis inter manus admodum Reverendi Patris Rectoris Pauli Lorthioit, segundum regulam nostram, et ad tenorem privilegiorum nostrorum, sponte nuncupavi vota simplicial paupertatis, castitatis, et obedientiae, una cum voto et juramento perseverandi ad mortem usque in praefacta congragatione, praesente tota Communitate, praesertim R. Francisco Masson et R. Josepho Chavatte. Ego Petrus Romero, manu propia"* (APRM. *Liber secundus inscriptionis Professionis Religiosae Perpetuae in Congregatione SS. Redemptoris,* Year 1890, n.º 48). [Translator's note: The Latin means: "I, Pedro Romero, from the village of Pancorbo, province of Burgos, a novice in the Congregation of the Most Holy Redeemer, on this 24th day of September, 1890, on this holy day of the Blessed Virgin Mary of Mercedes, in this formation community of St.Teresa, in the city of Nava del Rey, at the hands of Reverend Fr. Rector, Paul Lorthioit, according to our Rule, and in line with our Privileges, have taken of my own free will the simple Vows of Poverty, Chastity and Obedience, together with the Vow and Oath of Perseverance until death, in the aforesaid Congregation, in the presence of the whole Community, in particular before Reverend Francisco Masson and Reverend Joseph Chavatte. I, Pedro Romero, sign in my own hand."]

1177 D. DE FELIPE, 221.

1178 APRM. Mártires 0406007, *Ficha* 1.

1179 *Anales* III, 57.

del Palacio. Fr. Vicente was in delicate health and could not take life in Madrid.[1180] There Fr. Pedro began to be introduced to the life of a priest and on May 9, 1897, without having to be changed from that house, he began the second novitiate under the direction of Fr. Otmaro Allet. This was a period in which he not only refreshed his spiritual life for himself, but prepared his sermons for future missions.[1181] "Except for Saturdays and days of recreation, all the rest of the days the novices preached their sermons during supper. In addition,...it was they who preached almost all the sermons in the chapel."[1182] When they completed this time of probation in the month of October, the "young Fathers" were ready for the apostolic-missionary life. And it was then that Fr. Pedro Romero received his first assignment as a missionary: Granada.

Granada, Years of Travel as a Missionary (1897-1899)

Fr. Pedro arrived in Granada on November 4, 1897. The chronicler welcomed him by saying: "May he be welcome among us and remain many years."[1183] At that time the community was residing in the heart of Albayzín, in the historical church of San Juan de los Reyes.[1184] The superior entrusted to him responsibility for religious services in the church, with the title of church prefect. In addition, in the two years that Pedro was in this community, he was initiated into missionary ministry with grand campaigns throughout Granada and Almería.

The first series of missions preached by Fr. Pedro Romero was in el

....

1180 *Ib.*, III, 64 y 73.

1181 Some sermons of Fr. Pedro Romero remain from this period (cf. Fr. ROMERO, *12 Sermones* en: C. *Beatificationis—Escritos*).

1182 *Anales* III, 130.

1183 *Crónica de Granada* I, 269.

1184 Translator's note: The name of the church is translated "St. John of the Kings." The Albayzin area of Granada is the old Moorish quarter of town, declared a World Heritage Site.

Valle de Lecrín,[1185] up against the slope of the Sierra Nevada.[1186] He worked alongside veteran missionaries like Fr. Esteban Maret (a Swiss) and Fr. Juan Bautista Vidal. They began in Albañuelas[1187] on February 23, 1898, and continued there until March 13. The town had some 2,000 residents. Although the mission was not bad, it experienced difficulties because of the cold character of the people, the rainy season, the carnivals, and the absence of men at the religious services. In contrast to that, the fruit of the mission was the reconciliation of persons with each other. From there they went on to Durcál (Granada),[1188] from March 14 to April 3, where they conducted a great mission: "Unjust ways of acting were eliminated. We preached about the Seventh Commandment twice. There were some long consultations. Certain erroneous concepts about usury were corrected."[1189] A couple of days before finishing this mission, Pedro returned to Granada[1190] to preach the seven-day service in honor of Our Lady of Sorrows. In Holy Week he was sent to preach in the town of Dehesas Viejas[1191] (Granada).

The next missionary campaign was with Fr. Villoslada throughout Las Alpujarras.[1192] They began September 18, 1898, in Cástaras (Granada) and they ended November 23, on which day they returned to the community from Bubión (Granada).[1193] In Cástaras they reinforced the fruits of the mission by preaching a renewal from September 18 through 23. From

----

1185 Translator's note: El Valle de Lecrín is a tourist area in Granada and is made up of eight townships; the word *Lecrín* is a derivative of the Arabic *Iqlim*, meaning "gateway," and refers to a narrow stretch of land between two towns in the time of Moorish Spain. The passageway led to the rich sugar-producing lands of the Mediterranean coast.

1186 Translator's note: The Sierra Nevada, meaning "snowy mountain range," has the third highest point in continental Europe: Mount Mulhacén, 11,411 feet high (3,478 meters). The Sierra Nevada offers opportunities for skiing, while below are the warm coastal areas of the Mediterranean Sea.

1187 Cf. *Ib.,* I, 278-279.

1188 Cf. *Ib.,* I, 279-280. [Translator's note: another one of the townships in el Valle de Lecrín, as is Albañuelas.]

1189 *Ib.,* I, 280.

1190 Translator's note: the city of Granada, capital of the province of Granada.

1191 Translator's note: a small town known for its wine.

1192 Cf. *Ib.,* I, 290-293. [Translator's note: another area in the autonomous region of Andalusia. It is on the southern slope of the Sierra Nevada. It is fertile land that produces olives, grapes, citrus and other fruits.]

1193 Translator's note: Both of these very small towns have magnificent views of the Sierra Nevadas and offer today hiking trails and tourist accommodations.

September 23 through October 8, they remained in Nieles, a town of some 400 residents who in the majority participated in the mission services. On October 4 they moved on to Soportújar and they held a mission until October 16. At that time, 547 people made up that town. The next mission, in Cáñar, went on from October 18 until November 4. In this town of 900 inhabitants, the mission was only lightly attended because the people were busy with the harvest. But there were quality conversions. From there, there were mission renewals in Jubiles (from November 4 to 10), Pampaneira (from November 10 to 16), and Bubión (from November 16 to 21). In these apostolic campaigns, Fr. Pedro met people who were very poor. They were victims of usury and the exploitation of *caciques*,[1194] a theme that is repeated over and over in the chronicles of the mission. The year 1898 ended with the preaching of a mission in Pinos Genil (Granada)[1195] with Fr. Salvador from December 9 to 18. It was a mission that did not resonate well with the people.[1196]

In January 1899, Fr. Pedro went to preach in Las Alpujarras in Granada[1197] with Fr. Salvador. They began by strengthening the fruits of the mission with renewals in Pórtugos (January 11-19), Pitres (January 19-26), and Mecina Fondales (January 26 until February 3). In these missions they saw that "the efforts made during the mission against profanation of holy days were crowned with success, but not quite so much regarding blasphemy." On February 5 they traveled to Yegen to preach a mission until February 19. During that mission "many families which were at enmity against one another were reconciled. The Association of Las Hijas de María was established." They ended this particular missionary campaign in Las Alpujarras again with the mission in Válor (from February 19 until March 12). There was full attendance at the sermons and talks, and a solemn func-

---

1194 Translator's note: *Caciques* were local leaders in business and government who tended to have dominance over and to exploit the people.

1195 Cf. *Ib.*, I, 294.

1196 Translator's note: All these towns and others are part of a chain of small towns nestling in Las Alpujarras, featuring houses of distinctive flat, clay roofs, a carryover from the days of the Spanish Moors. Tourists hike through the area today, going from town to town.

1197 Cf. *Ib.*, I, 296-297.

tion was celebrated in honor of *Cristo de la Yerda*,[1198] a devotional crucifix that is very much venerated and visited in all of La Alpujarra. After celebrating Holy Week in their own community, Frs. Romero and Salvador left again to preach during April further into the interior of Las Alpujarras de Almería.[1199] From April 14 to 28 they were in Baycal and from there, on April 29, they went to Patrna until May 14. Before arriving in Granada they stopped to preach a mission in Nechite (Granada) from May 15 to 28.[1200]

When he was in Granada, Fr. Pedro Romero received a letter telling him of the illness of his mother. When he had things arranged so that he could go be with her in her final moments, he received another letter informing him that she had died. In spite of that, he went to Pancorbo to take care of several family matters.[1201] He left Granada on June 6 in the morning and would not be returning there. On June 16, he was intercepted by the Father Visitator[1202] at El Espino. Fr. Romero had gone there from Pancorbo. He was then told of his transfer to Astorga.[1203]

Astorga, Years of Glory as a Missionary (1899-1911)

Fr. Romero arrived in Astorga (León) on July 18, 1899, "from El Espino, where he had been temporarily since he had not ceased to be a member of the Granada community...He is coming to this community [Astorga] as a

....

1198 Translator's note: Cristo de la Yerda is the name of a particular crucifix that hangs today in the church of San Agostino in Montilla. Its origins are from medieval times in a hermitage on the outskirts of Baeza. The Jesuits promoted devotion to Christ under this title in the sixteenth and seventeenth centuries. At the time of the suppression of the Jesuits, the Augustinians took over the devotion and moved the crucifix to their church. Cristo de la Yerda is carried on Good Friday in procession through the streets of Montilla. Devotion to this crucifix can be found throughout Écija, Jerez de la Frontera, Vélez-Blanco, Válor, and Granada.

1199 Cf. *Ib.,* I, 299. Translator's note: on the other side of the Sierra Nevadas, this town and the other small towns mentioned offer picturesque views of the River Andarax, the vineyards, almond and cherry trees, and farmed fields up the side of the mountain to as far as the cultivators can reach before the area becomes too frigid for farming.

1200 Translator's note: The local parish church in Nechite, San Blas, is of Mudejar architecture—partly Gothic, partly Arabic—prevalent in Granada from the twelfth to the fifteenth centuries.

1201 Cf. *Ib.,* I, 300-301.

1202 Translator's note: One of the provincial consultors would accompany the provincial superior to make the Canonical Visitations, as required by the Rule. Or the provincial would designate another Redemptorist for particular official visits, such as to negotiate the transfer of an individual.

1203 Cf. *Crónica del Espino* II, 165-166; *Anales* III, 343.

missionary."[1204] The community was going through profound changes, especially among the professors of philosophy and theology: the older French professors were being replaced by Spanish Redemptorists. The emancipation of the Spaniards from those who had founded the province was not always met with understanding and cordiality. In this community, Pedro would have an intense missionary life. During his twelve years there, he would preach some one hundred missions.[1205] These would be chiefly in León and Galicia. Whether it is because of the chronicler or whether it is because of the small amount of time that he would actually be in the house, his name is seen in the house chronicles only as tied to evangelizing work.

The first missions preached by him within the first few months of his arrival were in small and poor Galician towns of the diocese of Santiago de Compostela[1206] (province of La Coruña) together with Fr. Antonio Mariscal: Moreira (100 households, from August 23 to September 10, 1899), Castro and Cira (244 households each, September 11-24) and Santa Eulalia de Oza (170 households, no date given). The two missionaries ended the year in the province of Zamora, in Vega de Tera[1207] (diocese of Astorga, two towns of some 100 households each) where they preached the mission from December 9 to 20.

With the year 1900, a new century began, as did an intense year of missions for Fr. Pedro. He preached fourteen missions and two mission renewals with Frs. Antonio Mariscal, Eduardo Bourel, and Ignacio Rodríguez Insúa in small towns of the dioceses of Astorga, Santiago, and Lugo.[1208]

....

1204 *Crónica de Astorga* I, 291.

1205 APRM. Mártires Cuenca, 0406007, *Ficha 2.*

1206 *Crónica de Astorga* I, 296. Translator's note: Santiago de Compostela is actually an Archdiocese, designated as such in the year 1120. It encompasses most of Galicia and includes the cities of La Coruña and Pontevedra. Its cathedral is the focal point of pilgrims since AD 812, when it was claimed that the remains of St. James the Apostle were found there.

1207 Cf. *Ib.,* I, 299.

1208 San Clemente de César (Coruña, February 3-5), La Baña (León, February 26 to March 10), Forna and Losadilla (León, March 10 to 19), Trabazos and Encinedo (León, March 19 to 29), Santa Eulalia (León, March 30 to April 7), Robledo de Losada (León, April 7 to 16), Nogar (León, April 16 to 24), Santa Columba de las Monjas (León, April 26 to May 4), [Translator's note: Missions are usually not requested for summertime.] Agrón (Lugo, September 6 to 16), Gónzar (Lugo, September 19 to 28), Chayán (Coruña, September 29 to October 7), Santo Tirso de Villanueva (Coruña, October 7 to 21), Augueriz (Lugo, November 2 to 11), Sofán (Coruña, November 11-25), Reguería (Pontevedra, November 27 to December 9) and Gulanes (Pontevedra, December 9 to 23) (cf. *Crónica de Astorga* II, 9-13. 22-23).

In these places he could experience the cultural poverty and difficulties for living the faith.

Pedro, with Frs. Marchal, A. Mariscal, Montuno, Fernández, Bartolomé, and Taboada preached eleven missions in 1901[1209] in the dioceses of Astorga and Santiago. In 1902, he was a bit lazier, and the house chronicle lists him with only seven periods of extraordinary preaching[1210] at the side of Frs. Llerena, Fernández, Gómez, Taboada, and Barona in the dioceses of Santiago and Orense. But some of the missions, such as the one in Villagarcía de Arosa, were in cities of greater size.[1211]

Apostolically speaking, 1903 was especially important for Fr. Pedro. He preached along with Frs. A. Mariscal and Lorenzo González in the dioceses of Astorga and Santiago, a total of ten events, both missions and renewals.[1212] The mission in Manzaneda merits special attention.[1213] It is a town in Orense, belongs to the diocese of Astorga and has 170 households. Frs. A. Mariscal and Romero preached a mission there from April 15 to 28. The town was divided and the reception of the two missionaries was very cold. On the day of reparation, Fr. Romero exposed the Blessed Sacrament. Meanwhile, Fr. Mariscal preached. When the preacher proclaimed the words of Isaiah, "I stretched out my hands to a rebellious people," those who were in the church felt a shudder and a child shouted in Galician: *Eu quero ver o neno.* ("I want to see the child.") Many of those present said that they had seen in the place of the Sacred Host the Child Jesus, dressed in white, with arms open, and his heart open in his chest. Others saw a great flash, and the priest said he saw the Crucified One. The event created great expectations among the people

....

1209 Boa (Coruña, January 28 to February 7), San Martín de Minostos (Coruña, February 7 to 17), Puebla de Caramiñal (Coruña, February 20 to March 9), Beade (Coruña, March 10 to 26), Albarellos (Coruña, March 26 to April 8), Gudín (Coruña, April 8 to 21), Sandín (Zamora), Palacios (León, October 7 to 17), Remesal (León, October 17 to 28), Aldaña (Coruña), Veldedo (León) (*Crónica de Astorga* II, 39-41. 54-57. 70; *Anales* IV, 98-104).

1210 Villagarcía (Pontevedra, April 20 to 26), Carabiñal (Coruña, from the 26th of April to the 9th of May), Forcas (Orense), Vilacha (Coruña), Dordaño (Coruña), Colinas (León), Montes y Uriales (León) (*Crónica de Astorga* II, 72-73. 82; *Anales* IV, 192-196).

1211 Translator's note: This city along the Atlantic coast had about 37,000 inhabitants in 2018.

1212 Cornazo (Coruña), San Lorenzo de Moraña (Pontevedra), Negreira (Coruña), Troitosenda (Coruña, February 26 to March 8), Arcos (Coruña, March 17 to 27), Muros (Coruña, March 28 to April 13), Brión (Coruña), renewal in Barcala (Coruña), Graba (Coruña) and Villarrubín (Orense) (*Crónica de Astorga* II, 93-98. 119-121; *Anales* IV, 294-297).

1213 Cf. *Anales* IV, 297-299.

of the place. Fr. Pedro, whose character was cold and pragmatic, showed himself to be indifferent to the whole thing, denying to the event any supernatural "halo," and ascribing it to the imagination of the Galician people.

In the following years, Pedro Romero continued with this missionary work. In 1904, all the towns that had missions were Galician, small townships belonging to the diocese of Santiago, Orense, and Astorga.[1214] The subject of our biography was accompanied by Frs. Pardo and Mariscal in these seven missions and renewals. In 1905, there were many missions in small towns, almost all in Galicia, and the majority of them in the diocese of Lugo. For this reason, all the missionaries in the house were involved in the apostolate. Fr. Pedro shared his apostolic work that year with Frs. Del Pozo, Victorino del Olmo, Bordagaray, Eriguoz, and Pitreguoz.[1215]

In 1906, he preached various Tridua, together with Fr. Mariscal, in towns around Astorga (Cuevas de Celada, Val de San Lorenza, Carral, Posadilla, Soto, Villoria, Palacios, Castrillo, Castrotierra, Tejados, and Valderrey). And he preached six events, divided between missions and renewals,[1216] with Frs. Vidal, Lorenzo, and Montuno in the dioceses of Astorga and Orense. In 1907, Fr. Pedro, with Fr. Lorenzo González, preached in the small towns of Galicia of the dioceses of Santiago and Orense,[1217] with one rare exception.

....

1214 Esgos (Orense, February 17 to 29), Carnota (Coruña, March 3 to 17), San Mamed de Carnota (Coruña, March 18 to April 3), renewals in Brión and in Beacan and Villarrubín; Valdana de Chaodocastro (Orense), Las Hermitas de Santa Cruz (Orense, October 30 to November 12), Sobrado and Trives (Orense), and Ruian (Orense), where he preached the Novena of Perpetual Help (*Crónica de Astorga* II, 126-127. 139-141; *Anales* IV, 397).

1215 Pino (Coruña, January 10 to 20), Arca (Coruña, January 20 to February 3), Budino (Coruña, February 3 to 15), Carnota - Sta. Columba (Coruña, February 18 to 25), Carnota - San Mamed (Coruña, February 25 to March 8), Vilocoba (Coruña, March 9 to 20), renewal in Santa Cruz (April 9 to 14), renewal in Las Hermitas (Orense, April 14 to 19), San Cristóbal de Souto (Lugo, April 24 to May 6), Santa María de Villaquinde (Lugo, May 7 to 19), Carracedo (León, November 2 to 16) (*Crónica de Astorga* II, 156-160. 170; *Anales* IV, 504).

1216 Laroco (Orense, March 1 to 16), Corneces (March 17 to 29), Porriño (Pontevedra, April 1 to 10), Lubián, (Zamora, December 4 to 17), Hermisende (province of Zamora), San Román el Antiguo (León) (*Crónica de Astorga* II, 182. 185. 201; *Anales* V, 36-39).

1217 Chaguazoso (Zamora, mission from January 7 to 21), Castromil (Orense, from January 20 to February 1), Beariz (Coruña, mission from February 13 to 21), Trasalba (Orense, February 25 to March 9), Pungín (Orense, March 9 to 20), Louredo (Orense, renewal from March 24 to 28), Macendo (Orense, renewal from March 29 to April 6), San Facundo (Orense, April 7 to 11), Partovía (Orense, mission from May 26 to June 8) and a novena to Mary Immaculate in Benavides de Órbigo (León) (*Crónica de Astorga* II, 213-214. 217. 221. 247; *Anales* V, 106-112).

In the following years new young priests were taken into the community of Astorga as missionaries. For this reason, little by little, Fr. Pedro waned in enthusiasm and found his voice diminishing.[1218] He was relegated to small towns and renewals until he was not assigned any missions at all. In 1908, he and Frs. Lorenzo González and Teófilo Escribano still preached thirteen missions and renewals in small Galician towns in the dioceses of Orense and Tuy.[1219] In 1909, the number was reduced to three renewals and three missions[1220] with Fr. Escribano. In 1910, we find him only preaching in the church of San Francisco, attached to the Redemptorist community of Astorga.[1221] And in 1911, he preached a mission in Val de San Román (León), from January 15 to 23, with Frs. Lorenzo González and Crescencio Ortiz. In Holy Week of that year we find him with Fr. José Javier Gorosterratzu preaching in Las Hermitas (Orense).[1222]

After twelve years of intense missionary activity—more than 100 missions—Pedro Romero left Astorga on May 28, 1911, for the community of San Miguel in Madrid.[1223] In the following period, his life began its downward slope "until his activity as a missionary was voided, while he himself was in full vigor in his strength and of a good age to work."[1224] Certainly, Fr. Romero did not have the intellectual and oratorical dispositions to be a missionary of first rank; in fact, he always went to the missions as second man or helper. Only once does the chronicle of Astorga record him as the

....

1218 Translator's note: Since preaching was done without a microphone, the preacher had to develop the strength of his voice. The less he preached, the more his voice weakened.

1219 San Salvador (Orense, from January 27 to February 5), Corneda (from February 6 to 18), in Ciudad (renewal from February 19 to 23), Sofán (Coruña, from March 21 to April 4), Rodis (Coruña, from April 5 to 15), Montemayor (Coruña, from April 19 to May 1), Castrelo (May 1 to 10), Rubín (Coruña, from September 8 to 22), Previdiños (Coruña, September 23 to 28), Santa María de Cejo (Orense, October 31 to November 9), San Adrián del Cejo (Orense, November 9 to 19), San Miguel de Bangueses (Orense, from November 19 to 30) and Nigrán (Pontevedra, December 1 to 8) (*Crónica de Astorga* II, 257-259. 274-275; *Anales* VI, 205-509).

1220 Renewals in Ardaña (January 10 to 17), Sofán (January 17 to 25), Montemayor (renewal from February 6 to 14) and missions in Soutullo and Golmar (January 26 to February 6), Viñodaguía (Orense, December 3 to 12), Villar de Canes (Orense, December 13 to 23) (*Crónica de Astorga* II, 303-304, 320-321; *Anales* V, 290-292).

1221 Cf. *Crónica de Astorga* II, 383.

1222 Cf. *Ib.*, III, 14.

1223 Cf. *Ib.*, III, 8.

1224 D. DE FELIPE, 221.

superior of a mission,[1225] in a town named Val de San Román. But on the fifth day of the mission he collapsed and Fr. Lorenzo González had to take charge of the direction of the mission.

Accepting Limitations: Madrid (1911-1913), El Espino (1913-1914), and Granada (1914-1921)

We have little data about the presence of Fr. Pedro in the community of San Miguel[1226] because the chronicle disappeared during the religious persecution.[1227] When Fr. Pedro arrived at No. 2 on the Plaza del Conde Miranda in Madrid,[1228] the community was involved in the religious services of the basilica of San Miguel. They had come to have some renown in the Villa and the Corte. Nevertheless, the missions, which were preached during those years in the dioceses of Madrid and Toledo, were scarcely a half dozen.[1229] The same did not happen with the novenas and the retreats. Although we do not have data to attribute them to Fr. Romero, it is not out of line to think that he participated in all the apostolic work of the community: worship, confessions, novenas, retreats, and missions.

In less than two years, he packed his suitcases again. In September 1913, Fr. Romero returned to his home territory of Burgos. He arrived in El Espino on September 22.[1230] No sooner did he move in than he took up

....

1225 Translator's note: According to the Redemptorist Rule, not only did local communities have a superior to control the business of a house, but mission bands, or teams, also had one man in charge.

1226 The ancient church of San Justo in Madrid, situated next to the palace of the bishop, on a corner of the Calle Sacramento, was conceded to the Nunciature in compensation for the Hospital of the Italians, which had been torn down to build the Palacio de las Cortes [Translator's note: Parliament.] The Secretary of State of the Vatican changed its name to the Pontifical Church of San Miguel and by express wish of Pope Leo XIII it was given to the Redemptorists. They built living accommodations for the community in the buildings to the rear of the property and had charge of the church until 1959 (Cf. R. TELLERÍA, *Un instituto misionero* [Madrid, 1932] 296-304).

1227 Data is obtained from the provincial chronicle, (*Anales* V, 505-509; *Anales* VI, 51-54. 113-116), records written in years anterior to the disappearance of the chronicles.

1228 Translator's note: This was the address of the living quarters of the Redemptorist community attached to the Pontifical Basilica of San Miguel.

1229 In the year 1911, the following were preached: three missions, three renewals, thirteen series of retreat talks, thirteen novenas; in 1912, six missions and one renewal were preached. In 1913, the number of missions rose to fourteen, thirteen novenas, and seventeen series of retreat talks (Cf. *Ib.*, VI).

1230 *Ib.*, IV, 106-107; *Crónica del Espino* IV, 248.

his missionary activity again in small villages and paired the preaching with series of retreat talks. We find him preaching two sermons in Fuente Burebo (Burgos) on September 23, and sermons for various occasions during the month of October in Miraveche (Burgos) and Ages (Burgos).[1231] From November 4 to 16 he was in Vileña (Burgos) to preach a series of retreat talks to the Cistercian nuns. After that, there was another series of retreat talks to the boys of La Salle High School in Bugedo (Burgos); and a final one beginning on November 29 to the girls of the Sister Oblates of San Sebastián (Guipúzcoa).[1232] Once this series was finished he preached a mission with Fr. Pedro del Palacio in Montoria (Álava), a town of some 130 inhabitants. There was good fruit from the mission.[1233]

Also in the year 1914, Fr. Pedro Romero is credited with strong missionary activity.[1234] In February he preached a Triduum in Tirgo (La Rioja), and on March 1 he went to Ujo (Asturias) to preach a mission until March 16. The success of the missionaries was so great and they were applauded so much that influential persons wrote to the Marqués de Comillas[1235] praising the activity of the Redemptorists. On his return on March 11, he preached a mission renewal in San Miguel de Guna (Cantabria) with a fair amount of satisfactory results. He celebrated Holy Week in Peñacerrada (Ávala). From then until September, there are only sporadic preaching events recorded in the chronicles.[1236] The chronicle of El Espino ends with a record that he had a mission in Villasuso de Mena (Burgos) from September 18 to 27 together with Fr. Enrique Chaubel. Through some misunderstanding, almost all the men and a good number of women did not take part in the mission activities. The missionaries had to be inventive

....

1231 Cf. *Crónica del Espino* IV, 254.

1232 *Ib.,* 257.

1233 *Ib.,* 264.

1234 *Ib.,* 265. 267. 270. 272. 277. 280. 290.

1235 Translator's note: Claudio López Bru was the second Marqués de Comillas (1853-1925). He was prominent as a Catholic in labor relations at the time.

1236 A sermon in Burgüenda (Álava) on May 31. In June, a sermon on Perpetual Help in El Espino and on June 14 a sermon on the Most Holy Trinity in San Miguel de Guna (Cantabria). On July 22, a sermon on St. Mary Magdalene in Suzana (Burgos) and on September 8 and 9 a sermon on the Virgin and another on the Holy Souls in Purgatory in Galbarros (Burgos) (*Ib.,* 293-294).

to gather in the people. In October he also preached a mission in Soto de Campo (Cantabria).[1237]

1237 *Ib.*, 302.

Community of Granada, 1914:
Fr. Romero, bottom row, first on left

Fr. Romero was once again assigned to Granada in November 1914, where he arrived on November 7, according to the chronicle, "with a lot of determination...assigned to the missions."[1238] Even though the city was familiar, the community had just moved from El Alabayzín to the center of the city, in the old church of the Congregation of the Sisters of St. Philip Neri,[1239] situated in front of the hospital of San Juan de Dios.[1240] In the internal organization of the community, Fr. Pedro[1241] held the positions of zelator (1915-1916 and 1921), librarian (1915-1920), prefect of the Brothers (1917-1920),[1242] and consultor (1921). He would remain in the city of Alhambra until December 30, 1921, when he again packed up his things and went off to Cuenca.[1243]

As regards his apostolic ministry, in 1915, besides a mission in Lupión (diocese and province of Jaén, of some 850 inhabitants, where he remained from April 16 to 26), he had a missionary campaign with Fr. Leoncio D. Yáñez throughout Las Alpujarras[1244] and another through the mountain range of Málaga with Fr. Francisco Echebarría.[1245] In 1916, he preached

....

1238 *Crónica de Granada* II, 368.

1239 Translator's note: the Congregation of the Sisters of St. Philip Neri was founded by siblings Marcos and Gertrudis Castañer y Seda in 1858 to address problems created by the Industrial Revolution, in particular giving education to poor girls.

1240 Due to the inaccessibility of Albayzín, after various attempts, the Redemptorists acquired the church of San Felipe, on the central street of San Jerónimo. San Felipe had been sold and unconsecrated and was a warehouse. Restored, it was opened to worship and consecrated on December 12, 1913. On August 26 of the same year the church of San Juan de los Reyes was handed over [to the Diocese] and the whole community began to live in the monastery next to the Church of San Felipe (Cf. R. TELLERÍA, *o. c.,* 324-328).

1241 *Crónica de Granada* III, 1. 55. 78. 99. 116.

1242 Translator's note: The prefect of the Brothers was in charge of certain community responsibilities for the Redemptorist Brothers living in his house.

1243 *Ib.,* III, 121.

1244 Pampaneira (130 households, mission from February 23 to March 6), Bubión (120 households, mission from March 6 to 16), Capileira (280 households, mission from March 16 to 27) and Mecina Fondales (120 households, mission from March 27 to April 7). (Cf. *Ib.,* II, 377-378).

1245 Towns of the Diocese and province of Málaga which had missions by Fr. Romero: Cartajima (250 households; renewal May 25 to 31), Júzcar (700 inhabitants, mission June 1 to 9), Faraján (200 households, renewal June 9 to 14), Alpandeire (900 inhabitants, mission October 10 to 21), Júzcar (renewal October 21 to 26), Jubrique (2,100 inhabitants, mission October 26 to November 7), Genalguacil (1,300 inhabitants, mission, November 7 to 17), Algatocín (1,800 inhabitants, mission November 17 to 26), Atajate (60 households, mission December 9 to 18), Fuentepiedra (renewal, December 19 to 24) (cf. *Ib.,* II, 379. 388-390).

in the dioceses of Granada[1246] and Almería.[1247] The next mission that he preached and was recorded in the chronicle was in 1920, during a general mission[1248] in the city of Granada at Lent, which he preached in the parish of El Salvador between February 18 and 29.[1249] From March 14 to 18, 1920, we find him preaching a mission with Fr. Barredo in Güejar Sierra (Granada).[1250] And in 1921 he was still going to preach two missions with Fr. Andrés Goy, in Beas in Granada (March 14 to 22, a very difficult mission) and in Huétor Santillán (normal mission).[1251]

As a curious piece of information and at the same time something that can give us an idea of the kind of image that the rest of his confreres in Granada had about Fr. Pedro, we transcribe a prankish poem of the community which they composed on January 6, 1919, to tease him. The Redemptorist community celebrated the feast of the Epiphany of the Lord as a day of recreation, which means giving some time for happy conversation without the rigor of regular order. It was also traditional that one of the religious be nominated "king." And the nominee would ask the superior for a favor in the name of the whole community. The joke that follows is a mixture of theater and song, which we transcribe such as it is from the chronicle of Granada:

Fr. Romero does not show up, and the couplet is intoned:

Stop our joy
End the sound
Fr. Romero's
Nowhere to be found.

....

1246 Towns of the diocese and province of Granada where he had a mission: La Malahá (1,000 inhabitants, mission January 23 to February 3 with Fr. Vega), Deifontes (1,000 inhabitants, mission April 10 to 23 with Fr. Echebarría), El Marqués (a country estate, mission from May 29 to June 3 with Fr. Macua) (cf. *Ib.,* III, 5-6).

1247 Towns of the diocese and province of Almería where missions were given with Fr. Echebarría: Lucainena (3,500 inhabitants, mission February 5 to 18), Uleila del Campo (1,800 inhabitants, mission February 18 to March 3) with the conversion of the parish priest (cf. *Ib.,* III, 35).

1248 Translator's note: A "general mission" is an areawide mission in which several mission preachers preach at several parishes.

1249 Cf. *Ib.,* III, 90-91.

1250 Cf. *Ib.,* III, 91.

1251 Cf. *Ib.,* III, 108.

They look: Can he be in the tower?
Soon they solve the mystery
As hosannahs and shouts
Relay triumph and victory

'...in the air
Joyous musical notes
Accompany sonnets
And clearly denote:

Play the tambourines
Make the trumpets blast
Because Fr. Romero
Has appeared at last.[1252]

The chronicle does not tell us how he took the joke, but we can guess by his serious, austere, and rigid character that he was not enthusiastic about it.

Services in the new shrine of Perpetual Help were acquiring prestige and promoted in the population the devotion to the sacred icon of the Mother of God. The increase in activity in turn at the shrine itself had the effect of relegating Fr. Romero to a second tier, in attending to a smaller number of requests for missions and with a community gifted with members more

....

1252 *Ib.*, III, 62. The original:

Cesen las alegrías,
acabe el ruido,
porque el Fr. Romero
¡ay! se ha perdido'.

Lo buscan: ¿Estará en la torre?
Los ayes tristes y lamentaciones lúgubres
se cambiaron en gritos de triunfo y de victoria,
en hosannas y alegrías...,

y en los aires,
a los estrépitos de los instrumentos musicales,
resonaron sonatas
a esta parecidas:

'Suenen las panderetas,
ruido y más ruido;
porque el Fr. Romero
ya ha aparecido

accomplished in apostolic activities. Fr. Pedro received a new assignment in December 1921, this time in Cuenca.[1253]

Missionary and Monk: Cuenca (1921-1936)

Fr. Pedro arrived in Cuenca at the end of 1921. A few months later, the community received the visit of the general government and, at the advice of the consultors, many changes were decided upon for the community members. The new year 1922 brought a new superior to the community of Cuenca, Fr. Inocencio Leoz, and with him a new epoch. Let us recall that in 1920, the community of San Pablo had been closed, leaving the Redemptorist presence in the city reduced to only San Felipe. Also in the diocese there were new changes with the arrival of the new prelate, Bishop Cruz Laplana. Moreover, in 1922 the Vincentian Fathers took over the community of San Pablo. As a result, the Redemptorists ceased being the only male religious in the city of Cuenca.

Although we do not have the house annals, since they disappeared during the religious persecution, we observe in the province chronicle that Fr. Pedro Romero is not mentioned in it as having had any mission of note in the following years.[1254] The community was getting fewer missions and busied itself with preparing for the pastoral visit of the new prelate by preaching a Triduum in the places where the pastor of the diocese was going to be coming. It seems that Fr. Pedro was at least in Rubielos Bajos (Cuenca), for which reason the sacristan of the town later would recognize him in jail.[1255]

Until this time, Fr. Pedro Romero in his life as a missionary "did not know how to supervise a mission but served in a subordinate position. In that position he offered missions in many country parishes...His capacity for giving missions grew as it was cultivated with prayer and sacrifice...He scrupulously practiced his oratorical pieces. One sees in his handwritten notebooks containing his sermons and talks how the text is repeatedly corrected. He brought forth from his chest treasures both old and new.

....

1253 Cf. *Anales* VII, 539-540.

1254 Cf. *Anales* VII, 39-40. 138-139. 206-207. 384.

1255 "Gabriel Lozano at that point recognized Fr. Romero...because he had gotten to know him in Rubielos Bajos when Romero was accompanying the Lord Bishop on a Pastoral Visit" (D. DE FELIPE, 226).

When Pope Pius X published his decree about eucharistic Communion, he began right away to preach that good news to the people."[1256]

But as Fr. Dionisio de Felipe points out, in Cuenca he experienced an "early retirement," since "he had little aptitude for the pulpit. His was an extremely old style of preaching, his voice fairly disagreeable, he lacked technical flexibility and adaptation to the social media, which every day were demanding more in every aspect. He had to struggle with the narrowness of his judgment, which made his ministry painful."[1257] To these personal deficiencies had to be united the disdain of certain members of the Congregation who disqualified him as rigorous and out of step in mission-preaching. They would frequently make fun of his style and his missionary resources. Fr. Romero kept quiet with great humility, but only God knows what he was suffering inside.

Dionisio Ruiz describes in this way this painful stage in the life of our Fr. Pedro Romero: "Prematurely retired from missionary activity quite a bit ahead of time, it did not extinguish the lamp of his ministry—Word and Sacrament—taking great care of the moral side of doctrine which he explained in our church in Cuenca and in rural churches."[1258] And indeed, in Cuenca, though he had outings for missions and preaching engagements,[1259] as he did in Holy Week. Each time afterward he would shut himself up again in the community.[1260] A witness tells us that in his preaching, "he did not have oratorical abilities. The poor man was very simple and very scrupulous: in his simplicity, he even seemed gullible; in his scrupulosity...he was very overly good; very serious and not very communicative; very much a simpleton."[1261] On Saturdays he usually had the preaching for Saturday devotions

----

1256 D. RUIZ, De camino 3, 2.

1257 D. DE FELIPE, 221.

1258 D. RUIZ, De camino 3, 3.

1259 "He was always ready to hear confessions; he also preached and went out on missions. He had the reputation of being austere; we could say, rather than austere, more like rigid." (M.ª CARMEN GARCÍA DE LA ROSA, C. Beatificationis—Declaraciones I, 118).

1260 Patrocinio Moya said that "since he was old, he used to not go out on missions, but in the church of the Fathers—in San Felipe—he took care of the services, of the confessions, and one or the other time in Holy Week helped at some parish. He went to litte towns" (PATROCINIO MOYA, Ib., II, 446).

1261 CONCEPCIÓN SÁENZ, Ib., II, 462.

in honor of the Virgin Mary,[1262] and the same for other preaching events of small importance among the services offered in the church. Also, he went to preach retreats and to hear the confessions at the diocesan seminary of Cuenca, where he got to know D. Camilo Fernández de Lelis: "I got to know Fr. Pedro Romero Espejo as a member of the residence of the Redemptorists in Cuenca, and I remember something of his apostolic work, especially confessions which he offered in the seminary and one or the other talk. This was in the years before the War, a little before the times of the Republic."[1263]

His ministerial life went on reducing itself to the confessional in the church of San Felipe Neri in Cuenca, where he spent long hours waiting for and attending to penitents who would come to him.[1264] According to various witnesses, he had a lot of patience in the confessional, and although he was scrupulous himself and looked for sincere contrition, he well understood human fragility. One witness who knew him assures: "This Father was, as was obvious, a little scrupulous, which reflected itself in his confession work; and that was the general opinion of everyone who saw his hesitance in assuring himself that there was sincere contrition. He did not have ability in preaching, and he only did that in giving missions, and in the Saturday devotions in the church, during which times he had a simple talk. He was in the confessional a great deal, he spent long silent hours there, hearing the confessions of many people and showing himself to be very hard-working and very solicitous."[1265]

Another witness asserts, "In the confessional he was very patient with the little girls"[1266] and another "believes that he enjoyed being a confessor, and would often repeat this phrase: 'We are not angels, we are not angels.'"[1267]

Also various convents of contemplative nuns in Cuenca benefitted from his spiritual ministry and his dedication to the sacrament of reconciliation, such as the Discalced Carmelites, the Justinians, and the Benedictines.

....

1262 "He dedicated himself to the confessional, and was accustomed to take the talks for Saturday devotions to the Virgin." (*Ib.*)

1263 CAMILO FERNÁNDEZ DE LELIS, *Ib.*, I, 287.

1264 Cf. JULIÁN CASTELLANOS, *Ib.*, II, 371.

1265 MARÍA GARCÍA MOYA, *Ib.*, I, 80.

1266 FELICIA MARTÍNEZ, *Ib.*, I, 227.

1267 TRIFÓN BELTRÁN DE MARCO, *Ib.*, I, 178.

They asked him to give them retreats, talks, and to hear the confessions of the nuns.[1268]

One confrere, with whom he lived his last years, summarizes the life of Fr. Pedro Romero in Cuenca in the following fashion: "He gave himself to the services in the church and to giving retreats to the women religious; he carried out these ministries well. He was timid by nature; and he ended up being scrupulous in the way he went about things, no doubt due to his kind of life, due to his own character. He was very observant as far as the Rule goes, and he almost drove people crazy with his scrupulosity. He had a lot of confessions. He was considered a good religious; he ended up being almost exaggerated in his spirit of poverty."[1269]

From that point on, he led the life of a Carthusian: silence, prayer, long hours in the confessional, and, of course, the daily celebration of the Holy Sacrifice of the Mass. Deprived of missionary activitiy, to which he had devoted many years of his life, Fr. Romero saw himself obligated to root himself in his religious life in a different way, leaning more toward the inner life of the community, which he wanted to be holy and observant of the Rule. "In that way, he had to enclose himself in the residence and to work almost exclusively in the confines of his own church. For the rest of his life, the role of victim was reserved to him because there was no doubt that in the mystery of his inner life, which he did not open up to anyone—except his spiritual director—he underwent anguish. He saw himself uprooted and inoperative, victim of the very same grace of which he relished for those within the community and for those outside the community."[1270] The martyrdom of Fr. Pedro Romero began many years prior to the sad events of Cuenca.

....

1268 Sr. Antonia del Niño Jesús, a Justinian, says, "I got to know Fr. Pedro Romero Espejo from his having given us retreats twice, somewhere around the years '32 or '33" (*Ib.*, II, 390). Sr. María Natividad Cuenca, a Benedictine, declared: "I knew Fr. Pedro Romero Espejo, on the occasion of his giving us two retreats, as well as during the War when I saw him at some time" (*Ib.*, II, 411). Sr. Mercedes del S.Corazón, Discalced Carmelite, says: "He sometimes came to hear confessions here...he seemed very good to me, a good confessor. As far as I recall it was around the year 1934 that he came here for confessions" (*Ib.*, II, 378-379).

1269 BENJAMÍN LÓPEZ DE MURGA, *Ib.*, II, 488.

1270 BENJAMÍN LÓPEZ DE MURGA, *Ib.*, II, 488.

Fr. Pedro Romero

The provincial superior Fr. José Machiñena found him in this situation, which he says about him in the report of his visit to the community in Cuenca: "Reverend Fr. Pedro Romero: old and sickly, with little talent and hardly any common sense, but pious and very fond of the observance of the Rule; exaggerated at times in the letter of the Rule."[1271] This was the general opinion of those who had dealt with him, whether laypeople or religious. Although he possessed a narrow vision of religious life and intellectually was anchored in the past, although at times he readily took on the role of censor of the faults of the community and of its members, everyone who knew him were unanimous in affirming that he was a model religious and a virtuous person:

Fr. Romero was admired by all for his modesty, his gravity, his religious virtues, his austerity of life and of comportment, and his practice of poverty which showed through all his person. He was shy in his behavior and his appearance. He was not made for the world, nor was the world made for him. He was complete seriousness, even in his words. It seemed he extended the vow of poverty even to them, and he economized them as if each were a coin. In him there stood out the sobriety in speech of Burgos which someone defined this way: subject, verb, and predicate.[1272]

To complete this picture of Pedro Romero we conclude with the testimony of a companion of his last days, Fr. Isidro Fernández Posado, with whom he lived some years in Cuenca and quite a few months in the refuge of the Little Sisters of the Poor:

I always saw him practicing the faith....He showed a particular submission to the documents and directives of the Church; he was most submissive to authority. I always observed in him a crazy confidence

---

1271 AHGR. 30150002,0034.

1272 D. DE FELIPE, 222. The same Fr. De Felipe recorded the testimony of a confrere along the same lines: "Serious as a juvenist, serious as a novice, serious as a theology student and serious as a priest and missionary. A religious most observant of the Rule, most fond of holy poverty, most vigilant in dealing with women. Never was he heard to say anything less than what was proper about a confrere...He was always most austere with himself. While I was preaching a series of missions with him which lasted nearly three months, never did I see him take a drink of coffee, much less liquor, not even on the days which the Rule permitted" (*Ib.,* 223).

in God, in the Most Holy Virgin, etc. Always moved by supernatural motives; nothing of human motives. As far as his relationship with God, his charity was shown in that he was always steeped in God, speaking about him continuously. He had a lot of charity toward others: with those on the outside and those within the house, with his inferiors and with everyone; strict with himself and with everyone else. My opinion is he was a just religious in every bit of his activity. And I never heard anything to the contrary—that is, to contradict this opinion. In every-thing he was most moderate; too much mortified. I never saw him involved in arguments, never saw him emotional; he was very morti-fied; but, in my understanding, without any imprudence about it. And I never heard of any incident contrary to that. He was not demanding of conveniences for himself, but just the opposite; he was austere, making do very well with everything that was the worst and what was available. He was very observant, with everyone in the community in agreement on this point. And, as I have now said many times, being demanding, very demanding of himself...self-abnegation as his most evident virtue.[1273]

Pedro Romero, Beggar and Martyr: Cuenca (1936-1938)

As we said before, Fr. Pedro Romero resisted leaving the monastery, claim-ing that he preferred to die before abandoning the monastery. But under obedience he left San Felipe and went underground as an old man with the Little Sisters of the Poor. He stayed there until September 20, 1937, pass-ing unnoticed among the old people and celebrating the Eucharist each day, hearing the confessions of the religious and the elderly and sometimes abandoning his asylum to give pastoral attention to the requests for spir-itual help that were made to him. It seems that on one of these visits he had an encounter with a group of militia. He was saved from them by the intervention of a lady who made the people who wanted to arrest and con-demn him to see that he was an old man. When his place of asylum had been confiscated, he risked danger and went out onto the street to feel free, to live as a religious, and to do apostolic work. It weighed on his constricted conscience to be in hiding in that paradise when he knew, in Cuenca (more than ever), there was need of priestly help.

1273 ISIDRO FDEZ. POSADO, C. *Beatificationis—Declaraciones* I, 167-168

On the street he could heed the call of whoever asked for him to take care of the sick, hearing their confessions, and giving them Communion. At first, he went to hide in the house of a friend, Bienvenida Herráez. While he lived there, whoever needed him went to that house to look for him, until he was denounced.[1274] Taken to the civil government, they interrogated him; there they treated him courteously and were impressed with his coherence. By way of administrative sentencing, he was interned at the city social services. But this new establishment was very small to him. He could not stand the blasphemies, nor the mockery and the attacks against God, and finally decided to leave there.

Although they offered to take him out of Cuenca, he refused the escape in order to live on the streets of the city of the Jucár, sleeping wherever he was for the night, eating what was offered him out of charity as alms. He was dressed in a threadbare and dirty soutane, a cross at his breast, the rosary in his hand, and the breviary under his arm. On the streets, Fr. Romero, known by everyone, was a missionary-beggar. Many days he was seen praying the rosary and mumbling prayers under the trees in the park. From that time on he determined he would not put in danger charitable people who offered him a roof to stay under. Nor did he wish to submit to controls. He chose to live his missionary consecration with total liberty and as a clear sign of faith in the midst of a city in which religious signs had disappeared. When hunger or cold hit him too hard, this beggar of the Divine sought refuge in some shelter such as Rupert's Inn or in the house of some pious person. Trinidad Ayala, one of the people that took him into her house during this stage of wandering, described him this way:

> In the short times in which he hid in our house and spoke with us, in the times of war, I could appreciate his virtues: he said nothing against his persecutors—he had an exquisite charity—he demonstrated great courage, much patience, very much charity; we remained edified with

....

1274 "I don't know either the circumstances when he abandoned the convent. I know he hid in the house of Mónica. Mónica was a grandmother, the owner of the house; and her daughter-in-law Bienvenida is still living (in Barcelona), who was there in the house, with her children then. The impression I have is that he would go out generally for motives of the apostolate...Although I know that for some time he walked around aimlessly—without my knowing now the exact period; and after that, he did not hide" (TRINIDAD AYALA, *Ib.*, I, 213-214).

his patience and the way he dealt with things....With regards to his attire, he carried a shawl; he went around as a beggar, I mean to say poorly, and it wasn't that he was disguised as a poor man, as a beggar. I mean that he had no interest in hiding the fact that he was a religious, he moved about without making a show of it, but without fear and without any special attempts at hiding anything.[1275]

Voluntarily Fr. Romero took on the life of a beggar. He preferred walking around the streets to lodging in the house of friendly families for whom his presence as a religious, which he was, could put them in danger. He preferred it over staying in places where others might offend God in their words or in what they did. In addition to those things was his obsession with the salvation of souls. Living on the street gave him the total liberty that he needed to go where his duties as a good shepherd called him.

A year went by that way, twelve months of persecution and of martyrdom with only the idea of being available in case someone needed his services as a priest. He had not been able to be a missionary in the easier moments because of his narrow conscience and his few qualities for the task, but he was a missionary in the difficult moments during which the Church had gone underground to the catacombs. His age and his appearance as a beggar were his allies. And because he was a missionary in Cuenca during the religious persecution, his poor bones ended up being put in jail. After being there a few months, he was able to celebrate his perseverance in the vocation he had been given.

His health, in a measure contrary to his faith and his availability for priestly service, continuously declined. His physical strength as a son of *campesinos*, farm workers, was getting less and less. Finally on June 6, 1938, he was imprisoned by the authorities in the jail established in the monastery of the Discalced Carmelites. The accusation against him: disaffection with the regime. It seems paradoxical but being in prison was a relief for Fr. Romero, since at least there he had a roof over his head, a plate of food, and the company of other priests and religious such as he. There he found two angels who took care of him during the months he was there: the sacristan of Rubielos Bajos (Cuenca) and D. Trifón Beltrán, a priest whose mother

---

1275 *Ib.*, I, 212-214.

had been assisted by Pedro Romero at the moment of her death. His health soon got worse because of dysentery, and on July 4 he died because of tuberculous enteritis.[1276] D. Trifón tells us:

> *Regarding what kind of person he was, I can say that what character-ized him was his simplicity, his childlike candor....Now, a few days after arriving in the jail, he caught dysentery or a sharp colitis—which finished him off: better said, I don't know if he got the sickness there or already had it, since he was pretty much finished off when he arrived at the jail, with his situation accented by his age. He was in the infirmary the majority of the time. I could go up to the infirmary to see him. It's certain that the flies were eating him....Yes, I believe that the life that he had prior to coming into the jail contributed a lot to the death of the Father: since I have heard later on and they continue to say, he lived the life of a homeless beggar. And so, I repeat, that when I saw him, I found he was near the end, very grave. Perhaps if they had taken care of him, he could have recovered. And I believe firmly that the great deal of suffering he had to endure and the minimal care that he got in jail contributed to his death. And I believe he can be considered a martyr from persecution by the Reds, by the Marxists, against the faith, against everything related to religion.[1277]*

Anyone who was able to have contact with him during that year in which Fr. Romero lived on the streets of Cuenca understood that his was a prolonged martyrdom. That is what María García Moya convincingly asserts when she said: "Yes, yes, I believe it. His was a true martyrdom, a slow martyrdom, that life of his of continuous suffering without a fixed home and under persecution; with the result that undoubtedly it would effect him in his agony and in his death."[1278]

....

1276 *Death Certificate of Pedro Romero Espejo*: REG. CIVIL DE CUENCA, Sec. 3.ª, T. 44, F. 300. N.º 599. [Translator's note: Tuberculous enteritis occurs in about 2 percent of people with pulmonary diseases. It is contracted by drinking unpasteurized milk or from being infected by others with tuberculosis.]

1277 TRIFÓN BELTRÁN, C. *Beatificationis—Declaraciones* I, 178-180.

1278 MARÍA GARCÍA MOYA, *Ib.*, I, 84.

Cross of Fr. Romero and a piece of his clothing

Appendices

Unedited Documents

DOCUMENT 1:
JOSÉ JAVIER GOROSTERRATZU JAUNARENA,

Letter addressed to his nephew José M. Nuin,
Cuenca 11 May 1936, 4 pp.

Letter manuscript on four sides, which was addressed to José Nuin Gorosterratzu, Redemptorist priest, nephew of Fr. Gorosterratzu. At the time, he was assigned to Pamplona (Navarra). In the letter the author uses figurative language to hide from view the letter's content. In doing so, he hides his own fear that it might fall into the hands of revolutionaries, for which reason he speaks about the Phillipian Center (Redemptorist community of San Felipe), friends (Vincentian Fathers of San Pablo), pastor Goñi (priest Miguel Goñi), family of Josefa (Benedictine Sisters; Josefa was his niece, a professed sister in the convent of the Benedictine Sisters in Cuenca). He tells in the letter about the explusion of the Vincentians, the persecution to which were subject Fr. Goñi and Br. Benjamin, and the rough situation in which he was living in Cuenca:

J.M.J.A
Cuenca 11 May 1936
Sr. D. José M. Nuin

My dear nephew; I believe that when this arrives to you, you will already find useless what it is going to tell you, because I gave the same information to a person from there some days ago, as my answer. It was meant to convey the essentials of what could have importance to you, so that you all would be at peace there. It surprises me that D.[1279] would not have already given it to you; but I am going to abbreviate the principal parts that might interest you directly.

On the first of this month they burnt the CEDA Center and in the afternoon they prepared and then began the unheard of expulsion of those friends who had talked about those things. Those friends advised the ones at the Phillipian Center that afternoon of the first, that something similar to what happened to them was going to befall these others. A pair[1280] was requested, who came to that Center at 11 at night. Almost everyone in the Center dispersed to stay with friends during the night. But while the Center of those others had been besieged by hundreds and thousands of adversaries in spite of there being many pairs inside, the Phillipian did not see anyone appear, not even in the following days, until now; although always a pair came to them at night.

Just the same I know for a fact that two members of that Center on the 2nd at 9:00 in the morning dared to visit the others, calling themselves tourists; the porter Benjamín, dressed like a picador's assistant; Pastor Goñi, was dressed like a High Knight. Things went poorly for them and they were on the point of being shot. Here is how it happened....

They could see everything that was happening and how those who had been dismissed prepared for the journey believing that the mobs were what they said they were. Moreover, once they had finished visiting at their ease, instead of returning by way of the bridge of San Pablo, the way by which they came, they went by the Puerta de Valencia. The mobs prowling about there suspected that they were two undercover men, who were going to the station. As they entered the city, the young men began to follow them. They were calling them by the nickname of those who had been expelled. They ran, trying to evade them. They crossed the walkway to the schools

----

1279 Translator's note: He is using an initial to refer to a person. We do not know who that person is.

1280 Translator's note: a pair of Civil Guard, who always patrolled in pairs.

of Palafox,[1281] because they were walking near the gangs. But a woman closed off the exit on them and they remained inside. They closed the entry door. Here there was a tremendous fight for an hour and a half defending themselves, since a great number of people who were extremely furious had gathered together. They finally broke down the door, which until that point pastor Goñi had bravely held shut. This one calmed down[1282] and capitulated under these conditions:

1st: To go the Commisary in front of all of them so that they could see that they were not what they were saying they were.

2nd: That they would not attack their persons with the clubs and iron bars, which they were waving at them in their anger.

One, the most formal and secretly right-wing, promised to comply with those terms, and with the help of a left-winger, but also an enemy of abuses. And they set off, out in front of the great crowd, which was of infinite size on the Highway. Here the old ones irritated the young ones because they were urging them to beat and finish off the two, and they received a few light punches. And they finally came into the hands of the guards, who took them (now free) to the Commissary, where they were well treated. It was verified that they were not among those who had been expelled as they were saying. They had them wear their clothes and they returned to their home by foot without their being bothered. At first, they were with the guards, and finally they went by themselves. That was the most dramatic and significant thing that happened that day.

The third, the day of the elections, tranquil. But the fourth was a day of rumors of poisonings, the same as in Madrid…here very much changed. All the convents upset. Even the Prelate spent the night away from the palace. Three from the family of Josefa went out; the others stayed, and Josefa stayed with them, because very late at night, a head-man of theirs assured them that nothing would be done against the convents.

I visited Josefa the other day. She is fine and at peace. The most agonizing thing that has happened, and the same for her companions, was during the

....

1281 Translator's note: The façade of a building constructed in 1776 is used as the entrance to two music schools dedicated to the memory of Bishop Antonio Palafox y Croy, who was Bishop of Cuenca in 1800.

1282 Translator's note: The editor of the letter has placed a disclaimer in the text, *sic*, because the author of the letter incorrectly used an accent mark: *serenáse* should be *serénase*.

hour and a half of the fight which they saw happening from their house on the day of the incident of Pastor Goñi and his companion. Because, from where they were watching, the crowd was in a frenzy.

Now everything is tranquil. Perhaps there may be some alarm when the Deputies publish something, which they are still looking at.

We still are not safe, not by any means. The horizon is menacing.

A thousand thanks to Mr. Paco and company and thousands of warm regards to all. Yours truly affectionately embraces you.

X. Goroste (Signed)

DOCUMENT 2: MIGUEL GOÑI ÁRIZ

Letter sent to his family
Cuenca 30 June 1936, 4 pp.

Typewritten letter on four sides arranged in landscape format. It is addressed to the family of the author, siblings and nephews and nieces. In it he uses a colloquial and direct tone. The contents revolve around various topics, such as in some cases family matters, the illness of the author, made a little worse before writing the letters, the explusion of the Vincentian Fathers from the monastery of San Pablo and the perse- cution which the author suffered when he went to offer shelter to those who had been expelled, the disturbing situation which they were going through in Cuenca when contrasted with the peace they were enjoying in Navarro, and, finally, a few strokes of the pen about his love for his condition as a Basque:

Cuenca 30 June 1936
Caballero, 2.

My dearest family:

As I got up from bed the day before yesterday, I hit my head on the bed and as I was conjuring up a disagreeable bump on my head I remembered that I had to write to you. How so? Very simple; when I felt the unpleasant blow on my head, this reminded me of the slaps to the neck that Santos[1283] used to give me there when I was about the age of Higinio[1284] now, and thinking of Santos, it was natural that I would remember the rest of you as well.

I decided then to bring you up to date on my life and my failings at the first moment free from business and from the bad mood that I was in, when, lo and behold, on that very day in the afternoon I received the letter from Marichu. (What I got from María Ángeles[1285] is very long, very pretentious and very old-style Castillian.) It demands of me in a very rigid and formal way that I send back a famous seal[1286] which I suspect would have belonged to Pablo Iglesias[1287] some time back. [Censured], as one says. Rumors of this letter have gone as far as Imarkoain.

So that today, in view of the resolution born from the bump on the head that I gave myself when I got out of bed and in view of the story which Marichu asks of me about the other bumps on the head, I have sat down at the typewriter, decided upon divulging the story of the bumps on the head until I disgorge the adventures of all the bumps on the head which ever were and which ever shall be. I have also decided to get rid of a "seal", one of the authentic ones, one which would be acceptable to Jovellanos,[1288] the only ones that can circulate on the front of letters in these lands of...Lenin and "La Pasionaria"[1289] without danger of being destroyed and even if I wear the soutaine of a priest. Now you see that I am generous; so that later Marichu can come and have it out with me, calling me stingy, lazy and robber of seals.

....

1283 Translator's note: Miguel's oldest brother.

1284 Translator's note: probably a relative.

1285 Translator's note: We do not know who Marichu or María Ángeles are.

1286 Translator's note: Letter seals were used on envelopes to indicate that letters intended only for the recipient had not been tampered with. Hot wax would be dropped on the fold of the envelope. The letter seal on a signet ring or seal die is pressed into the hot wax.

1287 Translator's note: Pablo Iglesias founded the Spanish Socialist Workers' Party in Madrid on May 2, 1879.

1288 Translator's note: Gaspar Melchor de Jovellanos was a Spanish lawyer and judge who in the eighteenth century advocated land reform, including taking away the property of the Church and redistributing it.

1289 Translator's note: Dolores Ibárruri was called La Pasionaria, "the Passion Flower." She was a Communist from the Basque Country who was elected to Las Cortes Generales (Parliament).

Well, enough. It was back on the 2nd of May, 1936, anniversary of that other May 2[1290] so much praised in another time in Spanish patriotism and which today praised almost only by the Basques of the upper Ebro region who have been "Castilianized." People of the lower Ebro region are interested more in burning churches and showing off red shirts. On that day, I was on the point of losing my hide. After the scuffle, I was talking with my companion in the misadventure. He is as Basque as I am. We were talking about our bad luck on a day which is so important in the annals of Castile. I told him that without doubt those persons who were enraged at these two real Basques, were *"manes"*[1291] of the heroes of the 2nd of May in Madrid. That for this reason they were taking revenge that way out of the fury they felt with the forgetfulness about the significance of the day that their compatriots were guilty of. It would not have surprised me at all if the *Diario de Navarra*[1292] (I call it *el Diario de Albacete*),[1293] might comment on our misfortune, if they came to hear about what happened!

The fact is that by a miracle we saved our precious lives...It can be said that until May 1 we enjoyed relative normalcy. Although already since the middle of April insults against the Right were reported almost daily (albeit, there exists few who are on the Right), they were not such as to inspire fear for the future. The 1st of May arrived and, conformable with the Marxist ritual, they celebrated the obligatory demonstration with a profusion of red shirts, fists uplifted, and empty stomachs.[1294] Once that was finished, I myself along with some friends witnessed how a group of rowdy individuals

----

1290 Translator's note: The city of Madrid rose up against Napolean on May 2, 1808. The day is commemorated as a holiday in Madrid as "the Day of Madrid."

1291 Translator's note: The ancient Romans believed that once a person died, he became a spirit, called a *mane*.

1292 Translator's note: El *Diario de Navarra* was an ultraconservative, anti-Basque newspaper that favored the restoration of the Carlist monarchy.

1293 Translator's note: The Communist International established paramilitary units to assist the Spanish Second Republic and in 1936 headquartered them in Albacete, the largest city in Castille-La Mancha. His intention is to say that as Basques they would be resented in Madrid. Socialists would also resent them.

1294 Translator's note: This reference to "empty stomachs" refers to the notion that socialism is not successful in providing for the needs of people.

separated themselves from the rest of the demonstrators. With total delib-
eration as if obeying some cue, they attacked the headquarters of the Acción
Popular party and threw anything they found there out into the street. They
put together a magnificent bonfire of chairs, tables, typewriters, 200,000
electoral ballots….And all this was done at a whisker's distance from the
Civil Guard, who watched from their quarters next to the place where all
this happened. Everyone else did the same. It was an unexpected spectacle.
They also tried to burn down a few churches; but somebody with guts and
who wasn't quite as wild managed to dissuade them for the moment. This
was the prelude to the meeting in which a little later Comrade Prietos[1295]
beat his breast and spoke in such governmental tones…

On the afternoon of that same day they tried to attack the monastery of
San Pablo located on the outskirts of the city and where a hundred Vincentian Fathers and students were living. This monastery is the school where in
another day Eleuterio, Segundo, and I studied. The Civil Guard, who a few
days before made as if they were guarding the place, heard the first shots
fired by the crowd. The Guard for their part fired into the air. As a result, the
crowds scampered away. This made things worse. In the confusion of their
escape, they trampled some overly curious children. That was enough for
them to cry to high heaven and to the ears of the Governor, and to spread
the rumor that it had been the priests disguised as Civil Guards who had
fired the shots. A general strike was called for the next day, demanding the
immediate expulsion from Cuenca of the Vincentians. In fact, the priests
were given the order to move out of the building by noon of the following
day. Some of them (and these were the most fortunate) with a view of what
could happen on the following morning, set out during the night across the
eleven kilometers[1296] between Cuenca and the next station.[1297] Meanwhile,
the rest spent the night packing up books, furniture, and sacred objects
for the purpose of transporting them in the early hours of the morning in
various trucks to Pamplona.

....

1295 Translator's note: Indalecio Prieto Tuero was a leading figure in the Spanish Socialist
Party (PSOE).

1296 Translator's note: a little more than six miles.

1297 Translator's note: train station.

But the next day and already from the earliest hours the mobs and the gunmen who had come from Madrid for the voting took over control of the city. They overturned the trucks that were carrying the furniture of the priests, they robbed whatever they wanted to, they desecrated the sacred vessels and ornaments, parading around the streets, and they instigated the savage beating of some of the Vincentians. And it was in the morning that day that I got a taste of and firsthand experience of how well they know how to hand out such barbaric caresses. I set out with a friend to see what direction events were taking and miraculously the excursion did not end in the other neighborhood. I sported a nice-looking suit and a beret. I found out later that hereabouts only the secret police wear these kinds of berets. My companion had on a brand-new pair of overalls. Someone told him that with those overalls no one would recognize him when he would go out onto the street. How mistaken he was! My companion was the one who gave me away. The first Communists who came upon us said about me that perhaps I was a policeman. But about him, because of his fine features, his way of walking and his new overalls, they said over and over that he was undoubtedly a Vincentian.

The first suspicions about us began around San Pablo where a big crowd had gathered to attack the monastery and to beat up the Vincentians. At first, I managed to convince some that we were from Madrid and that we had come in the night before for the elections. That day every unfamiliar face was considered a Vincentian priest. At the insistence of some of them, I let loose some gross remarks which had good results. But none of them could get it out of their heads that my companion was a priest. You aren't a priest, but this other fellow, he certainly is—they kept repeating nonstop. And with that the Assault Guard arrived and they demanded that they search us. That was the end for us. Seeing that we were unarmed and with my "prestige" as a policeman having dashed to the ground, they rushed at us. Yet by instinct we made as if we were drawing a gun. The crowd momentarily ran away. It was just enough time for us to take advantage of running into the first house. There we defended ourselves for two hours, with the hope that finally the police would come to our help. We could have escaped by the back door, but they shut it on us. Two doors came crashing down, reduced to splinters. Finally, having used up all the means of defense and seeing that no one was coming to our help, before the last door would be opened, which was already half destroyed, I decided to talk to them. I convinced them that it was the homeowner who was coming out of this thing with losses. I promised to go with them to the Civil Government where our identity could be verified, but on condition that they would not beat us. The leaders agreed. We went out and once we were in the midst of that mob, I thought that we would never live to tell about it. Thankfully some of the more understanding individuals did what they could to assure that we were not beaten more brutally. We arrived at the Civil Government with our lives, which was no small deed; and I without my beret from Bilbao, which ended up lost in the fracas.

The panic that overtook the right-wing elements was enormous. That day none of them went out onto the street. Some young men tried to call together all the men who favored good order to defend the monasteries, convents and churches, and only eight showed up. And this in a city of some 18,000 inhabitants. If that day (or any other) they wanted to burn down all the religious houses, they could do it with complete freedom.

And yet Cuenca is the best province in New Castile. In all the other provinces and in Andalusia and in Valencia the Soviet system has practically speaking been established for some time. The socialist and communist militias give orders in uniforms and carry guns around the highways and are the ones who control the life of the cities. In Murcia, Alicante, etc., there are hardly any churches and the priests have had to leave all the towns. Where you are, you would not be able to tell, and all the more with press censorship, how Spain is from Madrid and down....

Marichu told me in her letter that she had found out (she did not tell me how and I would like to know) that I had preached three days of the novena of Our Lady of Perpetual Help. It's true; they offered me the opportunity to preach the whole novena and, since there was a temporary improvement in things, I almost worked up the enthusiasm to preach it. But fearing that it might involve too much effort and might jeopardize my health, I decided to preach only three days. I wish I had never done it! Already on the second day I could tell my cure was pure illusion. I could hardly preach the third day; and my foolhardiness cost me a good relapse which has left me disabled for a while and from which I am still not completely recovered. It is clear that my lung infection is with me for the long run, but some day, God willing, I will manage to have it cured. For this reason, I have made the decision to not take on any commitment. The other day, the Board of Directors of the Daughters of Mary came with the proposal that I preach the novena of the Immaculate Conception for them next December. And I told them I was very grateful, but I did not want to commit myself to anything and that they should find somebody else. I have gone on two years this way, with more than 200 injections in my body, and without it doing absolutely any good. You can see that God, at least for part of my life, wants me to be this way. I myself am amazed at my good humor, in spite of illness. With the illusion that I had of working in the vineyard of the Lord....

Some days ago, Fr. Gorosterratzu showed me a copy of *El Diario de Navarra* and what could just as easily be the same in Cáceres or Albacete. It isn't my cup of tea, since it has no other interest except to "de-Basque" Navarre. In it I saw a report accompanied by a photograph of Ángel Goñi Navarcorena[1298] and naturally it piqued my curiosity to know who this young man is.

I was deeply affected to hear of the death of the mother of Victorino: I may very easily write on account of it, but anyway give my condolences to the family. My most affectionate greetings to D. Casimiro and everyone else in town who has taken an interest in myself. A hearty embrace, lots of kisses.

Miguel

Send this with my loving regards to Mutilva, Zabalza, Beriain, Lérruz, Olaz, Guerendiain, etc., so that they may hear how I am doing.

1298 Translator's note: Ángel Goñi Navarcorena was from the area of Imárcoain and died as a combatant in the Spanish Civil War in 1937. Since this letter was written in June 30, 1936, and the Spanish Civil War had not yet started (July 17, 1936), Ángel was not yet in combat when the photo was taken.

DOCUMENT 3: JULIÁN POZO RUIZ DE SAMANIEGO

Letter addressed to his siblings,
Cuenca July 1, 1936, 4 pp.

The letter is handwritten on four sides, addressed to a brother of the author named Joaquín and his wife Carmen, residents of Vitoria. Since the major part of the letter deals with family matters, we have transcribed only the part in which Fr. Julán talks about Cuenca. The author shows in the letter the clear knowledge that he has about the present time. He talks about a demonstration for women organized by the central unions UGT and CNT. He verifies the economic situation that the city was going through in view of the lack of pay for the mass of workers. What he most underlines is the situation of hatred for religion that they are living through and their ugly prospects. Certain indications of his awareness of the possibility of martyrdom can de detected in his saying, "here no new bloodshed":

Redemptorist Fathers
San Felipe-Cuenca
July 1, 1936

To my dear brother Joaquín and sister, Carmen-Vitoria.

Dear brother and sister: a thousand thanks for your letter. I see in it that you are enjoying good health, thanks be to God. I also have nothing new to report and I am happily marching along on my little mule,[1299] with the help of God.

[Family matters]

Here no new bloodshed; yesterday there was a demonstration by women who were asking that their husbands would receive their back-pay. At an initiative of the CNT and UGT, the husbands have been working on

....

1299 Translator's note: "My little mule" probably refers to his body. St. Francis of Assisi had called his body "brother donkey."

371

a highway and now they want the manager of the city government to pay them. They also want a raise in the daily wage and shorter work hours; these women show themselves to be aggressive and not well cultured.... Since the men do not get their salaries, business does not give out as credit what it needs, namely, money. Now the seeds of hatred and threats are being sowed, next comes the storm. On the other hand, those who are called "right wing" are people of order and propriety, but they don't practice their religion, which is the basis for mutual respect and justice.

That's all for today. Accept a hug from your brother. A thousand congratulations to Carmen, and I join my own to the millions of well wishes which will be the gift of our family on your saint's day.[1300]

Julián

[1300] Translator's note: In the Spain of 1936, birthdays were not celebrated as such. Rather, one's name's day was celebrated. But since many people were given at baptism the name of the saint whose feast it was when they were born, name's day and birthdays were often the same.

Redemptorists with a Special Relationship to the Martyrs

Agustín Pedrosa Misol

He was the superior of San Felipe in Cuenca when the religious persecution broke out. He had arrived in the city and taken on this charge in June 1936. He was born in Monfarracinos (Zamora) in 1871, enrolled in El Espino (Burgos), and professed his vows in 1888. He was ordained a priest in 1893 in Astorga (León). He was a professor in El Espino from 1893 to 1901 and named director of that same center, work which he did until 1904. From 1904 to 1907 he was master of novices in Nava del Rey; superior of El Espino in 1912; admonitor in Astorga in 1918; superior of Nava del Rey in 1921; provincial consultor in 1930; superior of Cuenca in 1936, where he would continue after the war until the community was suppressed in 1945; sent to Madrid-San Miguel, where he died on April 25, 1953, at the age of eighty-two. Kindness and a spirit of self-sacrifice characterized him throughout his life. When the religious persecution started, he accepted the hospitality of Doña Esperanza Molero. From there he went over to the refuge of the Little Sisters of the Poor, where he stayed until it fell under the control of the CNT. After leaving the asylum, he hid in various private homes, where he did ministry on behalf of some families in whom he had confidence. In 1938, Fr. Jose María Ibarrola made arrangements to bring him to Madrid, where he was at the time of the liberation (see *Necrology of R. Fr. Agustín Pedrosa*, BPE.IV, 46 [June 1953] 157-159).

Antonio Capocci Buoni

In Spain he was called Fr. Bueno. He was born in Italy in 1855 and professed his vows as a Redemptorist in France in 1874. He was ordained a priest on June 13, 1880, and sent to Spain in the following month where he remained until 1897, at which time he was sent to Argentina. There he left the Congregation. During the seventeen years that he lived in Spain he was in El Espino (1880-1883), Granada (1883-1890), Nava del Rey (1890-1892), Pamplona (1892-1894), Madrid (1894-1895), and Astorga (1895-1897). During his time in Pamplona, he preached a mission together with Fr. Prudencio Erviti in San Sebastián, and as a result of that mission Fr. Javier Gorosterratzu joined the Congregation. (see V. PÉREZ DE GAMARRA, *Anales Provinciae Hispanicae* C.SS.R. I, Madrid 1925, 133).

Antonio Girón González

He was director of the second novitiate for Miguel Goñi. He had been born in Campo (León) in 1871. After having studied theology for some years as a seminarian, he entered the Congregation of the Most Holy Redeemer and professed his vows in 1886. He was ordained a priest in 1894. During his years of ministry, he was a professor in the juvenate in El Espino and in the studentate, master of second novitiate for many years; local superior and provincial consultor. To help the young Fathers in the stage of second novitiate he published a book of sermons and missionary practice (A.GIRÓN GONZÁLEZ, *Sermones de Misión*[1301] [Madrid, 1932]). He died as a martyr in Madrid on August 31, 1936 (*Memorial of the Madrid Province of CSsR*, Madrid 2008, 126).

Benjamín López de Murga Eguíluz

He was one of the members of the community of Cuenca when the religious persecution began in 1936. He was called Rufino by his baptismal name. He was born in Bellogín (Álava) on November 16, 1909. His parents were

----

1301 Translator's note: "mission sermons"

Pedro López de Murga and Rafaela Eguíluz. He entered the Congregation of the Most Holy Redeemer in September 1922 as a juvenist and in 1924 he decided to direct his life toward being a coadjutor brother. For this purpose, he made the postulancy in order to enter the novitiate in August 1925. He professed his vows on August 14, 1926, with the name Br. Benjamin. He dedicated himself fundamentally to being porter and sacristan. His appointments in the Congregation were to: La Coruña (1926), Astorga (1928), La Coruña and Pamplona (1929), Nava del Rey (1930), El Espino (1932), Cuenca (1934), La Coruña (1940), Saragossa (1945), Vigo (1949), Madrid-Editorial PS (1953), Salamanca (1956), Portugal (1957), Saragossa (1958), Seville (1962), Madrid-Editorial PS (1964), and Pamplona (1976), where he died on March 3, 1992, at age eighty-three. In great measure the development of the process of martyrdom of the Redemptorists killed in Cuenca is owed to him since he lived in the city until he managed to cross the line of the Nationalists in 1938 (see J. J. Itoiz Leoz, *H. Benjamín López de Murga Eguíluz*: BPE. 135 [1992] 391-409; *Chronicle of Cuenca from the year 1936. Activities of Brother Benjamín: Annals XI*, 41; *NER* n° 359, April 1992, 5).

Clemente López Aguilló

Br. Clemente belonged to the Cuenca community in 1936. He had been born in San Martín de Galbocín (Burgos) in 1858; he enrolled in El Espino as a postulant in 1882, where he professed his vows as a Redemptorist in 1886. He was assigned to the foundation in Cuenca in 1895, where he remained for the rest of his life. He learned the job of cook in the community, but he contracted a skin disease that continued throughout his life. Because of this he had to give up the kitchen to become receptionist, to dedicate himself to maintenance work, or to take care of other needs. Among those who lived with him, he stood out because of his affability and patience. When the persecution started up, he entered the home run by the Little Sisters of the Poor as an elderly patient. He died there of severe bronchitis on December 19, 1937 (see APRM. Martyrs 0400200, 4 ff; *Chronicle of Cuenca for the year 1936. Activities of Brother Clemente: Annals XI*, 39; APRM. Martyrs 0400107, 10; V.PÉREZ DE GAMARRA, *Anales Provinciae Hispanicae C.SS.R.* I [Madrid, 1925] 151). *Acta de defunción de Clemente López Aguilló*: REG. CIVIL DE CUENCA, Sec. 3ª, T. 44, F. 56.

Eloy Gómez Jorge

He was one of the priests in the Redemptorist community of Cuenca in 1936. He was born in Moreruela de Tábara (Zamora) in 1910, son of Santiago and Lucila; he entered el Espino in 1923; he professed his vows as a Redemptorist in 1929 and was ordained a priest in Astorga on December 22, 1934. In August 1935, he made the second novitiate in Nava del Rey (Valladolid) which concluded at the end of January 1936, at which time he was assigned to Cuenca. When the religious persecution broke out he took asylum in the house of D. Acislo. From there he went to the Little Sisters of the Poor. He left there and was arrested by the SIM, who recognized his instability and fear, and they offered him the opportunity to collaborate with them. At the end of the civil strife he was arrested and submitted to an emergency summary judgment[1302] (see *Summary Judgment against Eloy G. Jorge*: AGET. CAJA 5927 / SUM.333). Condemned to thirty years of imprisonment (Sentence 14-9-1939: *Ib.*, 34) the bishop of Cuenca asked for a review of his condemnation and his sentence was commuted to twelve years and one day of lesser imprisonment (Sentence 27-12-1939: *Ib.*, 36). He did his time in prisons in Barcelona, Cuenca, Salamanca, and Carmona (Seville). He was released from prison in Seville on March 12, 1943. He was dispensed from his vows on April 16, 1940. For that reason, when he was free, he incardinated into the diocese of Zamora, where he lived the rest of his life as a priest.

Félix Ruiz de Samaniego Viana

He was uncle to Julián Pozo Ruiz de Samaniego. He was born in Payueta (Álava) in 1888; he enrolled in El Espino and professed vows with the Redemptorists in 1906; he was ordained a priest in 1911. In 1920, he was sent to Mexico; because of the persecution by Plutarco Calles, he left Mexico in 1927 and passed through the Central American republics as one of the founders of the Redemptorists in those countries. He died August 31, 1937, at age forty-nine in San Salvador (El Salvador). During his time in El Espino his sister visited him; it is through those contacts that he influenced the choice for religious life by Fr. Julián Pozo. Félix accompanied his nephew Julián when the nephew entered El Espino (*Memorial of the CSsR Province of Madrid*, Madrid 2008[6], 126).

1302 Translator's note: A "summary judgment" is a judgment rendered without a jury.

Inocencio Tirapu Leoz

He was superior in Cuenca until 1936. He had been born in Olcoz (Navarre), professed his vows as a Redemptorist in 1900 and was ordained a priest in 1905. He was sent to Cuenca as superior starting in 1921 until 1927, at which time he went to Nava del Rey (Valladolid). He returned to Cuenca in 1930 and was in the community of San Felipe until a few days before the religious persecution started up. During his stay in Cuecna, Fr. Leoz was the spiritual director for Paulina Muñoz, whom Br. Victoriano directed. When he came back to Cuenca in 1930, it seems he was only her confessor and that he gave permission to Br. Victoriano to do the spiritual accompaniment for Paulina. In 1937, he was sent as novice master for the coadjutor Brothers in El Espino. He died there on December 8, 1948. (*Necrology of R. Fr. Inocencio T. Leoz*: BPE III, 33 [April 1949] 94-95).

Isidro Fernández Posado

He belonged to the Cuenca community in 1936. He was born in San Adrián del Valle (León) in 1890. He entered El Espino and made his profession of vows in 1911. He was ordained to the priesthood in Astorga in 1917. Professor in El Espino from 1918 to 1919. Missionary in Nava del Rey (1918-1932), Cuenca (1932-1941), Granada (1941-1944), La Coruña (1944-1953), and Vigo (1953-1963). He died in Vigo on March 17, 1963, at age seventy-three. When the religious persecution began, he first hid in the house of D. Acisclo Domínguez. He didn't feel secure there and wanted to move to the seminary, but he smelled danger in that and took refuge instead with the Little Sisters of the Poor. When he had to leave his asylum, he played a trick on the militias. When they saw him on the street, they took him for a beggar and carried him off to their barracks. He slipped away from the barracks and, following along twists and turns through the streets, he ended up at the home of the Zanón family. He stayed there some months. Since he did not feel safe in the city, he decided to go off to the small towns, and arrived in Huete. After stays in various towns, he once again returned to the provincial capital.[1303] He wanted to go along with an expedition that was planning to join up with the Nationalist forces. They were surprised by the militias and were taken to the headquarters of the secret police on Calle

....

1303 Translator's note: Cuenca.

Sorni in Valencia. From there they were sent to the Modelo prison[1304] in the capital on the Turia.[1305] They again returned him to Cuenca, to the prison in the convent of the Discalced Carmelite Sisters. While he was there, the civil war came to an end (cf. *Necrology of R. Fr. Isidro Fernández Posado*: BPE. IX, 77 [June 1963] 131-132).

José María Machiñena Aríztegui

He was born in Urroz de Santesteban (Navarre) and enrolled in the juvenate in El Espino in 1900. He professed his vows in 1905 and was ordained to the priesthood in 1910. In 1911, he was assigned to Pamplona as a mission preacher in both Castilian and Basque, sharing many missions with his fellow countryman José Javier Gorosterratzu. In 1924, he was assigned to Granada as a mission preacher, consultor, and admonitor. Besides being of the same ethnic group and companions, he was related to Fr. Gorosterratzu, since a brother of José María was married to a sister of José Javier, resulting in the family called Machiñena-Gorosterratzu. In 1928, he was named provincial superior until 1936, at which time the religious persecution overtook him while he was rector of Perpetual Help in Madrid, and suffered imprisonment. In died in Madrid on November 20, 1962 (see *Anales VIII*, 422; *Memorial de la Provincia de Madrid CSSR*, Madrid 2008[6], 170).

Marcos Álvarez García

Member of the community in Cuenca in 1936. He was born in San Justo de Cubillas (León) in 1863. For a while he lived in Vigo (Pontevedra), working as a day laborer, where he was married to a certain "Petra." His wife died and they had had no offspring. He entered Astorga as a postulant in 1895; he professed his vows in Nava del Rey in 1902. He was cook in El Espino, Pamplona, Nava del Rey, and Cuenca. He was a very obliging and self-sacrficing man. For a long time, he had a stomach ailment. When the religious persecution broke out, he and Br. Clement hid out in the convalescent center of the Little Sisters of the Poor. On September 21, he left his hiding place and

....

1304 Translator's note: The "Modelo" prisons, product of the architect Joaquín María Belda, were considered around 1900 model prisons for their functionalism and architecture. Several were built, with the one in Valencia as one of the first.

1305 Translator's note: Valencia is the capital of the province of the same name. It is situated on the Turia River.

went off to the house of Doña Francisca Echevarría and there he died suddenly on November 23, 1937, as a consequence of pnueumonia (see APRM. Mártires 0400300, 7 ff; *Chronicle of Cuenca for the year 1936. Activities of Brother Clement: Anales* XI, 39; APRM. Mártires 0400115, 14; APRM. Mártires 0400105, 4, 20; APRM. Mártires 0400107, 10; *Acta de defunción de Marcos Álvarez García*: REG. CIVIL DE CUENCA, Sec. 3ª, T. 44, F. 37).

Pablo Lorthioit

Born in France in 1850. Professed his vows as a Redemptorist on October 9, 1870, and ordained to the priesthood on July 18, 1875. In 1885, he left France for Spain, where he remained until 1908, at which time he was sent to Mexico. In 1912, he returned to France, where he died on April 18, 1914. During the time that he was in Spain he lived at Nava del Rey (1885-1887), Granada (1887-1888), Astorga (1888-1890), and again in Nava del Rey (1890-1891). He was the founder and superior in Pamplona (1891-1895), Astorga (1895-1901), Granada (1901-1904), Madrid-San Miguel (1904-1907), and Pamplona (1907-1908). While he was superior in Pamplona, he welcomed José Javier Gorosterratzu and directed him toward being a brother Redemptorist (see V.PÉREZ DE GAMARRA, *Anales Provinciae Hispanicae C.SS.R.* I [Madrid, 1925] 140).

Prudencio Erviti Gorosterratzu

Born in Urroz de Santesteban (Navarre) on April 26, 1856. Ordained to the priesthood on April 2, 1881, he entered the Congregation of the Most Holy Redeemer, where he professed vows on July 17, 1893. He was the second citizen of Navarre to enter the Congregation, where he was a mission preacher in both Castilian and Euskera.[1306] After a short time in Astorga, he was sent in August 1893, to Pamplona; in 1895, he went to Madrid and El Espino; in 1896 he returned to Pamplona, where he died on May 4, 1913. He was a relative of José Javier Gorosterratzu. He preached a mission in Santesteban with Fr. Bueno. During this mission the father of J. J. Gorosterratzu introduced his son to the missionaries so that they would take him with them in order that he could become a Redemptorist (V. PÉREZ DE GAMARRA, *Anales Provinciae Hispanicae C.SS.R.* II [Madrid, 1927] 239).

....

1306 Translator's note: Euskera is another name for Basque.

Companions in Martyrdom to the Redemptorists of Cuenca

1. MARTYRED ON AUGUST 9, 1936, ON THE HIGHWAY TO TRAGACETE

Alfonso López-Guerrero Portocarrero

Priest; he had been born in Madrid in 1882. He was a Knight of Montesa,[1307] Infanzón de Villenas[1308] and Royal Chaplain. He had first been a Canon of the Cathedral of Ciudad Real and later of the Cathedral of Cuenca. With the coming of the Second Republic he volunteered to be a pastor and was appointed to be pastor-financial administrator of Barajas de Melo (Cuenca), where he remained for some time. The religious persecution caught up with him in the city of Cuenca. He was martyred on August 9, 1936, in Cuenca, at the nine-kilometer marker along the highway from Cuenca to Tragacete together with Francisco Torrijos Ruiz, a few meters forward from where Fr. Ju-

---

1307 Translator's note: The Knights of Santa María de Montesa y San Jorge de Alfama were a religious and military order founded by King James II of Aragon in the XIV century. Today it is an honorary title of nobility.

1308 Translator's note: "Infanzón" is a title of lower nobility, especially in Aragón.

lián Pozo and D. Crisóstomo Escribano died. We have not found the place where he was held. (see S. CIRAC ESTOPAÑÁN, *Martyrology of Cuenca. Diocesan Chronicle of the Red Era [Barcelona, 1947]* 197; *Report Number 2. City Hall of Cuenca. Listing of cadavers taken in in this municipal station, of persons not recognized as residents, who suffered violent death during the red regime. June 7, 1939*: CAUSA Leg. 1062, Exp. 10, 140).

Francisco Torrijos Ruiz

He was born in Cardenete (Cuenca) in 1883; he was married, the father of a family and was known as a man of strong Catholic convictions. On June 23, 1936, some militiamen came into his home in Cardenete and arrested and carried off him and his children. After they took them away, the militia burned down his home. Francisco and his children were transferred to Cuenca along with other Catholics and imprisoned in jail, where Francisco was tortured. He was martyred on August 9, 1936, in Cuenca, at kilometer 9 on the highway from Cuenca to Tragacete, some meters on from where Fr. Julián Pozo and D. Crisóstomo Escribano were killed. We have not found the place where he was detained. (see S. CIRAC ESTOPAÑÁN, 108; *Report Number 2. City Hall of Cuenca. Listing of cadavers taken in in this municipal station, d. c.,* 140).

Juan Crisóstomo Escribano García

He died sharing martyrdom with Julián Pozo, according to all the sources. He was born in El Provencio (Cuenca). When his career as a teacher came to an end, he entered the seminary of Cuenca and after that went on to the Spanish College in Rome,[1309] where he was ordained a priest on July 17, 1904. He took courses at the Gregorian University[1310] in the Eternal City, where in 1906 he received his doctorate in canon law. In his pastoral ministry he especially emphasized catechesis, publication, and popular

----

1309 Translator's note: The Pontifical College of St. Joseph was opened in 1892 in Rome by Blessed Manuel Domingo y Sol to serve the Church in Spain by offering higher studies to Spanish priests.

1310 Translator's note: The Pontifical Gregorian University, also known as the "Gregoriana," is part of the Roman College founded by St. Ignatius Loyola in Rome in 1556. It was relocated to grandiose new buildings in 1584 by Pope Gregory XIII, after whom it is named. Since the Italian revolution in 1870, it has offered only studies in philosophy and thelogy.

devotions. He was professor of sacred Scripture in the seminary, a canoni-cal prebendary,[1311] secretary, and administrator of the Diocesan Curia, and for some time before that he was episcopal vicar. He was very close to and friend of the Redemptorist community of San Felipe. The religious perse-cution came upon him unexpectedly in Cuenca. He had declined to take some days off with his family so that he could get some project ready for the diocesan prelate. On July 24 he left his home at Calle Obispo Valero, Number 6, and hid at the nursing home of the Little Sisters of the Poor, where he was some days. From there he sought shelter at the diocesan sem-inary, a building right next to that of the Little Sisters. It was believed to be safer because of the presence of the Civil Guard. He was taken out of the seminary and killed at the marker for kilometer eight on the highway from Cuenca to Tragacete as he cried out, "Viva Cristo Rey" (see S. CIRAC ESTOPAÑÁN, 188-189; APRM. Mártires 0405001, 2; APRM. Mártires 0405004, 19; CAUSA, Leg. 1062, Exp. 7, 131. 138-139).

2. MARTYRED ON AUGUST 10, 1936, ON THE ROAD TO THE CEMETERY

Fernando Pérez del Cerro

He was born in Valdeolivas (Cuenca) in 1889 and was ordained a priest in 1913. He carried out his pastoral ministry in El Picazo del Júcar, Huete, San Nicolás el Real and beginning in 1934 in Barajas de Melo, where he was act-ing pastor. Before the religious persecution began, he was threatened by the People's Committee and in June 1936, he went to Cuenca to have an inter-view with the bishop, staying at the Seminary of San Julián. There the on-set of the Civil War and persecution took him by surprise. He was dragged out in the early morning of August 10 along with various priests and the Redemptorists Javier Gorosterratzu and Victoriano Calvo. His body was picked up, as the others were, on the road to the cemetery (see S. CIRAC ESTOPAÑÁN, 61; *Report Number 2. City hall of Cuenca. Listing of cadavers taken in in this municipal station, d. c.,* 140).

....

1311 Translator's note: A *prebendary* is a senior Church cleric who is the theological consul-tant for a cathedral chapter; he must have a licentiate or doctorate in theology.

Juan Félix Bellón Parrilla

Brother of Lucio Bellón. Born in Villamanrique (Ciudad Real) in 1895 and was ordained a priest in 1918; he took an exam for and was awarded the benefice of the Cathedral of Cuenca.[1312] He worked in the ecclesiastical curia. He was arrested on the night of August 9 along with his brother and the rest of the priests. That is a fact that makes us believe he was a prisoner also in the seminary. He was killed with his brother near the cemetery, next to the shortcut that leads off from the road from Cuenca to the cemetery and leads to Arcos de la Cantera. Based on the fact that his body was found near Javier Gorosterratzu and Victoriano Calvo and also based on what Cirac Estopañán narrates, he was taken out and martyred in the same group as they (see S. CIRAC ESTOPAÑÁN, 181-182).

Lucio Bellón Parrilla

Brother of Juan Félix Bellón. Born in Villamanrique (Ciudad Real) en 1884, he was ordained a priest in 1908. He was canonical schoolmaster of the cathedral and professor of liturgy of the seminary of San Julián. At the time of the persecution, he was vicar general of the diocese and the provisor of the Curia. Arrested with his brother and the other priests, we presume he had taken refuge in the seminary and then was held prisoner there. He died together with his brother near the shortcut that goes out from the road from Cuenca to the municipal cemetery and leads to Arcos de la Cantera. We believe that he, just as his brother, shared martyrdom with Javier Gorosterratzu and Victoriano Calvo (cf. S. CIRAC ESTOPAÑÁN, 182).

Manuel Laplana Torres

He was born in 1895 in Puy de Cinca, in the mountanous region of Aragon called Huesca. He was the cousin of Bishop D. Cruz Laplana. He had been professor of the seminary in Barbastro and D. Cruz brought him to Cuenca to be his administrator and the administrator of the goods of the episcopal palace. He also gave him a benefice of the cathedral. At the time of the persecution he went with the bishop to the seminary of San Julián on July 28,

....

1312 Translator's note: Based on the model of the ancient Roman Empire, the Church in the West adopted in the Middle Ages a system of giving benefices, or rewards, for services, which included tenure in a position. This system was still in place in the days of the early twentieth century but was eliminated by the Second Vatican Council.

1936. On August 8 in the morning, he was distressed by what happened to his cousin[1313] and that he had not accompanied him. On August 9, he received a visit from a militiaman from Barbastro who asserted that he knew him. Before departing, he took leave of the Mercederian Sisters. Since he presumed that he would be martyred, he assured them that he had prayed the Way of the Cross and now was ready. His body was found on the road to the cemetery on August 10, 1936, together with the bodies of Victoriano Pérez, Javier Gorosterratzu, and Victoriano Calvo. S. Cirac Estopañán asserts that he was martyred with the Bellón Parrilla brothers (see *Report Number 1. City Hall of Cuenca. Listing of residents in this municipal station, who suffered violent death or disappeared and who are believed to have been assassinated during the red regime. Cuenca, June 7, 1939*: CAUSA Leg. 1062, Exp. 10, 136; S. CIRAC ESTOPAÑÁN, 195; S. CIRAC, *Life of D. Cruz Laplana, Bishop of Cuenca* (Barcelona, 1943) 71-72, 126).

Victoriano Pérez Muñoz

Born in 1873, he was canonical archpriest of the Cathedral of Cuenca and was sick for a fair amount of time. He was staying in the seminary and from there was violently taken out with the rest of the priests on August 10, 1936. His body was found on the road to the cemetery together with that of Javier Gorrosterratzu, Victoriano Calvo, and Manuel Laplana (see *Report Number 1. City Hall of Cuenca. Listing of residents in this municipal station, who suffered violent death or disappeared and who are believed to have been assassinated during the red regime. Cuenca, June 7, 1939*: CAUSA Leg. 1062, Exp. 10, 136; S. CIRAC ESTOPAÑÁN, 209).

3. OTHER MARTYRED PRIESTS WITH CONNECTIONS TO THE SIX BEATIFIED.

Antonio Cortés Moral

He was pastor of Horche (Guadalajara) and accompanied Br. Victoriano in the process of vocational discernment. He was born in Horche on Decem-

---

1313 Translator's note: The bishop had been taken out early on the morning of July 8 and had been killed.

ber 5, 1875. He was ordained to the priesthood on November 23, 1899, and celebrated his first Mass on January 1, 1900, in the parish church of Horche. He worked as a priest in Dos Barrios (Toledo), Malagulla (Guadalajara), and Torija (Guadalajara), before settling into Horche, his own hometown, where he was parish priest for twenty-six years, from 1910 until 1936. It was there that the religious persecution caught up with him. From July 22, 1936, he stayed hidden in the home of his relatives; he was arrested on the night of of September 29-30, 1936, and was taken out of the home where he had been hiding. He was transferred to Madrid and underwent various interrogations. He was martyred on October 4, 1936. Although he was not with him at the time of his martyrdom, we offer this reference because of the importance this man had in the life of Br. Victoriano.

Enrique María Gómez Jiménez

He was the priest who welcomed into his home Frs. Ciriaco Olarte and Miguel Goñi. He was born in Cuenca on June 15, 1865, and was baptized on June 17 in the parish of Santo Domingo de Silos. He entered the seminary of San Julián de Cuenca, where he did his priesthood studies—in an accelerated course—in the years 1883 to 1888. He was ordained a priest on May 26, 1888. The progression of his life after that was that he became coadjutor of Villaescusa de Palositos (Cuenca) and acting parish priest in Valdeganga (Cuenca). In 1890, he became chaplain in the convent of the Trinitarian Sisters in San Clemente (Cuenca). Then as priest administrator of Villar de Cantos (Cuenca), he was given a benefice in the collegiate church of Belmonte (Cuenca). In 1900, he was put in charge of the University (Cuenca) and in 1901 was given a benefice in the Cathedral of Cuenca. In 1903, he took the exam for the benefice of the Cathedral of Almería, where he became subchanter.[1314] In November 1910, he resigned his ecclesiastical office to become a missionary in Argentina. In the New World he worked in the dioceses of La Plata and in Chivilcoy.[1315] He came back temporarily to Al-

....

1314 Translator's note: another of many ecclesiastical titles and offices that made up the Church in Spain from the Middle Ages; the subchanter was the deputy for the preceptor of a cathedral, which means he was assistant to the dean of the cathedral school.

1315 Translator's note: La Plata is the capital of the Buenos Aires province of Argentina. Chivilcoy is also in Buenos Aires province, with a population of 60,000 or so.

mería[1316] in 1917 and returned to Argentina in 1918. He returned to Spain for good in 1923. He was assigned to the parish of San Pedro in Almería and qualified as subchanter again in 1924. Besides having this responsibility in the cathedral school, he was confessor at the seminary[1317] and at the nursing home of the Little Sisters of the Poor.[1318] When it became impossible for him to continue carrying out his duties at the cathedral of Almería, he returned to his native city,[1319] where he lived on Calle de los Pilares, next to the cathedral plaza. He was ensnared in the religious persecution. He died a martyr on August 13, 1936, at kilometer marker five on the highway from Cuenca to Alcázar (see S. CIRAC ESTOPAÑÁN, 232; *Beatificationis seu Declarationis Martyrii Servorum Dei Iosephi Álvarez-Benavides y de la Torre et CXVI sociorum in odium fidei, uti fertur, interfectorum (+1936-1938). Positio super martyrio et fama martyrii*, Roma 2003, I, 367-368; II, 1088-1096).[1320]

1316 Translator's note: Almería, Spain, is in the southern province of Andalusia.

1317 Translator's note: these were the cathedral and seminary in Almería, not in Cuenca.

1318 Translator's note: also in Almería, not in Cuenca.

1319 Translator's note: Cuenca.

1320 Translator's note: translation from the Latin for this title of the work by Cirac Estopañán— *On the declaration of Beatification and Martyrdom of the Servants of God Joseph Álvarez-Benavides y de la Torre and 116 of his companions killed in the odor of faith, as has been reported (+1936-1938). Position paper about their martyrdom and reputation as martyrs.*

APPENDIX FOUR

Documents Consulted from the Archives

I. REDEMPTORIST ARCHIVES

Historical Archives of the Redemptorist Generalate. ROME (AHGR)

30150002, 0006h *Informe enviado a Roma el año 1897.*

30150002, 0034 J. MACHIÑENA, *Informe enviado al Gobierno General de la Visita Canónica realizada en 1934.*

30150001, 1901 C. OTERO, C.SS.R., PROVINCIAL DE ESPAÑA, *Carta dirigida al Rvdmo. Fr. General Patricio Murray; El Espino (Burgos) 1 de septiembre de 1936.*

30150001, 1918 C. OTERO, C.SS.R., PROVINCIAL DE ESPAÑA, *Carta dirigida al Rvdmo. Fr. Murray, Superior General de los Redentoristas; Astorga (León) 6 de marzo de 1937.*

30150001, 1919 C. OTERO, C.SS.R., PROVINCIAL DE ESPAÑA, *Carta dirigida al Rvdmo. Fr. Murray, Superior General de los Redentoristas; Astorga (León) 12 de marzo de 1937.*

30150001, 1921 C. OTERO, C.SS.R., PROVINCIAL DE ESPAÑA, *Carta dirigida al Rvdmo. Fr. Murray, Superior General de los Redentoristas; Astorga (León) 13 de abril de 1937.*

30150001, 1922 C. OTERO, C.SS.R., PROVINCIAL DE ESPAÑA, *Carta dirigida al Rvdmo. Fr. Murray, Superior General de los Redentoristas; Astorga, 30 de abril de 1937.*

30150001, 1939 C. OTERO, C.SS.R., PROVINCIAL DE ESPAÑA, *Carta dirigida al Rvdmo. Fr. Murray, Superior General de los Redentoristas; El Espino, 13-12-1937.*

30150001, 1956 C. OTERO, C.SS.R., PROVINCIAL DE ESPAÑA, *Carta dirigida al Rvdmo. Fr. Murray, Superior General de los Redentoristas; Porto, 10-8-1938.*

30150009, 0601.5 R. TELLERÍA, C.SS.R., *Carta dirigida al Rvdmo.Fr. Murray, Superior General de los Redentoristas; Bruselas, 5 de diciembre de 1937.*

30150010, 011-1 A. PEDROSA, *Carta dirigida al Rvdmo. Fr. Murray, Superior General de los Redentoristas sobre el futuro de la comunidad de Cuenca, 6 de noviembre de 1941.*

30150009, 0290 F. COLLOUD, *Informe sobre el R. H. J. Javier Gorosterratzu para solicitar su profesión.*

30150010, A/4 *Óbolo de los Estudiantes de Astorga al Reverendísimo Padre con motivo de sus bodas de oro de profesión.*

30150001, 1282 O. ALLET, *Carta dirigida al Fr. General; Madrid, 7-9-1906.*

30150001, 1345 O. ALLET, *Carta al Superior General; 31 de Agosto de 1908.*

30150001, 1377 O. ALLET, *Carta al Fr. Van Rossum; 15 de Agosto de 1910.*

30150001, 1436 M. GIL, *Carta al Consultor General; 29 de Agosto de 1913.*

30150009, 170-21 E. CHAUBEL, *Carta al Superior General Fr. Murray; Pamplona 4-octubre-1920.*

30150002, 0033 Fr. SORDET, *Visita canónica della Provincia Spagnuola. 1934.*

30150009, 0451 N. MUTILOA, *Informe sobre el R. H. Ciriaco Olarte para solicitar su profesión.*

30150007, 0017-23 V. MIGUEL, *Informe sobre la vida del Estudiantado de Astorga; Astorga (León) 1912.*

30150001, 1546 N. MUTILOA, *Carta al Gobierno General. Octubre 1920.*

30150009, 0503 R. CAVERO, *Informe sobre el R. H. Julián Pozo para solicitar su profesión.*

30150009, 0287 R. CAVERO, *Informe sobre el R. H. Miguel Goñi para solicitar su profesión.*

30150007, 0027 C. OTERO, *Informe para solicitar la profesión perpetua del Estudiante Miguel Goñi; Astorga, 29-8-1923.*

30150001, 1626 Fr. MURRAY, *Admisión de Miguel Goñi a la profesión perpetua. Toma, 30-8-1923.*

ARCHIVE OF THE REDEMPTORIST PROVINCE OF MADRID (APRM)

File on the Martyrs (APRM. Mártires)

0400101 B. LÓPEZ DE MURGA, *Tarjeta dirigida a Lucas Pérez; La Coruña 23-8-1944; 1 p.*

0400102 T. VELASCO, *Carta dirigida a Lucas Pérez; Pancorbo (Burgos) 23-8-1944; 2 pp.*

0400103 B. LÓPEZ DE MURGA, *Carta dirigida a Lucas Pérez; La Coruña 4-8-1944; 2 pp.*

0400104 B. LÓPEZ DE MURGA, *Carta dirigida a Lucas Pérez; La Coruña 23-7-1944; 4 pp.*

0400105.1 B. LÓPEZ DE MURGA, *La casa de Cuenca;* 20 pp. 0400105.2 B. LÓPEZ DE MURGA, *Los sujetos de Cuenca; La Coruña 30-6-1944;* 16 pp.

0400105.3 B. LÓPEZ DE MURGA, *Peripecias propias;* 11 pp.

0400105.4 B. LÓPEZ DE MURGA, *Memorias de la Guerra Civil; El Espino (Burgos) 25-7-1944;* 39 pp.

0400106 J. M. IBARROLA, *Artículo sobre los PFr. Olarte y Goñi. Copia Revista Perpetuo Socorro año 1940, p. 307;* 1 p.

0400107 L. FDEZ. DE RETANA, *Notas sobre los Mártires de Cuenca;* 12 pp.

0400108 I. POSADO, *Carta a Lucas Pérez; Granada 26-6-1944;* 2 pp.

0400109 L. PÉREZ, *Anotaciones;* 1 p.

0400110 A. ARABADEJO, *Carta a Lucas Pérez; Tarancón (Cuenca) 3-8-1944;* 2 pp.

0400111 R. COLMENARES, *Carta dirigida a Remedios Acedo; Madrid 30-4-1953;* 1 p.

0400112 R. COLMENARES, *Cartas a las HH. Belinchón; Madrid 30-4-1953;* 1 p.

0400113 R. COLMENARES, *Apuntes sobre las impresiones de Cuenca;* 1 p.

0400114 R. COLMENARES, *Informe sobre mártires de Cuenca;* 5 pp.

0400115 J. ITURGÁIZ, *Informe sobre los mártires de Cuenca;* 15 pp.

0400116 D. DE FELIPE, *Apuntes del martirologio conquense;* 5 pp.

0400117 D. DE FELIPE, *Apuntes manuscritos sobre los PFr. Goñi y Olarte;* 1 p.

0400118 AA.VV., *Anotaciones sobre la persecución en Cuenca;* 9 ff.

0400119 M. GIL, *Solicitud de datos sobre milicianos al Tribunal militar; Madrid 18-9-1944;* 1 p.

0400120 AUTOR DESCONOCIDO, *Anotaciones sobre milicianos*; 1 p.

0400121 L. PÉREZ, *Plan de trabajo Mártires de Cuenca*; 3 pp.

0400122.1 J. ITURGÁIZ, *Notas manuscritas sobre San Felipe*; 8 pp.

0400122.2 J. ITURGÁIZ, *Carta al Fr. Lucas Pérez; Madrid 1-10-1956*; 2 pp.

400123 D. DE FELIPE, *Proyecto de trabajo de los mártires de Cuenca*; 4 pp.

0400124 D. RUIZ, *Boletines "De camino"—Años 1999-2003*; 6 boletines / 68 pp.

0400200 L. PÉREZ, *Notas sobre el H. Clemente López*; 4 pp.

0400300 L. PÉREZ, *Notas sobre el H. Marcos Álvarez*; 8 pp.

0400400 *Recorte de periódico sobre la muerte del Obispo de Cuenca*; 1 p.

0401001 AA.VV., *Fichas sobre el Fr. Javier Gorosterratzu*; 15 ff.

0401002 L. PÉREZ, *Anotaciones sobre el Fr. Gorosterratzu*; 2 pp.

0401004 ANÓNIMO, *Nota necrológica del Fr. Gorosterratzu*; 1 p.

0401005 J. ITURGÁIZ, *Notas sobre el Fr. J. Gorosterratzu*; 5 pp.

0401006 RELIGIOSA, *Carta al Fr. Lucas Pérez sobre Gorosterratzu*; 4 pp.

0402001 L. PÉREZ, *Anotaciones sobre el H. Victoriano*; 2 pp.

0402002 ANÓNIMO, *Perfil biográfico H. Victoriano*; 9 pp.

0402003 AA.VV., *Fichas sobre el H. Victoriano*; 6 ff.

0403001 L. PÉREZ, *Anotaciones sobre el Fr. Olarte*; 3 pp.

0403003 AA.VV., *Fichas con anotaciones sobre el Fr. Olarte*; 6 ff.

0404002 ANÓNIMO, *Necrología del Fr. Goñi*; 1 p.

0404003 AA.VV., *Fichas con anotaciones sobre el Fr. Goñi*; 20 ff.

0404004 J. ITURGÁIZ, *Anotaciones sobre el martirio del Fr. Goñi*; 2 pp.

0405001 L. PÉREZ, *Anotaciones sobre el Fr. Pozo*; 2 pp.

0405003 ANÓNIMO, *Perfil biográfico del Fr. Pozo*; 2 pp.

0405004 AA.VV., *Fichas sobre el Fr. Pozo*; 20 ff.

0406001 M. GARCÍA, *Carta al Fr. Lucas sobre Romero; Cuenca 30-8-1944*; 2 pp.

0406002 L. PÉREZ, *Anotaciones sobre el Fr. Romero*; 2 pp.

0406004 ANÓNIMO, *Perfil biográfico del Fr. Romero*; 2 pp.

0406005 J. ITURGÁIZ, *Anotaciones sobre el Fr. Romero; 4-1-1957*; 2 pp.

0406006 D. DE FELIPE, *Anotaciones sobre el Fr. Romero*; 1 p.

0406007 AA.VV. *Fichas sobre el Fr. Romero*; 19 ff.

Copy of the Actas from the Process of Canonization of J. Javier Gorosterratzu

—*Causa Beatificationis et Canonizationis seu Declarationis Martyrii Servorum Dei Josephi—Xaverii Gorosterrazu Jaunarena et Sociorum eius. Acta Processus Ordinarii Informativi super "Fama Martyrii".* Conchae 1962-1965; 3 vols / 896 pp. (*C. Beatificationis—Declaraciones*).

—*Causa Beatificationis et Canonizationis seu Declarationis Martyrii Servorum Dei Josephi—Xaverii Gorosterrazu Jaunarena et Sociorum eius. Acta Processus Ordinarii Diligentiarum seu super "De perquisitione scriptorum".* Conchae 1962-1965; 49 pp. y copia de los escritos (*C. Beatificationis—Escritos*).

—*Causa Beatificationis et Canonizationis seu Declarationis Martyrii Servorum Dei Josephi—Xaverii Gorosterrazu Jaunarena et Sociorum eius. Acta Processus Ordinarii Informativi super "Non cultu" muncupati.* Conchae 1962-1965; 142 pp.

—*Causa Beatificationis et Canonizationis seu Declarationis Martyrii Servorum Dei Josephi—Xaverii Gorosterrazu Jaunarena et Sociorum eius. Informe de la Comisión Histórica; Cuenca, 5-11-1998;* 14 pp. (*Causa Beatificationis, Informe Comisión Histórica*).

—*Xaverii Gorosterrazu Jaunarena et Sociorum eius. Informe de la Comisión Teológica; Cuenca, 5-11-1998;* 12 pp. (*Causa Beatificationis, Informes Comisión Teológica*).

—*Actas de la recognición y traslado de restos de J. Javier Gorosterratzu y cinco compañeros mártires (Copia)* (*Actas de la recognición y traslado*).

Provincial-General Correspondence

VIII, 6/1937 Fr. MURRAY, *Carta dirigida al Fr. Carlos Otero; Roma 10-12-1937;* 1 p.

Provincial Secretary

Liber Primus Inscriptionis Vestium mutationis Laicorum—1866-1967.

Liber Primus Inscriptionis Vestium mutationis Choristarum—1866-1934.

Libro de ingresos del Jovenado de El Espino (1887-1956).

Libro de postulantes coristas y legos I.

Libro de notas del Jovenado de San Pablo.

Liber secundus inscriptionis Professionis Religiosae Perpetuae in Congregatione SS. Redemptoris de la Provincia de Madrid CSSR.

Actus Authentici Renovationum 1921-1953 Professionis Temporariae. Estudiantado Astorga.

Actus Authentici Professionum a Votis Perpetuis I.

Libro de Calificaciones Estudiantado. Astorga 1901-1951.

Libro de objetos traídos por el sujeto al llegar al Noviciado. 1885-1933. Espino, Astorga, Nava del Rey.

Liber professionis perpetuae laicorum II.

Liber Secundus Professionis Perpetuae Laicorum.

Chronicles

Anales de la Provincia Española; vols. I-XI (*Anales*).

Crónica doméstica de la comunidad Redentorista de Cuenca. 1939- 1940 (*Crónica de Cuenca*).

Crónica doméstica de la comunidad Redentorista de Nava del Rey. Vols. I-III (*Crónica de Nava*).

Crónica doméstica de la comunidad Redentorista de Valencia—El Temple. Vol. I (*Crónica de Valencia*).

Crónica doméstica de la comunidad Redentorista de Vigo. Vol. I (*Crónica de Vigo*).

Crónica del Estudiantado de Astorga. Vols. I-II.

Crónica del Jovenado del Espino. Vols I-II.

Crónica de Cuenca—San Pablo. 1 vol.

Manuscripts

R. SARABIA, *Mis memorias.* 16 vols.

J. GOROSTERRATZU, *Ejercicios Espirituales.* 2 vols.

DOMESTIC ARCHIVES OF THE LOCAL COMMUNITIES

Astorga (León) *Crónica doméstica de la Comunidad Redentorista de Astorga.* Vols. I-III (*Crónica de Astorga*).

Coruña *Crónica doméstica de la Comunidad Redentorista de Coruña.* Vol. I (*Crónica de Coruña*).

El Espino (Burgos) *Crónica doméstica de la Comunidad Redentorista de El Espino.* Vols. I-IV (*Crónica del Espino*).

Fr. CARLOS OTERO, *Carta circular del a la Provincial; El Espino 8-7-1938.*

Granada *Crónica doméstica de la Comunidad Redentorista de Granada.* Vols. I-IV (*Crónica de Granada*).

Madrid—Fr. Socorro *Crónica doméstica de la Comunidad Redentorista de El Perpetuo Socorro de Madrid.* Vols.I-IV (*Crónica de Madrid-PS*).

Pamplona (Navarra) *Crónica doméstica de la Comunidad Redentorista de Pamplona.* Vols. I-IV (*Crónica de Pamplona*).

II. DIOCESAN ARCHIVES

Historial Archives of the Diocese of Vitoria (AHDV- GEAH)
Bautismo de Toribio Pozo *Libro de Bautizados de Villabuena. 1833-1891,* f. 279 r-v.

Matrimonio de Sixto y Micaela *Libro de desposorios de la Fr. de S. Miguel de Vitoria* VII, f. 374.

Diocesan Archives of Pamplona
Bautismo de Miguel Goñi *Libro de Bautismos de la Parroquia de Imarcoain* I, f. 160, n.º 4.

Defunción de Domingo Goñi *Libro de difuntos Imarcoain* I, 84, n.º 6.

Defunción de María Áriz *Libro de difuntos Imarcoain* I, 97 vto. n.º 1.

III. PAROCHIAL ARCHIVES

Parroquia de Urrotz (Navarra)

Bautismo de J. Javier Gorosterratzu *Libro de Bautismos* n.º 2.º, f. 96 vto., n.º 3.

Confirmación de J. Javier Gorosterratzu *Libro de Confirmados* n.º 1, ff. 30-31 (30-8-1881).

Hermanos Gorosterratzu -Jaunarena *Libro de Bautismos* n.º 2.

Libro de velaciones y casados.

Libro de Defunciones n.º 1.

Parroquia de Beinza-Labayen (Navarra)

Defunción de Juan Antonio Jaunarena *Libro de Defunciones* n.º IV, f. 46 vto., 2.

Parroquia de Gometxa (Vitoria-Álava)

Bautismo de Ciriaco Olarte *Libro de Bautismos* n.º II, f. 187.

Confirmación de Ciriaco Olarte *Libro de Confirmados* nº I, f. 1.

Parroquia de Payueta (Álava)

Matrimonio de Toribio Pozo y Micaela Ruiz de Samaniego *Libro de Matrimonios. 1886-1965,* f. 6 r-v.

Bautismo de Julián Pozo *Libro de Bautismos* 3, f. 47.

Confirmación de Julián Pozo *Libro de Bautismos* 3,f. 60.

Parroquia de Horche (Guadalajara)

Bautismo de Víctor Calvo *Libro de Bautismos* 17, f. 274 vto.

Confirmación de Víctor Calvo *Libro de Bautismos* 18, f. 63 vto., n.º 126.

Defunción de M.ª Candelas Lozano *Libro de difuntos* 18, f. 197 vto., n.º 45.

Parroquia de Pancorbo (Burgos)

Bautismo de Pedro Romero *Libro de bautismos* XVI, f. 129.

Confirmación *Libro de bautismos* de Pedro Romero XVI, f. 315ss.

IV. NATIONAL HISTORICAL ARCHIVES: CAUSA GENERAL (CAUSA)

Leg. 1538, Exp. 3, pp. 44-45 *Informe del Comité local de la Federación CNT de Cuenca; Cuenca, 19-4-1937,* en: CAUSA DE MADRID—PIEZA 5.ª —JUSTICIA ROJA, *Expediente General Informativo sobre la Rebelión Militar dentro del territorio de la República Española, instruido por el Juez del Tribunal Supremo Francisco Javier Elola y Díaz Varela.*

Leg. 675. Exp. 2, pp. 7-38 *Prisión Provincial de Cuenca; Relación nominal de personas que fueron encarceladas por razón político-terrorista durante la dominación marxista. Cuenca 7-4-1942* en: CAUSA DE CUENCA—PIEZA 3. CÁRCELES Y SACAS.

Leg. 675. Exp. 3, pp. 11-12 *Relación nominal de los milicianos que integraban el Comité local de Cuenca,* en: CAUSA DE CUENCA—PIEZA 4. CHECAS.

Leg. 1062, Exp. 10, pp. 136-139 *Estado número 1. Ayuntamiento de Cuenca. Relación de personas residentes en este término municipal, que durante la dominación roja fueron muertas violentamente o desaparecieron y se cree fueran asesinadas. Cuenca, 7 de junio de 1939,* en: CAUSA DE CUENCA—PIEZA PRINCIPAL—PARTIDO JUDICIAL DE CUENCA.

Leg. 1062, Exp. 10, pp. 140-143 *Estado número 2. Ayuntamiento de Cuenca. Relación de cadáveres recogidos en este término municipal, de personas no reconocidas como residentes en él, que sufrieron muerte violenta durante la dominación roja. Cuenca, 7 de junio de 1939,* en CAUSA DE CUENCA—PIEZA PRINCIPAL—PARTIDO JUDICIAL DE CUENCA.

Leg. 675. Exp. 9, pp. 19-22 *Informe de la Secretaría del Obispado de Cuenca sobre la persecución Religiosa contestando al cuestionario propuesto por el Fiscal Instructor Delegado de la Causa General; Cuenca, 18-8-1941,* en CAUSA DE CUENCA—PIEZA 10. PERSECUCIÓN RELIGIOSA.

Leg. 675, Exp. 11 *Pieza especial de milicianos,* en: CAUSA DE CUENCA.

V. GENERAL ARCHIVES OF THE ARMY (AGET)

Sum. 88 / Leg. 2045 *Sumario de urgencia contra Elías Cruz Moya, Benigno (a) El Cangrejero y Alberto (a)* El Cacharrero.

Sum. 161 / Leg. 2133 *Sumario de urgencia contra Juan García.*

Sum. 213 / Leg. 4364 *Sumario de urgencia contra Elías Cruz Moya.*

Sum. 261 / Leg. 2236 *Sumario de urgencia contra Eusebio del Río.*

Sum. 325 / Leg. 2062 *Sumario de urgencia contra Teodoro Delgado.*

Sum. 327 / Sig. 1258 *Sumario de urgencia contra Francisco Martínez.*

Sums. 386 / Sigs. 4866 *Sumario de urgencia contra Antonio Ros y 7496 Sallen.*

Sum. 417 / Leg. 6392 *Sumario de urgencia contra Alejandro Delgado.*

Sum. 497 / Leg. 672 *Sumario de urgencia contra Jaime (a)* Pambarato *y Agustín (a)* El Cestero.

Sum. 633 / Sig. 05969 *Sumario de urgencia contra Demetrio Muelas.*

Sum. 686 / Sig. 9148 *Sumario de urgencia contra Julián (a) El Polaco, Ángel (a)* El Vinagrero *y Teodoro (a)* El Guerra.

Sum. 741 / Sig. 4884 *Sumario de urgencia contra Mariano (a) El Pesca y Faustino Mollar.*

Sum. 1062 / Leg. 776 *Sumario de urgencia contra Emilio Martínez.*

Sum. 1064 / Leg. 4131 *Sumario de urgencia contra Crescencio (a) El Sustos.*

Sum. 1369 / Leg. 162 *Sumario de urgencia contra Apolonio Peñaranda.*

Sum. 1400 / Leg. 688 *Sumario de urgencia contra Elías Cruz Moya y Alberto (a)* El Cacharrero.

Sum. 1601/ Sig. 3221 *Sumario de urgencia contra Apolonio Peñaranda.*

Sum. 1771 / Sig. 3023 *Sumario de urgencia contra Julián López.*

Sum. 4918 / Leg. 4169 *Sumario de urgencia contra Alejandro Delgado.*

Sum. 5024 / Leg. 4464 *Sumario de urgencia contra Elías Cruz Moya*

Sum. 5276 / Leg. 562 *Sumario de urgencia contra Daniel (a) El Picias.*

Sum. 8008 / Leg. 823 *Sumario de urgencia contra Pedro Navarro.*

Sum. 11419 / Leg. 1785 *Sumario de urgencia contra Enrique Jiménez.*

Sum. 11444 / Sig. 5563 *Sumario de urgencia contra Ángel (a) El Vinagrero.*

Sum. 50360 / Leg. 472 *Sumario de urgencia contra José M.ª Carralero.*

Sum. 51050 / Leg. 4169 *Sumario de urgencia contra Alejandro Delgado.*

Sum. 141483 / Leg. 7304 *Sumario de urgencia contra Daniel (a)* El Picias.

VI. CIVIL AND MUNICIPAL COURT RECORDS

Cuenca

Acta de defunción de C. Olarte Sec. 3ª, T. 42, F. 304, Nº 603.

Acta de defunción de M. Goñi Sec. 3ª, T. 42, F. 304, Nº 604.

Acta de defunción de Julián Pozo Sec. 3ª, T. 42, F. 324, Nº 642.

Acta de defunción de V. Calvo Sec. 3ª, T. 42, F. 326, Nº 647.

Acta de defunción de J. Gorosterratzu Sec. 3ª, T. 42, F. 327, Nº 648.

Acta de defunción de Pedro Romero Sec. 3ª, T. 44, F. 300, Nº. 599.

Horche (Guadalajara)

Acta de nacimiento de Víctor Calvo Sec. 1ª, T. 9, F. 135, Nº 69.

Pancorbo (Burgos)

Acta de nacimiento de Pedro Romero Sec. 1ª, T. 1, F. 15, Nº 24.

Peñacerrada (Álava)

Acta de nacimiento de Julián Pozo Sec. 1ª, T. X, Nº 53.

Urrotz (Navarra)

Acta de nacimiento de J. Gorosterratzu Sec. 1ª, T. 1, F. 6.

Valle de Olorz (Navarra)

Acta de nacimiento de Miguel Goñi Sec. 1ª, T. 10, F. 126.

Vitoria (Álava)

Acta de nacimiento de Ciriaco Olarte Sec. 1ª, T. 50, Fr. 26.

VII. OTHER ARCHIVES

Archive General of the Administration (AGA)
Hoja de servicios de Sixto González en Expediente de depuración politico social de Sixto González Boix, Sig. (05)001.030, Caja 32/12428, Exp. 38.

Expediente personal y de título del maestro Sixto González Boix, Sig.31-18458-00038.

Statutory Delegation of Guipúzcoa, Koldo Mitxelena Library
J. J. GOROSTERRATZU, *Carta a Julio Urquijo; Pamplona, 26-12-1925;* 5 pp.

J. J. GOROSTERRATZU, *Carta a Julio Urquijo; Pamplona, 5-2-1926;* 4 pp.

J. J. GOROSTERRATZU, *Carta a Julio Urquijo; Madrid, 29-11-1929;* 4 pp.

Archive of the General Secretariate of the Oblate Sisters of the Holy Redeemer
Ficha personal de Elisa Pozo Ruiz de Samaniego.

Archive of the Secretary of the Marianist Province of Madrid
Ficha personal de Francisco González Ruiz de Samaniego.

Bibliography

I. BIBLIOGRAPHY ABOUT THE RELIGIOUS PERSECUTION

Works

A. B. RODRÍGUEZ PATIÑO Y R. DE LA ROSA RICO, *Represión y Guerra Civil en Cuenca. Nuevos testimonios y fotografías* (Cuenca, 2009).

A. MONTERO, *Historia de la persecución religiosa en España. 1936-1939* (Madrid, 1961).

A. B. RODRÍGUEZ PATIÑO, *La Guerra Civil en Cuenca (1936-1939). Vol. I. Del 18 de Julio a la Columna del Rosal* (Madrid, 20063).

A. B. RODRÍGUEZ PATIÑO, *La Guerra Civil en Cuenca (1936-1939). Vol. II. La pugna ideológica y la evolución* (Madrid, 2006).

Almerien. Beatificationis seu Declarationis Martyrii Servorum Dei Iosephi Álvarez-Benavides y de la Torre et CXVI sociorum in odium fidei, uti fertur, interfectorum (+1936-1938). Positio super martyrio et fama martyrii, Roma, 2003, I y II.

ARNALDO DE OYENART, MAULEONENSE, *Noticia de las dos Vasconias, la Ibérica y la Aquitana* (San Sebastián, 1929). Traducida al castellano y nota introductoria por J. GOROSTERRATZU, redentorista.

B. OLIVERA, *Martirio y consagración. Los mártires de Argelia* (Madrid, 20112).

C. MERA, *Guerra, exilio y cárcel de un anarcosindicalista. Memorias* (Francia, 1976).

Conchen. Beatificationis seu Declarationis Martyrii Servorum Dei Iosephi Xaverii Gorosterratzu et V sociorum e Congregatione SS.mi Redemptoris in odium fidei, uti fertur, interfectorum (+1936-1938).

Positio super martyrio (Roma, 2001).

D. DE FELIPE, *Nuevos Redentores* (Madrid, 1962).

J. GOROSTERRATZU, *D. Rodrigo Jiménez de Rada, gran estadista, escritor y prelado* (Pamplona, 1925).

J. GOROSTERRATZU, C.SS.R, *Una víctima de la caridad. Reseña biográfica de Sor Josefa de San Alfonso. Religiosa Oblata del Stmo. Redentor* (Zaragoza, 1927).

M. E. GONZÁLEZ, *Los doce obispos mártires del siglo XX en España* (Madrid, 2012).

R. CARR, *Historia de España, 12. La República y la Guerra civil* (Madrid, 1999).

S. CIRAC ESTOPAÑÁN, *Martirologio de Cuenca. Crónica diocesana de la época roja* (Barcelona, 1947).

S. CIRAC ESTOPAÑÁN, *Vida de D. Cruz Laplana, Obispo de Cuenca* (Barcelona, 1943).

V. CÁRCEL ORTÍ, *La persecución religiosa en España durante la Segunda República (1931-1939)* (Madrid, 1990).

Articles and collaborations in periodical publications

B. MARTÍNEZ PÉREZ, *Sin compasión, ¡¡A la picota!!*: Heraldo de Cuenca 83 (3-8-1936) 1.

B. MARTÍNEZ PÉREZ, *El sacrilegio de la clerecía española*: Heraldo de Cuenca 85 (10-8-1936) 1.

D. RUIZ, *Hacia los altares. Nuestros mártires*: BPE. XXVII, 151 (2000) 149-152.

Elenchus eorum qui Hispania saeviente persecutione perierunt: Analecta Congregationis SS. Redemptoris XVIII, 3 (mayo 1939) 150-153.

J. M. IBARROLA, *Un redentorista en el Madrid rojo*: PS (julio 1965) 211-214.

J. M. IBARROLA LATASA, C.Ss.R. *Nuestros Mártires*: El Perpetuo Socorro XLI (1940) 101-104. 132-137. 185-190. 309-310.

Necrológica. Las Comunidades bajo el poder rojo: BPE. 8 segunda época (2 de febrero de 1940) 3-7.

T. CEPEDAL, *Las Comunidades de la Provincia*: BPE XXVII, 151 (2000) 61-102.

II. OTHER CONSULTED WORKS

A. FLORISTÁN, *Recorridos por Navarra. Valle de Santesteban-Basaburúa menor* (Estella, 1992).

A. SOTÉS, *El convento de San Francisco de Astorga* (Madrid, 1934).

AA.VV., *Los Redentoristas y la persecución*: El Perpetuo Socorro XXXV, 425 (noviembre 1933) 467-520.

AA.VV., *Repensar el martirio*: Concilium 299 (2003).

J. COLÓN-R. BOLAÑOS, *Historia de los Misioneros Redentoristas en el Cono Norte de América Latina y el Caribe* (Santafé de Bogotá, 1995).

D. DE FELIPE, *De hojalatero a Obispo* (Madrid, 1945).

D. DE FELIPE, *Flor de Granada. Historia documentada de Conchita Barrecheguren* (Madrid, 1935).

D. DE FELIPE, *Fundación de los Redentoristas en España* (Madrid, 1965).

D. GÓMEZ PINEDO, *H. Martín Gorosterratzu (1885-1955)* (Madrid, 1956).

D. RUIZ, *50 años en Barcelona*: BPE. XV, 104 (1977) 112-157.

F. MUELAS, *Cuenca. "Tierras de sorpresa y encantamientos"* (León, 1983).

G. GONZÁLEZ RONDA, *Santuario de Barcelona. Restauración y decoración*: BPE. XVIII, 116 (1983) 48-55.

J. CAMPOS, *Grandes del Apostolado* (Madrid, 1965).

J. CAMPOS, *Por un México mejor. Cincuenta Años de Historia Redentorista* (México, 1959).

J. RAMÓN JIMÉNEZ, *Españoles de tres mundos (1914-1940)* (Madrid, 1969).

J. J. ITOIZ LEOZ, H. *Benjamín López de Murga Eguíluz*: BPE. 135 (1992) 391-409.

L. MIGUÉLEZ, *Los Redentoristas. Veinte lecturas sobre su historia* (México, 1986).

L. MIGUÉLEZ, *Viceprovincia de México*: BPE XXVII, 151 (2000) 351-359.

L. PÉREZ, *Los redentoristas en Granada 1879-1979. Historia corta de cien años largos*, s.e, s.f, 76.

L. FDEZ. DE RETANA, *Aún hay santos!* (Madrid, 1935) 226.

M. VIDAL, *Concilio Vaticano II y Teología pública* (Madrid, 2012).

Memorial de la Provincia de Madrid CSSR (Madrid, 20086).

Necrología del R. Fr. Agustín Pedrosa: BPE. IV, 46 (junio 1953) 157-159.

Necrología del R. Fr. Inocencio T. Leoz: BPE. III, 33 (abril 1949) 94-95.

Necrología del R. Fr. Isidro Fernández Posado: BPE. IX, 77 (junio 1963) 131-132.

OBLATAS DEL SANTÍSIMO REDENTOR, *Biblioteca Histórica OSR I. Orígenes de la Congregación, cronologías generales y documentos varios* (Madrid, 1981).

Fr. MADOZ, *Diccionario Geográfico-Estadístico-Histórico de España y sus posesiones de Ultramar* (Madrid, 1847)

R. TELLERÍA, *Un instituto misionero* (Madrid, 1932).

T. VEGA, *Historia de otra alma* (Madrid, 19443).

V. PÉREZ DE GAMARRA, *Anales Provinciae Hispanicae C.SS.R.* I (Madrid, 1925).

V. PÉREZ DE GAMARRA, *Anales Provinciae Hispanicae C.SS.R.* II (Madrid, 1927).

V. PÉREZ DE GAMARRA, *Anales Provinciae Hispanicae C.SS.R.* III (Madrid, 1928).

Fr. Gary Lauenstein, CSsR, was professed as a Redemptorist in 1966 and ordained to the priesthood in 1971. His assignments have included teaching Spanish in the high school seminary, pastoral work in predominantly Hispanic parishes, vocation ministry, and novice director for the North American Redemptorists. He currently serves as a parish priest.

CPSIA information can be obtained
at www.ICGtesting.com
Printed in the USA
FSHW021911160220
67076FS